D1602972

משלי
PROVERBS

SONCINO BOOKS OF THE BIBLE

EDITOR: REV. DR. A. COHEN M.A. Ph.D., D.H.L.

Proverbs

HEBREW TEXT & ENGLISH TRANSLATION
WITH AN INTRODUCTION
AND COMMENTARY

by

THE REV. DR. A. COHEN M.A. Ph.D., D.H.L.

Revised by

RABBI A. J. ROSENBERG

THE SONCINO PRESS

LONDON • JERUSALEM • NEW YORK

FIRST EDITION 1946 (Eight Impressions)
REVISED EDITION 1985

ISBN 0–900689-33-1

PUBLISHERS' NOTE

*Thanks are due to the
Jewish Publication Society of America
for permission to use their beautiful
English text of the Scriptures*

PRINTED IN THE UNITED STATES OF AMERICA

PUBLISHERS' INTRODUCTION TO THE REVISED SECOND EDITION

JUST over thirty-seven years ago THE PSALMS, the first in a series of the SONCINO BOOKS OF THE BIBLE, saw the light of day, to be followed in the next six years by the remaining thirteen books. Whereas the earlier edition drew from various non-Jewish, as well as Jewish, sources, the publishers now feel there is a need to acquaint the reader with the pure Jewish view of these holy books, and this revised edition therefore limits its scope to the traditional classic Jewish commentaries and source material.

We are indebted to The Judaica Press for allowing us to use material from the Judaica Books of the Prophets.

FOREWORD BY THE GENERAL EDITOR TO THE FIRST EDITION

THE second volume of THE SONCINO BOOKS OF THE BIBLE is herewith presented to the public. It will be followed after a short interval by the Five Megilloth (*Song of Songs*, *Ruth*, *Lamentations*, *Ecclesiastes* and *Esther*).

The series is distinctive in the following respects:

(*i*) Each volume contains the Hebrew text and English translation together with the commentary. (*ii*) The exposition is designed primarily for the ordinary reader of the Bible rather than for the student, and aims at providing this class of reader with requisite direction for the understanding and appreciation of the Biblical Book. (*iii*) The commentary is invariably based upon the received Hebrew text. When this presents difficulties, the most probable translation and interpretation are suggested, without resort to textual emendation. (*iv*) It offers a *Jewish* commentary. Without neglecting the valuable work of Christian expositors, it takes into account the exegesis of the Talmudical Rabbis as well as of the leading Jewish commentators.

All Biblical references are cited according to chapter and verse as in the Hebrew Bible. It is unfortunate that, unlike the American-Jewish translation, the English Authorized and Revised Versions, although made direct from the Hebrew text, did not conform to its chapter divisions. An undesirable complication was thereby introduced into Bible study. In the Hebrew the longer headings of Psalms are counted as a separate verse; consequently Ps. xxxiv. 12, e.g., corresponds to verse 11 in A.V. and R.V. It is also necessary to take into account a marginal note like that found against 1 Kings iv. 21, 'ch. v. 1 in Heb.', so that the Hebrew 1 Kings v. 14 tallies with iv. 34 in the English.

It is hoped that this Commentary, though more particularly planned for the needs of Jews, will prove helpful to all who desire a fuller knowledge of the Bible, irrespective of their creed.

A. COHEN

CONTENTS

	Page
Publishers' Introduction to the Revised Edition	v
Foreword by the Editor to the First Edition	vi
Preface	ix
Introduction	xi
THE TEXT	1–215
Authorities quoted	216
Terms and Abbreviations	217

PREFACE

While the aim of a popular commentary has been kept in mind in the preparation of this volume, I trust that it will also be found of interest and utility by students of the Hebrew text. The greater part of PROVERBS consists of disjointed verses and there is often no context to give aid in problems of exegesis. The gnomic sayings are usually expressed with a brevity which adds to the difficulty of their interpretation.

For the carrying out of my task I found it necessary to devote myself to a fresh study of the text. Giving due weight to what had been written by the leading Christian expositors, but rejecting their practice of emending the Hebrew when it baffles them, I have not infrequently departed from their interpretations and elucidated obscure passages in the light of the Jewish commentaries. Among these the *Metsudath David* by Rabbi David Altschul has been particularly helpful. I am also indebted to Dr. Eitan's *A Contribution to Biblical Lexicography* for suggestions which threw light on many doubtful phrases.

The labour expended upon this volume has been heavy, but it will be well rewarded if it tends to make this precious Biblical Book better understood and more widely read.

Apart from the value of the wisdom and practical guidance enshrined in the discourses and aphorisms which are to be read in this Book, it has an important lesson to teach which is characteristically Hebraic and particularly noteworthy in these times. Some of the contents may appear to lie beyond the purview of religion, dealing as they do with phases of everyday life which are normally regarded as secular. But religion of the Bible is all-embracing and does not exclude any part of human activity as outside its scope. *Humani nihil a me alienum puto* would well express its standpoint.

My thanks must again be expressed to Mr. J. Davidson, Director of the Soncino Press, for his unremitting care and attention to the host of technical problems which arose in the production of the volume.

A. Cohen

Birmingham
April 1945

INTRODUCTION

THE WISDOM LITERATURE

The Bible supplies evidence that three classes of teachers existed in ancient Israel. They are mentioned in Jeremiah xviii. 18: *Instruction shall not perish from the priest, nor counsel from the wise* (chacham), *nor the word from the prophet*; and in Ezekiel vii. 26: *They shall seek a vision of the prophet, and instruction shall perish from the priest, and counsel from the elders* (zekenim). The priest had the duty of providing the community with *instruction* (Torah) in the practices of religion, in the narrower connotation of the term (cf. Mal. ii. 7); the function of the prophet was to communicate to the people the Divine *word* or *vision* which he had received; and in addition there were the 'wise' or 'elders' who imparted *counsel*, guidance in the secular affairs of life.

What especially differentiated the last-named from the other two was the absence of Divine authority. The priest's responsibility was to adhere, and make the people adhere, strictly to the God-revealed code which regulated the national worship; the prophet claimed to speak in the name of God; but the 'wise' taught what they believed to be true and right. Never did they presume to insert *thus saith the LORD* in their messages. They were earnest seekers of the good life and taught their disciples in what this consisted.

If, however, they lacked the seal of unquestionable authority possessed by priest and prophet, the warrant for the validity of their teaching was its harmony with the precepts of Torah and prophecy. In no way did they regard themselves as antagonistic to the other classes of teacher, but rather as supplementing their instruction. They found it possible to establish closer contact with the masses, especially the youth, and were the means of translating into concrete and specific terms the way of life indicated in the Scriptures of Moses and his successors. If they deal more particularly with what we should call the secular life, it is always within the orbit of religion, recognizing that no sharp dividing line exists in Judaism between the secular and the religious. The identification of the two in their system of thought is emphasized in the maxim which may be considered the distinctive motto of these teachers: *The fear of the LORD is the beginning of knowledge* (i. 7; cf. Job xxviii. 28; Eccles. xii. 13).

As there is a literature of priests and of prophets, so is there a literature of these wise men. It has been given the general title of 'The Wisdom Literature.' Three works of this category are incorporated in the Biblical Canon: Proverbs, Job and Ecclesiastes. Excluded from the Hebrew Scriptures but preserved in the Apocrypha are: The Wisdom of Solomon and The Wisdom of Ben Sira, or Ecclesiasticus.

THE BOOK OF PROVERBS

No section of the Wisdom Literature so distinctly illustrates its characteristics as this Book. Its main contents formulate rules of practical ethics, which was the special concern of the 'wise.' In it are also found discourses on moral philosophy which typify the disquisitions addressed by these teachers to their pupils. The personal note is often struck by the addition of *my son*, so that we gain the impression of being in the presence of the instructor and listening to his words of advice and pleading.

The Book presents unmistakable evidence of being not one continuous work, but rather, as we might expect from the character of its material, the compilation of a number of documents. The clearly marked divisions are: I. The Introduction (i. 1-7), giving the title and stating the object of the Book, followed by a series of moral addresses (i. 8—vii. 27), and two discourses on the nature of wisdom (viii. ix). II. The first collection of aphorisms (x. 1—xxii. 16) introduced by the heading *The proverbs of Solomon*. III. The second collection of aphorisms (xxii. 17—xxiv. 34), prefaced by an introductory section (xxii. 17-21) and ending with an appendix (xxiv. 23-34) entitled *These also are sayings of the wise*. IV. The third collection of aphorisms (xxv-xxix), beginning with an editorial note, *These also are proverbs of Solomon, which the men of Hezekiah king of Judah copied out*. V. The words of Agur ben Jakeh (xxx). VI. The words of king Lemuel (xxxi. 1-9). VII. Praise of the ideal wife (xxxi. 10-31).

AUTHORSHIP

The initial introductory passage (i. 1-7) has the appearance of being by the hand of the compiler as a foreword to the Book as a whole. The last two chapters, which bear signs of the later stages of the Hebrew language and differ in style and contents from the rest, are undoubtedly an addendum. What reliance can be placed upon the ascription of the bulk of the chapters to Solomon?

A Rabbinic teaching asserts that the Israelite king wrote Song of Songs in his youth, Proverbs in middle age, and Ecclesiastes towards the end of his life (Midrash Shir ha-Shirim, i. 1, § 10). The tradition that Solomon was renowned for his wisdom is attested by 1 Kings iii. 28, v. 9ff., x. 1ff., 23, xi. 41. Even a critical scholar like Cheyne remarks, 'I see no reason for not accepting the substance of this tradition' (*Job and Solomon*, p. 131). It is explicitly told of Solomon that *he spoke three thousand proverbs* (mashal) (1 Kings v. 12). We also read of *the old men* (zekenim) *that had stood before Solomon* (1 Kings xii. 6) and, as we have seen above, *zekenim* is a synonym for the wise men who were responsible for the Wisdom Literature. There is consequently a presumption in favour of the hypothesis that the Book of Proverbs may, at least, have had its beginnings in the reign of Solomon and embodies material composed by the king and his *zekenim*.

Yet there is even Rabbinic warrant for the view that the Book, in its present form, is the product of a later date. The Talmud has the statement, 'Hezekiah and his colleagues wrote Isaiah, Proverbs, the Song of Songs and Ecclesiastes' (B.B. 15a), and by the term 'wrote' is probably to be understood 'compiled' or 'edited.' The mention of Hezekiah in xxv. 1 supports the opinion that the Book began to take shape in that king's reign.

It is noteworthy that as late as the first and second centuries C.E., the right of Proverbs, Song of Songs and Ecclesiastes to a place in the Biblical Canon was a subject of dispute among the Rabbis. In the case of Proverbs the reason was said to have been the contradiction between xxvi. 4 and 5, *Answer not a fool according to his folly* and *Answer a fool according to his folly* (Shabbath 30b). A conservative authority, I. H. Weiss, has suggested that the real point at issue was the doubt of the School of Shammai on Solomon's authorship of these Books (*Dor*, II., p. 88).

A plausible conclusion, therefore, seems to be that Proverbs is not the work of one author, but a collection of ethical writings originating from the age of Solomon, first edited in the period of Hezekiah, and issued in its final form with the incorporation of additional matter at a subsequent date, perhaps by the Sopherim, the 'scribes' who succeeded Ezra.

THE *MASHAL*

The English title *Proverbs* is the rendering of the Hebrew *mishlë*, a term which has a variety of significations. It corresponds to the word 'proverb' in 1 Sam. x. 12, xxiv. 14. Other meanings are: 'a prophetic discourse' (Num. xxiii. 7, 18, etc.; Isa. xiv. 4; Micah ii. 4); 'parable, allegory' (Ezek. xvii. 2, xxi. 5, xxiv. 3) and this is probably its sense in 1 Kings v. 12; 'ethical aphorism' (Job xiii. 12, xxvii. 1, xxix. 1; Eccles. xii. 9). It is mainly in this last connotation that the word is attached to this Book.

Toy undoubtedly goes too far when he maintains that 'none of the aphorisms —not even such as *Go to the ant, thou sluggard*, or *Answer a fool according to his folly*, or the tetrads in chapter xxx— are popular proverbs or folk-sayings. They are all reflective and academic in tone, and must be regarded as the productions of schools of moralists in a period of high moral culture' (p. xi). While most of the sentences are certainly of this type, some of the sayings appear to be genuine proverbs. Oesterley quotes as examples: *Hope deferred maketh the heart sick* (xiii. 12), *Where no oxen are, the crib is clean* (xiv. 4), *Pride goeth before destruction* (xvi. 18), *Wine is a mocker, strong drink is riotous* (xx. 1), and he adds, 'There are, doubtless, others' (p. lxxv).

As applied to chapters i-ix, however, *mashal* denotes a discourse and not an aphorism. But even where we have a genuine proverb, it is not left in its original form, but is elaborated into a poetical couplet. The effect is to heighten the force of the moral. For instance, the proverb *Hope deferred maketh the heart sick* receives the addition, *But desire fulfilled is a tree of life.*

In conformity with the general design of Hebrew poetry, the aphorisms are distinguished by the employment of parallelism. This may be:

(*i*) *Synonymous*, the second clause repeating the thought of the first in different words:

(*a*) *The evil bow before the good,*
(*b*) *And the wicked at the gates of the righteous* (xiv. 19).

(*a*) *A fool's mouth is his ruin,*
(*b*) *And his lips are the snare of his soul* (xviii. 7).

(*ii*) *Antithetic*, the second clause presenting a contrast to the first. This is by far the commonest form:

(*a*) *The righteous eateth to the satisfying of his desire;*
(*b*) *But the belly of the wicked shall want* (xiii. 25).

(*a*) *A merry heart is a good medicine;*
(*b*) *But a broken spirit drieth the bones* (xvii. 22).

(*iii*) *Synthetic*, the second clause continuing the thought of the first:

(*a*) *It is the discretion of a man to be slow to anger;*
(*b*) *And it is his glory to pass over a transgression* (xix. 11).

(*a*) *Love not sleep, lest thou come to poverty;*
(*b*) *Open thine eyes, and thou shalt have bread in plenty* (xx. 13).

Another frequent form which the aphorism takes is in agreement with the root-meaning of *mashal*, viz. 'to resemble.' The point of the lesson is made clear by the use of comparison:

(*a*) *As vinegar to the teeth, and as smoke to the eyes,*
(*b*) *So is the sluggard to them that send him* (x. 26).

(*a*) *A word fitly spoken*
(*b*) *Is like apples of gold in settings of silver* (xxv. 11).

Occasionally a verse consists of three clauses, but the normal is two. In this style of composition the aphorism comes 'trippingly on the tongue' and is the more easily memorized. This is a contributory cause, in addition to the intrinsic merit of the sayings, of the extraordinary popularity enjoyed by the Book of Proverbs and the passing of many of its phrases into current speech.

CHARACTERISTICS

'To polish commonplaces and give them a new lustre; to express in a few words the obvious principle of conduct, and to give to clear thoughts an even clearer expression; to illuminate dimmer impressions and bring their faint rays to a focus; to delve beneath the surface of consciousness to new veins of precious ore, to name and discover and bring to light latent and unnamed experience; and finally to embody the central truths of life in the breadth and terseness of memorable phrases—all these are the opportunities of the aphorist; and to take advantage of these opportunities, he must be a thinker, an accurate observer, a profound moralist, a psychologist, and an artist as well' (L. Pearsall Smith, *A Treasury of English Aphorisms*, pp. 13f.).

If these are taken to be the criteria of the excellence of this form of literary composition, the wise men who contributed to *Proverbs* may deservedly be placed in the highest class, and the quotation accurately describes their aim. To this must be added their intense moral purpose. Men's foibles are satirized and set against the opposing virtues. Vices of all kinds, which corrupt the mind and body, are relentlessly exposed and denounced. The benefits which accrue from sound principles of conduct are brought to the disciple's attention, to make their appeal to his self-interest when he is unable to rise to the plane where he perceives that goodness is its own reward.

The sages who impart their doctrines in this Book do not stand on a lofty height and preach impracticable ideals. On the contrary, their endeavour is to step down to a level which is easily accessible by the majority. Nor do they deal in vague abstractions, but apply the test of common sense and verifiable experience. They urge the fundamental thesis that the morally defective and wilfully perverted stand in their own light, deny themselves the real joys of living, bring avoidable troubles upon their head and, though they may at times have a momentary triumph, ultimately fall. On the other hand, to conduct oneself in the light of wisdom means to get the best out of life, discover sources of strength which assure final victory over calamity and evil, and become a blessing to oneself and society. Such, reduced to its simplest terms, is the message of these wise men of Israel.

Two outstanding features of their teaching have lastly to be noted. Naturally, being Hebrews who addressed themselves to Hebrews, they employed the language of Judaism. Wisdom or morality is defined as *the fear of the LORD* (i. 7); the highest excellence of character in the ideal woman is similarly described in the phrase she *feareth the LORD* (xxxi. 30) and the same would apply to the ideal man; a favourite term for an unethical act or a vicious person is *an abomination to the LORD* (iii. 32, vi. 16, xi. 1, etc.). Sin is rebellion against God's will and man is accountable to Him for his deeds; thus *the curse of the LORD is in the house of the wicked, but He blesseth the habitation of the righteous* (iii. 33).

Nevertheless no passage is addressed exclusively to the Hebrew. The tone of the Book is strikingly universalistic throughout. 'The word "Israel" does not occur once, the word *adam* "man" thirty-three times' (Cheyne, p. 119). Its teaching is applicable to all men everywhere and is true of life generally and not of any particular people or land. The Book of Proverbs is the Hebrew *vade mecum* offered to all travellers along the road of life.

Secondly, the comprehensiveness of outlook is indeed remarkable. No phase of human relationship seems to be overlooked. The king on his throne, the tradesman in his store and the farmer in the field, husband and wife and child, all receive wholesome instruction and exhortation. Advice is tendered on the treatment of friends, the poor, the rearing of children, the snares which lurk in the path of youth, the perils of overconfidence and self-commitment by standing surety for others. These and other contingencies provide occasion for shrewd counsel, based upon the central doctrine that wisdom is *a tree of life to them that lay hold upon her, and happy is every one that holdeth her fast* (iii. 18).

PROVERBS

PROVERBS

1 CHAPTER I א

1 **The proverbs of Solomon the son of David, king of Israel;**

2 **To know wisdom and instruction;**
To comprehend the words of understanding;

3 **To receive the discipline of wisdom,**
Justice, and right, and equity;

1 מִשְׁלֵי שְׁלֹמֹה בֶן־דָּוִד
מֶלֶךְ יִשְׂרָאֵל׃
2 לָדַעַת חָכְמָה וּמוּסָר
לְהָבִין אִמְרֵי בִינָה׃
3 לָקַחַת מוּסַר הַשְׂכֵּל
צֶדֶק וּמִשְׁפָּט וּמֵשָׁרִים׃

CHAPTER I

1 TITLE OF THE BOOK

VERSES 1–6 are the editor's prologue. The first verse is the title which he attached to his completed collection, and what follows summarizes the nature of its contents.

proverbs. For the various meanings of *mashal* and the senses in which it is employed in this Book, see Introduction.

Solomon the son of David. The common usage in Hebrew is to add *ben*, 'son of,' to a man's name. The heading in x. 1 is simply 'the proverbs of Solomon,' and similarly in xxv. 1. In his admiration of the Israelite king, the editor elaborated the title connoting that the Book was written by a wise man, the son of a wise man (Ibn Ezra).

2–6 PURPOSE OF THE BOOK

2. *to know.* i.e. the aim of the proverbs is for man to know. His first duty is to obtain a knowledge of wisdom; then it is hoped he will allow it to rule his life (Ibn Ezra).

wisdom. Hebrew *chochmah*, a key-word of the Book and the basis of the whole structure of its teaching. It has been defined as 'the knowledge of those truths which lead to the knowledge of God' (Maimonides). Not sagacity, abstract learning or philosophical speculation is intended, but an understanding of the principles which control and direct human living at its highest and best. Combined with the next term, *instruction*, it corresponds to ethics or moral philosophy (see Daath Mikra).

instruction. Hebrew *musar*, another crucial word in the Book which is better translated 'discipline' (cf. the use of the verb and noun in Deut. iv. 36, viii. 5, xi. 2 where, however, the rendering 'chasten, chastisement' is inadequate). Man is endowed with instincts and passions which must be kept under restraint or they make him brutish (see Malbim). 'The wicked are under the control of their impulses, but the righteous have their impulses under their control,' remarked the Rabbis; i.e. the former lacked, while the latter possessed, *musar*.

comprehend the words of understanding. Both the verb and the noun are connected with the Hebrew preposition meaning 'between,' and signify the ability to draw proper distinctions. Here is meant the distinction between right and wrong (Hirsch). A good illustration is found in Solomon's prayer, *Give Thy servant therefore an understanding heart to judge Thy people, that I may discern between good and evil* (1 Kings iii. 9). The interdependence of knowledge and understanding is taught in the Rabbinic aphorism, 'Where there is no knowledge, there is no understanding; where there is no understanding, there is no knowledge' (Aboth 3.21).

3. *receive.* Apprehend, find acceptable and apply in daily life (Gerondi).

4 To give prudence to the simple,
To the young man knowledge and discretion;

5 That the wise man may hear, and increase in learning,
And the man of understanding may attain unto wise counsels;

6 To understand a proverb, and a figure;
The words of the wise, and their dark sayings.

לָתֵת לִפְתָאיִם עָרְמָה
לְנַעַר דַּעַת וּמְזִמָּה׃
יִשְׁמַע חָכָם וְיוֹסֶף לֶקַח
וְנָבוֹן תַּחְבֻּלוֹת יִקְנֶה׃
לְהָבִין מָשָׁל וּמְלִיצָה
דִּבְרֵי חֲכָמִים וְחִידֹתָם׃

wisdom. Hebrew *haskel*; so A.V., but R.V. *wise dealing*. Perhaps 'insight' comes nearest to the original, but in a practical sense as defined in the terms that follow. The reader will be taught how to acquire the discipline which will enable him to perceive the line of conduct that is just and right (Ibn Ezra).

justice. [The three terms occur together in ii. 9, and the first two in Ps. lxxxix. 15, xcvii. 2 as the attributes upon which God's throne is based. There they are more literally translated *righteousness and justice.*] *Tsedek* includes the service of God and all good deeds (Ibn Ezra).

right. lit. 'judgment,' the application of righteousness in judicial decisions (Ibn Ezra).

4. *prudence.* The word is used in a bad sense of craftiness, as of the tempting serpent (Gen. iii. 1). Here it signifies 'shrewdness,' which is a safeguard against being misled (Malbim).

simple. A common word in Proverbs. [The root-meaning is 'to be wide open';] so he is a person of undecided views, susceptible to good or bad influence. He is one, therefore, who needs *prudence* if he is not to be led astray (see Meiri).

young man. Typifying an immature person without experience of the world (cf. Jeremiah's plea, *'Behold, I cannot speak, for I am a child,'* Jer. i. 6; the same Hebrew word) (Malbim, Metsudath David).

discretion. lit. 'power to devise,' to decide wisely for himself to attain a desired end (Meiri).

5. *that the wise man may hear.* [Better, 'let the wise man hear.'] Even he who is not simple and has acquired wisdom will find this Book advantageous to him (Metsudath David).

increase in learning. Rather, 'enlarge (his) teaching'; his instruction will be wider and deeper. It is the same word as in *I give you good doctrine* (iv. 2; see note, Metsudath David).

the man of understanding. [He also, to whom verse 2 does not apply, cannot dispense with this tuition.]

wise counsels. The Hebrew is connected with the word for 'rope' and is literally a chain of thoughts, one following the other. i.e. through this Book, he will learn many fundamentals, from which he will develop and widen his understanding (Malbim).

6. *to understand a proverb and a figure.* This Book was written so that people should strive to understand the double meaning of each verse, the proverb and the figure. They should understand what the author wished to bring out with his proverb, and also not neglect the figure itself, i.e. the way it was expressed. When he compares idolatry to a strange woman, the reader must not neglect the simple meaning of the verse to beware of a tempting adultress (Rashi).

7 The fear of the LORD is the beginning of knowledge;
But the foolish despise wisdom and discipline.

8 Hear, my son, the instruction of thy father,
And forsake not the teaching of thy mother;

7 יִרְאַת יְהוָה רֵאשִׁית דָּעַת
חָכְמָה וּמוּסָר אֱוִילִים בָּזוּ׃
8 שְׁמַע בְּנִי מוּסַר אָבִיךָ
וְאַל־תִּטֹּשׁ תּוֹרַת אִמֶּךָ׃

This fundamental enunciation of the Hebraic standpoint is repeated with variations in ix. 10; Ps. cxi. 10; Job xxviii. 28; Ecclus. i. 14. God is the Creator of the universe and of life; it is consequently impossible to obtain an understanding of man's place in the design and purpose of living without a humble approach to Him. (Cf. the Rabbinic teaching, 'Where there is no wisdom, there is no fear of God; where there is no fear of God, there is no wisdom' — Aboth 3.21).

7. *fear.* Books of Hebrew ethics divide fear of God into two categories, viz. fear of retribution, and reverence. Reverence is, naturally, the higher attainment. This verse, however, which deals with the prerequisite for attaining wisdom, refers to fear of retribution. Reverence for God is a result of that wisdom (Anaf Yosef on Aboth ad loc.).

beginning. Before learning knowledge, one must acquire fear of the Lord (Rashi, Metsudath David). Rashi explains too that fear of the Lord is the chief part of knowledge.

the foolish. As there is an ethical connotation in the 'wise' and 'wisdom' of Proverbs, so with the opposite, 'the foolish' and 'folly.' They are morally, rather than intellectually, defective, and *despise a father's correction* (xv. 5) (Elijah of Wilna).

despise wisdom and discipline. Since the fools despise wisdom and discipline, if one learns wisdom without acquiring fear of God, it will be of no avail (Metsudath David).

8. *hear.* Pay attention to and put into practice (cf. *all that the* LORD *hath spoken will we do and obey* (lit. hear), Exod. xxiv. 7) (Metsudath David).

my son. An endearing term in which the teacher addresses his pupil since he contributes to his essence, intellectually and spiritually (Ibn Caspi).

instruction. As in verse 2 *discipline*. The parallel word *teaching* is *Torah,* meaning 'direction' (Metsudath Zion).

father . . . mother. Before entering upon his course of instruction, the teacher exhorts the disciple, presumably a young man, to follow the guidance which his parents give him, because it is always well intentioned. Even wicked parents do not wish their children to follow their ways (J. Kimchi). In connection with the father the sterner word *musar* is employed for the reason that his discipline at times involves chastisement (xiii. 24, xxii. 15, xxiii. 13f.). The mother's *teaching* is denoted *Torah,* since she usually limits herself to verbal exhortation (Likkutei Yehudah). Ibn Nachmiash explains the verse as though it would read : 'Hear, my son, the instruction of thy father and thy mother, and forsake not their teaching.' This construction resembles that of Lev. xxv. 37. The intention is that he must first follow their instruction to eliminate evil deeds and then follow their teaching to do good. The Talmud (Ber. 35b) (so also Rashi) homiletically defines *father* as God, and *mother* as the nation of Israel; be obedient to the precepts revealed by God and the laws enacted by the Rabbis.

9 For they shall be a chaplet of grace
unto thy head,
And chains about thy neck.

10 My son, if sinners entice thee,
Consent thou not.

11 If they say: 'Come with us,
Let us lie in wait for blood,
Let us lurk for the innocent without cause;

12 Let us swallow them up alive as
the grave,
And whole, as those that go down
into the pit;

13 We shall find all precious substance,
We shall fill our houses with spoil;

14 Cast in thy lot among us;
Let us all have one purse'

כִּי ׀ לִוְיַת חֵן הֵם לְרֹאשֶׁךָ
וַעֲנָקִים לְגַרְגְּרֹתֶךָ׃
10 בְּנִי אִם־יְפַתּוּךָ חַטָּאִים אַל־תֹּבֵא׃
11 אִם־יֹאמְרוּ לְכָה אִתָּנוּ
נֶאֶרְבָה לְדָם נִצְפְּנָה לְנָקִי חִנָּם׃
12 נִבְלָעֵם כִּשְׁאוֹל חַיִּים
וּתְמִימִים כְּיוֹרְדֵי בוֹר׃
13 כָּל־הוֹן יָקָר נִמְצָא
נְמַלֵּא בָתֵּינוּ שָׁלָל׃
14 גּוֹרָלְךָ תַּפִּיל בְּתוֹכֵנוּ
כִּיס אֶחָד יִהְיֶה לְכֻלָּנוּ׃

9. *chaplet of grace.* A beautiful adornment; in iv. 9 the parallel is *a crown of glory*.

chains about thy neck. A decoration of honour (cf. of Joseph (Gen xli 42) and Daniel (Dan. v. 29).

10–19 WARNING AGAINST ROBBERY WITH MURDER

That this crime is treated first is an indication of its prevalence. The prophet Hosea, in particular, denounced the existence of organized gangs of bandits (iv. 2, vi. 9, vii. 1).

10. *sinners.* The form *chattaim,* as distinct from *choteim,* signifies men habitually addicted to crime. Ibn Ganah defines it as an adjective.

entice thee. To join them with the promise of rich loot (see Malbim, Yair Ohr).

11. *for blood.* To commit robbery though it entails bloodshed (again xii. 6).

the innocent. A harmless wayfarer who offers no resistance (Malbim).

without cause. To be joined with the verb: the ambush has no justification, such as self-defence against an enemy, but only the desire to steal the victim's possessions (see Rashi).

12. *swallow them up alive.* Take all the property they carry with them, in the same manner that the grave receives the body (Metsudath David).

go down into the pit. i.e. the grave (cf. Ps. xxviii. 1, and often). [The words put into the mouth of the enticer disclose an utter callousness about the value of human life.]

13. *all precious substance.* [The addition of *all* and the mention of *filling* their houses with plunder point to a scheme for a whole series of robberies. A career of crime is suggested, not a single act of violence.]

14. *cast in thy lot among us.* If you wish, we will divide the spoils by lot, and you will receive a share like any member of our band (Rashi). You may cast the lots to distribute the loot (Metsudath David).

15 My son, walk not thou in the way with them,
Restrain thy foot from their path;

15 בְּנִי אַל־תֵּלֵךְ בְּדֶרֶךְ אִתָּם
מְנַע רַגְלְךָ מִנְּתִיבָתָם׃

16 For their feet run to evil,
And they make haste to shed blood.

16 כִּי רַגְלֵיהֶם לָרַע יָרוּצוּ
וִימַהֲרוּ לִשְׁפָּךְ־דָּם׃

17 For in vain the net is spread
In the eyes of any bird;

17 כִּי־חִנָּם מְזֹרָה הָרָשֶׁת
בְּעֵינֵי כָּל־בַּעַל כָּנָף׃

18 And these lie in wait for their own blood,
They lurk for their own lives.

18 וְהֵם לְדָמָם יֶאֱרֹבוּ
יִצְפְּנוּ לְנַפְשֹׁתָם׃

19 So are the ways of every one that is greedy of gain;
It taketh away the life of the owners thereof.

19 כֵּן אָרְחוֹת כָּל־בֹּצֵעַ בָּצַע
אֶת־נֶפֶשׁ בְּעָלָיו יִקָּח׃

20 Wisdom crieth aloud in the street,
She uttereth her voice in the broad places;

20 חָכְמוֹת בַּחוּץ תָּרֹנָּה
בָּרְחֹבוֹת תִּתֵּן קוֹלָהּ׃

16. This verse is quoted from the first half of Isa. lix. 7 where, however, the reading is *innocent blood*. The omission of 'innocent' seems to imply that the words have been adopted with a different meaning. If so, *evil* does not signify 'wickedness,' but 'harm' to themselves: they will quickly be brought to a bad end by the arm of justice (so Rashi); and *to shed blood* does not refer to murder but the sentence of death passed upon them by the judges (Saadiah Gaon, quoted by Ibn Nachmiash). Such an interpretation suits the context.

17. *for in vain the net is spread.* The translation produces the opposite meaning of that required, since the nets are not spread in vain to trap birds, and many are caught in the snare. Rashi offers the correct interpretation: 'As in vain the net is sprinkled (with corn) in the sight of any bird,' i.e. the bird vainly imagines that here is food.

18. *lie in wait for their own blood.* 'They overreach themselves and become the executors of their own doom' (Ibn Nachmiash). Another possible rendering is: 'but they (the trappers) lie in wait for their (the birds') blood, they lurk for their lives.' Instead of picking up the corn which attracted them to the net, they find there death. So will it be with a man who is lured by the bandits' bait; not riches but destruction will come to him (Malbim).

19. *greedy of gain.* [By any means, however illegal.] The prospect of abundant loot has the same effect upon such men as the corn in the net has on birds which are tempted by it, viz. death (Rashi).

20–23 THE CALL OF WISDOM

Wisdom, which is personified as a woman, issues her proclamation to all and sundry, urging them to reform their ways and denouncing those who scornfully reject her plea.

20. *wisdom.* [The plural form of the word expresses the abstract idea; according to others, intensity, profound wisdom, or fulness, the perfection of wisdom. So again ix. 1, xxiv. 7; Ps. xlix. 4.]

21 She calleth at the head of the noisy streets,
At the entrances of the gates, in the city, she uttereth her words:

22 'How long, ye thoughtless, will ye love thoughtlessness?
And how long will scorners delight them in scorning,
And fools hate knowledge?

23 Turn you at my reproof;
Behold, I will pour out my spirit unto you,
I will make known my words unto you.

24 Because I have called, and ye refused,
I have stretched out my hand, and no man attended,

25 But ye have set at nought all my counsel,
And would none of my reproof;

בְּרֹאשׁ הֹמִיּוֹת תִּקְרָא 21
בְּפִתְחֵי שְׁעָרִים בָּעִיר
אֲמָרֶיהָ תֹאמֵר׃
עַד־מָתַי ׀ פְּתָיִם תְּאֵהֲבוּ־פֶתִי 22
וְלֵצִים לָצוֹן חָמְדוּ לָהֶם
וּכְסִילִים יִשְׂנְאוּ־דָעַת׃
תָּשׁוּבוּ לְתוֹכַחְתִּי 23
הִנֵּה אַבִּיעָה לָכֶם רוּחִי
אוֹדִיעָה דְבָרַי אֶתְכֶם׃
יַעַן קָרָאתִי וַתְּמָאֵנוּ 24
נָטִיתִי יָדִי וְאֵין מַקְשִׁיב׃
וַתִּפְרְעוּ כָל־עֲצָתִי 25
וְתוֹכַחְתִּי לֹא אֲבִיתֶם׃

21. *head.* The point where several streets branch off and so a suitable spot for attracting a large number (Isa. li. 20; Lam. ii. 19).

noisy streets. Cf. *a tumultuous city* (Isa. xxii. 2). Wherever a crowd of people is assembled wisdom proclaims her message (Metsudath David).

entrances of the gates. Eastern cities have deep gateways which are shaded from the sun, and there the elders sit to adjudicate and discuss local affairs. Accordingly the first half of the verse alludes to the general population, the second to its rulers (Rashi).

22. *ye thoughtless.* The same word as *simple* in verse 4.

scorners. Men who mock at moral principles, wilfully ignore them in their own conduct and corrupt others. The godly shun their company (Ps. i. 1).

fools. Defined as those easily enticed (Rashi, Metsudath Zion).

23. *turn you.* According to this translation, it is an imperative form (Ibn Nachmiash). He suggests also that we translate, 'when will you turn to me?' Accordingly, the word 'when' (the literal translation of 'how long'), in the preceding verse applies to this verse as well.

pour out my spirit. Spirit has the same meaning as 'mind' in the phrase, 'I will speak my mind to you' (Meiri).

make known my words. Although you may pay no attention to them, yet I address my words to you so that you are forewarned (Meiri).

24. *because I have called.* [As the words *how long?* (verse 22) indicate, wisdom has repeatedly issued her appeal. Since it has been in vain, the denunciation is warranted, because the deafness of the people has been deliberate.]

stretched out my hand. A gesture of appeal to approach (Rashi).

25. *set at nought.* [Better, 'neglected'; lit. 'let go.']

I also, in your calamity, will laugh,
I will mock when your dread cometh;

When your dread cometh as a storm,
And your calamity cometh on as a whirlwind;
When trouble and distress come upon you.

Then will they call me, but I will not answer,
They will seek me earnestly, but they shall not find me.

For that they hated knowledge,
And did not choose the fear of the LORD;

They would none of my counsel,
They despised all my reproof.

Therefore shall they eat of the fruit of their own way,
And be filled with their own devices.

26 גַּם־אֲנִי בְּאֵידְכֶם אֶשְׂחָק
אֶלְעַג בְּבֹא פַחְדְּכֶם׃
27 בְּבֹא כשאוה ׀ פַּחְדְּכֶם
וְאֵידְכֶם כְּסוּפָה יֶאֱתֶה
בְּבֹא עֲלֵיכֶם צָרָה וְצוּקָה׃
28 אָז יִקְרָאֻנְנִי וְלֹא אֶעֱנֶה
יְשַׁחֲרֻנְנִי וְלֹא יִמְצָאֻנְנִי׃
29 תַּחַת כִּי־שָׂנְאוּ דָעַת
וְיִרְאַת יְהוָה לֹא בָחָרוּ׃
30 לֹא־אָבוּ לַעֲצָתִי
נָאֲצוּ כָּל־תּוֹכַחְתִּי׃
31 וְיֹאכְלוּ מִפְּרִי דַרְכָּם
וּמִמֹּעֲצֹתֵיהֶם יִשְׂבָּעוּ׃

v. 27 כשואה ק׳

26. *your calamity.* Which is the sequel of neglecting the advice (Ralbag).

will laugh. As they had laughed and mocked at wisdom's warnings (Elijah of Wilna).

27. *storm.* The Hebrew signifies 'a storm which causes devastation' (Kimchi, Shorashim).

28. *I will not answer.* Since they neglected the study of the Torah during their youth, they will no longer be able to grasp it in old age, as the Rabbis state: 'He who learns Torah when he is old — what is he like? He is like ink written on erased paper' (Aboth 4.25). This may also mean that when they are dead, there is no learning wisdom in the grave (Ibn Nachmiash). Elijah of Wilna explains : 'If they pray to Me to help them understand the wisdom of the Torah, I will no longer answer them.'

they shall not find me. If they delve into its wisdom, they will no longer be able to grasp it (Elijah of Wilna). Meiri explains that, although repentance is always accepted, sometimes it does not save the sinner from punishment in this world.

29. *did not choose.* [The doctrine of free will is implied; the choice of godliness or wickedness is in each person's own hands.]

30. *would none of.* As in verse 25.

despised. Rejected with contempt (Metsudoth).

31. *eat of the fruit.* Under God's law of retribution, the reaping will be according to their sowing (Metsudath David).

way. Manner of living.

devices. Except in xxii. 20 the word always has a bad sense.

32 For the waywardness of the thoughtless shall slay them,
And the confidence of fools shall destroy them.

33 But whoso hearkeneth unto me shall dwell securely,
And shall be quiet without fear of evil.'

32 כִּי מְשׁוּבַת פְּתָיִם תַּהַרְגֵם
וְשַׁלְוַת כְּסִילִים תְּאַבְּדֵם:
33 וְשֹׁמֵעַ לִי יִשְׁכָּן־בֶּטַח
וְשַׁאֲנַן מִפַּחַד רָעָה:

2 CHAPTER II ב

1 My son, if thou wilt receive my words,
And lay up my commandments with thee;

2 So that thou make thine ear attend unto wisdom,
And thy heart incline to discernment;

1 בְּנִי אִם־תִּקַּח אֲמָרָי
וּמִצְוֺתַי תִּצְפֹּן אִתָּךְ:
2 לְהַקְשִׁיב לַחָכְמָה אָזְנֶךָ
תַּטֶּה לִבְּךָ לַתְּבוּנָה:

32. *waywardness.* lit. 'turning back,' apostasy (Meiri).

confidence. lit. 'quietness, condition of ease and well-being; here the feeling of security which such circumstances create. It brings about their undoing (Rashi), [because where society is not built upon sound moral foundations, it eventually collapses.]

33. *securely.* Free from danger.

evil. Calamity. The call of wisdom ends on a hopeful note. To hearken at the outset is to avert the sequel of rejection; but if the mistake has been made, the warning stands for the future (Daath Mikra).

CHAPTER II

THE FRUITS OF WISDOM

HAVING described the calamitous effects of rejecting wisdom's direction, the teacher proceeds to recount the happy results which accrue from its acceptance. Here it is an instructor, not wisdom, who speaks.

1. *my son.* See on i. 8.

my words. [Of instruction. It is to be noted that whereas the Prophets merely regarded themselves as messengers of God speaking His words (*thus saith the* LORD*),* in Proverbs the teacher imparts his own doctrine derived from wisdom. Not that there is a conflict between the two, but the teacher does not presume to give the impression that he has received a call to speak in God's name.]

2. *heart.* In Hebrew psychology the seat of man's intellect.

incline. It is insufficient for the *ear* to *attend*; the *heart* (i.e. mind) must also *incline* as evidence of eagerness to absorb what is being taught (Ibn Nachmiash).

discernment. Another form of *binah,* 'understanding,' in i. 2. They are parallel to each other in the next verse. [As with the others of this series of terms, it has to be given an ethical sense.]

3 Yea, if thou call for understanding,
And lift up thy voice for discernment;

3 כִּי אִם לַבִּינָה תִקְרָא
לַתְּבוּנָה תִּתֵּן קוֹלֶךָ׃

4 If thou seek her as silver,
And search for her as for hid treasures;

4 אִם־תְּבַקְשֶׁנָּה כַכָּסֶף
וְכַמַּטְמוֹנִים תַּחְפְּשֶׂנָּה׃

5 Then shalt thou understand the fear of the LORD,
And find the knowledge of God.

5 אָז תָּבִין יִרְאַת יְהוָה
וְדַעַת אֱלֹהִים תִּמְצָא׃

6 For the LORD giveth wisdom,
Out of His mouth cometh knowledge and discernment;

6 כִּי־יְהוָה יִתֵּן חָכְמָה
מִפִּיו דַּעַת וּתְבוּנָה׃

7 He layeth up sound wisdom for the upright,

7 וצפן לַיְשָׁרִים תּוּשִׁיָּה

v. 7. יצפון ק׳

3. *call for.* Some render 'call to.' In either case the meaning is to invite to come.

lift up thy voice. A weaker form of *call,* indicative of less intensity (Malbim).

4. *silver.* The Hebrew may denote silver ore or silver coins. Preference should perhaps be given to the former, because the parallelism favours the thought of exerting oneself to possess what has to be brought up from the depths. A graphic description of the process of mining for silver and other precious metals occurs in Job xxviii. as a preface to the question, *'But wisdom where shall it be found? And where is the place of understanding?'* (According to Daath Mikra).

hid treasures. Valuables were deposited in secret places, often being buried, as a protection against theft (cf. Isa. xlv. 3).

5. *the fear of the* LORD. As it is the *beginning of knowledge* (i. 7), so it is the goal of the search for wisdom. One can only understand what *the fear of the* LORD means and attain to *the knowledge of God* through moral perfection (Malbim).

the knowledge of God. This refers to the secrets of the Torah (Metsudath David). Malbim elaborates and explains that this refers to knowledge of the Creation and the Heavenly Chariot, the profound intricacies of theology.

6. *the* LORD *giveth wisdom.* He is its source and assists those who strive to achieve it (Ibn Nachmiash).

out of his mouth. Whatever He commands is distinguished by *knowledge and discernment.* By conforming to His precepts, man lives in the light of these ethical principles (Daath Mikra).

7. *He layeth up.* So the *kerë*; the translation of the *kethib* is 'and He had laid up.' The search for wisdom as for a hidden treasure cannot be fruitless, because He has deposited it and it is there to be discovered (see Rashi, Metsudath David). The Midrash explains that when a person is formed in his mother's womb, the Torah he is destined to learn is laid up for him.

sound wisdom. Hebrew *tushiyyah,* a common term in Proverbs and Job. Targum renders it 'glory,' LXX 'deliverance,' or 'salvation.' Ibn Nachmiash derives it from *yesh,* there is. This refers to the Torah which is the essence of this world and its preservation as well as the preservation of the soul in the hereafter. Gerondi explains it as 'foundation,' for the Torah is the foundation of the world (Ibn Nachmiash).

He is a shield to them that walk in integrity;

8 That He may guard the paths of justice,
And preserve the way of His godly ones.

9 Then shalt thou understand righteousness and justice,
And equity, yea, every good path.

10 For wisdom shall enter into thy heart,
And knowledge shall be pleasant unto thy soul;

11 Discretion shall watch over thee,
Discernment shall guard thee;

12 To deliver thee from the way of evil,
From the men that speak froward things;

מָגֵן לְהֹלְכֵי תֹם׃
לִנְצֹר אָרְחוֹת מִשְׁפָּט
וְדֶרֶךְ חֲסִידָו יִשְׁמֹר׃
אָז תָּבִין צֶדֶק וּמִשְׁפָּט
וּמֵישָׁרִים כָּל־מַעְגַּל־טוֹב׃
כִּי־תָבוֹא חָכְמָה בְלִבֶּךָ
וְדַעַת לְנַפְשְׁךָ יִנְעָם׃
מְזִמָּה תִּשְׁמֹר עָלֶיךָ
תְּבוּנָה תִנְצְרֶכָּה׃
לְהַצִּילְךָ מִדֶּרֶךְ רָע
מֵאִישׁ מְדַבֵּר תַּהְפֻּכוֹת׃

v. 8. חסידיו ק׳

8. *that He may guard.* The Hebrew is literally 'to guard,' which may mean 'that they may keep' (R.V. margin) intact. If this is accepted, the continuation is: 'and the way of His godly ones He will preserve.' By their adoption of *sound wisdom* they maintain the right paths, and these will in turn be guarded by God (Rashi, Ibn Ezra).

godly ones. Hebrew *chasid,* the singular in a collective sense according to the *kethib,* the *kerë* being plural. This word is used only here in Proverbs but common in the Psalms. [The word defines one who loves God and is therefore loved by Him.]

9. *righteousness . . . equity.* See on i. 3.

good path. In walking through life. The Hebrew for *path* is less common. Some explain it as a straight path (Ibn Nachmiash). Others, as a circuitous path (Malbim, Wertheimer).

10. *enter into thy heart.* Taking up her abode there, that you do not forget her (Elijah of Wilna).

shall be pleasant. [And therefore freely welcomed to stay without being forced to do so.]

11. *watch . . . guard.* Man must provide this guardianship over himself to avoid wrongdoing. It does not come to him unbidden (Ibn Nachmiash, Elijah of Wilna).

12. *to deliver thee.* As in i. 10 a warning is given against corrupting companionship, there which may lead him into a life of crime, here which may lure him to heresy (Metsudath David).

way of evil. The parallelism suggests that by *evil* is to be understood false doctrine, the opposite of wisdom (Malbim).

froward things. lit. 'things which are upside down,' contrary to what is true and proper. Rashi plausibly interprets the word as referring to the ideas of the Epicureans which ran counter to the Hebraic ethical doctrine. Epicurus, the Athenian philosopher of the fourth and third centuries B.C.E., taught that physical pleasure was the aim of life. This hedonistic outlook, of course, antedated him, and is alluded to in Isa. xxii. 13, *Let us eat and drink, for tomorrow we shall die.*

13 הַעֹזְבִים אָרְחוֹת יֹשֶׁר
לָלֶכֶת בְּדַרְכֵי־חֹשֶׁךְ׃

Who leave the paths of uprightness,
To walk in the ways of darkness;

14 הַשְּׂמֵחִים לַעֲשׂוֹת רָע
יָגִילוּ בְּתַהְפֻּכוֹת רָע׃

Who rejoice to do evil,
And delight in the frowardness of evil;

15 אֲשֶׁר אָרְחֹתֵיהֶם עִקְּשִׁים
וּנְלוֹזִים בְּמַעְגְּלוֹתָם׃

Who are crooked in their ways,
And perverse in their paths;

16 לְהַצִּילְךָ מֵאִשָּׁה זָרָה
מִנָּכְרִיָּה אֲמָרֶיהָ הֶחֱלִיקָה׃

To deliver thee from the strange woman,
Even from the alien woman that maketh smooth her words;

17 הַעֹזֶבֶת אַלּוּף נְעוּרֶיהָ
וְאֶת־בְּרִית אֱלֹהֶיהָ שָׁכֵחָה׃

That forsaketh the lord of her youth,
And forgetteth the covenant of her God;

13. *ways of darkness.* In Proverbs the path of virtue is illumined and the way of wickedness shrouded in darkness (iv. 18f.).

14. *rejoice . . . delight.* The verbs are significant and lend support to Rashi's interpretation of verse 12. Here is no rejection of wisdom from ignorance or simplicity; it is a wilful decision due to a false conception of happiness.

evil. As in the *way of evil* (verse 12).

15. *crooked in their ways.* The Hebrew construction is different from xxviii. 6, and there is no preposition *in*. Render: 'whose ways are crooked and they are perverse in their paths.'

16. *strange woman.* Despite Rashi's insistence that the phrase is used metaphorically of heretical doctrine, the numerous warnings in the Book have a literal interpretation as well (see i. 6). Immorality is a frequent subject of prophetical reproof, particularly when it involved the sin of adultery (Jer. xxiii. 10, 14; Hos. iv. 14). In Proverbs the warning is against consorting with married women who are dissolute. They are described as *strange* or *alien* either in contempt or because they were usually less moral when of non-Israelite origin (cf. *strange god,* Ps. xliv. 21 and *the foreign gods of the land,* Deut. xxxi. 16). Solomon's wives are called *foreign women* (1 Kings xi. 1, 8). In Rabbinic language a person of this class is spoken of as 'an Aramean woman.' The disciple of wisdom is expected to live a chaste life.

maketh smooth her words. Uses seductive language, of which an illustration is given in vii. 14ff.

17. *the lord of her youth.* Her husband whom she had married in girlhood, marriage taking place in the Orient at an early age. The phrase is applied by Israel to God in Jer. iii. 4.

forgetteth. [Better, 'is forgetful of.' A woman cannot forget that she had a husband, but may be unmindful of her duty to him.]

covenant of her God. The prohibition of adultery formed part of God's covenant with Israel (Exod. xx. 13) (Ibn Ezra).

18 For her house sinketh down unto death,
And her paths unto the shades;

19 None that go unto her return,
Neither do they attain unto the paths of life;

20 That thou mayest walk in the way of good men,
And keep the paths of the righteous.

21 For the upright shall dwell in the land,
And the whole-hearted shall remain in it.

22 But the wicked shall be cut off from the land,
And the faithless shall be plucked up out of it.

כִּי שָׁחָה אֶל־מָוֶת בֵּיתָהּ 18
וְאֶל־רְפָאִים מַעְגְּלֹתֶיהָ׃
כָּל־בָּאֶיהָ לֹא יְשׁוּבוּן 19
וְלֹא־יַשִּׂיגוּ אָרְחוֹת חַיִּים׃
לְמַעַן תֵּלֵךְ בְּדֶרֶךְ טוֹבִים 20
וְאָרְחוֹת צַדִּיקִים תִּשְׁמֹר׃
כִּי־יְשָׁרִים יִשְׁכְּנוּ־אָרֶץ 21
וּתְמִימִים יִוָּתְרוּ בָהּ׃
וּרְשָׁעִים מֵאֶרֶץ יִכָּרֵתוּ 22
וּבוֹגְדִים יִסְּחוּ מִמֶּנָּה׃

18. *her house.* An immoral resort (Rashi). Ibn Ezra renders: 'For she sinketh down into death, (which is) her house.'

sinketh down unto death. Life is shortened for those who frequent it (Metsudath David).

the shades. Mentioned again in this sense in Isa. xiv. 9; Ps. lxxxviii. 11; Job xxvi. 5. The inhabitants of Sheol (see on i. 12), the dead. (According to Metsudath David, Ibn Ezra, Rashi).

19. *return.* From their evil courses (Ibn Ezra); but more probably, return from the gates of Sheol to resume their normal life (cf. Ps. xxx. 4) Daath Mikra).

attain unto the paths of life. i.e. the paths of the life of the soul (Ibn Ezra).

20. This and the following verses summarize the ultimate purpose of wisdom's call in this chapter.

21. *dwell in the land.* viz. the land of Israel in which the people dwelt as the fulfilment of God's promise. Residence there consequently implied the continuance of His favour and the enjoyment of His blessings (Daath Mikra).

whole-hearted. The word in God's exhortation to Abraham, *Walk before Me, and be thou whole-hearted* (Gen. xvii. 1), i.e. steadfast in loyalty to God and resolute against temptation to unfaithfulness (Malbim).

22. *be cut off from the land.* [Forfeit all the privileges which the virtuous enjoy.]

plucked up. For the verb, cf. xv. 25.

3 CHAPTER III ג

My son, forget not my teaching;
But let thy heart keep my commandments;

For length of days, and years of life,
And peace, will they add to thee.

Let not kindness and truth forsake thee;
Bind them about thy neck,
Write them upon the table of thy heart;

1 בְּנִי תּוֹרָתִי אַל־תִּשְׁכָּח
וּמִצְוֺתַי יִצֹּר לִבֶּךָ׃
2 כִּי אֹרֶךְ יָמִים וּשְׁנוֹת חַיִּים
וְשָׁלוֹם יוֹסִיפוּ לָךְ׃
3 חֶסֶד וֶאֱמֶת אַל־יַעַזְבֻךָ
קָשְׁרֵם עַל־גַּרְגְּרוֹתֶיךָ
כָּתְבֵם עַל־לוּחַ לִבֶּךָ׃

CHAPTER III

1–10 BLESSINGS OF OBEDIENCE

In extolling the virtue of obedience to his instruction, the teacher utters an emphatic warning against the common fault of the young, viz. excessive self-confidence and a sense of being all-wise. Without Divine guidance man is liable to go astray.

1. *my teaching . . . commandments.* See on ii. 1.

2. *length of days.* Cf. the promise for honouring parents, *that thy days may be long upon the land* (Exod. xx. 12), and the exhortation of Moses, *to love the* Lord *thy God, to hearken to His voice, and to cleave unto Him; for that is thy life and the length of thy days* (Deut. xxx. 20). Walking in God's chosen path, the disciple will earn God's approval and protection, and thereby live even longer than his appointed years without coming to a violent and premature end, to which they who choose evil ways are exposed (Ibn Caspi).

years of life. i.e. of happiness (cf. xvi. 15).

peace. Hebrew *shalom* is a comprehensive term meaning 'wholeness,' all the factors which make existence complete and worthwhile. Health, prosperity and a happy domestic life lose their value when conditions threaten their destruction. Consequently the supreme blessing which God can bestow is *peace,* since it is the foundation upon which everything desirable rests. The Rabbis (Uktsin iii. 3) depict peace as the only vessel that contains blessing.

3. *kindness and truth.* Divine attributes characteristic of God's relationship with man (Gen. xxiv. 27, xxxii. 11; Exod. xxxiv. 6), they are recommended for man's relationship with his fellow (xvi. 6, xx. 28). *Kindness* (Hebrew *chesed*) has its root in love; and *truth* in this connection has the same meaning as faithfulness (Daath Mikra).

bind them. viz. kindness and truth, or as some commentators hold, *teaching* and *commandments* of verse 1 (Ibn Ezra).

about thy neck. Carry them about thy person like the signet, attached to a cord, which is worn about the neck (Gen. xxxviii. 18) and is always visible (Meiri).

write . . . heart. Again in vii. 3 (cf. Jer. xvii. 1). A metaphorical phrase based upon the law of Deut. vi. 9, to express the idea of keeping the instruction ever fresh in mind (Ralbag).

4 So shalt thou find grace and good favour
In the sight of God and man.

5 Trust in the LORD with all thy heart,
And lean not upon thine own understanding.

6 In all thy ways acknowledge Him,
And He will direct thy paths.

7 Be not wise in thine own eyes;
Fear the LORD, and depart from evil;

8 It shall be health to thy navel,
And marrow to thy bones.

וּמְצָא־חֵן וְשֵׂכֶל טוֹב 4
בְּעֵינֵי אֱלֹהִים וְאָדָם׃
בְּטַח אֶל־יְהוָה בְּכָל־לִבֶּךָ 5
וְאֶל־בִּינָתְךָ אַל־תִּשָּׁעֵן׃
בְּכָל־דְּרָכֶיךָ דָעֵהוּ 6
וְהוּא יְיַשֵּׁר אֹרְחֹתֶיךָ׃
אַל־תְּהִי חָכָם בְּעֵינֶיךָ 7
יְרָא אֶת־יְהוָה וְסוּר מֵרָע׃
רִפְאוּת תְּהִי לְשָׁרֶּךָ 8
וְשִׁקּוּי לְעַצְמוֹתֶיךָ׃

4. *so shalt thou find.* lit. 'and (in consequence) find'; the imperative of the verb (Ibn Ezra, Meiri).

good favour. Cf. xiii. 15 and Ps. cxi. 10 where it is translated *good understanding*. Here the intention seems to be 'a reputation for prudent and good behavior, a favourable impression' (see Ibn Nachmiash).

in the sight of God and man. An important declaration indicative of the Hebraic standpoint that the service of God cannot be kept separate from the service of one's fellow-men. The two are intertwined resulting in the approval of both God and man. 'He in whom the spirit of his fellow-creatures takes delight, in him the Spirit of the All-present takes delight; and he in whom the spirit of his fellow-creatures takes not delight, in Him the Spirit of the All-present takes not delight' (Aboth 3.10).

5. *trust in the* LORD. For a knowledge of the true way of living and for guidance in correct behaviour (Malbim).

with all thy heart. With an undivided heart, completely and at all times. Do not accept His direction only when it conforms with your own inclination (Ibn Caspi).

6. *ways.* The various activities and pursuits of life (Metsudath David).

acknowledge Him. lit. 'know Him'; have Him in mind and walk in the light of the knowledge which he has imparted (Gerondi).

direct. lit. 'make straight,' i.e. remove obstacles. If the paths which have been chosen are approved by Him, He will help man to walk therein (Gerondi).

7. *be not wise . . . eyes.* In making the choice of *thy ways*; another form of *lean not upon thine own understanding* (cf. xxvi. 12; Isa. v. 21 (Gerondi).

fear the LORD. That being *the beginning of knowledge* (i. 7) which guides man to a virtuous life.

depart from evil. Since being wise in one's own eyes often leads to the acceptance of evil (Ibn Nachmiash).

8. *health.* lit. 'healing.' The advice given, if adopted, will result in the body being invigorated, with a corresponding effect upon the will-power. He will be firm in his resolution to choose the good and reject what is wrong (see Meiri, Metsudath David).

9 Honour the LORD with thy substance,
And with the first-fruits of all thine increase;

10 So shall thy barns be filled with plenty,
And thy vats shall overflow with new wine.

11 My son, despise not the chastening of the LORD,
Neither spurn thou His correction;

9 כַּבֵּד אֶת־יְהוָה מֵהוֹנֶךָ
וּמֵרֵאשִׁית כָּל־תְּבוּאָתֶךָ׃
10 וְיִמָּלְאוּ אֲסָמֶיךָ שָׂבָע
וְתִירוֹשׁ יְקָבֶיךָ יִפְרֹצוּ׃
11 מוּסַר יְהוָה בְּנִי אַל־תִּמְאָס
וְאַל־תָּקֹץ בְּתוֹכַחְתּוֹ׃

9. The writer evidently had the law of Deut. xviii. 4, xxvi. 2 in mind. What one has acquired is God's bounty and must be utilized in ways which He approves, e.g. helping the poor. If the manner in which wealth is spent honours God, it can never be ill-spent (Rashi, Gerondi).

10. The doctrine that adherence to God's precepts brings material reward is often repeated in Proverbs, as elsewhere in the Bible; but such reward is not held out as an inducement to good conduct. Disinterested love and service of God is fundamental in Judaism and has been well summarized in the Talmudic comment on, Ps. cxii. 1, *Happy is the man that feareth the* LORD, *that delighteth greatly in His commandments* — in His commandments, not in the reward of His commandments! [The correct interpretation of the passage is: where morality bears sway, the sequel is a secure, happy and contented life for the community as a whole and its members individually. Conversely, where vice is prevalent, the standard of happiness and prosperity is inevitably reduced.]

11–12 GOD'S CHASTENING

The insertion of this brief section apparently has the purpose of forestalling a question which the pupil may well have asked his teacher, viz. 'You tell me that fidelity to wisdom, which reflects God's will, is followed by happiness and prosperity; how is it, then, that we see men enduring adversity who have displayed such faithfulness?' [The answer given coincides with that offered to Job by his friends Eliphaz and Elihu (Job v. 17, xxxiii. 12ff.)] (Ibn Nachmiash).

11. *despise not.* Rather, 'reject not.' What God sends upon thee has a beneficent purpose; do not refuse to put it to proper use (Ralbag).

chastening of the LORD. Should misfortune befall thee, accept it as a manifestation of His love in a submissive spirit because it is His method of exercising discipline upon thee (Rashi). This interpretation is in no way inconsistent with that of Ibn Ezra on the following verse: happy is the man who has acquired wisdom, because through it he will withhold himself from sinning, and sufferings will not come upon him. Adversity may produce one of two reactions: it can be understood as Divine discipline and induce the person to amend his ways; or it can make him defiant and confirm him in his evil. The teacher appeals to his disciple to adopt the first interpretation (cf. *It is good for me that I have been afflicted, in order that I might learn Thy statutes,* Ps. cxix. 71).

spurn. lit. 'feel a loathing for,' and so create a feeling of resentment and rebelliousness (Meiri).

12 For whom the LORD loveth He correcteth,
Even as a father the son in whom he delighteth.

13 Happy is the man that findeth wisdom,
And the man that obtaineth understanding.

14 For the merchandise of it is better than the merchandise of silver,
And the gain thereof than fine gold.

15 She is more precious than rubies;
And all the things thou canst desire are not to be compared unto her.

16 Length of days is in her right hand;

כִּי אֶת אֲשֶׁר יֶאֱהַב יְהֹוָה יוֹכִיחַ 12
וּכְאָב אֶת־בֵּן יִרְצֶה׃
אַשְׁרֵי אָדָם מָצָא חָכְמָה 13
וְאָדָם יָפִיק תְּבוּנָה׃
כִּי טוֹב סַחְרָהּ מִסְּחַר־כָּסֶף 14
וּמֵחָרוּץ תְּבוּאָתָהּ׃
יְקָרָה הִיא מפניים 15
וְכָל־חֲפָצֶיךָ לֹא יִשְׁווּ־בָהּ׃
אֹרֶךְ יָמִים בִּימִינָהּ 16

מפנינים ק׳ v. 15.

12. *whom the* LORD *loveth.* This exhortation is deservedly famous. It is one of the deepest sayings in the Bible. The Rabbis coined the beautiful phrase 'chastenings of love' to explain the sufferings of the righteous.

even as a father. Based on Deut. viii. 5.

13–18 BLESSINGS OF WISDOM

13. *happy is.* lit. 'the happiness of.' The phrase is frequent in the Bible, signifying either the pleasurable effect of God's material bounty, or the spiritual joy and tranquility of heart which result from trustfulness in Him. The writer may have had a combination of both senses in mind (see Kimchi, Ps. i. 1).

14. *the merchandise of it.* The profit which accrues from wisdom is of greater value than monetary gain. Silver and gold do no one any good until they leave his possession to be exchanged for something else. Wisdom, however, benefits him immediately (Ibn Nachmiash).

fine gold. The Hebrew, which is literally 'yellow (metal)', is only a poetical synonym for gold. As usual, identifying 'wisdom' with Torah, Rabbinic literature relates: Rabbi José the son of Kisma said, "I was once walking by the way, when a man met me and saluted me, and I returned the salutation. He said to me, 'Rabbi, from what place art thou?' I said to him, 'I come from a great city of sages and scribes.' He said to me, 'If thou art willing to dwell with us in our place, I will give thee a thousand thousand golden dinars and precious stones and pearls.' I said to him, 'Wert thou to give me all the silver and gold and precious stones and pearls in the world, I would not dwell anywhere but in a home of the Torah" (Aboth 6.9).

15. *rubies.* Modern authorities prefer the translation 'corals,' which were obtained from the Red Sea and India. The verse is almost identical with viii. 11 (Daath Mikra).

16. *length of days.* Cf. verse 2.

In her left hand are riches and honour.

בִּשְׂמֹאולָהּ עֹשֶׁר וְכָבוֹד׃

17 Her ways are ways of pleasantness,
And all her paths are peace.

17 דְּרָכֶיהָ דַרְכֵי־נֹעַם
וְכָל־נְתִיבוֹתֶיהָ שָׁלוֹם׃

18 She is a tree of life to them that lay hold upon her,
And happy is every one that holdeth her fast.

18 עֵץ־חַיִּים הִיא לַמַּחֲזִיקִים בָּהּ
וְתֹמְכֶיהָ מְאֻשָּׁר׃

19 The LORD by wisdom founded the earth;
By understanding He established the heavens.

19 יְהוָה בְּחָכְמָה יָסַד־אָרֶץ
כּוֹנֵן שָׁמַיִם בִּתְבוּנָה׃

20 By His knowledge the depths were broken up,
And the skies drop down the dew.

20 בְּדַעְתּוֹ תְּהוֹמוֹת נִבְקָעוּ
וּשְׁחָקִים יִרְעֲפוּ־טָל׃

riches. Although verse 14 had declared the intellectual and moral fruits of wisdom to be of higher value than financial profit, it is now asserted that material advantages are also gained.

honour. When combined with *riches,* the Hebrew word always signifies the splendour of luxury. It is used with this meaning of the priestly vestments (Exod. xxviii. 2, 40) and the cedars of Lebanon (Isa. xxxv. 2).

17. *pleasantness.* A pleasant life which yields satisfaction and is free of worries (Daath Mikra). This verse and the next are included in the Jewish liturgy for recital when the Scroll of the Torah is returned to the Ark in the Synagogue (*P.B.*, p. 71).

18. *tree of life.* A source of life; an allusion to the tree in the Garden of Eden (Gen. ii. 9) (Ibn Ezra). The phrase is repeated in xi. 30, xiii. 12, xv. 4.

and happy . . . fast. lit. 'and they that grasp her, each one is made happy,' the verb being singular. Possessing wisdom a man holds the key to the true wealth of life. A Midrashic proverb (Num. Rabbah 19.3) declares, 'Lackest thou wisdom, what hast thou acquired? Hast acquired wisdom, what lackest thou?'

19–20 WISDOM AND CREATION

The part which wisdom played in the creation of the universe is elaborated in viii. 22ff. As it then changed chaos to order, so it can affect each human life. That seems to be the purpose of the introduction of these verses at this point.

19. *by wisdom.* The creation of wisdom preceded that of the universe (viii. 23).

understanding. Identical with wisdom (Meiri); it was present when the heavens were established (viii. 27). This concept of the role of wisdom at the inception of the world will be discussed in the notes on chapter viii.

20. *His knowledge.* Also identical with wisdom as the controlling force of the physical universe (Meiri).

depths. Subterranean stores of water. These were *broken up* (cf. Gen. vii. 11) to provide the water of seas and rivers (Meiri).

skies. Poetical word for 'heaven,' with the literal meaning of 'powdered dust.' Meiri defines it as clouds. The Talmud (Hagigah 12b), however, considers it the third heaven.

21 My son, let not them depart from thine eyes;
Keep sound wisdom and discretion;

22 So shall they be life unto thy soul,
And grace to thy neck.

23 Then shalt thou walk in thy way securely,
And thou shalt not dash thy foot.

24 When thou liest down, thou shalt not be afraid;
Yea, thou shalt lie down, and thy sleep shall be sweet.

25 Be not afraid of sudden terror,
Neither of the destruction of the wicked, when it cometh;

21 בְּנִי אַל־יָלֻזוּ מֵעֵינֶיךָ
נְצֹר תֻּשִׁיָּה וּמְזִמָּה׃
22 וְיִהְיוּ חַיִּים לְנַפְשֶׁךָ
וְחֵן לְגַרְגְּרֹתֶיךָ׃
23 אָז תֵּלֵךְ לָבֶטַח דַּרְכֶּךָ
וְרַגְלְךָ לֹא תִגּוֹף׃
24 אִם־תִּשְׁכַּב לֹא־תִפְחָד
וְשָׁכַבְתָּ וְעָרְבָה שְׁנָתֶךָ׃
25 אַל־תִּירָא מִפַּחַד פִּתְאֹם
וּמִשֹּׁאַת רְשָׁעִים כִּי תָבֹא׃

dew. [The phenomenon of dew, which falls very heavily in the East, was more impressive to the Oriental than rain. During the long dry seasons the soil depends upon it for moisture.]

21–26 FURTHER BLESSINGS OF WISDOM

21. *let not them depart.* If this section is connected with the foregoing verses, the object *them* must refer to 'wisdom and understanding.' The disciple is advised to keep a constant watch on them as one guards a treasure (Meiri).

sound wisdom. See on ii. 7.

discretion. See on i. 4.

22. *life.* Cf. verse 18.

unto thy soul. Perhaps a Hebraism for 'unto thee.' If taken literally the sense is that as the dew from heaven gives life to the soil, wisdom from God vitalizes the soul (Meiri).

grace to thy neck. Cf. i. 9. For the neck is apparent to all. It is like saying, 'With them shalt thou find favour in everyone's eyes' (Meiri). Strictly speaking, *gargerothecha* refers to the rings of the trachea. This denotes speech. When thou speakest of wisdom, thou wilt find favour in everyone's eyes (Malbim).

23. *securely.* Free from anxiety and danger (cf. i. 33) (Malbim).

dash thy foot. Cf. Ps. xci. 12, *lest thou dash thy foot against a stone,* where, however, the protective agency is angels.

24. *when thou liest down.* A reminiscence of Ps. xci. 5, *thou shalt not be afraid of the terror by night.* The Hebrew is: 'when thou shalt lie down (to sleep), and (when) thou hast laid down' (Malbim).

shall be sweet. Because undisturbed (cf. Jer. xxxi. 26).

25. *sudden terror.* A frightening experience which comes unexpectedly (Daath Mikra).

destruction of the wicked. Devastation (cf. i. 27) caused by wicked men (Isaiah da Trani). Some commentators interpret it as the devastating storm of retribution which overthrows the wicked but leaves the devotee of wisdom unharmed (Rashi).

26 כִּֽי־יְהֹוָה יִהְיֶה בְכִסְלֶךָ
וְשָׁמַר רַגְלְךָ מִלָּכֶד׃

For the LORD will be thy confidence,
And will keep thy foot from being caught.

27 אַל־תִּמְנַע־טוֹב מִבְּעָלָיו
בִּהְיוֹת לְאֵל יָדֶיךָ לַעֲשׂוֹת׃

Withhold not good from him to whom it is due,
When it is in the power of thy hand to do it.

28 אַל־תֹּאמַר לְרֵעֶיךָ ׀ לֵךְ וָשׁוּב
וּמָחָר אֶתֵּן וְיֵשׁ אִתָּךְ׃

Say not unto thy neighbour: 'Go, and come again,
And to-morrow I will give'; when thou hast it by thee.

29 אַל־תַּחֲרֹשׁ עַל־רֵעֲךָ רָעָה
וְהוּא־יוֹשֵׁב לָבֶטַח אִתָּךְ׃

Devise not evil against thy neighbour,
Seeing he dwelleth securely by thee.

30 אַל־תָּרוּב עִם־אָדָם חִנָּם
אִם־לֹא גְמָלְךָ רָעָה׃

Strive not with a man without cause,
If he have done thee no harm.

31 אַל־תְּקַנֵּא בְּאִישׁ חָמָס
וְאַל־תִּבְחַר בְּכָל־דְּרָכָיו׃

Envy thou not the man of violence,
And choose none of his ways.

32 כִּי תוֹעֲבַת יְהֹוָה נָלוֹז
וְאֶת־יְשָׁרִים סוֹדוֹ׃

For the perverse is an abomination to the LORD;
But His counsel is with the upright.

v. 27. ידך ק׳ v. 28. לרעך ק׳ v. 30. תריב ק׳

26. *thy confidence.* [Reliance upon Him will prevent a feeling of helplessness.]

27–35 DUTY TO ONE'S FELLOWS

27. *him to whom it is due.* lit. 'its owners.' The Jewish commentators understand the allusion to be to charity upon which the poor have a claim. The LXX similarly renders 'to the poor,' and most moderns agree with this interpretation.

28. *neighbour.* The *kethib* was construed as plural and the *kerë* as singular.

29. *seeing he dwelleth securely.* [He is unsuspecting and has complete trust; therefore he takes no measures for self-protection.]

30. *without cause.* Do not pick a quarrel and stir up contention hastily because you believe that your neighbour has done you harm. Perhaps it is untrue and there is no cause for it (J. Kimchi). A warning against contentiousness is often mentioned in this Book (cf. x. 12, xiii. 10, xv. 18, xvii. 14, xx. 3, etc.).

31. *envy thou not.* Men who have gained riches by illegal means (cf. i. 11ff.) and so be tempted to follow their evil example (cf. Ps. lxxiii. 3) (Rashi).

32. *perverse.* The word is found in ii. 15.

abomination. Something repellent to God (Meiri).

33 The curse of the LORD is in the house of the wicked;
But He blesseth the habitation of the righteous.

34 If it concerneth the scorners, He scorneth them,
But unto the humble He giveth grace.

35 The wise shall inherit honour;
But as for the fools, they carry away shame.

מְאֵרַת יְהוָה בְּבֵית רָשָׁע
וּנְוֵה צַדִּיקִים יְבָרֵךְ׃
אִם־לַלֵּצִים הוּא־יָלִיץ
וְלַעֲנִיִּים יִתֶּן־חֵן׃
כָּבוֹד חֲכָמִים יִנְחָלוּ
וּכְסִילִים מֵרִים קָלוֹן׃

v. 34. ולענוים ק׳

counsel. lit. 'secret,' intimate relationship (cf. Ps. xxv. 14) (Meiri).

33. *curse of the* LORD. Although you see that the wicked has a permanent house, you should be aware that the curse of the LORD will be upon it to diminish it and totally destroy it (Malbim).

but He blesseth. On the other hand, the righteous, although they may have only a temporary makeshift dwelling, like a shepherd's hut, will experience the blessing of the LORD (Malbim). Elijah of Wilna, too, explains the difference in this manner, but metaphorically. This world, which is to the wicked as a permanent dwelling, will be cursed by the LORD, surely the hereafter, which is to him as a temporary dwelling. On the other hand, the righteous, who consider this world temporary, will enjoy God's blessing even in this world; surely in the hereafter, which they consider their permanent dwelling. This attitude is plainly illustrated by the anecdote concerning the sainted Chafetz Chaim, who, upon being questioned concerning his meager furniture, replied that he was merely a wayfarer passing through.

34. *if it concerneth the scorners.* The meaning of the Hebrew is uncertain. Perhaps the translation should be: 'if (He giveth an award) to the scorners, He showeth (them) scorn.' For *scorners,* see in i. 22. God pays them back in kind. The rabbinic interpretation is: if men wish to lead evil lives, the door is open for them to do so; God neither helps nor impedes them.

the humble. Opposite of *scorners,* they who humbly submit to God's will. The *kerë* is *anavim,* 'meek,' and the *kethib* reads *aniyyim,* 'poor, afflicted.'

He giveth grace. i.e. that the *humble* obtain favour in the sight of others (Metsudath David).

35. *the wise.* [In an ethical sense, the followers of wisdom.]

inherit. Better, 'acquire.'

honour. The respect and approbation of their fellows. [The high qualities of the wise being recognized, they will be accorded an honoured position in the community] (Meiri).

they carry away. The form is singular; each one of them carries away shame as his allotted portion. [He earns the contempt of his fellow-men, and his status among them is a degraded one] (Metsudath David).

Hear, ye children, the instruction of a father,
And attend to know understanding.

For I give you good doctrine;
Forsake ye not my teaching.

For I was a son unto my father,
Tender and an only one in the sight of my mother.

And he taught me, and said unto me:
Let thy heart hold fast my words,
Keep my commandments, and live;

1 שִׁמְעוּ בָנִים מוּסַר אָב
וְהַקְשִׁיבוּ לָדַעַת בִּינָה׃
2 כִּי לֶקַח טוֹב נָתַתִּי לָכֶם
תּוֹרָתִי אַל־תַּעֲזֹבוּ׃
3 כִּי־בֵן הָיִיתִי לְאָבִי
רַךְ וְיָחִיד לִפְנֵי אִמִּי׃
4 וַיֹּרֵנִי וַיֹּאמֶר לִי
יִתְמָךְ־דְּבָרַי לִבֶּךָ
שְׁמֹר מִצְוֹתַי וֶחְיֵה׃

CHAPTER IV

1–9 A FATHER'S ADMONITION

IN this beautiful cameo we are allowed a glimpse into a pious Israelite's home. Here it is not a teacher 'assuming the character of a father,' as some moderns hold, who addresses his pupil, but a father giving earnest and loving advice to his children (Malbim). His exhortation is made the more impressive by the autobiographical detail which he included. We see how the injunction of Deut. vi. 7 was faithfully observed.

1. *children.* Plural as in v. 7, vii. 24.

instruction of a father. Cf. i. 8, *the instruction of thy father.* The absence of 'your' in this verse may indicate that he is imparting to them paternal instruction which he had himself received from his father (Malbim). Rashi explains *father* as God, as he does in i. 8. See below how he explains verses 3ff.

to know understanding. In addition to hearkening to the instruction I received from my father, try to know what I have understood and deduced therefrom. Through this, you will know everything thoroughly (Malbim).

2. *doctrine.* Hebrew *lekach,* from a root 'to receive.' It accordingly represents not original teaching but that which is traditional, transmitted from the past. In this verse, it appropriately describes the lessons which his own father had taught him (Malbim).

teaching. Hebrew *Torah,* in its original meaning of 'direction.'

my teaching. This represents the original teaching of the father (Malbim). Rashi explains that the prophet is speaking in the name of God, Who gave the Torah to Israel.

3. *a son unto my father.* A dutiful and obedient son (Gerondi). Rashi explains that God called Solomon his son (2 Samuel vii. 14).

tender and an only one. His mother showered her love upon him, but did not spoil him by letting him do as he pleased. She corrected his failings, and he reciprocated with filial respect and devotion (Meiri).

4. *he taught me.* Better, 'he directed me.'

live. i.e. live worthily and happily (Daath Mikra).

5 Get wisdom, get understanding;
Forget not, neither decline from the words of my mouth;

קְנֵה חָכְמָה קְנֵה בִינָה
אַל־תִּשְׁכַּח וְאַל־תֵּט מֵאִמְרֵי־פִי׃

6 Forsake her not, and she will preserve thee;
Love her, and she will keep thee.

אַל־תַּעַזְבֶהָ וְתִשְׁמְרֶךָּ
אֱהָבֶהָ וְתִצְּרֶךָּ׃

7 The beginning of wisdom is: Get wisdom;
Yea, with all thy getting get understanding.

רֵאשִׁית חָכְמָה קְנֵה חָכְמָה
וּבְכָל־קִנְיָנְךָ קְנֵה בִינָה׃

8 Extol her, and she will exalt thee;
She will bring thee to honour, when thou dost embrace her.

סַלְסְלֶהָ וּתְרוֹמְמֶךָּ
תְּכַבֵּדְךָ כִּי תְחַבְּקֶנָּה׃

9 She will give to thy head a chaplet of grace;
A crown of glory will she bestow on thee.'

תִּתֵּן לְרֹאשְׁךָ לִוְיַת־חֵן
עֲטֶרֶת תִּפְאֶרֶת תְּמַגְּנֶךָּ׃

10 Hear, O my son, and receive my sayings;
And the years of thy life shall be many.

שְׁמַע בְּנִי וְקַח אֲמָרָי
וְיִרְבּוּ לְךָ שְׁנוֹת חַיִּים׃

11 I have taught thee in the way of wisdom;
I have led thee in paths of uprightness.

בְּדֶרֶךְ חָכְמָה הֹרֵתִיךָ
הִדְרַכְתִּיךָ בְּמַעְגְּלֵי־יֹשֶׁר׃

5. *get wisdom.* lit. 'acquire, purchase' at whatever price (cf. verse 7, xxiii. 23).

6. *forsake her not. Her* refers to wisdom (Ibn Ezra, Meiri).

7. *beginning of wisdom.* Unless one realizes how essential it is to possess this mental and ethical endowment, he will be disinclined to make the effort. Having appreciated its essential place in life, he will leave nothing undone to acquire it (see Isaiah da Trani).

with all thy getting. Better, 'with all thy possession,' at the price of all thou hast, seeing that its worth exceeds all material riches (Ibn Ezra).

8. *extol her.* Rather, 'esteem her highly' (Ibn Ezra).

exalt thee. As the parallelism shows, it means 'raise thee' in the repute of thy fellows (Meiri).

10–19 THE PATHS OF WISDOM AND EVIL

The teacher draws two vivid sketches, one of life guided by wisdom and the other instigated by vice. He contrasts them and insists how much happier the former is.

11. *taught.* Better, 'directed.'

uprightness. Whereas the beginning of the verse refers to the study of the Torah, the end refers to the performance of good deeds. No matter how one studies the Torah, it is commendable. Therefore, Scripture states: 'in the *way* of wisdom,' in the singular, since it is all one way. As regards good deeds, however, each commandment must be dealt with individually and safeguards must be undertaken to prevent transgressing them. Therefore, the plural *'paths'* is used, for this includes 'justice, right, and equity' (Elijah of Wilna).

12 When thou goest, thy step shall not be straitened;
And if thou runnest, thou shalt not stumble.

13 Take fast hold of instruction, let her not go;
Keep her, for she is thy life.

14 Enter not into the path of the wicked,
And walk not in the way of evil men.

15 Avoid it, pass not by it;
Turn from it, and pass on.

16 For they sleep not, except they have done evil;
And their sleep is taken away, unless they cause some to fall.

17 For they eat the bread of wickedness,
And drink the wine of violence.

12 בְּלֶכְתְּךָ לֹא־יֵצַר צַעֲדֶךָ
וְאִם־תָּרוּץ לֹא תִכָּשֵׁל׃
13 הַחֲזֵק בַּמּוּסָר אַל־תֶּרֶף
נִצְּרֶהָ כִּי־הִיא חַיֶּיךָ׃
14 בְּאֹרַח רְשָׁעִים אַל־תָּבֹא
וְאַל־תְּאַשֵּׁר בְּדֶרֶךְ רָעִים׃
15 פְּרָעֵהוּ אַל־תַּעֲבָר־בּוֹ
שְׂטֵה מֵעָלָיו וַעֲבֹר׃
16 כִּי לֹא יִשְׁנוּ אִם־לֹא יָרֵעוּ
וְנִגְזְלָה שְׁנָתָם אִם־לֹא יכשולו׃
17 כִּי לָחֲמוּ לֶחֶם רֶשַׁע
וְיֵין חֲמָסִים יִשְׁתּוּ׃

v. 16. יכשילו ק'

12. *not be straitened.* The road of wisdom is broad and allows for free movement (Meiri).

not stumble. Because God removed the stumbling-blocks in the path (see on iii. 6).

13. *she is thy life.* Cf. viii. 35.

14. *the wicked.* Those who sin against God (Elijah of Wilna).

evil men. Those who sin against their fellowmen (Elijah of Wilna).

15. *avoid it.* lit. 'leave it alone.' The advice is to keep far from temptation by intentionally avoiding the company of evil-doers (Elijah of Wilna).

turn from it. lit. 'from upon it,' which implies that one must not even set foot in it, and certainly not walk along it, though only a short distance (Elijah of Wilna).

16. *they sleep not.* They are unable to sleep through vexation and disappointment if the day has passed without gain from an act of violence (Meiri). [As against this restlessness, the innocent man's sleep is sweet (iii. 24).] Ibn Nachmiash contrasts this verse with Psalms cxxxii. 4f, where King David states: *'I will not give sleep to mine eyes, Nor slumber to mine eyelids; Until I find out a place for the Lord.'*

they cause some to fall. [Rendering of the *kerë*; the *kethib* means 'unless they fall (lit. stumble)' from innocence by a lawless deed.]

17. *they eat.* Their livelihood is derived from the proceeds of wickedness, and similarly in the next clause (Metsudath David).

18 But the path of the righteous is as the light of dawn,
That shineth more and more unto the perfect day.

וְאֹרַח צַדִּיקִים כְּאוֹר נֹגַהּ
הוֹלֵךְ וָאוֹר עַד־נְכוֹן הַיּוֹם׃

19 The way of the wicked is as darkness;
They know not at what they stumble.

דֶּרֶךְ רְשָׁעִים כָּאֲפֵלָה
לֹא יָדְעוּ בַּמֶּה יִכָּשֵׁלוּ׃

20 My son, attend to my words;
Incline thine ear unto my sayings.

בְּנִי לִדְבָרַי הַקְשִׁיבָה
לַאֲמָרַי הַט־אָזְנֶךָ׃

21 Let them not depart from thine eyes;
Keep them in the midst of thy heart.

אַל־יַלִּיזוּ מֵעֵינֶיךָ
שָׁמְרֵם בְּתוֹךְ לְבָבֶךָ׃

22 For they are life unto those that find them,
And health to all their flesh.

כִּי־חַיִּים הֵם לְמֹצְאֵיהֶם
וּלְכָל־בְּשָׂרוֹ מַרְפֵּא׃

23 Above all that thou guardest keep thy heart;
For out of it are the issues of life.

מִכָּל־מִשְׁמָר נְצֹר לִבֶּךָ
כִּי־מִמֶּנּוּ תּוֹצְאוֹת חַיִּים׃

18. *light of dawn.* lit. 'light of brightness.' Wisdom is likened to illumination, and when it brightens a man's path, he is as though he walks in the sunlight which grows more brilliant from dawn until it pours down in fullest splendour at noon (Metsudath David).

the perfect day. I.e. midday, for the light of the soul, although first clouded by the obstructions of the physical being, and its light covered and hidden, little by little, the soul bursts forth between the clouds of the body's physical being and the darkness of materialism, and bursts forth into a brilliant spiritual light (Malbim).

19. *darkness.* Although the way of the wicked appears wide and straight in the beginning, it is, nevertheless, like pitch darkness, even darker than ordinary darkness, so that they. . . (Malbim).

they know not at what they stumble. Sooner or later they fall, since they have not the light which would enable them to avoid the obstacles in their path (Metsudath David).

20–27 KEEP TO THE STRAIGHT PATH

21. *let them not . . . eyes.* As in iii. 21, with a different form of the verb.

in the midst of thy heart. Deep in mind, whence they are less likely to be removed (Bechaye).

22. *unto those that find them.* Cf. viii. 35.

health to all their flesh. A variant of iii. 8.

23. *keep thy heart.* i.e. watch thy heart, the central organ which conditions all man's activities, and upon whose correct functioning depends the character of his living. When a Rabbi set his disciples the problem, 'Go forth and see which is the good way to which a man should cleave,' he gave preference to the answer 'a good heart' because it included all the other replies (Aboth 2.13). 'God demands the heart' in man's relationship with Him, declares the Talmud. i.e. keep thy mind from straying either right or left from the path I have instructed thee (Meiri).

Put away from thee a froward mouth,
And perverse lips put far from thee.

Let thine eyes look right on,
And let thine eyelids look straight before thee.

Make plain the path of thy feet,
And let all thy ways be established.

Turn not to the right hand nor to the left;
Remove thy foot from evil.

24 הָסֵר מִמְּךָ עִקְּשׁוּת פֶּה
וּלְזוּת שְׂפָתַיִם הַרְחֵק מִמֶּךָּ׃
25 עֵינֶיךָ לְנֹכַח יַבִּיטוּ
וְעַפְעַפֶּיךָ יַיְשִׁרוּ נֶגְדֶּךָ׃
26 פַּלֵּס מַעְגַּל רַגְלֶךָ
וְכָל־דְּרָכֶיךָ יִכֹּנוּ׃
27 אַל־תֵּט־יָמִין וּשְׂמֹאול
הָסֵר רַגְלְךָ מֵרָע׃

for out of it. i.e. out of this keeping (Isaiah da Trani). Ibn Ezra explains, 'for out of the hearts,' which is like the king of the body.

issues of life. Perhaps 'sources of life,' the impulses which determine the nature of a man's existence (Malbim).

24. *a froward mouth.* lit. 'crookedness of mouth' (again in vi. 12), which utters dissembling speech, falsification of the truth (Ibn Nachmiash, Isaiah da Trani).

perverse lips. lit. 'turning aside of lips,' with the same meaning as the parallel clause. Gerondi explains the parallel to mean one who does not admit the truth, and this clause to mean one who perverts the truth. Ibn Nachmiash explains it to mean one who says 'Yes,' and then changes it to 'No,' or vice versa. Other commentators, as well as the Talmud (Kethuboth 22b), explain this verse to mean that a person must beware of performing any deed that will cause people to spread gossip, suspecting him of wrongdoing (Rashi, Meiri, Metsudath David).

25. *look right on.* Evidence of a truthful mind; telling lies is revealed by shifty eyes (Daath Mikra).

eyelids. Metaphorical for 'eyes,' since raising the eyelids is the beginning of sight (Meiri).

straight. [In contrast to the 'crookedness' of speech condemned in the previous verse.]

26. *make plain.* lit. 'weigh.' the sense is: do not wander about aimlessly, but mentally weigh up the alternatives and, having decided upon the right way, walk firmly therein (Rashi, Ibn Ezra).

established. Correct (Metsudath David).

27. *turn not.* From the path described in the preceding verse (Ibn Ezra).

remove thy foot from evil. By refusing to deviate from the right way. Some Jewish ethicists found in this verse support for the doctrine of the Aristotelian 'mean,' according to which virtue is the middle path between two harmful extremes. Malbim, for example, interprets the text in this sense.

1 My son, attend unto my wisdom;
Incline thine ear to my understanding;

2 That thou mayest preserve discretion,
And that thy lips may keep knowledge.

3 For the lips of a strange woman drop honey,
And her mouth is smoother than oil;

4 But her end is bitter as wormwood,
Sharp as a two-edged sword.

1 בְּנִי לְחָכְמָתִי הַקְשִׁיבָה
לִתְבוּנָתִי הַט־אָזְנֶךָ׃
2 לִשְׁמֹר מְזִמּוֹת
וְדַעַת שְׂפָתֶיךָ יִנְצֹרוּ׃
3 כִּי נֹפֶת תִּטֹּפְנָה שִׂפְתֵי זָרָה
וְחָלָק מִשֶּׁמֶן חִכָּהּ׃
4 וְאַחֲרִיתָהּ מָרָה כַלַּעֲנָה
חַדָּה כְּחֶרֶב פִּיּוֹת׃

CHAPTER V

A PLEA FOR CHASTITY

AGAIN the teacher repeats his earnest caution against the allurement of immorality. Having the welfare of the young particularly at heart, he feels that repetition is necessary. This chapter consists of five parts: 1) An introduction and an appeal to the individual (1–6); 2) the description of the peril in store for one who is enticed by the charms of the strange woman, viz. the loss of his freedom and his health (7–11); 3) the confession of the one who regrets his sins in due time (12 ff.); 4) praise of one who is faithful to the wife of his youth (15–19); 5) conclusion, moral of the wages of sin (20–23) (Daath Mikra).

1. *my wisdom.* The only place in the Book where the suffix is added. It means: the doctrine of wisdom which I teach. According to Metsudath David, this is King David instructing his son Solomon.

2. *discretion.* See on i. 4. [Here the word is plural to indicate intensification.]

thy lips may keep knowledge. That the fear of heaven be upon them and they never break off the yoke. This verse matches the Rabbinic maxim (Aboth iii. 7):

3. *strange woman.* See on ii. 16.

drop honey. As honey drips from the comb: she utters enticing words (Metsudath David).

mouth. lit. 'palate,' a poetical synonym (Metsudath Zion).

smoother than oil. Cf. Ps. lv. 22. Her words will appear attractive, unless by the aid of wisdom the tempted is able to appraise them at their true value and recognize their deadly nature (Meiri).

4. *her end.* [The sequel of consorting with her.]

wormwood. Cf. Deut. xxix. 17; Jer. ix. 14; Amos v. 7. 'Of this well-known genus of the composite plants *(Artemisia)* several species grow in Palestine' (Tristram). It is always used in the Bible as a symbol of what is bitter and harmful. Bitterness is the reality as compared with the honeyed sweetness of her words (Malbim).

sharp. Contrasted with her mouth which is *smoother than oil* (Malbim).

two-edged sword. lit. 'sword of mouths,' probably 'an all-devouring sword' (see Jud. iii. 16).

Her feet go down to death;
Her steps take hold on the nether-world;

5 רַגְלֶיהָ יֹרְדוֹת מָוֶת
שְׁאוֹל צְעָדֶיהָ יִתְמֹכוּ׃

Lest she should walk the even path of life,
Her ways wander, but she knoweth it not.

6 אֹרַח חַיִּים פֶּן־תְּפַלֵּס
נָעוּ מַעְגְּלֹתֶיהָ לֹא תֵדָע׃

Now therefore, O ye children, hearken unto me,
And depart not from the words of my mouth.

7 וְעַתָּה בָנִים שִׁמְעוּ־לִי
וְאַל־תָּסוּרוּ מֵאִמְרֵי־פִי׃

Remove thy way far from her,
And come not nigh the door of her house;

8 הַרְחֵק מֵעָלֶיהָ דַרְכֶּךָ
וְאַל־תִּקְרַב אֶל־פֶּתַח בֵּיתָהּ׃

Lest thou give thy vigour unto others,
And thy years unto the cruel;

9 פֶּן־תִּתֵּן לַאֲחֵרִים הוֹדֶךָ
וּשְׁנֹתֶיךָ לְאַכְזָרִי׃

Lest strangers be filled with thy strength,
And thy labours be in the house of an alien;

10 פֶּן־יִשְׂבְּעוּ זָרִים כֹּחֶךָ
וַעֲצָבֶיךָ בְּבֵית נָכְרִי׃

5. *her feet go down to death.* Cf. ii. 18, vii. 27. Her immoral life hastens her end, [and they who associate with her meet with a like fate] (Ibn Nachmiash).

6. *lest she should walk the even path of life.* The text is difficult and of uncertain meaning, but is evidently intended to be set against what was stated in iv. 26, *make plain the path of thy feet,* where the same verb occurs. The prefix *she* can also signify 'thou,' and if this is adopted, the meaning of the verse is: 'lest thou (thinkest to) make plain the path of life (i.e. if such be thine intention, thou art sure to fail by association with this woman because) her ways wander, thou knowest not where' (see Rashi, Malbim).

7. *ye children.* The plural as in iv. 1, but in the following verses we have the singular 'thou,' 'thy.' He invokes them collectively, but addresses himself to each personally (Isaiah da Trani).

8. *remove thy way far from her.* Take care to keep beyond reach of her temptation, on the principle 'do not play with fire lest you be burnt' (see Alshich).

9. *thy vigour.* Usually the word signifies 'majesty, splendour'; but also in Dan. x. 8 it means 'virility.' This will be dissipated by an immoral life. Jewish commentators, however, explain this to mean either, 'thy spiritual splendour,' which thou wilt lose through immorality (Elijah of Wilna, Malbim), or 'thy possessions,' which thou wilt give to ransom thyself from her husband or from the court (Isaiah da Trani).

the cruel. Some expositors take the word figuratively as describing the relentless consequences of the sin, a corrupted body and impoverishment (see Malbim). Others, perhaps with greater probability, understand it in a collective sense of the woman and her accomplices who grow rich at the expense of the victim and strip him of his possessions (see Ibn Nachmiash).

10. *lest strangers . . . strength.* What he had earned by his labours will not go into his own home, if he takes to this kind of life; he will be reduced to poverty (vi. 26) (Ibn Nachmiash, Meiri).

11 And thou moan, when thine end cometh,
When thy flesh and thy body are consumed,

12 And say: 'How have I hated instruction,
And my heart despised reproof;

13 Neither have I hearkened to the voice of my teachers,
Nor inclined mine ear to them that instructed me!

14 I was well nigh in all evil
In the midst of the congregation and assembly.'

15 Drink waters out of thine own cistern,
And running waters out of thine own well.

16 Let thy springs be dispersed abroad,
And courses of water in the streets.

17 Let them be only thine own,
And not strangers' with thee.

18 Let thy fountain be blessed;
And have joy of the wife of thy youth.

וְנָהַמְתָּ בְאַחֲרִיתֶךָ 11
בִּכְלוֹת בְּשָׂרְךָ וּשְׁאֵרֶךָ׃
וְאָמַרְתָּ אֵיךְ שָׂנֵאתִי מוּסָר 12
וְתוֹכַחַת נָאַץ לִבִּי׃
וְלֹא־שָׁמַעְתִּי בְּקוֹל מוֹרָי 13
וְלִמְלַמְּדַי לֹא־הִטִּיתִי אָזְנִי׃
כִּמְעַט הָיִיתִי בְכָל־רָע 14
בְּתוֹךְ קָהָל וְעֵדָה׃
שְׁתֵה־מַיִם מִבּוֹרֶךָ 15
וְנֹזְלִים מִתּוֹךְ בְּאֵרֶךָ׃
יָפוּצוּ מַעְיְנֹתֶיךָ חוּצָה 16
בָּרְחֹבוֹת פַּלְגֵי־מָיִם׃
יִהְיוּ־לְךָ לְבַדֶּךָ 17
וְאֵין לְזָרִים אִתָּךְ׃
יְהִי־מְקוֹרְךָ בָרוּךְ 18
וּשְׂמַח מֵאֵשֶׁת נְעוּרֶךָ׃

11. *when thine end cometh.* Better, 'at thy fate.'

flesh . . . consumed. When thy physical powers are exhausted by dissolute living and thy financial position is ruined (Isaiah da Trani).

12. *and say.* i.e. filled with remorse (Isaiah da Trani).

14. [The verse is best explained in the light of Deut. xxii. 22, *If a man be found lying with a woman married to a husband, then they shall both of them die*; *so shalt thou put away the evil from Israel.* The concluding phrase often occurs in Deut. in connection with sin which is regarded as a demoralizing element in the community that has to be removed. On reflection it will be brought home to this man that he had been such an *evil in the midst of the congregation* and incurred the danger of being 'put away.']

15. *drink waters.* The language is symbolic of marital intercourse. In Cant. iv. 15 the beloved is called *a well of living waters.* The intention is: find contentment in thy lawful wife (Ibn Ezra).

16. *springs . . . courses of water.* As Ibn Ezra explains, these terms are an image for numerous children. Through fidelity to his wife and his increasing love for her, he will be rewarded with many children (Meiri).

dispersed abroad. A picture of young children playing happily in the streets of the city (cf. Jer. ix. 20; Zech. viii. 5).

17. *only thine own.* Legitimate children (Ibn Ezra).

and not strangers' with thee. Children of doubtful paternity (Ibn Nachmiash).

18. *thy fountain.* The source of thy children, thy wife (Ibn Ezra).

19 אַיֶּלֶת אֲהָבִים וְיַעֲלַת חֵן
דַּדֶּיהָ יְרַוֻּךָ בְכָל־עֵת
בְּאַהֲבָתָהּ תִּשְׁגֶּה תָמִיד׃

A lovely hind and a graceful doe,
Let her breasts satisfy thee at all times;
With her love be thou ravished always.

20 וְלָמָּה תִשְׁגֶּה בְנִי בְזָרָה
וּתְחַבֵּק חֵק נָכְרִיָּה׃

Why then wilt thou, my son, be ravished with a strange woman,
And embrace the bosom of an alien?

21 כִּי נֹכַח ׀ עֵינֵי יְהוָה דַּרְכֵי־אִישׁ
וְכָל־מַעְגְּלֹתָיו מְפַלֵּס׃

For the ways of man are before the eyes of the LORD,
And He maketh even all his paths.

22 עֲוֺנוֹתָיו יִלְכְּדֻנוֹ אֶת־הָרָשָׁע
וּבְחַבְלֵי חַטָּאתוֹ יִתָּמֵךְ׃

His own iniquities shall ensnare the wicked,
And he shall be holden with the cords of his sin.

23 הוּא יָמוּת בְּאֵין מוּסָר
וּבְרֹב אִוַּלְתּוֹ יִשְׁגֶּה׃

He shall die for lack of instruction;
And in the greatness of his folly he shall reel.

19. *lovely hind . . . graceful doe.* Such a comparison is frequent in Oriental poetry. 'I have often stopped to admire the grace, ease, and fearless security with which these pretty animals bound along the high places of the mountains. They are amiable, affectionate, and loving, by universal testimony' (Thomson).

ravished. lit. 'reel' (of a drunkard) (cf. xxi. 1), hence *be thou intoxicated* (see Ibn Nachmiash). Even with your own wife, if you spend too much time with her, this is regarded as a fault (Metsudath David).

20. *be ravished with a strange woman.* If overindulgence even with thine own wife is regarded as a fault, why wilt thou be ravished with a strange woman and embrace the bosom of an alien? (Metsudath David, Ibn Ezra).

21ff. The exhortation concludes with a statement on Divine retribution. Virtue has God's approval and He comes to the aid of those who adhere to it, while the vicious are punished.

before the eyes of the LORD. God is aware of what man does, contradicting the thought of the wicked that He is indifferent to human conduct (Ps. lxxiii. 11ff.) (Metsudath David).

maketh even all his paths. Rather, 'weigheth all his paths.'

22. *ensnare.* Drive him from one misdeed to another until he ends in ruin. 'It is sin itself that causes death. With allusion to Prov. v. 22, the Rabbis teach, "As man throws out a net whereby he catches the fish of the sea, so the sins of man become the means of entangling and catching the sinner"' (Midrash).

cords of his sin. 'At first the evil inclination is like a spider's web, but finally it grows into something like cart-ropes' (Talmud, Sukkah 52a). If a vicious practice, easily checked in the beginning, is allowed to become a rooted habit, it becomes unbreakable.

23. *die.* [Prematurely.]

reel. Totter helplessly like a drunken man while he lives, pursuing no properly planned line of conduct (see Ralbag).

1 My son, if thou art become surety
for thy neighbour,
If thou hast struck thy hands for a
stranger—

2 Thou art snared by the words of
thy mouth,
Thou art caught by the words of
thy mouth—

1 בְּנִי אִם־עָרַבְתָּ לְרֵעֶךָ
תָּקַעְתָּ לַזָּר כַּפֶּיךָ׃
2 נוֹקַשְׁתָּ בְאִמְרֵי־פִיךָ
נִלְכַּדְתָּ בְּאִמְרֵי־פִיךָ׃

CHAPTER VI

ILLUSTRATIONS OF FOLLY

THE last chapter ended with the statement, *and in the greatness of his folly he shall reel.* Now the teacher proceeds to deal with some common examples of folly to which they who lack experience of life are prone. Verses 1–5 treat of agreeing to become a surety for his fellow; verses 6–11 of slothfulness; verses 12–15 of mischief-making; verses 16–19 of seven vices which are hateful to God.

1–5 THE FOLLY OF SURETYSHIP

The Mosaic law advocated the virtue of mutual help. Assistance was to be freely and readily given to those who suffered from a reverse of fortune, and when the aid took the form of a loan, no interest was to be charged (Lev. xxv. 35f.). When, at a later stage of the national life, conditions changed and men engaged in business transactions of a speculative character, they would occasionally need financial support. This they were unable to obtain by loans on interest, and so they resorted to the method of getting a friend to stand surety for any loss incurred or for non-payment. It must frequently have happened that the surety was called upon to surrender more than he could afford and inflicted hardship upon his own dependants. Hence the numerous warnings against taking this risk which are found in Proverbs xi. 15, xvii. 18, xx. 16, xxii. 26f., xxvii. 13. The Book does not advise excessive prudence which would check the practice of philanthropy; but that extreme piety should not bring a person to deplete his inheritance, surely with a practice from which he derives no benefit. This is discipline of foolishness, rather than 'discipline of wisdom.' Although acts of kindness are a precept of the Torah, and especially making loans to one's brethren, this is only in the case of lending money with security, but not orally or becoming surety for another's loan (Meiri).

1. *become surety.* As Judah offered to become for Benjamin (Gen. xliii. 9) but with his own person. Here it is a guarantee for a sum of money in the event of default.

stranger. i.e. whether you have become surety for your neighbour, or struck your hands for a stranger who is not your neighbour (Meiri). Others identify the 'neighbour' as the borrower, for whom the young man becomes surety. The 'stranger' is the lender to whom he makes himself responsible (Ibn Ezra, Ibn Nachmiash).

2. *thou art snared.* Know that thou art snared by the words of thy mouth (Isaiah da Trani).

words of thy mouth. With which the request to stand surety was granted (Malbim).

thou art caught. Should you stand surety for your neighbour, you are snared, i.e. a snare has been laid for you, but it is possible to avoid it. Should you strike your hands for a stranger, however, you are caught (Meiri).

3 עֲשֵׂה זֹאת אֵפוֹא ׀ בְּנִי וְהִנָּצֵל
כִּי בָאתָ בְכַף־רֵעֶךָ
לֵךְ הִתְרַפֵּס וּרְהַב רֵעֶיךָ׃

Do this now, my son, and deliver thyself,
Seeing thou art come into the hand of thy neighbour;
Go, humble thyself, and urge thy neighbour.

4 אַל־תִּתֵּן שֵׁנָה לְעֵינֶיךָ
וּתְנוּמָה לְעַפְעַפֶּיךָ׃

Give not sleep to thine eyes,
Nor slumber to thine eyelids.

5 הִנָּצֵל כִּצְבִי מִיָּד
וּכְצִפּוֹר מִיַּד יָקוּשׁ׃

Deliver thyself as a gazelle from the hand [of the hunter],
And as a bird from the hand of the fowler.

6 לֵךְ־אֶל־נְמָלָה עָצֵל
רְאֵה דְרָכֶיהָ וַחֲכָם׃

Go to the ant, thou sluggard;
Consider her ways, and be wise;

7 אֲשֶׁר אֵין־לָהּ קָצִין שֹׁטֵר וּמֹשֵׁל׃

Which having no chief,
Overseer, or ruler,

3. *do this now.* To be extricated from a perilous situation.

thy neighbour. The man for whom surety was given. He must be induced to free the guarantor of his obligation (Meiri).

humble thyself. A strong word with the literal meaning 'trample upon thyself'; consider not thy dignity but be prepared to humiliate thyself to secure a release from the pledge (Ibn Nachmiash, Metsudath David).

urge. Another strong word, 'give him superiority over you' (Metsudath David).

4. *give not sleep.* Do it at once; do not leave it over until the next day, and let nothing else take precedence to cause thee to defer this most urgent matter (Metsudath David, Daath Mikra).

5. *as a gazelle from the hand* [of the hunter]. [The addition of the words 'of the hunter' is unnecessary. Literally the Hebrew is 'from hand,' and the idiom occurs again in 1 Kings xx. 42 with the meaning 'from restraint.']

6–11 FOLLY OF SLOTHFULNESS

This homily is to be compared with xxiv. 30–34, where the same subject is treated and verses 10f. are repeated.

6. *ant.* Referred to again in xxx. 25 for its industry and foresight in laying up stores of food during the summer for its needs in winter. In Job xii. 7ff. man is also told that he has something to learn from the beasts, birds and fishes.

sluggard. The Hebrew word is only used in Proverbs, but the cognate verb is found in Judges xviii. 9 and the abstract noun in Eccles. x. 18. This type of person is amusingly satirized in xix. 24.

7. *having no chief.* To force it to toil, yet instinctively stores the provisions it will need (Ibn Ezra).

overseer. The word is used of Egyptian taskmasters (Exod. v. 6, 10, 14). Aristotle also asserted that ants laboured without rulers to direct them. It is now known that they live in highly organized communities. Perhaps Scripture means that there is no coercion.

8 Provideth her bread in the summer,
And gathereth her food in the harvest.

9 How long wilt thou sleep, O sluggard?
When wilt thou arise out of thy sleep?

10 'Yet a little sleep, a little slumber,
A little folding of the hands to sleep'—

11 So shall thy poverty come as a runner,
And thy want as an armed man.

12 A base person, a man of iniquity,
Is he that walketh with a froward mouth;

8 תָּכִין בַּקַּיִץ לַחְמָהּ
אָגְרָה בַקָּצִיר מַאֲכָלָהּ׃
9 עַד־מָתַי עָצֵל ׀ תִּשְׁכָּב
מָתַי תָּקוּם מִשְּׁנָתֶךָ׃
10 מְעַט שֵׁנוֹת מְעַט תְּנוּמוֹת
מְעַט ׀ חִבֻּק יָדַיִם לִשְׁכָּב׃
11 וּבָא־כִמְהַלֵּךְ רֵאשֶׁךָ
וּמַחְסֹרְךָ כְּאִישׁ מָגֵן׃
12 אָדָם בְּלִיַּעַל אִישׁ אָוֶן
הוֹלֵךְ עִקְּשׁוּת פֶּה׃

8. *provideth.* [The tense of the verb signifies 'she is accustomed to provide.']

in the summer. 'Two of the most common species of the Holy Land *(Atta barbara,* the black ant, and *Atta structor,* a brown ant) are strictly seed feeders, and in summer lay up large stores of grain for winter use' (Tristram).

in the harvest. 'Leave a bushel of wheat in the vicinity of one of their subterranean cities, and in a surprisingly short time the whole commonwealth will be summoned to plunder. A broad black column stretches from the wheat to their hole, and you are startled by the result. As if by magic, every grain seems to be accommodated with legs, and walks off in a hurry along the moving column. The farmers remorsely set fire to every ant city they find in the neighbourhood of their threshing-floors' (Thomson).

9. *how long wilt thou sleep.* During the waking hours of the day. A Rabbi included 'morning sleep' among the faults which 'put a man out of the world' (Aboth).

10. *yet a little sleep.* On waking or being aroused, he does not get up to work, but pleads for a longer stay in bed (see Metsudath David).

folding of the hands. Cf. Eccles. iv. 5. It is the attitude which is commonly adopted when one settles down for a siesta (Rashi, Metsudath David).

11. *runner.* A doubtful translation; the word is an intensive form of the verb 'to walk.' Perhaps Rashi's definition, 'a man walking fast,' is meant. Others render: 'a guest,' a traveler who comes suddenly without previous notice (Ibn Ezra, Metsudath David).

an armed man. lit. 'a man of shield,' an invading soldier against whom you cannot defend yourself (Isaiah da Trani, Malbim).

12–15 FOLLY OF MISCHIEF-MAKING

12. *a base person.* lit. 'a man without worth,' a good-for-nothing (Ibn Nachmiash). Perhaps the translation should be: 'A man of iniquity is a good-for-nothing walking with a froward mouth.'

froward mouth. So in iv. 24, but here it means a mischievous tongue (Ibn Nachmiash).

13 That winketh with his eyes, that scrapeth with his feet,
That pointeth with his fingers;

14 Frowardness is in his heart, he deviseth evil continually;
He soweth discord.

15 Therefore shall his calamity come suddenly;
On a sudden shall he be broken, and that without remedy.

16 There are six things which the LORD hateth,
Yea, seven which are an abomination unto Him:

13 קֹרֵץ בְּעֵינָו מֹלֵל בְּרַגְלוֹ
מֹרֶה בְּאֶצְבְּעֹתָיו׃
14 תַּהְפֻּכוֹת ׀ בְּלִבּוֹ
חֹרֵשׁ רָע בְּכָל־עֵת
מִדְנִים יְשַׁלֵּחַ׃
15 עַל־כֵּן פִּתְאֹם יָבוֹא אֵידוֹ
פֶּתַע יִשָּׁבֵר וְאֵין מַרְפֵּא׃
16 שֶׁשׁ־הֵנָּה שָׂנֵא יְהוָה
וְשֶׁבַע תּוֹעֲבוֹת נַפְשׁוֹ׃

v. 13. בעיניו ק׳ v.13. ברגליו ק׳ v. 14. מדינים ק׳ v. 16. תועבת ק׳

13. *winketh.* Again in x. 10, Ps. xxxv. 19. All the expressions in the verse indicate an act of insinuation. His purpose is to draw attention to a fellowman with evil intent (Metsudath David).

scrapeth. This is more correct than A.V. and R.V. *speaketh.* It is to be connected with a root in Rabbinic Hebrew meaning 'to rub (ears of corn).' A malicious indication to confederates directed against a victim (Rashi).

feet. So the *kerē*; the *kethib* is sing (see Ibn Ezra).

pointeth. With the object of directing invidious notice to a person (Rashi, Metsudath David).

14. Daath Mikra suggests that the verse be divided differently as follows: 'Frowardness doth the evil man devise in his heart, continually doth he send forth discord.'

frowardness. See on ii. 12; here it alludes to thoughts and devices contrary to what is right (Metsudath David).

soweth. lit. 'sendeth forth' (cf. xvi. 28).

15. *his calamity come suddenly.* Cf. i. 27. Retribution will overtake him unexpectedly. He will, therefore, be unable to avoid it (Elijah of Wilna).

without remedy. For he will not repent (Malbim).

16–19 SEVEN VICES HATEFUL TO GOD

Some authorities explain this section as a continuation of the preceding which recounts in detail the characteristics of the *base person.* Meiri understands it as a separate paragraph attached to the foregoing because it gives the cause of the preceding, viz. haughtiness.

16. *six things . . . yea, seven.* A form of enumeration used four times in chapter xxx, and also in Job v. 19. The Rabbis of the Midrash (Lev. Rabbah xvi.) disagree on its interpretation. Rabbi Meir sees the 'six' as the aforementioned, and the 'seven' those mentioned further. The Sages count the 'six' as those mentioned further, and the 'seven' as the seventh one listed.

an abomination. So the *kerē,* the *kethib* being plural. For the signification of the word, see on iii. 32.

17 Haughty eyes, a lying tongue,
And hands that shed innocent blood;

18 A heart that deviseth wicked thoughts,
Feet that are swift in running to evil;

19 A false witness that breatheth out lies,
And he that soweth discord among brethren.

עֵינַיִם רָמוֹת לְשׁוֹן שָׁקֶר 1
וְיָדַיִם שֹׁפְכוֹת דָּם־נָקִי׃
לֵב חֹרֵשׁ מַחְשְׁבוֹת אָוֶן 1
רַגְלַיִם מְמַהֲרוֹת לָרוּץ לָרָעָה׃
יָפִיחַ כְּזָבִים עֵד שָׁקֶר 1
וּמְשַׁלֵּחַ מְדָנִים בֵּין אַחִים׃

17. *haughty eyes.* Cf. xxx. 13. The sin of pride was especially denounced by Jewish teachers who considered humility to be the foundation upon which a virtuous, God-fearing life could alone be based. 'Be exceedingly lowly of spirit, since the hope of man is but the worm,' and 'A lowly spirit is an attribute of the disciples of Abraham our father' (Aboth) express the Hebraic doctrine. Of the many Rabbinic dicta against pride, perhaps the most forceful is: 'Whoever is possessed of an arrogant spirit, the Holy One, blessed be He, says, I and he cannot dwell in the world together' (Sotah 5a).

a lying tongue. Reproved in xii. 19, xxi. 6, xxvi. 28. The vice was severely censured by the Rabbis in such statements as: 'There are seven classes of thieves, and first among them all is he who steals the mind of his fellow-creatures (by lying words' (Tosefta Baba Kamma); 'Whoever equivocates in his speech is as though he worshipped idols' (Sanhedrin 92a); 'God hates the person who speaks one thing with his mouth and another in his heart (Pesahim 113b).'

innocent blood. Murder, to exclude the capital sentence passed by the Court. Homicide was held to be justified in Jewish law only in self-defence. On the heinousness of murder the Rabbis expressed this striking thought: 'How were the Ten Commandments given? There were five on one tablet and five on the other. On the one was inscribed, *I am the* LORD *thy God,* and over against it, *Thou shalt not murder.* The inference to be drawn is that if one sheds blood, Scripture imputes it to him as though he had diminished the likeness of the King' (Mechilta Yithro).

18. *a heart . . . thoughts.* Cf. verse 14.

swift in running. The combination of the two verbs, lit. 'hurrying to run,' is also used in Ps. cxlvii. 15. It does not mean 'running swiftly,' but 'making haste to run,' displaying eagerness to do evil (Meiri, Isaiah da Trani).

19. *false witness.* The Pharasaic law on perjury, as against the view of the Sadducees, is stated by Josephus *(Antiquities* IV, viii. 15): 'If any one be believed to have borne false witness, let him, if convicted, suffer the very same punishment which he, against whom he bore witness, would have suffered.' This ruling is based on Deut. xix. 15–21 (Metsudath David). The first clause of the verse is repeated in xiv. 5.

soweth discord. Cf. verse 14.

brethren. i.e. friends, associates.

20 My son, keep the commandment of thy father,
And forsake not the teaching of thy mother;

21 Bind them continually upon thy heart,
Tie them about thy neck.

22 When thou walkest, it shall lead thee,
When thou liest down, it shall watch over thee;
And when thou awakest, it shall talk with thee.

23 For the commandment is a lamp, and the teaching is light,
And reproofs of instruction are the way of life;

20 נְצֹר בְּנִי מִצְוַת אָבִיךָ
וְאַל־תִּטֹּשׁ תּוֹרַת אִמֶּךָ׃
21 קָשְׁרֵם עַל־לִבְּךָ תָמִיד
עָנְדֵם עַל־גַּרְגְּרֹתֶךָ׃
22 בְּהִתְהַלֶּכְךָ ׀ תַּנְחֶה אֹתָךְ
בְּשָׁכְבְּךָ תִּשְׁמֹר עָלֶיךָ
וַהֲקִיצוֹתָ הִיא תְשִׂיחֶךָ׃
23 כִּי נֵר מִצְוָה וְתוֹרָה אוֹר
וְדֶרֶךְ חַיִּים תּוֹכְחוֹת מוּסָר׃

20–35 FOLLY OF IMMORALITY

Again the author turns to admonish his listeners to beware of the pitfalls of immorality. He depicts the smooth talk and the seduction of the harlot, and the fate in store for one who falls into her clutches (Meiri).

20. *father . . . mother.* See on i. 8. [His parents are significantly recalled in this connection that he may have in mind an example of pure family life which he should set against the evil consequences of illicit passion.]

21. *tie them about thy neck.* See on iii. 3. The verb is used again only in Job xxxi. 36.

22. *walkest.* The form of the verb signifies 'goest about hither and thither' on thy daily tasks (Daath Mikra).

it shall lead thee. The subject *it,* although singular, as against the plural in the last verse, refers to *commandment* in verse 20 (Meiri, Isaiah da Trani).

liest down. In the night, when there is danger of unexpected attack (cf. iii. 24) (Meiri).

talk with thee. Advising and encouraging (Meiri). The Rabbis interpret this verse as an indication that 'in the hour of man's departure neither silver nor gold nor precious stones accompany him, but only Torah and good works, as it is said, *When thou walkest it shall lead thee etc. — when thou walkest it shall lead thee — in this world; when thou liest down it shall watch over thee — in the grave; and when thou awakest it shall talk with thee* — in the world to come (Aboth 6.9).

23. *commandment . . . teaching.* Isaiah da Trani understands this verse as referring to the commandment of the father and the teaching of the mother, mentioned above. The commandment of thy father is a lamp before thee, and the teaching of thy mother is light in all thy ways. Meiri, however, states explicitly that this refers to the commandment and the teaching in general since all this is included in the commandment of the father.

reproofs of instruction. The latter word is *musar,* 'discipline' (see on i. 2). [The warnings which restrain a man from unwise conduct act as a guide for the proper way of living.]

24 To keep thee from the evil woman,
From the smoothness of the alien tongue.

25 Lust not after her beauty in thy heart;
Neither let her captivate thee with her eyelids.

26 For on account of a harlot a man is brought to a loaf of bread,
But the adulteress hunteth for the precious life.

27 Can a man take fire in his bosom,
And his clothes not be burned?

28 Or can one walk upon hot coals,
And his feet not be scorched?

24 לִשְׁמָרְךָ מֵאֵשֶׁת רָע
מֵחֶלְקַת לָשׁוֹן נָכְרִיָּה׃
25 אַל־תַּחְמֹד יָפְיָהּ בִּלְבָבֶךָ
וְאַל־תִּקָּחֲךָ בְּעַפְעַפֶּיהָ׃
26 כִּי בְעַד־אִשָּׁה זוֹנָה עַד־כִּכַּר לָחֶם
וְאֵשֶׁת אִישׁ נֶפֶשׁ יְקָרָה תָצוּד׃
27 הֲיַחְתֶּה אִישׁ אֵשׁ בְּחֵיקוֹ
וּבְגָדָיו לֹא תִשָּׂרַפְנָה׃
28 אִם־יְהַלֵּךְ אִישׁ עַל־הַגֶּחָלִים
וְרַגְלָיו לֹא תִכָּוֶינָה׃

24. *the evil woman.* lit. 'the woman of evil,' one who has abandoned the true moral standards (Meiri).

the alien tongue. i.e. the language used by the *alien* woman (see on ii. 16).

25. *in thy heart.* According to a Talmudic proverb, 'The heart and eye are the two agents of sin.' If a man lets his mind become engrossed with thoughts of a woman who is forbidden to him, he wilfully places himself in the way of temptation.

her eyelids. If *eyelids* is not a poetical substitute for 'eyes' as in verse 4, and it is probably not, its use has been explained by the custom of Oriental women blackening the eyelids for the purpose of adding brilliance to the eyes (cf. 2 Kings ix. 30). Against this explanation is the fact that chaste women also indulged in the practice. More probably it refers to using the eyelids with seductive intent, and the phrase is illustrated by, 'The harlotry of a woman is in the lifting up of her eyes, and it shall be known by her eyelids' (Ecclus. xxvi. 9). (so Rashi, Metsudath David.)

26. *brought to a loaf of bread.* Deprived of the means of enjoying comforts and forced to keep himself alive with the minimum food which his depleted means allow. In other words, he is reduced to extreme poverty (cf. v. 10ff.). (so Rashi.)

adulteress. lit. 'wife of a man.' Since she is a married woman, his sin entails adultery which makes it the more serious (Malbim).

hunteth. Cf. Ezek. xiii. 18, 20.

the precious life. More than the shortening of life by dissipation (ii. 18, v. 5) is intended. The sinner is liable to the death penalty (Lev. xx. 10; Deut. xxii. 22). Jewish exegetes, however, explain this as an allusion to the hereafter (Meiri).

27. *bosom.* The Hebrew word also applies to a fold in the garment used as a pocket. Such is the meaning here and in xvi. 33, xxi. 14 (cf. the English proverb, 'He who plays with fire will be burnt').

28. *walk.* [Barefooted.]

29 So he that goeth in to his neighbour's wife;
Whosoever toucheth her shall not go unpunished.

30 Men do not despise a thief, if he steal
To satisfy his soul when he is hungry;

31 But if he be found, he must restore sevenfold,
He must give all the substance of his house.

32 He that committeth adultery with a woman lacketh understanding;
He doeth it that would destroy his own soul.

29 כֵּ֗ן הַ֭בָּא אֶל־אֵ֣שֶׁת רֵעֵ֑הוּ
לֹ֥א יִ֝נָּקֶ֗ה כָּל־הַנֹּגֵ֥עַ בָּֽהּ׃
30 לֹא־יָב֣וּזוּ לַ֭גַּנָּב כִּ֣י יִגְנ֑וֹב
לְמַלֵּ֥א נַ֝פְשׁ֗וֹ כִּ֣י יִרְעָֽב׃
31 וְ֭נִמְצָא יְשַׁלֵּ֣ם שִׁבְעָתָ֑יִם
אֶת־כָּל־ה֖וֹן בֵּית֣וֹ יִתֵּֽן׃
32 נֹאֵ֣ף אִשָּׁ֣ה חֲסַר־לֵ֑ב
מַֽשְׁחִ֥ית נַ֝פְשׁ֗וֹ ה֣וּא יַעֲשֶֽׂנָּה׃

29. *unpunished.* If not by law, then through the husband's vengeance, as is depicted below (Ralbag).

30. *men do not despise.* If this rendering is adopted, the argument is: Should a person steal because he is driven to it by sheer necessity, his fellow-men may feel sympathy with him. Moreover, if he is caught, he can redeem himself with monetary payment, at the most, sevenfold. . . . Even if he must give all the substance of his house, he still has a way of redeeming himself, since he sinned in the beginning because of hunger. An adulterer, however, has no such excuse. Only he who would destroy his own soul does this. Therefore, he does not escape punishment when he is caught (Rashi).

his soul. So literally, but in such a context the word implies 'desire' (Ibn Ezra).

31. *sevenfold.* According to the law of Exod. xxi. 37, xxii. 3, the restoration is double, fourfold or fivefold, and there is nowhere mention of a sevenfold restitution. The term must therefore be understood as 'manifold' (cf. Gen. iv. 15; Lev. xxvi. 28) (Isaiah da Trani).

all the substance of his house. An indication of the culprit's poverty. Although what he stole was intrinsically of small value, yet the consequence will be the forfeiture of all he possesses (see Malbim).

32. *lacketh understanding.* For he is not compelled by necessity (Rashi).

destroy his own soul. [Destroy himself. It is assumed that the would-be adulterer is one who rejects the discipline of wisdom, to whom arguments on higher grounds — moral, social and national — made no appeal. The author consequently employs reasoning which might prove an effective deterrent, the man's self-interest.]

33 Wounds and dishonour shall he get, And his reproach shall not be wiped away.	33 נֶגַע וְקָלוֹן יִמְצָא וְחֶרְפָּתוֹ לֹא תִמָּחֶה׃
34 For jealousy is the rage of a man, And he will not spare in the day of vengeance.	34 כִּי־קִנְאָה חֲמַת־גָּבֶר וְלֹא יַחְמוֹל בְּיוֹם נָקָם׃
35 He will not regard any ransom; Neither will he rest content, though thou givest many gifts.	35 לֹא־יִשָּׂא פְּנֵי כָל־כֹּפֶר וְלֹא־יֹאבֶה כִּי תַרְבֶּה־שֹׁחַד׃

33. *wounds.* Many Jewish commentators, such as Rashi, Ibn Ezra, and Ibn Nachmiash, explain it in a sense it often has, 'punishments inflicted by God'. Ralbag and Isaiah da Trani, however, explain it to mean bodily punishment caused by the outraged husband. The latter mentions also that it may refer to bodily punishment inflicted by the court. [Although we find scourging as a punishment only in Rabbinic times, when the death penalty ordained in the Pentateuch fell into abeyance, it may have been prevalent in early times as well, when the situation did not warrant the death penalty.]

dishonour. He will incur the censure of his fellow-men (Ibn Ezra, Ralbag).

reproach . . . away. For the rest of his life he will bear the stigma of his offence (Ibn Ezra).

34. *jealousy.* Aroused by the wife's infidelity gives rise to implacable fury which relentlessly seeks revenge (cf. xxvii. 4; Cant. viii. 6).

rage of a man. The Hebrew for *man* is *geber,* expressing the aspect of his strength (Wertheimer).

he will not spare. Infuriated by jealousy and resentment, the husband will have no pity on the culprit, and will reject every plea advanced to save him from the legal consequences of his act (Malbim).

35. *ransom.* [Monetary compensation. Hebrew law did not countenance the expiation of adultery by payment of money to the husband. In actual practice such an offer might be made in order to stop him from laying a charge. He would be acting illegally if he accepted, and no honourable man would agree to such a course.]

neither . . . gifts. Better, 'neither will he consent though thou multipliest bribes.' The point is that the husband will not hear of accepting money, however large the sum, to wipe out the affront to his honour, unlike the victim of theft, who will exonerate the thief upon acceptance of payment (Ralbag).

7 CHAPTER VII ז

My son, keep my words,
And lay up my commandments with thee.

Keep my commandments and live,
And my teaching as the apple of thine eye.

Bind them upon thy fingers,
Write them upon the table of thy heart.

Say unto wisdom: 'Thou art my sister,'
And call understanding thy kinswoman;

That they may keep thee from the strange woman,
From the alien woman that maketh smooth her words.

1 בְּנִי שְׁמֹר אֲמָרָי
וּמִצְוֺתַי תִּצְפֹּן אִתָּךְ׃
2 שְׁמֹר מִצְוֺתַי וֶחְיֵה
וְתוֹרָתִי כְּאִישׁוֹן עֵינֶיךָ׃
3 קָשְׁרֵם עַל־אֶצְבְּעֹתֶיךָ
כָּתְבֵם עַל־לוּחַ לִבֶּךָ׃
4 אֱמֹר לַחָכְמָה אֲחֹתִי אָתְּ
וּמֹדָע לַבִּינָה תִקְרָא׃
5 לִשְׁמָרְךָ מֵאִשָּׁה זָרָה
מִנָּכְרִיָּה אֲמָרֶיהָ הֶחֱלִיקָה׃

CHAPTER VII

THE TEMPTRESS

A REALISTIC and detailed picture is drawn of a phase of contemporaneous life. The teacher describes what he sees when he looks through the window of his house, and the sight impels him to utter yet another warning against vice.

3. *bind them upon thy fingers.* If one wishes to do something and fears he will forget, he ties a string around his finger in order to remember. Therefore, Scripture uses the expression, 'bind them upon thy fingers.' This corresponds to the Rabbinic maxim, 'If anyone asks you something, do not hesitate, but tell him immediately.' This may also mean that the commandments shall be to thee for an ornament, as in i. 9. It is likened to a ring, bound around the finger (Ibn Nachmiash). The figure is a ring made of pure gold, which is pliable and wound around the finger. Such rings have been discovered in excavations and many are in museums (Daath Mikra.)

4. *my sister.* Keep wisdom near in an affectionate way as one regards his sister (Ibn Nachmiash). Alternatively, be familiar with wisdom as one is familiar with his sister (Metsudath David).

5. Cf. ii. 16, vi. 24. Whereas Rashi explains both these verses as figurative of heretical doctrine, in this chapter he admits the possibility of a literal interpretation. Maimonides, on the other hand, in the Introduction of his *Guide for the Perplexed,* understands it as a simile: 'The author compares the body, which is the source of all sensual pleasures, to a married woman who at the same time is a harlot. And this figure he has taken as the basis of his entire Book.' [It cannot be doubted, however, that we have an account of a social evil of the time which was demoralizing the community and against which the writer felt it his duty to conduct a vigorous campaign.]

6 For at the window of my house
I looked forth through my lattice;

7 And I beheld among the thoughtless ones,
I discerned among the youths,
A young man void of understanding,

8 Passing through the street near her corner,
And he went the way to her house;

9 In the twilight, in the evening of the day,
In the blackness of night and the darkness.

6 כִּי בְּחַלּוֹן בֵּיתִי
בְּעַד אֶשְׁנַבִּי נִשְׁקָפְתִּי׃
7 וָאֵרֶא בַפְּתָאיִם
אָבִינָה בַבָּנִים נַעַר חֲסַר־לֵב׃
8 עֹבֵר בַּשּׁוּק אֵצֶל פִּנָּהּ
וְדֶרֶךְ בֵּיתָהּ יִצְעָד׃
9 בְּנֶשֶׁף־בְּעֶרֶב יוֹם
בְּאִישׁוֹן לַיְלָה וַאֲפֵלָה׃

6. *window.* lit. 'the perforated part' of the wall into which a movable latticework was fitted; this could be opened if required (2 Kings xiii. 17) but was usually kept closed because it did not present a view of the street. See below.

I looked forth. [Not on one particular occasion. The writer describes a customary sight.]

lattice. The word is met with again only in Judges v. 28. This translation follows Saadiah Gaon, quoted by Ibn Nachmiash (see Daath Mikra, Mandelkern).

7. *thoughtless ones.* [See on i. 4. The teacher is not concerned at the moment with the vicious who set out with the intention of gratifying their lust. His aim is to rescue young men who lack an understanding of the danger which besets them and walk into the trap laid for them.]

the youths. lit. 'the sons.'

8. A.J. has retained the translation of A.V. and R.V. which gives the impression that the young man intentionally walked in that direction. This is indeed Meiri's explanation. Daath Mikra explains: 'Passing along the street near her corner (i.e. the corner where her house was located), strolling in the direction of her house.' He may have known that it was a locality of ill-repute and wandered there without any thought of wrong-doing. He did not have the sense to avoid it and keep out of temptation.

9. *twilight.* lit. '(cool) breeze' which springs up in the East as the afternoon declines (Mandelkern).

evening. i.e. sunset (Malbim).

blackness. The same word as that translated 'apple (of the eye)' in verse 2; the period after the sun had disappeared and darkness set in (Meiri).

darkness. More intensive blackness of the night. The series of words describes the successive stages from the late afternoon to midnight. So foolish is the youth that, instead of returning home when the hour was late, he goes on exposing himself to the risk of temptation (see Malbim, Yair Or).

And, behold, there met him a woman
With the attire of a harlot, and wily of heart.

She is riotous and rebellious,
Her feet abide not in her house;

Now she is in the streets, now in the broad places,
And lieth in wait at every corner.

So she caught him, and kissed him,
And with an impudent face she said unto him:

Sacrifices of peace-offerings were due from me;
This day have I paid my vows.

Therefore came I forth to meet thee,
To seek thy face, and I have found thee.

I have decked my couch with coverlets,
With striped cloths of the yarn of Egypt.

10 וְהִנֵּה אִשָּׁה לִקְרָאתוֹ
שִׁית זוֹנָה וּנְצֻרַת לֵב׃
11 הֹמִיָּה הִיא וְסֹרָרֶת
בְּבֵיתָהּ לֹא־יִשְׁכְּנוּ רַגְלֶיהָ׃
12 פַּעַם ׀ בַּחוּץ פַּעַם בָּרְחֹבוֹת
וְאֵצֶל כָּל־פִּנָּה תֶאֱרֹב׃
13 וְהֶחֱזִיקָה בּוֹ וְנָשְׁקָה לּוֹ
הֵעֵזָה פָנֶיהָ וַתֹּאמַר לוֹ׃
14 זִבְחֵי שְׁלָמִים עָלָי
הַיּוֹם שִׁלַּמְתִּי נְדָרָי׃
15 עַל־כֵּן יָצָאתִי לִקְרָאתֶךָ
לְשַׁחֵר פָּנֶיךָ וָאֶמְצָאֶךָּ׃
16 מַרְבַדִּים רָבַדְתִּי עַרְשִׂי
חֲטֻבוֹת אֵטוּן מִצְרָיִם׃

10. *attire of a harlot.* Cf. Gen. xxxviii. 14f. (Metsudath David).

wily. lit. 'guarded,' or 'besieged.' Just as a besieged city is surrounded by a besieging army, so is her heart surrounded by lewdness and folly (Rashi). Targum renders: 'exciting the hearts of the youths.' Meiri renders: 'with a reserved heart.' She claims that her heart was reserved only for him, that he is her only love.

11. *riotous.* Lacking the staidness of the respectable woman (Ralbag).

rebellious. The word is used of a refractory heifer (Hos. iv. 16) which struggles to break loose from the yoke upon her neck. Similarly this type of woman chafes at moral restraint (Daath Mikra footnote).

12. *streets . . . broad places.* See on i. 20f., *corner* corresponding to *head* of the streets.

14. *sacrifices of peace-offerings.* According to the law of Lev. vii. 15f. the flesh of these sacrifices had to be eaten by the person who offered them on that day or the next. Hence the statement *this day have I paid my vows* implied that she had a good supply of meat at home and invited her intended victim to share it with her. This was the bait to attract him into her house (Metsudath David).

15. *therefore.* [Having this sumptuous meal ready and not wishing to eat it alone.]

seek thy face. Hebrew idiom for 'look for thee.' Having tempted him with food, she proceeds to suggest additional allurements (Malbim).

16. *couch.* [More strictly, 'bedstead.']

striped cloths. Rather, 'cut-out cloths' (Metsudath David). Others render: 'curtains' (Isaiah da Trani, Meiri).

17 I have perfumed my bed
With myrrh, aloes, and cinnamon.

18 Come, let us take our fill of love until the morning;
Let us solace ourselves with loves.

19 For my husband is not at home,
He is gone a long journey;

20 He hath taken the bag of money with him;
He will come home at the full moon.'

21 With her much fair speech she causeth him to yield,
With the blandishment of her lips she enticeth him away.

22 He goeth after her straightway,
As an ox that goeth to the slaughter,
Or as one in fetters to the correction of the fool;

נַפְתִּי מִשְׁכָּבִי 1
מֹר אֲהָלִים וְקִנָּמוֹן׃
לְכָה נִרְוֶה דֹדִים עַד־הַבֹּקֶר 1
נִתְעַלְּסָה בָּאֳהָבִים׃
כִּי אֵין הָאִישׁ בְּבֵיתוֹ 1
הָלַךְ בְּדֶרֶךְ מֵרָחוֹק׃
צְרוֹר־הַכֶּסֶף לָקַח בְּיָדוֹ 2
לְיוֹם הַכֶּסֶא יָבֹא בֵיתוֹ׃
הִטַּתּוּ בְּרֹב לִקְחָהּ 2
בְּחֵלֶק שְׂפָתֶיהָ תַּדִּיחֶנּוּ׃
הוֹלֵךְ אַחֲרֶיהָ פִּתְאֹם 2
כְּשׁוֹר אֶל־טָבַח יָבֹא
וּכְעֶכֶס אֶל־מוּסַר אֱוִיל׃

17. *perfumed.* lit. 'besprinkled.' For the aromatic spices, cf. Ps. xlv. 9; Cant. iv. 14 (Ibn Nachmiash, Metsudoth).

19. *my husband.* lit. 'the man,' a contemptuous reference to the husband for the purpose of creating the impression that she had no affection for him (Meiri, Ibn Ezra). She mentions the fact of his absence to assure the youth that he need not fear such consequences as are detailed in vi. 33ff. (Metsudath David).

20. *bag of money.* This indicated that he had gone on a long business journey and would not surprise them by an unexpected return (Metsudath David).

the full moon. This translation is accepted by all moderns. The traditional commentators, however, render it either as 'on the appointed day,' 'on the festival,' 'on the new moon,' 'at the end of the month,' or 'on the day of slaughtering,' meaning the festive day, when many animals are slaughtered (Ibn Nachmiash, Meiri, Ibn Ezra, Rashi).

21. *fair speech.* Hebrew *lekach* (see on iv. 2), but used here in a very different sense. [It may have been deliberately chosen in sarcastic contrast to the true and ennobling doctrine of wisdom.

causeth him to yield. lit. 'causeth him to incline (towards her)'; she overcomes his scruples and breaks down his opposition (Metsudath David).

22. *straightway.* Hebrew 'suddenly'; in a moment of weakness his resistance suddenly gives way (Malbim).

or as one . . . fool. A very difficult clause to construe which modern commentators alter with a variety of emendations. The word for *fetters* occurs again only in Isa. iii. 18 where it is used of anklets worn by women. Both the Targum and LXX have 'dog' (*keleb*), but it is inexplicable how so common a Hebrew word should have been corrupted into a most unusual one. In Rabbinic Hebrew *eches* means 'a viper,' and Rashi adopts it here but with a forced interpretation. The general sense is: he unresistingly follows her to his ultimate undoing, like an animal led to slaughter and a fettered criminal to his punishment (Isaiah da Trani).

23 Till an arrow strike through his liver;
As a bird hasteneth to the snare—
And knoweth not that it is at the cost of his life.

24 Now therefore, O ye children, hearken unto me,
And attend to the words of my mouth.

25 Let not thy heart decline to her ways,
Go not astray in her paths.

26 For she hath cast down many wounded;
Yea, a mighty host are all her slain.

27 Her house is the way to the nether-world,
Going down to the chambers of death.

23 עַד יְפַלַּח חֵץ כְּבֵדוֹ
כְּמַהֵר צִפּוֹר אֶל־פָּח
וְלֹא־יָדַע כִּי־בְנַפְשׁוֹ הוּא׃
24 וְעַתָּה בָנִים שִׁמְעוּ־לִי
וְהַקְשִׁיבוּ לְאִמְרֵי־פִי׃
25 אַל־יֵשְׂטְ אֶל־דְּרָכֶיהָ לִבֶּךָ
אַל־תֵּתַע בִּנְתִיבוֹתֶיהָ׃
26 כִּי־רַבִּים חֲלָלִים הִפִּילָה
וַעֲצֻמִים כָּל־הֲרֻגֶיהָ׃
27 דַּרְכֵי שְׁאוֹל בֵּיתָהּ
יֹרְדוֹת אֶל־חַדְרֵי־מָוֶת׃

23. *liver.* In Hebrew the organ which is 'heavy' through being charged with blood, and therefore the seat of vitality. Cf. *my liver is poured upon the earth* (Lam. ii. 11). The meaning of the phrase is: till he is mortally stricken (Isaiah da Trani).

bird . . . snare. Cf. i. 17.

at the cost of his life. His actual existence is involved, because the adulterer's soul is doomed (Metsudath David).

24. *now therefore.* The author draws the moral of what he has just related (Metsudath David).

O ye children. Addressing himself to the people, who are to him as children (Ibn Ezra).

25. *decline.* The verb used in Num. v of an unfaithful wife.

26. *for . . . wounded.* Better, 'for many are the killed she hath cast down (to Sheol)' in agreement with the statement of the next verse (Meiri, Targum, Metsudath David).

27. *way.* The Hebrew is plural, signifying that all the ways that lead to her house eventually lead to Sheol (Ralbag, Meiri).

chambers of death. [A poetical synonym of Sheol.]

8 CHAPTER VIII ח

1 Doth not wisdom call,
And understanding put forth her voice?

1 הֲלֹא־חָכְמָה תִקְרָא
וּתְבוּנָה תִּתֵּן קוֹלָהּ׃

2 In the top of high places by the way,
Where the paths meet, she standeth;

2 בְּרֹאשׁ־מְרֹמִים עֲלֵי־דָרֶךְ
בֵּית נְתִיבוֹת נִצָּבָה׃

3 Beside the gates, at the entry of the city,
At the coming in at the doors, she crieth aloud:

3 לְיַד־שְׁעָרִים לְפִי־קָרֶת
מְבוֹא פְתָחִים תָּרֹנָּה׃

4 'Unto you, O men, I call,
And my voice is to the sons of men.

4 אֲלֵיכֶם אִישִׁים אֶקְרָא
וְקוֹלִי אֶל־בְּנֵי אָדָם׃

5 O ye thoughtless, understand prudence,
And, ye fools, be ye of an understanding heart.

5 הָבִינוּ פְתָאִים עָרְמָה
וּכְסִילִים הָבִינוּ לֵב׃

CHAPTER VIII

THE EXCELLENCE OF WISDOM

PASSING from chapter vii. to this chapter is like leaving a stuffy, overheated room for fresh air. No more vivid contrast could be imagined than between the poisonous *lekach* (see on vii. 21), which entices youth to ruin, and the pure, vitalizing doctrine offered to them by wisdom. Unlike the harlot who lurks furtively in the darkness to trap her prey, wisdom issues her call publicly and produly. She, too, has tempting delights, but they are of the kind which increases life's beauty and true happiness, not destroying them as does vice.

1–3 WISDOM'S CALL

1. *doth not.* [A rhetorical question to stress the fact that wisdom does call.]

2. *top of high places.* Wisdom selects the most conspicuous sites, such as elevated ground, for the purpose of attracting the largest number of listeners (cf. ix. 3, 14).

where the paths meet. lit. 'the house of the paths,' the cross-roads (Metsudath David).

standeth. [Not the usual word for 'stand,' but one meaning 'taketh her stand.']

3. *the gates.* See on i. 21.

city. The Hebrew is the unusual word *kereth,* common in Aramaic, which is part of the place-name Carthage (again ix. 3, 14; xi. 11).

doors. Better, 'entrances.'

4–5 INTRODUCTORY APPEAL

4. *men.* Hebrew *ish* with a plural form, found elsewhere in Isa. liii. 3; Ps. cxli. 4. It is not synonymous with *sons of men,* but denotes those who belong to the higher social status (Ibn Ezra, Malbim).

sons of men. [lit. 'sons of *adam,*' connected with *adamah* 'the earth,'] a term for the masses. In combination the two comprise persons of all classes (cf. Ps. xlix. 3) (Ibn Ezra).

5. *thoughtless . . . prudence.* See on i. 4.

6 שִׁמְעוּ כִּי־נְגִידִים אֲדַבֵּר
וּמִפְתַּח שְׂפָתַי מֵישָׁרִים׃

Hear, for I will speak excellent things,
And the opening of my lips shall be right things.

7 כִּי־אֱמֶת יֶהְגֶּה חִכִּי
וְתוֹעֲבַת שְׂפָתַי רֶשַׁע׃

For my mouth shall utter truth,
And wickedness is an abomination to my lips.

8 בְּצֶדֶק כָּל־אִמְרֵי־פִי
אֵין בָּהֶם נִפְתָּל וְעִקֵּשׁ׃

All the words of my mouth are in righteousness,
There is nothing perverse or crooked in them.

9 כֻּלָּם נְכֹחִים לַמֵּבִין
וִישָׁרִים לְמֹצְאֵי דָעַת׃

They are all plain to him that understandeth,
And right to them that find knowledge.

10 קְחוּ מוּסָרִי וְאַל־כָּסֶף
וְדַעַת מֵחָרוּץ נִבְחָר׃

Receive my instruction, and not silver,
And knowledge rather than choice gold.

11 כִּי־טוֹבָה חָכְמָה מִפְּנִינִים
וְכָל־חֲפָצִים לֹא יִשְׁווּ־בָהּ׃

For wisdom is better than rubies,
And all things desirable are not to be compared unto her.

12 אֲנִי־חָכְמָה שָׁכַנְתִּי עָרְמָה
וְדַעַת מְזִמּוֹת אֶמְצָא׃

I wisdom dwell with prudence,
And find out knowledge of devices.

6–11 WISDOM'S MORAL WORTH

6. *excellent things.* lit. 'princes,' i.e. 'princely utterances' (Ibn Ezra). Others explain: words that attract the heart (Meiri, Ibn Nachmiash).

right things. Cf. i. 3.

7. *shall utter.* Better, 'uttereth' (Targum).

abomination to my lips. Something which is repellent to my lips (see on iii. 32) (Metsudath David).

8. *in righteousness.* i.e. in accordance with righteousness, never deviating from its standard (Ralbag).

perverse. lit. 'twisted'; a noun from this root is *pathil,* 'thread' (Kimchi).

9. *plain.* lit. 'in front'; i.e. straightforward. Although fools may misunderstand them or fail to grasp them entirely, to him that understandeth they are plain (Meiri).

10. *receive.* Here equals 'prefer.'

choice gold. Purest, unalloyed gold (Daath Mikra). For the word for *gold,* see on iii. 14.

12–21 WISDOM'S HIGH CLAIMS

12. *I wisdom.* Up to this point the teacher has been extolling the virtues of wisdom; now, personified, she speaks for herself.

dwell with prudence. Therefore, whoever associates with wisdom will become familiar with that desirable quality (Metsudath David).

devices. See on i. 4 where it is rendered *discretion,* and for the plural, see v. 2.

13 The fear of the LORD is to hate evil;
Pride, and arrogancy, and the evil way,
And the froward mouth, do I hate.

14 Counsel is mine, and sound wisdom;
I am understanding, power is mine.

15 By me kings reign,
And princes decree justice.

16 By me princes rule,
And nobles, even all the judges of the earth.

17 I love them that love me,
And those that seek me earnestly shall find me.

יִרְאַת יְהוָה שְׂנֹאת רָע
גֵּאָה וְגָאוֹן ׀ וְדֶרֶךְ רָע
וּפִי תַהְפֻּכוֹת שָׂנֵאתִי׃
לִי־עֵצָה וְתוּשִׁיָּה
אֲנִי בִינָה לִי גְבוּרָה׃
בִּי מְלָכִים יִמְלֹכוּ
וְרוֹזְנִים יְחֹקְקוּ צֶדֶק׃
בִּי שָׂרִים יָשֹׂרוּ
וּנְדִיבִים כָּל־שֹׁפְטֵי אָרֶץ׃
אֲנִי אֹהֲבַיהָ אֵהָב
וּמְשַׁחֲרַי יִמְצָאֻנְנִי׃

v. 17. אהבי ק'

13. *the fear of the* LORD *is to hate evil.* This is the instruction that wisdom announces to the people (Rashi). 'Evil' includes all faults, as elaborated in the latter half of the verse (Ibn Ezra). Others render: 'to hate the wicked,' for, since he is a wicked man, one should hate him, as David also states: *Do not I hate them, O* LORD, *that hate Thee?* (Psalms cxxxix. 21). Solomon, too, states further: *Those that forsake the law praise the wicked; But such as keep the law contend with them* (xxviii. 4). The righteous and the wicked are diametrically opposite, each hating the other, for everyone loves his kind and hates his opposite (Bechayah).

14. *counsel is mine.* Through wisdom, one can find ways of saving himself from temptation (Metsudath David).

I am understanding. The fundamental of wisdom is understanding. It is as though wisdom is understanding (Ibn Nachmiash).

15. *reign.* i.e. justly, as the next clause implies, not despotically without regard of right and wrong (cf. 1 Kings iii. 9).

16. *of the earth.* Hebrew editions are not identical with regard to this word. Some read 'of righteousness,' a similar ending as in the previous verse, and both the Targum and LXX support this variant. But *of the earth* gives the statement a more general and forceful significance. This is indeed Meiri's reading. Daath Mikra, contends, however, that not all judges of the earth judge with wisdom. Ibn Nachmiash and Isaiah da Trani, as well as many manuscripts, read, 'righteousness.'

17. *love me.* In most editions, so the *kerē*, the *kethib* reading 'love her.'

seek me . . . find me. This is true only of wisdom's faithful lovers (contrast i. 28). The author wishes to encourage people to study, not to fear that the task will be too difficult, too time consuming, and will require too much preparation, for this is the way of the slothful. Whoever is eager to learn, however, will not fear these drawbacks, as the Rabbis say (Megillah 6b): 'I toiled and did not find,' do not believe (Meiri).

Riches and honour are with me;
Yea, enduring riches and righteousness.

My fruit is better than gold, yea, than fine gold;
And my produce than choice silver.

I walk in the way of righteousness,
In the midst of the paths of justice;

That I may cause those that love me to inherit substance,
And that I may fill their treasuries.

18 עֹשֶׁר־וְכָבוֹד אִתִּי
הוֹן עָתֵק וּצְדָקָה׃
19 טוֹב פִּרְיִי מֵחָרוּץ וּמִפָּז
וּתְבוּאָתִי מִכֶּסֶף נִבְחָר׃
20 בְּאֹרַח־צְדָקָה אֲהַלֵּךְ
בְּתוֹךְ נְתִיבוֹת מִשְׁפָּט׃
21 לְהַנְחִיל אֹהֲבַי ׀ יֵשׁ
וְאֹצְרֹתֵיהֶם אֲמַלֵּא׃

18. *riches and honour.* Cf. iii. 16.

enduring riches. The adjective may mean either 'surpassing,' i.e. 'abundant riches,' or 'ancient,' that which will grow old in the possession of the owner, hence 'enduring.' Both yield an appropriate sense. All Jewish exegetes adopt the former.

and righteousness. Some expositors explain this to mean that the pursuit of wisdom will bring both temporal success and exemplary character traits (Ralbag). Others explain that one's riches will not be diminished by the charity he performs, rendering: 'abundant riches along with charity' (Meiri). Metsudath David explains that, although God will grant the wisdom seeker temporal success as a reward, He will reward him in the hereafter as charity.

19. *my fruit.* Cf. the figure of wisdom as a tree (iii. 18).

gold. As in verse 10.

fine gold. The term is used in a similar statement with regard to the Divine ordinances (Ps. xix. 11).

produce. Cf. iii. 14.

choice silver. See on verse 10.

20. *I walk.* The mood of the verb is intensive: 'I walk firmly' (Daath Mikra).

in the way of righteousness. As an assurance that the inducements which wisdom offers to her devotees will be fully discharged (see Daath Mikra).

21. *substance.* lit. 'that which exists, is real,' hence 'possessions, property' (cf. the English phrase 'real estate'). Worldly possessions are never denounced in the Bible as an evil in themselves. Man is commanded to work for the purpose of enjoying the comforts which God's universe has in store for him, but let him seek them in a worthy manner as advocated by wisdom, and not by resorting to evil ways (see Ibn Ezra).

22 The Lord made me as the beginning of His way,
The first of His works of old.

23 I was set up from everlasting, from the beginning,
Or ever the earth was.

יְהוָה קָנָנִי רֵאשִׁית דַּרְכּוֹ
קֶדֶם מִפְעָלָיו מֵאָז׃
מֵעוֹלָם נִסַּכְתִּי
מֵרֹאשׁ מִקַּדְמֵי־אָרֶץ׃

22–31 WISDOM'S ROLE AT THE CREATION

To justify the high claims which wisdom had asserted on her behalf, the author advances a still loftier claim. Wisdom, he declares, was created by God before the universe, because He ordained for her a part in His creative work which changed chaos into order. The same principles which the Creator applied in the formation of the universe have to be employed by man in the development of his highest self. In a word, wisdom, i.e. morality, has been appointed by God to be the controlling force of all life, both of the universe and of mankind, individually and collectively.

The later author of Ecclesiasticus took up the same theme and identified wisdom with the Mosaic Torah (xxiv. 23f.), and this thought was greatly elaborated by the Rabbis. Without Torah, they taught, there would be chaos, and for that reason Torah must have been created before the creation of the world. Basing themselves upon this section of Proverbs, they remarked: 'The Torah said, I was the architectural instrument of the Holy One, blessed be He. It is customary when a human king erects a palace that he does not build it according to his own ideas, but according to the ideas of an architect. The architect likewise does not depend upon the thoughts of his mind, but has parchments and tablets to know how he is to plan the rooms and entrances. So did the Holy One, blessed be He, look into the Torah and created the universe accordingly' (Gen. Rabbah 1.1). In the light of these concepts the verses that follow have to be understood.

22. *made me.* The verb *kanah,* usually 'acquire,' has the meaning *create* (the universe, or Israel, by God) in Gen. xiv. 19, 22; Deut. xxxii. 6; Ps. cxxxix. 13. This is to be explained in the same manner as *the* Lord *by wisdom founded the earth* (iii. 19), meaning that for the sake of wisdom He founded the earth. The entire intention of the Creation was wisdom. Hence, it is called 'the beginning,' since it was the intention which came before the act. If we say that He created the world with His wisdom we will necessarily assume that His wisdom preceded the Creation. This is the intention of the Rabbis, who state: 'The Torah said, I was the architectural instrument of the Holy One, blessed be He' (Meiri). Ibn Ezra, too, explains 'before' to mean that wisdom preceded the Creation in the sense of its necessity, not in the sense of time, for time itself is a creation, not existing before the Creation of the world.

way. The process of creation (Rashi).

of old. [Must be attached to *made me,* not to *works.*]

23. *was set up.* Usually explained as literally 'was poured out' like molten metal into a mould, hence 'fashioned.' This is perhaps the Targum's intention. Others connect with an Assyrian root and translate 'was installed.' Jewish exegetes derive it from *'nasich,'* a prince, rendering, 'I was made to rule' (Rashi, Metsudath David), or 'I was chosen' (Ibn Ezra).

24 When there were no depths, I was brought forth;
When there were no fountains abounding with water.

24 בְּאֵין־תְּהֹמוֹת חוֹלָלְתִּי
בְּאֵין מַעְיָנוֹת נִכְבַּדֵּי־מָיִם׃

25 Before the mountains were settled,
Before the hills was I brought forth;

25 בְּטֶרֶם הָרִים הָטְבָּעוּ
לִפְנֵי גְבָעוֹת חוֹלָלְתִּי׃

26 While as yet He had not made the earth, nor the fields,
Nor the beginning of the dust of the world.

26 עַד־לֹא עָשָׂה אֶרֶץ וְחוּצוֹת
וְרֹאשׁ עַפְרוֹת תֵּבֵל׃

27 When He established the heavens, I was there;
When He set a circle upon the face of the deep,

27 בַּהֲכִינוֹ שָׁמַיִם שָׁם אָנִי
בְּחוּקוֹ חוּג עַל־פְּנֵי תְהוֹם׃

28 When He made firm the skies above,
When the fountains of the deep showed their might,

28 בְּאַמְּצוֹ שְׁחָקִים מִמָּעַל
בַּעֲזוֹז עִינוֹת תְּהוֹם׃

24. *depths.* The waters, mentioned in Gen. i. 2, which made their appearance at the first stage of the world's creation.

fountains. Subterranean reservoirs which fed the oceans and rivers. When these were *broken up* and the *windows of heaven were opened,* the deluge overwhelmed the earth; when the fountains and windows were *stopped,* the flood of water began to lessen (Gen. vii. 11, vii. 2).

25. *setteled.* lit. 'sunk.' According to the ancient cosmogony, the mountains rested fundamentally upon the subterranean waters (Jonah ii. 7; Ps. xviii. 8).

26. *fields.* lit. 'outside places.' The word has this meaning of *fields* in Ps. cxliv. 13; Job v. 10. According to Siphre, it means deserts, or wildernesses.

dust of the world. As in Isa. xl. 12, the matter of which the physical world was constructed.

27. *a circle.* Cf. Job xxii. 14, the vault of heaven. [To the ancients the earth appeared as a circular disc, covered by the sky which had the shape of a vaulted canopy, and surrounded by the *deep,* i.e. the ocean.]

28. *skies.* See on iii. 20.

fountains. A slightly different form of the word in verse 24.

showed their might. lit. 'became strong,' i.e. firmly fixed in their place beneath the earth.

29 When He gave to the sea His decree,
That the waters should not transgress His commandment,
When He appointed the foundations of the earth;

30 Then I was by Him, as a nursling;
And I was daily all delight,
Playing always before Him,

31 Playing in His habitable earth,
And my delights are with the sons of men.

32 Now therefore, ye children, hearken unto me;
For happy are they that keep my ways.

בְּשׂוּמוֹ לַיָּם ׀ חֻקּוֹ 29
וּמַיִם לֹא יַעַבְרוּ־פִיו
בְּחוּקוֹ מוֹסְדֵי אָרֶץ׃
וָאֶהְיֶה אֶצְלוֹ אָמוֹן 30
וָאֶהְיֶה שַׁעֲשׁוּעִים יוֹם ׀ יוֹם
מְשַׂחֶקֶת לְפָנָיו בְּכָל־עֵת׃
מְשַׂחֶקֶת בְּתֵבֵל אַרְצוֹ 31
וְשַׁעֲשֻׁעַי אֶת־בְּנֵי אָדָם׃
וְעַתָּה בָנִים שִׁמְעוּ־לִי 32
וְאַשְׁרֵי דְּרָכַי יִשְׁמֹרוּ׃

29. *when He gave . . . decree.* Better, 'when He set for the sea its decreed limit' (Ralbag).

His commandment. viz. *let the waters under the heaven be gathered together unto one place, and let the dry land appear* (Gen. i. 9) (Ralbag).

appointed. lit. 'decreed'; R.V. 'marked out' (Rashi, Metsudath David).

30. *nursling.* A foster-child; so Rashi and many moderns who compare Lam. iv. 5. Others regard it as a form of the word in Cant. vii. 2, translated *skilled workman.* This latter interpretation is supported by tradition. The author of the Wisdom of Solomon (viii. 6), perhaps with this verse in mind, described prudence as a 'cunning (skilful) workman'; and the Rabbis, in the passage quoted in the introductory note, understood it as 'architect.'

I was daily all delight. For the idiom, see on verse 14. [Wisdom was delight personified while watching the progressive stages of the world's formation.] *Daily,* lit. 'day, day,' is an allusion to the two millenia preceding the Revelation (Rashi).

playing always. [The emotion of exultation, as it were, impelled wisdom to exhibit that delight in movement, jumping about in excited pleasure.]

31. *His habitable earth.* lit. 'habitable world of His earth'; the completed universe made fit as the habitation of living creatures (see Kimchi, Ps. xxv. 1).

my delights . . . men. The pleasure which wisdom experienced during the period of creation was subsequently transferred to the human race, the crown of God's designs; therefore she offers herself as a guide that men may discover true happiness in the world. Hence the plea which follows (Ralbag).

32–36 WISDOM'S CLOSING APPEAL

32. *now therefore.* Because of what I have just related to you. Repeated from vii. 24.

happy. Cf. iii. 18.

Hear instruction, and be wise,
And refuse it not.

Happy is the man that hearkeneth
to me,
Watching daily at my gates,
Waiting at the posts of my doors.

For whoso findeth me findeth life,
And obtaineth favour of the
LORD.

But he that misseth me wrongeth
his own soul;
All they that hate me love death.'

שִׁמְעוּ מוּסָר וַחֲכָמוּ 33
וְאַל־תִּפְרָעוּ׃
אַשְׁרֵי אָדָם שֹׁמֵעַ לִי 34
לִשְׁקֹד עַל־דַּלְתֹתַי יוֹם ׀ יוֹם
לִשְׁמֹר מְזוּזֹת פְּתָחָי׃
כִּי מֹצְאִי מֹצְאִי* חַיִּים 35
וַיָּפֶק רָצוֹן מֵיְהוָה׃
וְחֹטְאִי חֹמֵס נַפְשׁוֹ 36
כָּל־מְשַׂנְאַי אָהֲבוּ מָוֶת׃

* י׳ יתיר, read מָצָא v. 35.

33. *instruction.* Hebrew *musar* (see on i. 2).

and be wise. Or, 'and get wisdom,' as in vi. 6.

refuse. Rather, 'neglect,' lit. 'let go.'

34. *gates . . . doors.* Of the house which wisdom built (ix. 1). Keep a constant look-out for her, and whenever possible be in close attendance upon her. Stress is laid upon an unfailing conformity with wisdom's teachings. The tenets are to be borne in mind and practised in all circumstances, not only when they are agreeable to one's wishes (see Meiri).

35. *life.* Wisdom being the *tree of life* (iii. 18; cf. Eccles. vii. 12).

favour. i.e. his manner of life finds acceptance with God; so the Jewish commentators. Alshich, however, suggests that the Hebrew word denotes 'will,' i.e. he fulfills God's will, which is only to benefit others. By studying the Torah diligently, He allows God to bestow His bounty upon mankind.

36. *misseth.* Opposite of *findeth* in the last verse. The Hebrew is the common verb for 'sin'; hence A.V. and R.V., *but he that sinneth against me.* The root-meaning, however, is 'to miss' a target at which one aims, either literally or metaphorically of the standard of right and goodness. (Both are suggested by Ibn Ezra).

his own soul. i.e. 'himself'; does himself harm (Midrash).

hate. The verb signifies a wilful turning away from the precepts of wisdom, not just indifference to them. The intensive conjugation denotes action, not only hatred in mind. Kimchi on Psalms cxxxix. 21, equates this form with 'those who rise up.' Malbim explains that he despises him before others, inducing them to hate him as well (Daath Mikra).

death. Since *he who misseth me wrongeth his own soul,* it follows that all they that hate me love death (Meiri). This is the opposite of the preceding verse. *For whoso findeth me findeth life* (Malbim).

1 Wisdom hath builded her house,
She hath hewn out her seven pillars;

2 She hath prepared her meat, she hath mingled her wine;
She hath also furnished her table.

3 She hath sent forth her maidens, she calleth,
Upon the highest places of the city:

1 חָכְמוֹת בָּנְתָה בֵיתָהּ
חָצְבָה עַמּוּדֶיהָ שִׁבְעָה׃
2 טָבְחָה טִבְחָהּ מָסְכָה יֵינָהּ
אַף עָרְכָה שֻׁלְחָנָהּ׃
3 שָׁלְחָה נַעֲרֹתֶיהָ תִקְרָא
עַל־גַּפֵּי מְרֹמֵי קָרֶת׃

CHAPTER IX

RIVAL INVITATIONS

WITH this chapter the first division of the Book closes. It summarizes all that has gone before under the form of two invitations extended to simpletons, one by wisdom and the other by folly. As a judge, who, after hearing the cases of the litigants and wishing to deliver the verdict, sums up the claims, so does the author sum up the invitations of wisdom and folly (Meiri). The essential difference is that wisdom labors diligently, builds a beautiful house, sets a rich table, and then invites the guests to enjoy the bounty. Folly, on the other hand, is like a lazy woman, who does not prepare a feast; i.e. she understands nothing. She apes wisdom by making a similar announcement, inviting her guests to a frugal meal, which is not even hers, but stolen water and bread hidden away in her cabinet (Daath Mikra).

1. *wisdom.* The Hebrew is plural (see on i. 20).

her house. [For the reception of guests. The imagery may have been suggested as a contrast to the house of immorality described in chapter vii.] Rashi sees the house as the world, built through wisdom.

seven pillars. [Indicative of a mansion built around a court-yard, the structure being supported by three pillars on each side and one in the centre on the third side facing the open space which was the entrance.]

2. *prepared her meat.* lit. 'slaughtered her slaughtered (food)'; had animals slain for the repast. [The author seems to have in mind what he had written in vii. 14. The language is, of course, figurative; food for thought will really be provided.]

mingled her wine. With spices to flavour it and increase its potency (cf. Isa. v. 22; Ps. lxxv. 9; Cant. viii. 2) (Ibn Ganah).

furnished her table. [The same Hebrew phrase as in Ps. xxiii. 5, *preparest a table,* and it should be so translated here. In fact, the *shulchan,* 'table,' was nothing more than a mat of skin spread out before the guest who sat on the ground or reclined on a low couch, and to whom the dishes were presented in turn from which he helped himself with his fingers.]

3. *her maidens.* As messengers to invite the guests. Wisdom does not come directly to the person; he must receive it from the Sages, the prophets, and the teachers. These are the maidens whom she sends out in every generation, through whom 'she calleth upon the highest places of the city' (Malbim).

highest places. See on viii. 2.

city. See on viii. 3.

'Whoso is thoughtless, let him turn in hither';
As for him that lacketh understanding, she saith to him:

4 מִי־פֶתִי יָסֻר הֵנָּה
חֲסַר־לֵב אָמְרָה לּוֹ׃

'Come, eat of my bread,
And drink of the wine which I have mingled.

5 לְכוּ לַחֲמוּ בְלַחֲמִי
וּשְׁתוּ בְּיַיִן מָסָכְתִּי׃

Forsake all thoughtlessness, and live;
And walk in the way of understanding.

6 עִזְבוּ פְתָאיִם וִחְיוּ
וְאִשְׁרוּ בְּדֶרֶךְ בִּינָה׃

He that correcteth a scorner getteth to himself shame,
And he that reproveth a wicked man, it becometh unto him a blot.

7 יֹסֵר ׀ לֵץ לֹקֵחַ לוֹ קָלוֹן
וּמוֹכִיחַ לְרָשָׁע מוּמוֹ׃

4. *thoughtless.* A simpleton (see on i. 4).

lacketh understanding. And is willing to learn. *Understanding* is literally 'heart,' the seat of intellect (Ibn Nachmiash).

5. *come, eat.* For the form of the invitation, cf. Isa. lv. 1. In Ecclus. xv. 3 it is said of the God-fearing man that 'with bread of understanding shall she (wisdom) feed him, and give him water of discernment to drink.'

6. *forsake all thoughtlessness.* Better, 'forsake simpletons,' since it is doubtful whether the plural noun can be employed here in the abstract sense, in view of the use of a special form for it in verse 13. The type of young men wisdom seeks to influence is exhorted to leave the class of the unintelligent. Let them come to her to acquire understanding by which they will *live,* in the higher interpretation of that term (Ibn Ezra suggests both interpretations).

7–12 SCORNERS ARE UNTEACHABLE

The men, called *scorners,* are consciously and wilfully perverse. Knowing the better way, they prefer evil; consequently wisdom deems it prudent to exclude them from the banquet. The attitude of the scornful, to jest over serious matters, makes them impervious to correction and reproof. A popular adage states: One scornful word wards off one hundred reproofs.

7. *shame.* For he will deride him and insult him (Metsudath David).

it becometh unto him a blot. lit. 'his blemish.' The wicked man's blemish attaches itself to the reprover, in that he will be met with the rejoinder, 'Who are you to presume to correct me? You are not better than I!' A Rabbi, the Talmud (Baba Bathra 15b) reported, lamented the fact that nobody in his generation accepted correction, and if one told his fellow, 'Remove the splinter from thine eye,' the retort was, 'Remove the beam from thine eye' (after Metsudath David).

8 Reprove not a scorner, lest he hate thee;
Reprove a wise man, and he will love thee.

9 Give to a wise man, and he will be yet wiser;
Teach a righteous man, and he will increase in learning.

10 The fear of the LORD is the beginning of wisdom,
And the knowledge of the All-holy is understanding.

11 For by me thy days shall be multiplied,
And the years of thy life shall be increased.

12 If thou art wise, thou art wise for thyself;
And if thou scornest, thou alone shalt bear it.'

13 The woman Folly is riotous;
She is thoughtlessness, and knoweth nothing.

8 אַל־תּוֹכַח לֵץ פֶּן־יִשְׂנָאֶךָּ
הוֹכַח לְחָכָם וְיֶאֱהָבֶךָּ׃
9 תֵּן לְחָכָם וְיֶחְכַּם־עוֹד
הוֹדַע לְצַדִּיק וְיוֹסֶף לֶקַח׃
10 תְּחִלַּת חָכְמָה יִרְאַת יְהוָה
וְדַעַת קְדֹשִׁים בִּינָה׃
11 כִּי־בִי יִרְבּוּ יָמֶיךָ
וְיוֹסִיפוּ לְּךָ שְׁנוֹת חַיִּים׃
12 אִם־חָכַמְתָּ חָכַמְתָּ לָּךְ
וְלַצְתָּ לְבַדְּךָ תִשָּׂא׃
13 אֵשֶׁת כְּסִילוּת הֹמִיָּה
פְּתַיּוּת וּבַל־יָדְעָה מָּה׃

8. *reprove not a scorner.* Because *a scorner loveth not to be reproved* (xv. 12). In all other cases, however, the Rabbis urged the necessity to give reproof. 'Whence is it to be learnt that if one detects something reprehensible in his neighbour, he has the duty to correct him? As it is stated, *Thou shalt surely rebuke thy neighbour* (Lev. xix. 17). And from the phrase *surely rebuke* (lit. rebuking thou shalt rebuke) it is to be deduced that if he reject the reproof, it must be repeated' (Talmud, Berachoth 31a).

9. *give to a wise man.* Cf. xviii. 15.

10. *the fear . . . wisdom.* Cf. i. 7, but with two variants. A different word is employed for *beginning*. Here it signifies the essential prerequisite; there it denotes the principal constituent. *Wisdom* is substituted for *knowledge* as better adapted to the context which related to the 'wise man' (see Ibn Nachmiash and Malbim).

All-holy. In Hebrew the plural of 'holy,' the plural of majesty (again xxx. 3; Hos. xii. 1) (Ibn Ezra).

11. *by me.* viz. wisdom (Ibn Ezra).

12. The verse teaches the doctrine of personal responsibility. Each individual has it within his power to choose wisdom and reap its reward, or to remain a scorner and incur the penalty.

thou alone shalt bear it. Thou alone shalt bear the penalty for it (Ibn Ezra).

13–18 FOLLY'S INVITATION

13. *the woman Folly.* lit. 'a woman of folly,' i.e. a foolish woman. *Folly* must be defined in an ethical sense, so that the phrase denotes a harlot in antithesis to chaste wisdom. We accordingly have the same contrast as in preceding chapters: wisdom calling to a virtuous life and vice seducing to debauchery (see Malbim).

14 And she sitteth at the door of her house,
On a seat in the high places of the city,

15 To call to them that pass by,
Who go right on their ways:

16 'Whoso is thoughtless, let him turn in hither';
And as for him that lacketh understanding, she saith to him:

17 'Stolen waters are sweet,
And bread eaten in secret is pleasant.'

18 But he knoweth not that the shades are there;
That her guests are in the depths of the nether-world.

14 וְיָשְׁבָה לְפֶתַח בֵּיתָהּ
עַל־כִּסֵּא מְרֹמֵי קָרֶת׃
15 לִקְרֹא לְעֹבְרֵי־דָרֶךְ
הַמְיַשְּׁרִים אֹרְחוֹתָם׃
16 מִי־פֶתִי יָסֻר הֵנָּה
וַחֲסַר־לֵב וְאָמְרָה לּוֹ׃
17 מַיִם־גְּנוּבִים יִמְתָּקוּ
וְלֶחֶם סְתָרִים יִנְעָם׃
18 וְלֹא־יָדַע כִּי־רְפָאִים שָׁם
בְּעִמְקֵי שְׁאוֹל קְרֻאֶיהָ׃

riotous. The description applied to the unfaithful wife (vii. 11).

thoughtlessness. lit. 'simplicity,' without acumen or knowledge, easily enticed (Malbim).

knoweth nothing. Heedless of consequences, reckless (Ibn Nachmiash).

14. *high places of the city.* Like wisdom (verse 2) she seeks publicity to make herself known to the many.

15. *go right on their ways.* Without thought of deliberately indulging in unlawful pleasures; but she leads them astray (Meiri).

16. Identical with wisdom's invitation (verse 4.)

17. Seductive imagery to suggest the attractiveness of the forbidden.

stolen waters are sweet. Relations with a single woman are not as pleasing as relations with a married woman. Concerning apostasy, too, they feared to sin in public, and sinned clandestinely (Rashi). This follows Rashi's interpretation of the chapter as figurative of apostasy. lit., 'stolen waters will be sweet.' The sinner imagines the sweetness of sin before committing it, only to be disappointed after committing the sin (Chatham Sofer to Nedarim).

18. *he knoweth not.* Being a simpleton, the tempted man is unaware that a reckoning must follow his partaking of the *stolen waters* and *bread eaten in secret* (Ibn Ezra).

the shades. See on ii. 18.

there. In that house (Ralbag); it is the gateway to Sheol (ii. 19, vii. 27).

her guests . . . nether-world. Although still living they are depicted as actually incurring their ultimate fate (cf. the Rabbinic dictum, 'The wicked are accounted as dead even while alive').

1 **The proverbs of Solomon.**
A wise son maketh a glad father;
But a foolish son is the grief of his mother.

2 **Treasures of wickedness profit nothing;**
But righteousness delivereth from death.

מִשְׁלֵי שְׁלֹמֹה
בֵּן חָכָם יְשַׂמַּח־אָב
וּבֵן כְּסִיל תּוּגַת אִמּוֹ׃
לֹא־יוֹעִילוּ אוֹצְרוֹת רֶשַׁע
וּצְדָקָה תַּצִּיל מִמָּוֶת׃

CHAPTER X

MISCELLANEOUS PROVERBS

THE first nine chapters constitute a preface to the central and main section of the Book which extends from the beginning of this chapter down to xxii. 16. The break is not only marked by the new heading, *the proverbs of Solomon,* but by a difference in contents and structure. Hitherto, the Book provided discourses by wisdom on fundamentals. Now follows a collection of proverbs in the accepted sense of the term: pithy sayings which express wise rules of conduct, warnings, lessons drawn from experience, and moral reflections. These are not presented in systematic order, and no logical sequence is generally followed. Like the varied phases of human life, for which they offer guidance, the proverbs are of a miscellaneous character. Although the general religious principles advocated in the foregoing dissertations underlie them, many of them deal with social behaviour. The general trend of the verses is to present first the advantage of the good and then the contrasting disadvantage of the evil. This category extends as far as xv. 20. Thereafter, as a rule, each verse deals with one topic. This category extends to the end of the section. They are, however, intermingled with other verses, dealing with two topics each, both dealing with virtuous deeds, and others dealing with wrongdoings, also constructed in the same manner.

1 SON AND PARENTS

a wise son. [Both *wise* and *foolish* must be interpreted as having an ethical connotation. Perhaps 'good-living, ill-living' expresses the force of the Hebrew.]

grief of his mother. Poetical contrast to *maketh a glad father*; but the words may imply the thought that the mother, being less pre-occupied out of doors than her husband and having fuller opportunity of seeing the son's conduct, grieves more deeply when it is unseemly. It is noteworthy that the first of the miscellaneous proverbs deals with the effects of a young man's behaviour upon his home. The larger social life is coloured by the character of the home circle (Metsudath David, Ibn Ezra).

2 GAINS OF LAWLESSNESS AND REWARD OF RIGHTEOUSNESS

profit nothing. The statement may be interpreted generally in accordance with the English proverb, 'Ill got, ill gone.' Money so acquired brings no genuine happiness. But in xi. 4, we seem to have another form of the verse, *Riches profit not in the day of wrath; but righteousness delivereth from death.* Accordingly it is more probable to understand *profit nothing* as relating to the account which the human being has eventually to give of himself: of what use will his dishonest gains be to him on the day of judgment? (Metsudath David).

3 The LORD will not suffer the soul of the righteous to famish;
But He thrusteth away the desire of the wicked.

4 He becometh poor that dealeth with a slack hand;
But the hand of the diligent maketh rich.

5 A wise son gathereth in summer;
But a son that doeth shamefully sleepeth in harvest.

3 לֹא־יַרְעִיב יְהוָה נֶפֶשׁ צַדִּיק
וְהַוַּת רְשָׁעִים יֶהְדֹּף׃
4 רָאשׁ עֹשֶׂה כַף־רְמִיָּה
וְיַד חָרוּצִים תַּעֲשִׁיר׃
5 אֹגֵר בַּקַּיִץ בֵּן מַשְׂכִּיל
נִרְדָּם בַּקָּצִיר בֵּן מֵבִישׁ׃

righteousness. Clearly the opposite of *wickedness* and so to be understood. As sin causes death, virtue protects man from it and defers its advent. The Hebrew word *tsedakah,* 'righteousness,' quite early received the special sense of 'charity, almsgiving.' In Ecclus. iii. 14, 'For *the relieving* of thy father shall not be forgotten,' the Hebrew text has *tsedakah,* and Ecclus vii. 10, 'Neglect not to give *alms,*' the original reads, 'In *tsedakah* be not behindhand.' Some scholars find this meaning also in Dan. iv. 24, *Break off thy sins by alms-giving, and thine iniquities by showing mercy to the poor.* The clause here was so treated traditionally by the Jews in agreement with the doctrine commonly enunciated by the Rabbis that benevolence safeguards life and is a shield against the angel of death. The Targum renders: 'rescueth from a bad death,' the opposite of a peaceful and natural ending of life.

3 DESIRE OF RIGHTEOUS AND WICKED

suffer the soul of the righteous to famish. As in xiii. 25, xxvii. 7 *soul* indicates 'desire for food,' and the clause restates the declaration of Ps. xxxvii. 25, *I have been young, and now am old; yet have I not seen the righteous forsaken, nor his seed begging bread* (see Daath Mikra, Ibn Nachmiash).

He thrusteth away . . . wicked. This translation follows Ibn Nachmiash. When their desire appears to be within their grasp, God thrusts it away from them.

4–5 INDUSTRY AND IDLENESS

4. *slack hand.* Cf. the same adjective in xix. 15, *The idle soul shall suffer hunger.* Jewish thought consistently stresses the dignity of work and its essential place in the scheme of life. *Six days thou shalt labour and do all thy work* (Exod. xx. 9) is as much a Divine command as *Remember the sabbath day to keep it holy.* Consequently indolence was censured as a serious fault; but in Proverbs its disadvantages are dwelt upon. It is the cause of poverty. 'Who hath not worked shall not eat,' is a Rabbinic aphorism (Abodah Zarah 3a).

5. *gathereth in summer.* Corresponding to 'makes hay while the sun shines.' Unless he toils to gather in the crops during the season of fine weather, they will be ruined by the heavy rains of the autumn (after Metsudath David). Malbim explains that the summer follows the harvest. After the harvest, the wise son gathers the remaining kernels of grain lying on the ground.

but a son . . . harvest. Better, 'who sleepeth soundly in the harvest is a son that acteth shamefully' (Ibn Ezra, Targum). It may also be rendered: 'but a slothful son sleepeth. . .' (Ralbag, Malbim).

6 Blessings are upon the head of the righteous;
But the mouth of the wicked concealeth violence.

7 The memory of the righteous shall be for a blessing;
But the name of the wicked shall rot.

8 The wise in heart will receive commandments;
But a prating fool shall fall.

9 He that walketh uprightly walketh securely;
But he that perverteth his ways shall be found out.

6 בְּרָכוֹת לְרֹאשׁ צַדִּיק
וּפִי רְשָׁעִים יְכַסֶּה חָמָס׃
7 זֵכֶר צַדִּיק לִבְרָכָה
וְשֵׁם רְשָׁעִים יִרְקָב׃
8 חֲכַם־לֵב יִקַּח מִצְוֹת
וֶאֱוִיל שְׂפָתַיִם יִלָּבֵט׃
9 הוֹלֵךְ בַּתֹּם יֵלֶךְ בֶּטַח
וּמְעַקֵּשׁ דְּרָכָיו יִוָּדֵעַ׃

6–7 THE RIGHTEOUS AND WICKED CONTRASTED

6. *blessings are upon the head.* Either God rewards the righteous with blessings (cf. Gen. xlix. 26; Deut. xxxiii. 16), or, as the next verse states, the effect of his good life is the earning of his fellow-men's blessings (Ibn Ezra).

but the mouth . . . violence. This follows Ibn Ezra. Repeated in verse 11. The Hebrew may also be rendered: 'but violence covereth the mouth of the wicked' (so Rashi). Both translations offer the required contrast. [According to A.J. the meaning is that the wicked plot their neighbours' ruin and consequently earn their curses, not blessings. Alternatively the sense is that like produces like. The life of the righteous is full of blessing to others and blessings crown their own life; the life of the wicked is full of violence, and their malicious speech, which plots violence against others, will eventually be stopped by an act of violence practised upon them.]

7. *the memory . . . blessing.* After death the remembrance of his good deeds will endure, and men will recall his name with respect and gratitude (Isaiah da Trani). The deeds of the righteous shall be remembered forever, as the Rabbis stated.' The righteous, even in death, are called living.' The ethicists state: 'No one is dead, whose words keep him alive, for his memory will be known, and the practice of his life famed during the real life' (Meiri).

8 THE WISE ACCEPT INSTRUCTION

will receive commandments. Better, 'accepteth commandments,' viz. the precepts which regulate a well-ordered life. He recognizes his limitations and is willing to learn (Ralbag).

but a prating fool shall fall. Repeated in verse 10. *Prating fool* is literally 'foolish of lips,' a person who indulges in senseless talk. By his babbling he tries to give the impression that he is wise and has nothing to learn. Such as he rejects the earnest instruction of wisdom, and his fate is 'to be brought to ruin.' That is the force of the verb, as in Hos. iv. 14. Without the guidance of wisdom's *commandments* he comes to a calamitous end (after Ibn Ezra).

9 SAFETY IN UPRIGHTNESS

shall be found out. lit. 'shall be known.' i.e. he shall become known to others that he perverteth his ways, when evil befalls him. In this way, he is contrasted with 'walketh securely' (after Ibn Ezra).

10 He that winketh with the eye
causeth sorrow;
And a prating fool shall fall.

11 The mouth of the righteous is a
fountain of life;
But the mouth of the wicked
concealeth violence.

12 Hatred stirreth up strifes;
But love covereth all transgressions.

13 In the lips of him that hath
discernment wisdom is found;
But a rod is for the back of him
that is void of understanding.

10 קֹרֵץ עַיִן יִתֵּן עַצָּבֶת
וֶאֱוִיל שְׂפָתַיִם יִלָּבֵט׃
11 מְקוֹר חַיִּים פִּי צַדִּיק
וּפִי רְשָׁעִים יְכַסֶּה חָמָס׃
12 שִׂנְאָה תְּעֹרֵר מְדָנִים
וְעַל כָּל־פְּשָׁעִים תְּכַסֶּה אַהֲבָה׃
13 בְּשִׂפְתֵי נָבוֹן תִּמָּצֵא חָכְמָה
וְשֵׁבֶט לְגֵו חֲסַר־לֵב׃

walketh securely. Because *He is a shield to them that walk in integrity* (ii. 7). *Securely* means free from danger and anxiety, as in iii. 23 (after Ibn Ezra).

perverteth his ways. Cf. ii. 15.

10 MISCHIEF-MAKING

winketh with the eye. Cf. vi. 13.

causeth sorrow. More lit. 'giveth pain.' The pain of malicious innuendo is to cause the victim mental anguish and possibly material injury (Ralbag). This includes anyone who causes injury to his neighbour clandestinely (Meiri).

and a prating fool shall fall. Once he discloses his intentions, people are able to beware of him. Thus, he will meet his downfall (Meiri).

11 SPEECH WISE AND UNWISE

mouth of the righteous. The words which issue from a man who is instructed by wisdom (Meiri).

fountain of life. A source of vitality to those who listen to his exhortation and advice, in the same way that a well supplies refreshment to them who draw its waters (Ibn Ezra).

but the mouth . . . violence. From verse 6. Here the clause is used to mark the difference between the good and the wicked in the effect they produce upon their fellow-men. From the former comes *life,* from the latter *violence* (Daath Mikra).

12 HATE AND LOVE

hatred stirreth up strifes. By making mountains out of molehills (Ralbag).

covereth. Puts out of sight and enables one to overlook insults and wrongs (cf. xvii. 9) (Ralbag).

13–14 USE AND ABUSE OF SPEECH

13. *that hath discernment.* lit. 'understanding' (see on i. 2). From the lips of a man who has the insight to draw correct distinctions between right and wrong, truth and error, can words of wisdom be heard even concerning matters that he did not learn (Gerondi).

a rod is for the back. Cf. xxvi. 3. Whereas the intelligent have well-established principles which guide their conduct, they who lack this equipment have to be forcibly led in the right direction, like an animal upon whose back the driver's blows fall (Gerondi).

14. *lay up knowledge.* They keep

14 Wise men lay up knowledge;
But the mouth of the foolish is an imminent ruin.

15 The rich man's wealth is his strong city;
The ruin of the poor is their poverty.

16 The wages of the righteous is life;
The increase of the wicked is sin.

17 He is in the way of life that heedeth instruction;
But he that forsaketh reproof erreth.

18 He that hideth hatred is of lying lips;
And he that uttereth a slander is a fool.

14 חֲכָמִים יִצְפְּנוּ־דָעַת
וּפִי אֱוִיל מְחִתָּה קְרֹבָה׃
15 הוֹן עָשִׁיר קִרְיַת עֻזּוֹ
מְחִתַּת דַּלִּים רֵישָׁם׃
16 פְּעֻלַּת צַדִּיק לְחַיִּים
תְּבוּאַת רָשָׁע לְחַטָּאת׃
17 אֹרַח לְחַיִּים שׁוֹמֵר מוּסָר
וְעֹזֵב תּוֹכַחַת מַתְעֶה׃
18 מְכַסֶּה שִׂנְאָה שִׂפְתֵי־שָׁקֶר
וּמוֹצִא דִבָּה הוּא כְסִיל׃

knowledge in their hearts lest they forget it (Rashi, Ibn Ezra). Others, 'conceal knowledge.' They are not talkative and do not reveal their knowledge to those who may not comprehend it (Ralbag, Metsudath David).

15. *the rich . . . city.* Repeated in xviii. 11. A man's wealth is a protection against many troubles in life in the same way that a fortified city safeguards its inhabitants (Ibn Ezra).

ruin of the poor. The lack of wealth places disabilities upon a man and exposes him to misfortunes (Ibn Ezra). Metsudath David explains *rich* as 'rich in Torah,' and *poor* as 'poor in Torah.' Others explain: The rich man trusts in his wealth as a strong city, the poor feel that they are broken because of their poverty. The truth is, however, that they both err, for everything depends on God's will, as the next verse states (Meiri, Gerondi).

16. *wages.* earnings from honest toil (Gerondi).

is life. More lit. 'is for life,' but *life* must be understood in the sense which the word has in xxvii. 27, *maintenance.* What the clause declares is that honest earnings are normally devoted by a man to procuring the necessities of life for himself and his family (Gerondi).

increase. lit. 'produce'; perhaps a significant contrast to *wages,* implying what is acquired, even that which is not from crime (Gerondi).

18 ANIMOSITY AND SLANDER

is of dying lips. He has to profess a friendliness which he does not feel, and so must dissimulate his speech (Metsudath David).

a fool. Morally defective (see on i. 22). Applied to the serious sin of calumny a stronger word than *fool* might have been expected. Furthermore, the connection between the two halves of the verse has puzzled the commentators. The only antithesis here is between concealment (of hatred which exists) and outspokenness (of a slander which does not exist), and yet each is a thoroughly bad thing (Ibn Nachmiash); so there is no true antithesis. The translation proposed by Daath Mikra regards the whole verse as continuous: 'He that with lying lips hideth hatred, and he that uttereth a slander, is a fool.' Only a brainless person indulges in these practices, because the sensible man knows that sooner or later the truth will be out.

19 In the multitude of words there
wanteth not transgression;
But he that refraineth his lips is
wise.

20 The tongue of the righteous is as
choice silver;
The heart of the wicked is little
worth.

21 The lips of the righteous feed
many;
But the foolish die for want of
understanding.

22 The blessing of the LORD, it
maketh rich,
And toil addeth nothing thereto.

19 בְּרֹב דְּבָרִים לֹא יֶחְדַּל־פָּשַׁע
וְחוֹשֵׂךְ שְׂפָתָיו מַשְׂכִּיל׃
20 כֶּסֶף נִבְחָר לְשׁוֹן צַדִּיק
לֵב רְשָׁעִים כִּמְעָט׃
21 שִׂפְתֵי צַדִּיק יִרְעוּ רַבִּים
וֶאֱוִילִים בַּחֲסַר־לֵב יָמוּתוּ׃
22 בִּרְכַּת יְהוָה הִיא תַעֲשִׁיר
וְלֹא־יוֹסִף עֶצֶב עִמָּהּ׃

19–20 RIGHT AND WRONG SPEECH

19. *wanteth not transgression.* See on verse 14.

refraineth his lips. Keeps a check on his tongue. Some rabbinic dicta on this theme are: 'Silence is a healing for all ailments' (Meg. 18a); 'Silence is good or the wise; how much more so for the foolish' (Yerushalmi Pesahim, ch 9); 'The Holy One, blessed bh He, said to the tongue, "All the limbs of man are erect but you are horizontal; they are all outside the body but you are inside. More than that, I have surrounded you with two walls, one of bone (the teeth) and the other of flesh (the lips)".' (Arachin 15b).

20. *choice silver.* Refined and free of dross; similarly the words of the righteous are of pure intent and without guile (Ibn Nachmiash).

heart. In contrast to the tongue of the righteous, the mind of the wicked is at best like common metal which is of little value (Meiri, Ibn Nachmiash).

21 LIFE-GIVING INSTRUCTION

feed. Rashi takes the word in its literal sense: the merit and prayers of the righteous so weigh with God that He sends abundance to earth from which the many satisfy their needs. Ibn. Ezra, however, understands it figuratively: give instruction.

the foolish die. [Not only do they not *feed* others, but perish from lack of spiritual nourishment.]

22 TRUE RICHES ARE FROM GOD

it maketh rich. [The word *it* is emphatic in the Hebrew.] Real prosperity emanates from God, and He bestows it upon those who are worthy (see Meiri).

and toil addeth nothing thereto. So R.V. margin which agrees with Rashi. Enjoying the Divine favour, one has no need to labour for the acquisition of wealth. A.V. and R.V., *and He addeth no sorrow therewith,* seems preferable. When one's good fortune is a blessing from God, he is free of the anxieties which ill-gotten riches create for their possessor, because these do not yield genuine happiness. (This follows Ibn Ezra).

23 It is as sport to a fool to do wickedness,
And so is wisdom to a man of discernment.

24 The fear of the wicked, it shall come upon him;
And the desire of the righteous shall be granted.

25 When the whirlwind passeth, the wicked is no more;
But the righteous is an everlasting foundation.

23 כִּשְׂחוֹק לִכְסִיל עֲשׂוֹת זִמָּה
וְחָכְמָה לְאִישׁ תְּבוּנָה׃
24 מְגוֹרַת רָשָׁע הִיא תְבוֹאֶנּוּ
וְתַאֲוַת צַדִּיקִים יִתֵּן׃
25 כַּעֲבוֹר סוּפָה וְאֵין רָשָׁע
וְצַדִּיק יְסוֹד עוֹלָם׃

23 PLEASURE OF THE FOOL AND WISE

it is as sport. lit. 'like laughing,' that in which he finds amusement and satisfaction (Ibn Ezra). He suggests further: Just as laughing is easy for the fool to do, so is doing wickedness, and so is wisdom to a man of discernment.

24–25 FATE OF RIGHTEOUS AND WICKED

24. *the fear of the wicked.* What the wicked man fears and seeks ways and means of avoiding, will, nevertheless, befall him, for his plans will not avail him (Malbim). Rashi gives as an example the generation that built the tower of Babel, who feared that they would be scattered over the face of the earth and met that very fate.

and the desire . . . granted. Even what the righteous merely desire, God will grant although they do nothing to acquire it. In this way, the author contrasts the righteous with the wicked, in that the wicked will fall prey to the very thing they dread and seek means of avoiding, whereas the righteous will receive what they merely desire in their hearts (Malbim). Ibn Ezra explains that the desire of the righteous is to destroy the wicked as is evidenced by the following verse.

25. *when the whirlwind passeth.* The wicked man is likened to an unstable building which is left in ruins when a storm sweeps over it (cf. Ps. xxxvii. 10).

an everlasting foundation. He survives the whirlwind because his virtue gives him resilience and power of endurance. The thought is the same as in Ps. i. 3ff. The Targum renders, 'the righteous man is the support of the world,' in agreement with a traditional Jewish doctrine, found in the Talmud, 'If there be but one righteous man, the continuance of the world is assured.' Should the righteous be totally lacking, the universe reverts to chaos.

26 As vinegar to the teeth, and as
smoke to the eyes,
So is the sluggard to them that
send him.

26 כַּחֹמֶץ ׀ לַשִּׁנַּיִם וְכֶעָשָׁן לָעֵינָיִם
כֵּן הֶעָצֵל לְשֹׁלְחָיו׃

27 The fear of the LORD prolongeth
days;
But the years of the wicked shall
be shortened.

27 יִרְאַת יְהוָה תּוֹסִיף יָמִים
וּשְׁנוֹת רְשָׁעִים תִּקְצֹרְנָה׃

28 The hope of the righteous is
gladness;
But the expectation of the wicked
shall perish.

28 תּוֹחֶלֶת צַדִּיקִים שִׂמְחָה
וְתִקְוַת רְשָׁעִים תֹּאבֵד׃

29 The way of the LORD is a stronghold to the upright,
But ruin to the workers of
iniquity.

29 מָעוֹז לַתֹּם דֶּרֶךְ יְהוָה
וּמְחִתָּה לְפֹעֲלֵי אָוֶן׃

30 The righteous shall never be
moved;
But the wicked shall not inhabit
the land.

30 צַדִּיק לְעוֹלָם בַּל־יִמּוֹט
וּרְשָׁעִים לֹא יִשְׁכְּנוּ־אָרֶץ׃

26 THE SLUGGARD

vinegar to the teeth. Something that causes irritation (Ibn Ezra).

27–32 RIGHTEOUS AND WICKED CONTRASTED

27. *fear of the* LORD.. Which is *the beginning of knowledge* (i. 7) and *of wisdom* (ix. 10), the correct rule of living.

shortened. Although the wicked live without worries, and indulge the desires of the flesh, their years are shortened (Gerondi, Elijah of Wilna).

28. *gladness.* In the realization of the hope (Rashi).

29. *the way . . . upright.* Some authorities, ignoring the accentuation, translate: 'The Lord is a stronghold to the man who is upright in (his) way'; but this is unnecessary. *Way of the Lord* can bear two interpretations. It may denote the path of life commanded by God (Ibn Ezra): the upright man who walks therein finds courage and fortitude so that he is strengthened to face difficulties and dangers; to the evil-doers, on the other hand, it is *ruin* because they forsake it and so incur punishment (Rashi, Ibn Ezra). Possibly, however, *way* should be understood in the light of Moses' plea, *Show me Thy ways* (Exod. xxxiii. 13) and his declaration, *All His ways are justice* (Deut. xxxii. 4), i.e. His dealings with man. The way of the Lord serves as encouragement for the upright, who witness how He supports the fallen and cares for the crushed, and all His ways are kindness and mercy, for so God guides the world. It is ruin to the workers of iniquity, who behave in just the opposite manner (Malbim).

30. *moved.* An assurance frequently found in the Psalms (e.g. xv. 5, xxi. 8, lv. 23), indicating that the righteous withstand the attacks of the wicked, and though they fall, they rise again (Rashi,

31 The mouth of the righteous buddeth with wisdom;
But the froward tongue shall be cut off.

32 The lips of the righteous know what is acceptable;
But the mouth of the wicked is all frowardness.

פִּֽי־צַדִּיק יָנוּב חָכְמָה
וּלְשׁוֹן תַּהְפֻּכוֹת תִּכָּרֵת׃
שִׂפְתֵי צַדִּיק יֵדְעוּן רָצוֹן
וּפִי רְשָׁעִים תַּהְפֻּכוֹת׃

Metsudath David). Or, as Ibn Ezra suggests, after their death, their descendants remain.

shall not inhabit the land. Cf. *For the upright shall dwell in the land, but the wicked shall be cut off from the land* (ii. 21f.; see note). Although now they prosper, they will not remain long (Metsudath David).

31. *buddeth with wisdom.* The mouth is compared to a tree, and its words to flowers and fruit (cf. *the mouth of the righteous uttereth wisdom,* Ps. xxxvii. 30). A more literal rendering would be, 'The mouth of the righteous bears wisdom as fruit' (after Ibn Ezra, Meiri, Malbim).

froward tongue. Cf. *froward mouth* (vi. 12) which distorts the words of the Torah to apostasy (Metsudath David).

cut off. Severed from its roots and wither. It will not be able to execute its plans (Meiri).

32. *know what is acceptable.* 'They know how to appease their Maker, and how to pacify their fellow-creatures, promoting peace in their midst' (Rashi). The word *acceptable* can signify that which gives satisfaction either to God or man. Where in this Book it refers to God, the Divine name is always specified (cf. viii. 35, xi. 1, etc.). It is therefore probable that in this verse the intention is: the righteous man knows how to speak what will give satisfaction to his fellows as well (so Ralbag).

is all frowardness. A.V. and R.V. '(speaketh) frowardness' is unnecessary. For the idiom, see on viii. 14. The point made in the two verses is that a man's speech is the reflection of his character, and therefore his character reveals itself in his speech. Seneca, the Roman philosopher of the first century C.E., observed, 'Speech is the index of the mind.' Ibn Ezra explains: 'But the mouth of the wicked knows frowardness.

A false balance is an abomination
to the LORD;
But a perfect weight is His
delight.

When pride cometh, then cometh
shame;
But with the lowly is wisdom.

The integrity of the upright shall
guide them;
But the perverseness of the faithless shall destroy them.

1 מֹאזְנֵי מִרְמָה תּוֹעֲבַת יְהֹוָה
וְאֶבֶן שְׁלֵמָה רְצוֹנוֹ׃
2 בָּא זָדוֹן וַיָּבֹא קָלוֹן
וְאֶת־צְנוּעִים חָכְמָה׃
3 תֻּמַּת יְשָׁרִים תַּנְחֵם
וְסֶלֶף בֹּגְדִים וְשַׁדֵּם׃

v. 3. ישדם ק׳

CHAPTER XI

1 BUSINESS HONESTY

1. *a false balance.* lit. 'scales of deceit.' For the Pentateuchal exhortations in this connection, cf. Lev. xix. 35f.; Deut. xxv. 15. The necessity of honest trading is stressed in Hebrew ethics. This Book refers to the subject again in xvi. 11, xx. 10, 23. Prophetical denunciations of the use of false weights and measures are found in Amos viii. 5; Micah vi. 11. The Talmud includes several regulations to ensure straight dealing between seller and buyer. One only need be quoted to indicate the demand for the most scrupulous care against fraud: 'The shopkeeper must wipe his measures twice a week, his weights once a week, and his scales after every weighing' (Baba Bathra 88a).

His delight. That which has His approval. It is not merely abstinence from evil, and therefore not an abomination, but it is counted as though he performs a positive commandment. In the words of the Sages: 'Whoever refrains from committing a sin is accounted as having performed a precept' (Malbim from Makkoth 23b).

2 FALSITY OF PRIDE

2. *pride.* Better, 'arrogance.' For this vice, see on vi. 17; cf. also xiii. 10, xvi. 18f., xviii. 12.

shame. Rather, 'contempt'; the man s end is to be lightly esteemed by his fellows (Isaiah da Trani).

lowly. The Hebrew root occurs again only in Micah vi. 8, in the sublime answer to the question, *What doth the* LORD *require of thee?* viz. *to walk humbly with thy God.* Here the word defines one who walks humbly with God and man.

is wisdom. The thought is beautifully expressed in a Rabbinic dictum, 'As water leaves a high level and goes to a lower level, so Torah abandons him whose mind is haughty and cleaves to him whose mind is humble.'

3–6 SAVING POWER OF RIGHTEOUSNESS

3. *integrity of the upright.* They who are *upright* chose *integrity* as their standard of conduct; it will prove a reliable guide and be a safeguard against error (Ibn Nachmiash) and danger (Meiri).

perverseness. [If men resort to dubious methods to gain their ends, they will be ultimately ruined by their intrigues.]

shall destroy them. lit. 'shall rob them.' Shall rob them of their souls (Metsudath David). They will be destroyed by divine retribution, not by chance (Meiri). Ibn Nachmiash quotes exegetes who render: 'shall compel them.' i.e., their perverseness compels them to continue on that path.

4 Riches profit not in the day of wrath;
But righteousness delivereth from death.

לֹא־יוֹעִיל הוֹן בְּיוֹם עֶבְרָה
וּצְדָקָה תַּצִּיל מִמָּוֶת׃

5 The righteousness of the sincere shall make straight his way;
But the wicked shall fall by his own wickedness.

צִדְקַת תָּמִים תְּיַשֵּׁר דַּרְכּוֹ
וּבְרִשְׁעָתוֹ יִפֹּל רָשָׁע׃

6 The righteousness of the upright shall deliver them;
But the faithless shall be trapped in their own crafty device.

צִדְקַת יְשָׁרִים תַּצִּילֵם
וּבְהַוַּת בֹּגְדִים יִלָּכֵדוּ׃

7 When a wicked man dieth, his expectation shall perish,
And the hope of strength perisheth.

בְּמוֹת אָדָם רָשָׁע תֹּאבַד תִּקְוָה
וְתוֹחֶלֶת אוֹנִים אָבָדָה׃

8 The righteous is delivered out of trouble,
And the wicked cometh in his stead.

צַדִּיק מִצָּרָה נֶחֱלָץ
וַיָּבֹא רָשָׁע תַּחְתָּיו׃

4. *profit not.* lit. 'have no use.'

day of wrath. Usually in the Bible this phrase indicates a time of calamity which comes upon the nation as punishment for sin (cf. Zeph. i. 15ff.). In such a time of crisis, the wealth for which a man bartered his honour does not protect him from the sufferings which befall the population; all he possesses is taken from him. The parallel *from death,* however, suggests that the words mean the day when life is ended by an act of God. Indeed, the Talmud (Shabbath 156b) explains this verse to mean that charity saves one from death.

5. *sincere.* The Hebrew word is cognate with *integrity* (verse 3), and the thought of that verse is repeated here.

7 PLACE NO RELIANCE UPON THE WICKED

wicked man. [As often in Proverbs and Psalms, the *wicked man* is one who holds a position of authority and influence which he abuses by acting lawlessly. Fearing his power of doing them harm with impunity, people are disposed to curry favour with him and buy his protection and help. The verse utters a warning against this tendency.]

his expectation shall perish. Cf. x. 28, but the phrase now receives a different application. Rashi's interpretation is the most acceptable: the expectation perishes which they who relied upon him entertained. The influence he wielded in his lifetime at once ceases on his death, and so they are disappointed who put their trust in him.

8–9 RIGHT VINDICATED

8. If we give *righteous* and *wicked* their ordinary ethical definition, the intention is that sometimes evil is decreed upon a righteous man, and a wicked man is put in his place as ransom or redemption from this misfortune. Cf. Isaiah xliii. 3, infra xxi. 18 (Gerondi). Elijah of Wilna offers the examples of Mordecai, who was replaced by Haman, and Hananiah, Mishael, and Azariah, who were replaced in the furnace by those who had informed upon them. In this context it is cited in numerous places in Talmud and Midrash. Rashi explains that this verse is connected to the preceding one. When the wicked dies, a righteous man is delivered from trouble and a wicked one cometh in his place.

9 With his mouth the impious man destroyeth his neighbour;
But through knowledge shall the righteous be delivered.

10 When it goeth well with the righteous, the city rejoiceth;
And when the wicked perish, there is joy.

11 By the blessing of the upright a city is exalted;
But it is overthrown by the mouth of the wicked.

12 He that despiseth his neighbour lacketh understanding;
But a man of discernment holdeth his peace.

בְּפֶה חָנֵף יַשְׁחִת רֵעֵהוּ 9
וּבְדַעַת צַדִּיקִים יֵחָלֵצוּ׃
בְּטוּב צַדִּיקִים תַּעֲלֹץ קִרְיָה 10
וּבַאֲבֹד רְשָׁעִים רִנָּה׃
בְּבִרְכַּת יְשָׁרִים תָּרוּם קָרֶת 11
וּבְפִי רְשָׁעִים תֵּהָרֵס׃
בָּז־לְרֵעֵהוּ חֲסַר־לֵב 12
וְאִישׁ תְּבוּנוֹת יַחֲרִישׁ׃

9. *with his mouth.* Uttering false accusations (Ibn Ezra).

the impious man. lit. 'polluted,' a Godless person who lacks all sense of honour. He pretends to be a friend, but then betrays those he has befriended (Meiri).

destroyeth. Better, 'would destroy,' seeks to ruin (Ibn Ezra). Targum and Ibn Nachmiash, however, render according to A.J.

his neighbour. His fellow. The one the impious man seeks to ruin by slandering him (Meiri).

through knowledge. His integrity provides him with the understanding that enables him to penetrate the flattery and false friendship of the impious (Ibn Nachmiash).

10–11 THE RIGHTEOUS IN CIVIC LIFE

10. *the city rejoiceth.* Because the prosperity of the righteous is not selfishly enjoyed; they share it with their fellow-citizens (Metsudath David).

there is joy. In the removal of a disturbing element in the civic life (Metsudath David).

11. *blessing.* When the upright are blessed with prosperity, and they alone govern the city justly, the city is exalted (Metsudath David). They will build up the city. It may also mean that the people of the city will be exalted (Ibn Ezra).

mouth of the wicked. Which speaks falsehood or tale-bearing (Ibn Ezra); it upsets the unity of the city and undermines its stability.

12–13 MISUSE OF SPEECH

These two verses illustrate the second clause of verse 11 and instance the effect produced by *the mouth of the wicked.*

12. *despiseth his neighbour.* Openly displays his contempt for him. A Rabbi advised, 'Despise not any man, for there is not a man who has not his hour' (Aboth 4.3).

lacketh understanding. He acts foolishly, because he makes an enemy of the despised person who may have an opportunity to retaliate (Meiri).

holdeth his peace. If he was insulted by another, he keeps his peace and does not return the insult (Ibn Ezra, Metsudath David).

13 He that goeth about as a tale-bearer revealeth secrets;
But he that is of a faithful spirit concealeth a matter.

14 Where no wise direction is, a people falleth;
But in the multitude of counsellors there is safety.

15 He that is surety for a stranger shall smart for it;
But he that hateth them that strike hands is secure.

16 A gracious woman obtaineth honour;
And strong men obtain riches.

הולך רכיל מגלה־סוד
ונאמן־רוח מכסה דבר׃
באין תחבלות יפל־עם
ותשועה ברב יועץ׃
רע ירוע כי־ערב זר
ושנא תוקעים בוטח׃
אשת חן תתמך כבוד
ועריצים יתמכו־עשר׃

13. *he that goeth . . . secrets.* Repeated in a different form in xx. 19. For the prohibition of this slanderous practice, cf. Lev. xix. 16. This social pest is gravely censured in Hebrew literature, even when he is not actuated by malice.

of a faithful spirit. He whose spirit is faithful to God concealeth a matter although it was not confided to him as a secret (Metsudath David). Solomon warns not to confide a secret to a tale-bearer but to one of faithful spirit (Ibn Nachmiash).

14 PEOPLE'S NEED OF WISE DIRECTION

wise direction. [See on i. 5 where the word is translated *wise counsels.* We likewise speak of 'the ship of State' which needs skilled navigation.]

but in the multitude . . . safety. The clause recurs in xxiv. 6 where the last word is translated *victory,* to fit in with an illustration of the general principle which is stated in the present verse, viz. *For with wise advice thou shalt make thy war.* The proverb has a parallel in the English saying, 'Two heads are better than one' (cf. also xv. 22).

15 WARNING AGAINST SURETY

surety. See on vi. 1.

for a stranger. Whom you do not know to be honest (Ibn Ezra, Metsudath David).

shall smart for it. lit. 'shall surely suffer harm' (Targum). Ibn Ezra, however, renders, 'be broken.'

who hateth. Whoever avoids being surety even for his friends (Metsudath David).

secure. He is not burdened by worry or liable to pay his guarantee to his financial embarrassment.

16 TRIBUTE TO A GOOD WOMAN

and strong men. Better, 'whereas strong men.' A gracious woman, who is charming because of her talent is wont to preserve her honour by increasing her skill, whereas the strong men seek to preserve their riches lest it be lost (Metsudath David).

17 The merciful man doeth good to his own soul;
But he that is cruel troubleth his own flesh.

17 גֹּמֵל נַפְשׁוֹ אִישׁ חָסֶד
וְעֹכֵר שְׁאֵרוֹ אַכְזָרִי׃

18 The wicked earneth deceitful wages;
But he that soweth righteousness hath a sure reward.

18 רָשָׁע עֹשֶׂה פְעֻלַּת־שָׁקֶר
וְזֹרֵעַ צְדָקָה שֶׂכֶר אֱמֶת׃

19 Stedfast righteousness tendeth to life;
But he that pursueth evil pursueth it to his own death.

19 כֵּן־צְדָקָה לְחַיִּים
וּמְרַדֵּף רָעָה לְמוֹתוֹ׃

20 They that are perverse in heart are an abomination to the LORD;
But such as are upright in their way are His delight.

20 תּוֹעֲבַת יְהוָה עִקְּשֵׁי־לֵב
וּרְצוֹנוֹ תְּמִימֵי דָרֶךְ׃

21 My hand upon it! the evil man shall not be unpunished;
But the seed of the righteous shall escape.

21 יָד לְיָד לֹא־יִנָּקֶה רָּע
וְזֶרַע צַדִּיקִים נִמְלָט׃

17 ON KINDLINESS

to his own soul. 'To himself'; his gracious deeds are a blessing to others and also to himself, since he benefits his soul (Malbim).

18-21 EFFECTS OF GOODNESS AND EVIL

18. *deceitful wages.* lit. 'wages of falsehood,' so described because they possess only temporary value. Such *riches profit not in the day of wrath* (verse 4) (after Rashi).

19. *stedfast righteousness.* The first word in the Hebrew, *ken,* has two meanings: 'so,' used in drawing a comparison, hence R.V. margin 'so righteousness'; or 'firm,' adopted by R.V. 'he that is stedfast in righteousness.' The first translation follows Ibn Ezra. It appears, however, that he renders: 'so charity.' The second follows Elijah of Wilna. Perhaps the best translation is obtained by adopting the second meaning of *ken* with adverbial force, as in Joshua ii. 4, 'yea, righteousness.' The sense is clear and yields a familiar doctrine of the Book, viz. righteousness prolongs life, evil shortens it. This follows Meiri and Gerondi.

20. Cf. xv. 9. God being the perfection of holiness, only they whose lives are disciplined by the laws of holiness can have His approval.

upright in their way. Better, 'upright in the way' (cf. Ps. cxix. 1).

21. *my hand upon it!* lit. 'hand to hand,' which Rashi explains: from the hand of God to the hand of the wicked shall come the penalty he has incurred. The expression is found once more in xvi. 5, and is now taken to be an exclamatory remark with the meaning 'assuredly' (cf. the English saying, 'Here's my hand upon it'). For its possible origin, see on vi. 1 (see Likutei Yehudah).

seed of the righteous. Normally *seed* signifies descendants; but the comparison is now between the wicked and the righteous themselves. Saadiah explains that not only do the righteous escape, but also their children in their merit.

22 **As a ring of gold in a swine's snout,**
So is a fair woman that turneth aside from discretion.

23 **The desire of the righteous is only good;**
But the expectation of the wicked is wrath.

24 **There is that scattereth, and yet increaseth;**

נֶזֶם זָהָב בְּאַף חֲזִיר
אִשָּׁה יָפָה וְסָרַת טָעַם׃
תַּאֲוַת צַדִּיקִים אַךְ־טוֹב
תִּקְוַת רְשָׁעִים עֶבְרָה׃
יֵשׁ מְפַזֵּר וְנוֹסָף עוֹד

22 REFINEMENT ESSENTIAL IN WOMAN

The Hebrew lacks anything which corresponds to *as* and *so,* and in its terseness is more forceful than the translation. It sets side by side two separate incongruities, leaving the reader to associate them.

ring of gold. A nose-ring was a common adornment of Oriental women (cf. Gen. xxiv. 22; Isa. iii. 21). According to the taste of the time it was considered to beautify the wearer. Imagine it, however, in a swine's snout; how out of place! The swine is chosen for the illustration as the most unclean of animals in its habits (see Malbim).

discretion. lit. 'taste.' Perhaps 'refinement' best expresses its meaning in this context, combining the ideas of good sense and good taste. The Rabbis of the Midrash applied the verse to the disciple: 'If thou puttest a golden ornament into the nose of a pig, he will dirty it with mud and refuse; so is the student of Torah if he abandon himself to immorality, he defiles his Torah.'

23 FATE OF RIGHTEOUS AND WICKED

is only good. The verse suggests two interpretations: what the righteous long for is limited to the good and they have no desire for anything that could debase their character. What the wicked strive after is *arrogance* (for this sense of the word, cf. Isa. xvi. 6), i.e. the power to enrich themselves at the expense of others (Rashi). The alternative reading is: the righteous desire only what is intrinsically good, not what is pleasant for a fleeting moment, or that which is beneficial in the future. The wicked, however, desire what is pleasant now, yet their end is to bring upon themselves the Divine *wrath* (Elijah of Wilna).

24–26 LIBERALITY AND AVARICE

24. *scattereth.* The verb occurs in *he hath scattered abroad, he hath given to the needy* (Ps. cxii. 9), and so it was natural for the traditional interpretation to apply the clause to charity. He who devotes his money to benevolence, becomes the richer and not the poorer for it. The author intimates, however, that not everyone who scattereth increaseth. This is an allusion to the Rabbinical ruling (Kethuboth 67b) that one may not give away more than a fifth of his money to charity (Alschich). After giving one fifth of his property, he may thereafter give a fifth of his earnings. The usual, recommended amount, however, is a tenth, reminiscent of the tithes given the Levites.

And there is that withholdeth more than is meet, but it tendeth only to want.

וְחוֹשֵׂךְ מִיֹּשֶׁר אַךְ־לְמַחְסוֹר׃

25 The beneficent soul shall be made rich,
And he that satisfieth abundantly shall be satisfied also himself.

25 נֶפֶשׁ־בְּרָכָה תְדֻשָּׁן
וּמַרְוֶה גַּם־הוּא יוֹרֶא׃

26 He that withholdeth corn, the people shall curse him;
But blessing shall be upon the head of him that selleth it.

26 מֹנֵעַ בָּר יִקְּבֻהוּ לְאוֹם
וּבְרָכָה לְרֹאשׁ מַשְׁבִּיר׃

27 He that diligently seeketh good seeketh favour;
But he that searcheth for evil, it shall come unto him.

27 שֹׁחֵר טוֹב יְבַקֵּשׁ רָצוֹן
וְדֹרֵשׁ רָעָה תְבוֹאֶנּוּ׃

withholdeth more than is meet. Gives less charity than it is proper to give according to his means (Metsudath David).

only to want. The Rabbis (Tanchuma, R'eh 10) relate an incident of one who inherited a field and failed to give the prescribed tithes to the Levites. His punishment was that the following year the field produced only one tenth of the crops it had produced previously. His friends told him that since he withheld the tithe, God took away the field from him, becoming the owner of the field and giving him the tithe like the Levite. This verse tells us that the same is true of charity; if one withholds charity from the poor, 'it tendeth only to want' (Alschich).

25. *the beneficent soul.* lit. 'soul of blessing,' a kindly and sympathethic disposition which responds to the call for help from those in need (Daath Mikra).

made rich. lit. 'shall be made fat,' a word commonly employed for the idea of prosperity (cf. xiii. 4, xxviii. 25).

satisfieth abundantly . . . be satisfied. A.V. and R.V. more lit. 'watereth . . . be watered,' a metaphor from agriculture. If a man irrigates his land, he has his reward in a good harvest. Similarly the benevolent have their recompense in the Divine bounty which is bestowed upon them. 'Whoever runs after charity (to practise it), the Holy One, blessed be He, provides him with the means wherewith to do it' (Talmud, B.B. 9b).

26. *withholdeth corn.* In a time of scarcity to inflate the price. The practice is denounced in the Talmud.

blessing shall be upon the head. See on x. 6. He forgoes the opportunity of making high profits from the emergency; but God will give him his reward (Ibn Ezra).

27 WORKING FOR THE GOOD OF OTHERS

good. The happiness of his fellow-men (Metsudath David).

seeketh favour. Probably the meaning is: desires to obtain and wins their goodwill. The Jewish commentators understand it of God's favour.

searcheth for evil. Opposite of the phrase *seeking the good of his people* (Esther x. 3). If he plans to harm others, the injury will recoil upon his own head (Metsudath David).

28 He that trusteth in his riches shall fall;
But the righteous shall flourish as foliage.

29 He that troubleth his own house shall inherit the wind;
And the foolish shall be servant to the wise of heart.

30 The fruit of the righteous is a tree of life;
And he that is wise winneth souls.

31 Behold, the righteous shall be requited in the earth;
How much more the wicked and the sinner!

28 בּוֹטֵחַ בְּעָשְׁרוֹ הוּא יִפּוֹל
וְכֶעָלֶה צַדִּיקִים יִפְרָחוּ׃
29 עֹכֵר בֵּיתוֹ יִנְחַל־רוּחַ
וְעֶבֶד אֱוִיל לַחֲכַם־לֵב׃
30 פְּרִי־צַדִּיק עֵץ חַיִּים
וְלֹקֵחַ נְפָשׁוֹת חָכָם׃
31 הֵן צַדִּיק בָּאָרֶץ יְשֻׁלָּם
אַף כִּי־רָשָׁע וְחוֹטֵא׃

28. TRUST NOT IN RICHES

in his riches. The intention is that one must not trust in his riches and take away his trust from God. Should one do so, he will fall, his riches not availing him. The righteous who trust in God and not in their riches will flourish like foliage (Ibn Ezra).

as foliage. lit. 'a leaf.' For the imagery, cf. Ps. i. 3, xcii. 13.

29 FOLLY OF A MISER

troubleth his own house. By his miserly disposition and denies his family necessities of life for the purpose of saving money (Gerondi).

shall inherit the wind. Or, 'will have the wind as his possession.' His niggardliness deprives him of what is worth having, viz. a comfortable home-life, and he is left with money which has no real value because it is hoarded. *Wind* is a figure of what lacks substance, as in Jer. v. 13, and the phrase of Eccles. *a striving after wind* (after Meiri).

and the foolish . . . heart. [This clause continues the thought of the preceding: and being a fool, he becomes a slave to the wise-hearted. He toils hard to accumulate money the fruits of which he does not enjoy; and so he is practically a slave working for those who will inherit his wealth and, being more sensible than he, will spend it liberally.]

30 EFFECT OF THE RIGHTEOUS

fruit of the righteous. The effect produced upon others by the exalted principles of his life (Elijah of Wilna).

a tree of life. See on iii. 18.

winneth souls. Attracts people and imparts to them sound advice (Rashi).

31 DIVINE RETRIBUTION

requited. lit. 'repaid.' Even the righteous man is not perfect (Eccles. vii. 20), and the faults of which he is guilty are judged by God and punished (Rashi).

in the earth. During his lifetime (Rashi).

how much more. Will God not overlook the misdeeds of the wicked and exact a full penalty (Rashi).

Whoso loveth knowledge loveth correction;
But he that is brutish hateth reproof.

A good man shall obtain favour of the LORD;
But a man of wicked devices will He condemn.

A man shall not be established by wickedness;
But the root of the righteous shall never be moved.

A virtuous woman is a crown to her husband;
But she that doeth shamefully is as rottenness in his bones.

1 אֹהֵב מוּסָר אֹהֵב דָּעַת
וְשׂוֹנֵא תוֹכַחַת בָּעַר׃
2 טוֹב יָפִיק רָצוֹן מֵיְהוָה
וְאִישׁ מְזִמּוֹת יַרְשִׁיעַ׃
3 לֹא־יִכּוֹן אָדָם בְּרֶשַׁע
וְשֹׁרֶשׁ צַדִּיקִים בַּל־יִמּוֹט׃
4 אֵשֶׁת חַיִל עֲטֶרֶת בַּעְלָהּ
וּכְרָקָב בְּעַצְמוֹתָיו מְבִישָׁה׃

CHAPTER XII

1 LOVE CORRECTION

correction. Hebrew *musar* (see on i. 2). That is the meaning required by the translation of A.J. to make the antithesis with the second clause; and the point of the verse is the necessity for a man to be willing to accept criticism of his conduct and benefit therefrom (this follows Ibn Ezra). A.V. and R.V. reverse the subject and predicate: 'whoso loveth correction loveth knowledge; but he that hateth reproof is brutish,' i.e. will remain brutish (Metsudath David).

brutish. A person in whom animal instincts overrule the spiritual elements (cf. Ps. lxxiii. 22, xcii. 7). The Hebrew *ba'ar* is related to the Aramaic *b'ir,* a beast (Ibn Nachmiash, Gerondi, Metsudath Zion). The intention of the verse is that if a person errs in his deeds, but is pleased when others reprove him, he is an intelligent person. He erred merely because his desires overpowered him. Therefore, when he is reproved, he will improve his ways, and we can hope that he will learn to overpower his temptation. One who 'hateth reproof,' however, shows that he lacks intelligence and is like a beast that follows its lusts (Gerondi).

2–3 FATE OF RIGHTEOUS AND WICKED

2. *obtain favour.* And be blessed with His protection and help (Meiri).

wicked devices. lit. 'devices,' but wherever the word is used in chapters i-ix (e.g. i. 4) it has a good sense, and thereafter a bad sense.

condemn. God will not allow him to escape punishment (Meiri).

3. *not be established.* The prophets applied this doctrine to nations as well as individuals (cf. *In righteousness shalt thou be established,* Isa. liv. 14).

4 WIFE'S EFFECT ON HER HUSBAND

a virtuous woman. More lit. 'a wife of strong character.' The same phrase is met with in xxxi. 10. It combines the ideas of virtuous disposition and sound intellectual capacity (see Ralbag, Ibn Nachmiash).

a crown. Such a wife adds to the social status of her husband and elevates him in the esteem of his neighbours (Ibn Ezra).

5 The thoughts of the righteous are right;
But the counsels of the wicked are deceit.

מַחְשְׁבוֹת צַדִּיקִים מִשְׁפָּט
תַּחְבֻּלוֹת רְשָׁעִים מִרְמָה׃

6 The words of the wicked are to lie in wait for blood;
But the mouth of the upright shall deliver them.

דִּבְרֵי רְשָׁעִים אֱרָב־דָּם
וּפִי יְשָׁרִים יַצִּילֵם׃

7 The wicked are overthrown, and are not;
But the house of the righteous shall stand.

הָפוֹךְ רְשָׁעִים וְאֵינָם
וּבֵית צַדִּיקִים יַעֲמֹד׃

8 A man shall be commended according to his intelligence;
But he that is of a distorted understanding shall be despised.

לְפִי־שִׂכְלוֹ יְהֻלַּל־אִישׁ
וְנַעֲוֵה־לֵב יִהְיֶה לָבוּז׃

9 Better is he that is lightly esteemed and hath a servant,
Than he that playeth the man of rank, and lacketh bread.

טוֹב נִקְלֶה וְעֶבֶד לוֹ
מִמִּתְכַּבֵּד וַחֲסַר־לָחֶם׃

5–6 THOUGHTS AND WORDS OF RIGHTEOUS AND WICKED

5. *thoughts.* Or, 'designs'; they are well-intentioned and morally sound, because the mind of the righteous man is disciplined by wisdom. Their sole intention is to perform justice (Meiri, Isaiah da Trani).

6. *lie in wait for blood.* Rashi explains the verse of false evidence in a court of law which may result in the forfeiture of an innocent life. According to Ibn Ezra, the intention is more general: the wicked conspire together and plot murder (cf. i. 11).

7 INSTABILITY OF THE WICKED

the wicked are overthrown. lit. 'to overthrow the wicked.' The teaching is that being once overthrown, that is their end; they have not the power of recovery (cf. x. 25).

8 MAN ESTEEMED FOR HIS INTELLIGENCE

intelligence. Ability to form a sound judgment in everyday matters, common sense. Since people benefit from his intelligence, his behavior, and his counsel, they recognize his superiority and commend him (Meiri).

9 FALSE PRIDE CONDEMNED

and hath a servant. The interpretation of the verse depends on the way this phrase is understood. One possible reading is: Better to be held in low social esteem by not living beyond one's means, and yet possess a slave to do the menial work and so have a comfortable life, than make a pretence of wealth, mixing with the rich and spending what is necessary for food on maintaining a place in such society. This yields a satisfactory meaning and a sensible admonition which many need today. On the other hand, the words *and hath a servant* may signify 'and is a slave to himself,' i.e. he does for himself the humble tasks which are usually relegated to a slave, and spends the money on feeding his body well. In either case, the point is the futility of inflicting privations upon oneself to preserve an outward show of affluence which does not correspond with reality. The second interpretation is accepted by most exegetes.

A righteous man regardeth the life of his beast;
But the tender mercies of the wicked are cruel.

He that tilleth his ground shall have plenty of bread;
But he that followeth after vain things is void of understanding.

The wicked desireth the prey of evil men;
But the root of the righteous yieldeth fruit.

10 יוֹדֵעַ צַדִּיק נֶפֶשׁ בְּהֶמְתּוֹ
וְרַחֲמֵי רְשָׁעִים אַכְזָרִי׃
11 עֹבֵד אַדְמָתוֹ יִשְׂבַּע־לָחֶם
וּמְרַדֵּף רֵיקִים חֲסַר־לֵב׃
12 חָמַד רָשָׁע מְצוֹד רָעִים
וְשֹׁרֶשׁ צַדִּיקִים יִתֵּן׃

10 CONSIDERATION FOR ANIMALS

regardeth the life. lit. 'knoweth the soul,' pays attention to its needs and is careful that it is sufficiently supplied with food (Metsudath David). For this use of *soul,* see on x. 3. On this subject, cf. Deut. xxv. 4. As God provides for animals (Ps. civ. 14, 27), so must man. From the words, *And I will give grass in thy fields for thy cattle, and thou shalt eat and be satisfied* (Deut. xi. 15, note the sequence), the Rabbis (Gittin 62a) deduced the regulation that a man must feed his animals before feeding himself.

11 ADVANTAGE OF AGRICULTURE

tilleth his ground. The verse is repeated in xxviii. 19 with a different ending. Meiri explains that Scripture exhorts the person to take care of his property and till his ground. In this manner, he is assured by God that he will earn a livelihood. [But it would accord with the facts of Hebrew history to understand it as an exhortation to follow agriculture as a livelihood, particularly in view of the tendency to drift into other occupations. In a later period, doubtless because of the insecurity of land tenure, we find Rabbis advocating the advantages of commerce over husbandry. Yet others took the contrary view and declared, 'A landless man is not a man' (Yebamoth 63a); while one of them adopted a middle course and advised, 'Let every man divide his money into three parts, investing a third in land, a third in business, and holding a third in reserve' (Baba Metsia 42a).]

vain things. If he idles and wastes his time (Ibn Nachmiash). Alternatively, if he follows things which serve no benefit (Metsudath David).

12 STABILITY OF THE RIGHTEOUS

prey. Modern commentators find the verse unintelligible, but it can be made to produce a satisfactory interpretation. The Hebrew *matsod* is assumed by most commentators to be a form of *metsodah,* 'net,' hence what is caught in a net, viz. 'prey.' Accordingly, they explain that the wicked desires to prey on the innocent, as the evil men do (Rashi, Ibn Ezra, Isaiah da Trani, Ibn Nachmiash). Others explain it as a form of *metsodah,* 'stronghold' (cf. Isa. xxix. 7; Ezek. xix. 9). The sense of the first clause is: 'The wicked covets the stronghold of evil men'; i.e. the stronghold where the evil men fortify themselves to direct their robbing (Metsudath David). This may also be interpreted as the company of the evil (Saadiah Gaon, Meiri).

13 In the transgression of the lips is a snare to the evil man;
But the righteous cometh out of trouble.

בְּפֶשַׁע שְׂפָתַיִם מוֹקֵשׁ רָע
וַיֵּצֵא מִצָּרָה צַדִּיק׃

14 A man shall be satisfied with good by the fruit of his mouth,
And the doings of a man's hands shall be rendered unto him.

מִפְּרִי פִי־אִישׁ יִשְׂבַּע־טוֹב
וּגְמוּל יְדֵי־אָדָם יָשׁוּב לוֹ׃

15 The way of a fool is straight in his own eyes;
But he that is wise hearkeneth unto counsel.

דֶּרֶךְ אֱוִיל יָשָׁר בְּעֵינָיו
וְשֹׁמֵעַ לְעֵצָה חָכָם׃

16 A fool's vexation is presently known;
But a prudent man concealeth shame.

אֱוִיל בַּיּוֹם יִוָּדַע כַּעְסוֹ
וְכֹסֶה קָלוֹן עָרוּם׃

v. 14 ישיב ק'

yieldeth fruit. lit. 'gives.' The verb may also be understood as Targum, 'but the root of the righteous endureth. [He depends upon the integrity of his life, and it does not fail him. The verse, accordingly, expresses a thought common in Proverbs: the instability of the bad man and the security of the righteous (cf. verse 7).]

13–14 THE FRUITS OF SPEECH

13. *transgression of the lips.* False and mischievous talk, aimed at ensnaring others, ends in the speaker himself being trapped by his words (cf. xviii. 7) (Metsudath David).

cometh out of trouble. His lips speak only what is true, and truth will out. He is finally vindicated (Metsudath David).

14. *by the fruit of his mouth.* [If he belongs to the category mentioned in the preceding clause, viz. the righteous.]

shall be rendered unto him. The *kethib* is 'shall return to him,' the *kerë* 'he shall cause to return to him,' the subject being either God or indefinite 'one shall cause' etc., which has the force of the passive as in the translation of A.J.

15–16 CHARACTERISTICS OF A FOOL

15. *straight in his own eyes.* Cf. iii. 7. The fool is self-opinionated and rejects advice (Ibn Ezra). [He does not act on the principle 'two heads are better than one.']

hearkeneth unto counsel. Cf. xv. 22.

16. *presently.* lit. 'in the (same) day,' immediately. Should he be affronted, he at once makes a retort. Doing this in the heat of anger, he arouses contention (Rashi).

prudent man. See on i. 4.

concealeth shame. He exercises restraint and disregards an insult. 'Happy is he who hears and ignores; a hundred evils pass him by' (Talmud).

He that breatheth forth truth uttereth righteousness,
But a false witness deceit.

There is that speaketh like the piercings of a sword;
But the tongue of the wise is health.

The lip of truth shall be established for ever;
But a lying tongue is but for a moment.

Deceit is in the heart of them that devise evil;
But to the counsellors of peace is joy.

17 יָפִיחַ אֱמוּנָה יַגִּיד צֶדֶק
וְעֵד שְׁקָרִים מִרְמָה׃
18 יֵשׁ בּוֹטֶה כְּמַדְקְרוֹת חָרֶב
וּלְשׁוֹן חֲכָמִים מַרְפֵּא׃
19 שְׂפַת־אֱמֶת תִּכּוֹן לָעַד
וְעַד־אַרְגִּיעָה לְשׁוֹן שָׁקֶר׃
20 מִרְמָה בְּלֶב־חֹרְשֵׁי רָע
וּלְיֹעֲצֵי שָׁלוֹם שִׂמְחָה׃

17–19 RIGHT AND WRONG SPEECH

17. *breatheth forth.* The verse relates to the testimony of a witness in a court of law, and the verb is used of giving evidence in vi. 19, xiv. 5, 25, xix. 5, 9 (after Targum, Rashi, Ibn Ezra).

uttereth righteousness. The noun must be understood in its forensic sense of 'justice.' A true witness supports the cause of justice by contributing to a right verdict (Rashi).

a false witness deceit. lit. 'a witness of lies (uttereth) deceit.' He misleads the judges and is responsible for a miscarriage of justice (after Rashi).

18. *speaketh.* (Cf. its use in Lev. v. 4; Num. xxx. 7, 9 of a rash vow).

like the piercings of a sword. Unweighed words may have most harmful, and even fatal, consequences. Ibn Ezra connects with the foregoing verse and explains the reference to be to legal evidence; but it is better understood generally (so Rashi, Ralbag).

19. *established for ever.* A proverb in the Talmud (Shabbath 104a) affirms, 'Truth stands, falsehood does not stand'; and a Rabbinic aphorism reads, 'Truth is the seal of God' (ibid. 54a) and, partaking of His nature, must endure.

is but for a moment. For afterwards the falsehood is revealed (Metsudath David). Meiri suggests: 'but forever I shall silence a lying tongue,' or 'forever I shall break a lying tongue.' The first denotes that the lying tongue will not continue to function, to cause trouble. The second denotes the punishment of the lying tongue. He also suggests our translation which is a more fitting antithesis to the beginning of the verse.

20–23 FALSEHOOD AND FOLLY

20. *deceit.* Rashi's explanation provides the antithesis to *joy* which modern expositors cannot find and try to supply by resorting to textual emendation. They who *devise evil,* which creates social disturbance, have hearts filled with *deceit*; and where this bad quality exists there can be no tranquility of mind which is an essential constituent of personal happiness. On the other hand, *counsellors of peace* work for a harmonious society and their endeavours bring them a feeling of *joy.*

21 There shall no mischief befall the righteous;
But the wicked are filled with evil.

לֹא־יְאֻנֶּה לַצַּדִּיק כָּל־אָוֶן
וּרְשָׁעִים מָלְאוּ רָע׃

22 Lying lips are an abomination to the LORD;
But they that deal truly are His delight.

תּוֹעֲבַת יְהוָה שִׂפְתֵי־שָׁקֶר
וְעֹשֵׂי אֱמוּנָה רְצוֹנוֹ׃

23 A prudent man concealeth knowledge;
But the heart of fools proclaimeth foolishness.

אָדָם עָרוּם כֹּסֶה דָּעַת
וְלֵב כְּסִילִים יִקְרָא אִוֶּלֶת׃

24 The hand of the diligent shall bear rule;
But the slothful shall be under tribute.

יַד־חָרוּצִים תִּמְשׁוֹל
וּרְמִיָּה תִּהְיֶה לָמַס׃

25 Care in the heart of a man boweth it down;
But a good word maketh it glad.

דְּאָגָה בְלֶב־אִישׁ יַשְׁחֶנָּה
וְדָבָר טוֹב יְשַׂמְּחֶנָּה׃

21. The interpretation turns on the words *mischief* and *evil.* They may mean 'harm, calamity,' and in this sense the first clause is paralleled by Ps. xci. 10 and the second by Ps. xxxii. 10. Alternatively, the terms have the ethical definition of 'iniquity, badness,' in which case the thought is: an atrocious act will not chance to a righteous man because his nature will instinctively recoil from it, but wicked persons are 'full of badness' and so readily succumb to the lure of sin. Rashi favours the second explanation which seems the preferable.

22. *an abomination . . . His delight.* Cf. xi. 20. Ibn Ezra understands *lying lips* as false witnesses, and *they that deal truly* as conscientious judges. The intention is doubtless wider: God hates anything that is perverse and delights in what is straightforward (see Gerondi).

23. *prudent . . . knowledge.* See on xi. 13.

24 REWARD OF DILIGENCE

shall bear rule. Through his industry a man reaches the position where he becomes the employer of labour (Gerondi).

under tribute. An employee to a master (Daath Mikra).

25 EFFECT OF A KIND WORD

boweth it down. Hebrew *yashchennah.* An interesting homiletical explanation is found in the Talmud (Yoma 75a) where a Rabbi pointed the verb *yesichennah,* i.e. 'Should there be care in the heart of a man, *let him speak of it* (to others)'; he should not keep it to himself, but unburden his heart to a sympathetic listener.

a good word. Better, 'a kind word.' One of the superior features of benevolence over almsgiving, said the Rabbis, is that the former can be practised with words (Baba Bathra 9b). A word of encouragement may prove a real help in time of trouble.

'he righteous is guided by his friend;
ut the way of the wicked leadeth them astray.

'he slothful man shall not hunt his prey;
ut the precious substance of men is to be diligent.

ı the way of righteousness is life,
nd in the pathway thereof there is no death.

יֹתֵר מֵרֵעֵהוּ צַדִּיק 26
וְדֶרֶךְ רְשָׁעִים תַּתְעֵם׃
לֹא־יַחֲרֹךְ רְמִיָּה צֵידוֹ 27
וְהוֹן־אָדָם יָקָר חָרוּץ׃
בְּאֹרַח צְדָקָה חַיִּים 28
וְדֶרֶךְ נְתִיבָה אַל־מָוֶת׃

26 TRUE AND FALSE GUIDANCE

s guided. The Hebrew *yather* is either ın adjective or a verb. If the former, it ignifies 'superior to' and is so undertood by the Targum and A.V. 'The righteous man is more excellent than his neighbour.' Apart from the triteness of this rendering, it bears no relationship to the sequel. Metsudath David explains: 'The righteous man is more excellent than his neighbour, but the way of the wicked (which prospers) leadeth them astray to follow it).' As a verb the word has to be connected with *ur,* 'spy out, explore,' hence R.V. 'is a guide to his neighbour.' But the preposition means 'from' not 'to.' A good explanation is suggested by Malbim: 'let a righteous man search out (his way) from his friend,' by consulting him.

hem. The object refers back to *the wicked* who resemble the fool described in verse 15. They are opinionated and refuse advice, with the consequence that they are misled (Malbim).

27 VIRTUE OF DILIGENCE

unt. The verb occurs nowhere else in he Bible. It is connected by some with an Arabic root 'to set in motion,' and he mention of *prey* therefore suggests he idea of hunting. A.V. and R.V. roast' is a sense which the verb has in Rabbinic Hebrew. Whichever translaion is adopted, the clause satirizes the lothful person. Rashi explains: 'will not roast,' meaning that he will not succeed in his hunt and not catch any fowl to roast. Or, as Ibn Ezra explains, it will be stolen from him.

the precious . . . diligent. A difficult clause. A.V. 'but the substance of a diligent man is precious' agrees with Rashi, but it is based upon a different order of the words in the original. [More faithful to the text is the translation: 'but the wealth of a man is precious (when he is) diligent,' and this follows well on the first part which spoke of a man catching an animal in the hunt but too indolent to roast it as food; consequently what he owns has no value for him at all. Similarly a man may possess wealth, but it likewise is worthless to him unless he is diligent and makes sensible use of it.]

28 EFFECT OF RIGHTEOUSNESS

life. Since death is the penalty for sin. Life is prolonged for the righteous — a basic teaching of this Book (Ibn Ezra).

no death. To reproduce the original, the words should be hyphened 'no-death.' This can only be an allusion to immortality which follows the ending of a righteous life upon earth. Many Hebrew MSS. point *el* instead of *al,* which gives the meaning: 'but there is a way (viz. of evil) which is a path to death,' hastening its advent to the sinner. This reading is supported by the Targum and other ancient Versions.

1 A wise son is instructed of his father;
But a scorner heareth not rebuke.

2 A man shall eat good from the fruit of his mouth;
But the desire of the faithless is violence.

3 He that guardeth his mouth keepeth his life;
But for him that openeth wide his lips there shall be ruin.

4 The soul of the sluggard desireth, and hath nothing;
But the soul of the diligent shall be abundantly gratified.

בֵּן חָכָם מוּסַר אָב
וְלֵץ לֹא־שָׁמַע גְּעָרָה׃
מִפְּרִי פִי־אִישׁ יֹאכַל טוֹב
וְנֶפֶשׁ בֹּגְדִים חָמָס׃
נֹצֵר פִּיו שֹׁמֵר נַפְשׁוֹ
פֹּשֵׂק שְׂפָתָיו מְחִתָּה־לוֹ׃
מִתְאַוָּה וָאַיִן נַפְשׁוֹ עָצֵל
וְנֶפֶשׁ חָרֻצִים תְּדֻשָּׁן׃

CHAPTER XIII

1 PATERNAL CORRECTION

a wise father. The Hebrew is literally 'a wise son discipline of a father.' A.V. 'a wise son *heareth* his father's instruction' supplies the verb from the second clause. Rashi offers two explanations: verbs like 'asks and loves' have to be understood; or, the meaning is that on account of the father's discipline the son is wise. The latter agrees better with the text: 'a son is wise (as the effect of) a father's discipline.'

heareth not. Pays no attention to (Rashi). Ibn Ezra explains the verse more literally: 'But a scorner heareth not rebuke,' for his father, knowing that he will not accept it, does not rebuke him.

2 FRUIT OF CONDUCT

a man . . . mouth. Similar to xii. 14, and, as in that verse, we have to think of a righteous man. Ibn Ezra renders: 'A good man shall eat good from the fruit of his mouth,' doubling the word *'tob,'* good. Rashi explains that from the reward of his Torah study he benefits in this world and the principal remains for the hereafter. This is recited every morning after the blessings for the Torah.

faithless. Treacherous men who devise evil schemes to encompass the ruin of others. As their longing is to commit acts of violence, they will themselves experience them. (Ibn Ezra).

3 CAUTIOUS SPEECH

guardeth his mouth. Not from speaking evil (Ibn Ezra), but from rash talk (Ibn Nachmiash). The first clause is expanded into a whole verse in xxi. 23.

keepeth his life. While this is true in a general way, the writer may have had in mind more particularly the prudence of keeping a still tongue under autocratic rule. An incautious word may then easily cost a man his life (cf. xviii. 21).

4 LAZINESS AND DILIGENCE

soul. Appetite for food (see on x. 3). The lazy man hungers but is unable to supply his want. A favourite text of the Hebrew teachers was, *when thou eatest the labor of thine hands, happy shalt thou be, and it shall be well with thee* (Ps. cxxviii. 2).

A righteous man hateth lying;
But a wicked man behaveth vilely and shamefully.

5 דְּבַר־שֶׁקֶר יִשְׂנָא צַדִּיק
וְרָשָׁע יַבְאִישׁ וְיַחְפִּיר׃

Righteousness guardeth him that is upright in the way;
But wickedness overthroweth the sinner.

6 צְדָקָה תִּצֹּר תָּם־דָּרֶךְ
וְרִשְׁעָה תְּסַלֵּף חַטָּאת׃

There is that pretendeth himself rich, yet hath nothing;
There is that pretendeth himself poor, yet hath great wealth.

7 יֵשׁ מִתְעַשֵּׁר וְאֵין כֹּל
מִתְרוֹשֵׁשׁ וְהוֹן רָב׃

The ransom of a man's life are his riches;
But the poor heareth no threatening.

8 כֹּפֶר נֶפֶשׁ־אִישׁ עָשְׁרוֹ
וְרָשׁ לֹא־שָׁמַע גְּעָרָה׃

5 UNETHICAL CONDUCT CENSURED

lying. lit. 'a word (or, matter) of falsehood.' Probably the phrase implies more than the act of speaking lies, and includes any action which is morally wrong (Daath Mikra).

behaveth vilely. lit. 'causeth a stench,' acts odiously. Jewish commentators, however, render: 'But a wicked man disgraces and embarrasses (people by lying)' (Rashi). Or, 'the wicked man disgraces and embarrasses (the righteous)' (Ibn Ezra). Or the object may be 'the one about whom the lies were told' (Metsudath David).

6 RIGHTEOUSNESS OFFERS TRUE DIRECTION

overthroweth the sinner. An impossible translation. The verb occurs in xix. 3, 'the foolishness of man *perverteth* his way,' and that is the correct significance. *Sinner* is apparently literally 'sin' and is forced to have the sense of a man who commits a sin, which is most improbable. In order to avoid this difficulty, Rashi explains that the completely wicked is given the appellation 'sin.' He is sin personified. His wickedness overthrows him and humbles him.

7 SOCIAL PRETENCE

pretendeth himself rich . . . pretendeth himself poor. That seems to be the correct force of the mood of the verbs. Some men wish to give the impression of being richer than they are for social reasons (cf. xii.9), while others with a miserly disposition live as though they were poor although possessing wealth. A less probable interpretation is that a man owning little may be in a real sense rich because he is contented, whereas another man may own much and in fact be poor because his desires exceed his means (after Rashi and Isaiah da Trani).

8 THE RICH BLACKMAILED

heareth no threatening. The Hebrew is identical with the end of verse 1, *heareth not rebuke,* and the same translation should be retained in this verse. A fact of life under unscrupulous government is exposed, viz. for self-enrichment governors penalize the wealthy. What in a poor man would not incur even a *rebuke* is made an occasion to extract *the ransom of a man's life* if he happens to be rich (Ibn Nachmiash, Meiri).

9 The light of the righteous rejoiceth;
But the lamp of the wicked shall be put out.

10 By pride cometh only contention;
But with the well-advised is wisdom.

11 Wealth gotten by vanity shall be diminished;
But he that gathereth little by little shall increase.

12 Hope deferred maketh the heart sick;
But desire fulfilled is a tree of life.

אוֹר־צַדִּיקִים יִשְׂמָח
וְנֵר רְשָׁעִים יִדְעָךְ׃
רַק־בְּזָדוֹן יִתֵּן מַצָּה
וְאֶת־נוֹעָצִים חָכְמָה׃
הוֹן מֵהֶבֶל יִמְעָט
וְקֹבֵץ עַל־יָד יַרְבֶּה׃
תּוֹחֶלֶת מְמֻשָּׁכָה מַחֲלָה־לֵב
וְעֵץ חַיִּים תַּאֲוָה בָאָה׃

9 HAPPINESS OF THE RIGHTEOUS

rejoiceth. The verb is clearly inappropriate, and the parallel *be put out* requires the translation 'burneth brightly'; accordingly modern exegetes emend the text. But Eitan points out that a cognate root in Arabic means 'to be high' and translates: 'the light (flame) of the righteous shall rise,' and so give a steady light. Light is a symbol of joy and prosperity (cf. Job xviii. 5f.; Esther viii. 16). Daath Mikra compares it to the Hebrew root, *'tsamach,'* to grow. Ibn Ganah, too, defines it as 'addition.'

10 ARROGANCE CAUSES STRIFE

cometh. Hebrew 'giveth.' Translate: 'only through arrogance cometh contention.' One whose deeds are only through arrogance and wickedness, brings contention (Metsudath David). Ibn Ezra explains: 'Only through arrogance of one man over another, does the arrogant man cause contention.' [A quarrel, which could easily be avoided if the parties involved were reasonable, flares up when they are arrogant men, neither of them willing to admit himself in the wrong.]

but with the well-advised is wisdom. Cf. xi. 2, where *lowly (tsenuim)* occurs for *well-advised (noatsim).* The letters of the Hebrew words are the same but in different order. Here the intention is that men who are disposed to ask for and accept advice are in the opposite category to the arrogant. They possess *wisdom,* the application of which helps avoid a quarrel (Metsudath David).

11 INSECURITY OF QUICKLY GOTTEN WEALTH

by vanity. Ibn Ezra comments: by robbery with violence and by theft. While such criminal methods may not be excluded, the Hebrew rather signifies methods which have no real worth, such as rash speculation. In this way a fortune can be quickly made, but as quickly lost (Elijah of Wilna).

little by little. lit. 'by a hand,' which some understand as 'by labour' (A.V. and R.V.), by manual toil. In post-Biblical Hebrew the phrase is an idiom for 'gradually,' and if accepted here the lesson is that wealth steadily accumulated grows in amount, while the get-rich-quick way ends in ruin (after Elijah of Wilna).

Whoso despiseth the word shall suffer thereby;
But he that feareth the commandment shall be rewarded.

13 בָּז לְדָבָר יֵחָבֶל לוֹ
וִירֵא מִצְוָה הוּא יְשֻׁלָּם׃

The teaching of the wise is a fountain of life,
To depart from the snares of death.

14 תּוֹרַת חָכָם מְקוֹר חַיִּים
לָסוּר מִמֹּקְשֵׁי מָוֶת׃

Good understanding giveth grace;
But the way of the faithless is harsh.

15 שֵׂכֶל־טוֹב יִתֶּן־חֵן
וְדֶרֶךְ בֹּגְדִים אֵיתָן׃

Every prudent man dealeth with forethought;
But a fool unfoldeth folly.

16 כָּל־עָרוּם יַעֲשֶׂה בְדָעַת
וּכְסִיל יִפְרֹשׂ אִוֶּלֶת׃

13 EAGER OBEDIENCE OF GOD'S LAW

word. viz. of God, His Revelation to Israel (Rashi, Metsudath David).

shall suffer thereby. The verb may have this meaning and was so understood by Ibn Ezra; accordingly, infidelity to the Divine ordinances results in penalties, while faithfulness is rewarded. R.V. margin, in agreement with Rashi, renders: 'maketh himself a debtor thereto,' and this is preferred by most modern commentaries. [It was customary for a debtor to deposit a pledge which was forfeited in the event of default. Similarly one who is negligent of his duty to obey the Torah is, as it were, held as a pledge; if on reconsideration he redeems himself by carrying out his obligation, well and good, otherwise he forfeits his pledge, i.e. his life.]

feareth. Shows respect for the Torah by *immediate* compliance. Such as he receives a reward, whereas the former, by his belated obedience, only averts punishment. 'Be strong as a leopard, light as an eagle, fleet as a hart, and strong as a lion, to do the will of thy Father Who is in heaven' (Aboth 5.23).

14 WISDOM PRESERVES LIFE

the wise. See on i. 5.

snares of death. i.e. fatal snares, the pitfalls along the road of life which, if not avoided, bring one to a premature death (Metsudath David). An illustration is the allurement of *the alien woman* (v. 5, vii. 22f.).

15 VALUE OF INTELLIGENCE

good understanding. The same phrase as in iii. 4 translated *good favour.* Here it denotes erudition in Torah and excellence in character traits. Such a quality of mind *giveth* (i.e. produces) *grace.* All who see him are charmed by him (Elijah of Wilna).

harsh. The usual signification is 'permanent'; but the Talmud supports the sense of 'hard, rugged,' by so understanding it in Deut. xxi. 4, '*rough* valley' and Num. xxiv. 21, 'though *firm* be thy dwelling place.' The contrast is: whereas the character of the refined man is graceful, the manner of them who are *faithless* to wisdom's discipline and act boorishly is uncouth and harmful both to himself and to others (after Rashi, Ibn Nachmiash, Isaiah da Trani).

16 CHARACTERISTIC OF PRUDENCE

dealeth with forethought. lit. 'acts with knowledge'; he weighs the circumstances and consciously decides his course of action (after Rashi).

17 A wicked messenger falleth into evil;
But a faithful ambassador is health.

18 Poverty and shame shall be to him that refuseth instruction;
But he that regardeth reproof shall be honoured.

19 The desire accomplished is sweet to the soul;
And it is an abomination to fools to depart from evil.

20 He that walketh with wise men shall be wise;
But the companion of fools shall smart for it.

מַלְאָךְ רָשָׁע יִפֹּל בְּרָע
וְצִיר אֱמוּנִים מַרְפֵּא׃
רֵישׁ וְקָלוֹן פּוֹרֵעַ מוּסָר
וְשׁוֹמֵר תּוֹכַחַת יְכֻבָּד׃
תַּאֲוָה נִהְיָה תֶּעֱרַב לְנָפֶשׁ
וְתוֹעֲבַת כְּסִילִים סוּר מֵרָע׃
הָלוֹךְ אֶת־חֲכָמִים וחכם
וְרֹעֶה כְסִילִים יֵרוֹעַ׃

v. 20. הולך ק' v. 20. יחכם ק'

17 BAD AND GOOD AGENCY

falleth into evil. When of low ethical character, a representative may easily go beyond his instructions and act wickedly, thereby doing injury to the person who deputed him (Isaiah da Trani).

is health. If he perceives any weak point in his errand, he will diplomatically rectify it, thus rescuing the person who deputed him from any harm (Metsudath David).

18 SUCCESS DEPENDS UPON WILLINGNESS TO LEARN

poverty . . . instruction. More exactly, 'Poverty and disgrace (result if) one refuseth instruction.' The maxim relates to the wicked messenger. If he persists in acting on his own opinions, rejecting the guidance of persons more experienced than himself, and divulges the secrets of him who deputed him, the effect is likely to be failure which impoverishes him since it earns him the contempt of his fellow-men, who will refrain from sending him on errands (Gerondi).

shall be honoured. Better, 'will be made rich' (cf. the use of the word in Gen. xiii. 2 and Num. xxii. 17, where *I will promote thee unto very great honour* should be *I will make thee very rich,* as the context shows) (see Heidenheim to Gen. xiii. 2).

19 FULFILLED DESIRE

the desire accomplished. lit. 'a longing which has come into existence.' When a goal has been reached or a wish realized, the whole of man's nature becomes suffused with a feeling of satisfaction (cf. the second clause of verse 12).

and it is . . . evil. To obtain the sense of the verse the conjunction should be translated 'so' instead of *and.* Since to accomplish one's aim is a most pleasant experience, it follows that to *depart from evil* must be *an abomination to fools.* Their aspirations can only be achieved by bad methods, and were they to abandon *evil,* they would be denied the pleasure of ever fulfilling their wishes (after Rashi).

20 EFFECT OF ASSOCIATION

he . . . wise. So the *kerë*; the translation of the *kethib* is: 'walk with wise men and become wise' (cf. the Rabbinic maxim, 'Let thy house be a meeting place for the wise; sit amidst the dust of their feet, and drink their words with thirst' (Aboth 1.4).

il pursueth sinners;
t to the righteous good shall
be repaid.

21 חַטָּאִים תְּרַדֵּף רָעָה
וְאֶת־צַדִּיקִים יְשַׁלֶּם־טוֹב׃

good man leaveth an inheritance to his children's children;
d the wealth of the sinner is
laid up for the righteous.

22 טוֹב יַנְחִיל בְּנֵי־בָנִים
וְצָפוּן לַצַּדִּיק חֵיל חוֹטֵא׃

uch food is in the tillage of the
poor;
it there is that is swept away by
want of righteousness.

23 רָב־אֹכֶל נִיר רָאשִׁים
וְיֵשׁ נִסְפֶּה בְּלֹא מִשְׁפָּט׃

e that spareth his rod hateth his
son;
ut he that loveth him chasteneth
him betimes.

24 חוֹשֵׂךְ שִׁבְטוֹ שׂוֹנֵא בְנוֹ
וְאֹהֲבוֹ שִׁחֲרוֹ מוּסָר׃

'he righteous eateth to the
satisfying of his desire;
ut the belly of the wicked shall
want.

25 צַדִּיק אֹכֵל לְשֹׂבַע נַפְשׁוֹ
וּבֶטֶן רְשָׁעִים תֶּחְסָר׃

21 RECOMPENSE OF THE BAD AND GOOD

but to the righteous . . . repaid. lit. 'and the righteous he shall reward good,' or 'and good (fortune) shall reward the righteous' (Gerondi). If the former, the subject is either God (Ibn Ezra) or indefinite, giving the verb a passive character (see on xii. 14) (see Ibn Nachmiash).

22 DESCENDANTS OF RIGHTEOUS BENEFIT

children's children. A good man is able to leave his inheritance to his grand-children, whereas a sinner does not leave over his property even to his chil-dren for his property is preserved for the righteous, e.g. Haman's property that was given to Mordecai (Rashi).

23 INJUSTICES IN THE WORLD

This verse baffled the commentators, both ancient and modern. The latter declare the text to be beyond elucida-tion. Of the former, the simplest interpretation was suggested by the medieval Jewish expositor, Levi ben Gershon: 'The tillage of the poor (yields) abundance of food.' They work hard for the landowners who enjoy the fruits of their toil while they themselves remain poor with little to eat. That is the first injustice, and the second is: 'It happens that (an innocent man) is destroyed through the want of justice,' being condemned unjustly.

24 A PARENT SHOULD NOT SPARE THE ROD

hateth. The verb is sometimes used merely with the comparative intention of not loving, or not loving so much, rather than of actual hating (cf. Gen. xxix. 31; Deut. xxi. 15; Mal. i. 2f.). A man displays no love for a child by fail-ing to correct him (Metsudath David).

chasteneth him betimes. i.e. every morn-ing (Rashi, Ibn Ezra), or in his early youth (Metsudath David, Ralbag). He does not overlook the child's faults and exercises disciplinary measures to eradi-cate them (Meiri).

25 MODERATION OF THE RIGHTEOUS

his desire. lit. 'his soul' (see on x. 3). The teaching of the verse, as the Rabbis explain, is that the righteous man eats to satisfy his hunger; the wicked man never has enough (Rashi, Metsudath David).

1 Every wise woman buildeth her house; But the foolish plucketh it down with her own hands.	חכמות נשים בנתה ביתה ואולת בידיה תהרסנו׃
2 He that walketh in his uprightness feareth the LORD; But he that is perverse in his ways despiseth Him.	הולך בישרו ירא יהוה ונלוז דרכיו בוזהו׃
3 In the mouth of the foolish is a rod of pride; But the lips of the wise shall preserve them.	בפי־אויל חטר גאוה ושפתי חכמים תשמורם׃
4 Where no oxen are, the crib is clean; But much increase is by the strength of the ox.	באין אלפים אבוס בר ורב־תבואות בכח שור׃

CHAPTER XIV

1 INFLUENCE OF WOMAN ON THE HOME

every wise . . . house. lit. 'the wise ones of women (each) buildeth her house.' The economy of the home was controlled by the woman (cf. xxxi. 13ff.), and upon her capacity depended its welfare. *Buildeth* is employed in a figurative sense, of increasing the prosperity of the household (Ralbag).

2 RIGHT CONDUCT DEPENDS UPON PIETY

The moral of the verse is better expressed in the translation: 'He who reverences the Lord walks in his uprightness; but he who is perverse in his ways despises Him (Meiri, Isaiah da Trani).

despiseth Him. Ibn Ezra explained 'despises him who reverences God.' In the Bible, sin is always held to be an offence against God and therefore an affront to Him. Typical of the Hebraic standpoint was Joseph's remark, *How then can I do this great wickedness, and sin against God?* (Gen. xxxix.). This follows Rashi, Meiri, and Isaiah da Trani).

3 FOOLISH AND WISE TALK

rod. The word is found again only in Isa. xi. 1, where it signifies a new branch growing from the trunk of the tree. If rod was intended, as a symbol of punishment, another Hebrew word, *shebet,* would have been more appropriate. It is better, therefore, to translate: 'a branch (producing) pride.' From the fool's mouth issues haughty speech which has the effect of getting him into trouble (Gerondi).

4 DISADVANTAGE OUTWEIGHED BY ADVANTAGE

strength of the ox. This animal was employed for ploughing and threshing the corn (Deut. xxii. 10, xxv. 4). The point of the verse is neither the importance of agricultural work (Ibn Ezra) nor the value of work as opposed to slothfulness (Meiri). As sometimes happens with a proverb, the abstract thought is presented by means of a concrete example. So here, the ox is used as an illustration. Having no ox is, from one point of view, an advantage because a man is then freed from attending to its care; but as against that there is the great advantage of having an ox for the provision of essential food. Consequently, the disadvantage of having to look after the animal is far outweighed by the benefits which accrue from its employment in the field (Alshich).

faithful witness will not lie;
ut a false witness breatheth forth lies.

5 עֵד אֱמוּנִים לֹא יְכַזֵּב
וְיָפִיחַ כְּזָבִים עֵד שָׁקֶר׃

scorner seeketh wisdom, and findeth it not;
ut knowledge is easy unto him that hath discernment.

6 בִּקֶּשׁ־לֵץ חָכְמָה וָאָיִן
וְדַעַת לְנָבוֹן נָקָל׃

o from the presence of a foolish man,
or thou wilt not perceive the lips of knowledge.

7 לֵךְ מִנֶּגֶד לְאִישׁ כְּסִיל
וּבַל־יָדַעְתָּ שִׂפְתֵי־דָעַת׃

he wisdom of the prudent is to look well to his way;
ut the folly of fools is deceit.

8 חָכְמַת עָרוּם הָבִין דַּרְכּוֹ
וְאִוֶּלֶת כְּסִילִים מִרְמָה׃

5 TRUE AND FALSE TESTIMONY

With this verse cf. xii. 17.

a false . . . lies. Repeated from vi. 19.

6 CHARACTER NECESSARY FOR WISDOM

a scorner . . . not. Better, 'should a scorner seek wisdom, then it is not,' i.e. it does not exist for him. He cannot find it because, being a scorner, he lacks the essential prerequisite, viz. *the fear of the* LORD (Ps. cxi. 10) (Gerondi). Alshich identifies the scorner as one who learned wisdom but then neglected it. Should he seek the wisdom he once learned, he will find that he has forgotten it.

unto him that hath discernment. The same word as *the man of understanding* (i. 5). He possesses the right temperament for knowledge and so it comes easily to him (see Meiri).

7 ASSOCIATE NOT WITH A FOOL

go from the presence. Do not make an intimate of such a man and spend your time in his company (Ralbag).

lips of knowledge. [Uttering words of wisdom which are worth hearing.]

8 THE PRUDENT ARE CONSCIOUSLY RIGHT

look well to his way. lit. 'to understand his way,' which Rashi correctly identifies with 'to weigh one's steps' (see on iv. 26). The prudent man does not walk on blindly, but carefully notes the various paths before him and deliberately chooses the one he believes to be right.

deceit. The verb, from which this noun is derived, means 'to mislead.' Translate: 'but the folly of fools (results in) misdirection.' Not possessing the wisdom of the prudent and urged on by folly, fools are led to ways of deceit and guile (Ibn Ezra).

9 Amends pleadeth for fools;
But among the upright there is good will.

10 The heart knoweth its own bitterness;
And with its joy no stranger can intermeddle.

11 The house of the wicked shall be overthrown;
But the tent of the upright shall flourish.

12 There is a way which seemeth right unto a man,
But the end thereof are the ways of death.

אֱוִלִים יָלִיץ אָשָׁם
וּבֵין יְשָׁרִים רָצוֹן׃
לֵב יוֹדֵעַ מָרַּת נַפְשׁוֹ
וּבְשִׂמְחָתוֹ לֹא־יִתְעָרַב זָר׃
בֵּית רְשָׁעִים יִשָּׁמֵד
וְאֹהֶל יְשָׁרִים יַפְרִיחַ׃
יֵשׁ דֶּרֶךְ יָשָׁר לִפְנֵי־אִישׁ
וְאַחֲרִיתָהּ דַּרְכֵי־מָוֶת׃

9 BOND BETWEEN THE BAD AND BETWEEN THE GOOD

The translation of A.J. follows most of the classical exegetes. The intention is that when fools sin against their fellowmen and must make amends, the money they pay for amends pleads for them to expiate their sin. But among the righteous there is good will without the necessity of amends (Rashi, Metsudath David). A.V.'s translation 'fools make a mock at sin' and R.V.'s 'the foolish make a mock at guilt' follow Ibn Ezra. Daath Mikra renders: 'Guilt joins the fools, but between the upright, good will.' Between the upright, deeds acceptable to God are the link that joins them. Others render: 'As for the fools (each one) speaks of (his neighbour's) guilt, but among the upright there is good will (Ibn Nachmiash).

10 FEELING OF SORROW AND JOY INCOMMUNICABLE

its own bitterness. lit. 'the bitterness of its soul, of itself.' Nobody can make another understand exactly how he feels in a time of bitter sorrow (Isaiah da Trani). Others explain this as a reference to the toil a person puts into his study of Torah. He alone knows how much effort he must exert in order to gain knowledge and understanding of Torah. Therefore, when he rejoices with the reward God will give him, no one will share this joy with him, for he alone will receive it (Rashi, Metsudath David).

can intermeddle. 'can mingle himself.' Just as others did not share his sorrow, they will not share his joy (Isaiah da Trani). Rashi presents a Midrashic explanation of this verse. The Jews, whose souls were embittered and who sacrificed their lives in order to sanctify God's name — no stranger will be intermingled in their joy in the hereafter.

11 THE BAD PERISH, THE GOOD ENDURE

house . . . tent. As Ibn Ezra remarks, there may be more than poetical parallelism in the choice of these words. The *house,* inhabited by the *wicked,* is a substantial building which they can afford to erect and occupy on their dishonest gains; but the upright, who adhere to honesty, dwell in a humble *tent.* Yet the former will be *overthrown* and the latter will *flourish.*

12 EVIL LEADS TO DEATH

right. i.e. ethically correct; but probably the translation should be 'straight.' As compared to the way of wisdom, the way of the fool appears straight, without obstacles to overcome. Not so, the way of wisdom, upon which one must overcome his lusts and his bad character traits (Malbim).

Even in laughter the heart acheth;
And the end of mirth is heaviness.

The dissembler in heart shall have his fill from his own ways;
And a good man shall be satisfied from himself.

The thoughtless believeth every word;
But the prudent man looketh well to his going.

A wise man feareth, and departeth from evil;
But the fool behaveth overbearingly, and is confident.

13 גַּם־בִּשְׂחֹק יִכְאַב־לֵב
וְאַחֲרִיתָהּ שִׂמְחָה תוּגָה׃
14 מִדְּרָכָיו יִשְׂבַּע סוּג לֵב
וּמֵעָלָיו אִישׁ טוֹב׃
15 פֶּתִי יַאֲמִין לְכָל־דָּבָר
וְעָרוּם יָבִין לַאֲשֻׁרוֹ׃
16 חָכָם יָרֵא וְסָר מֵרָע
וּכְסִיל מִתְעַבֵּר וּבוֹטֵחַ׃

13 BLEND OF JOY AND SORROW IN LIFE

The rendering of A.J. is too positive, and states a point of view with regard to the character of life which is inconsistent with Hebraic thought. The stark pessimism of Ecclesiastes is exceptional. It is therefore better to substitute 'may ache' and 'may be heaviness.' As a day which begins with bright sunshine may grow cloudy, so it is with the happiness of man because existence is full of uncertainty.

the end of mirth is heaviness. lit. 'and as for its end rejoicing (may turn to) heaviness.' i.e. if one engages in excessive rejoicing and levity, although it may not be a sin, it will likely lead to sin and immorality, bringing heartache and sadness in its wake (Meiri).

14 SATISFACTION OF THE BAD AND GOOD

dissembler. lit. 'turned away of heart' (cf. Ps. xliv. 19), a man whose mind is wilfully kept away from the right (Metsudath David).

shall have his fill. Better, 'has satisfaction.' His one desire is to enjoy the profit which he obtains from his manner of living, and he is indifferent to questions of ethics and the account which he will have later to render (Gerondi).

and a good man . . . himself. lit. 'and (or, but) from upon him a good man.' This is usually taken to mean that the good man derives his satisfaction from himself, i.e. from the consciousness that he leads a moral life, irrespective of material considerations. Such an interpretation yields a good contrast and teaches an excellent lesson, but it is questionable whether the Hebrew can mean 'from himself.' The alternative is to relate 'him' to the *dissembler*; and since the preposition denotes 'detachment from,' the intention may be: 'but a good man is apart from him,' does not accept his standpoint in that he has a higher view of life's purpose and opportunities (Gerondi).

15 TRUSTFULNESS OF THE SIMPLE

believeth every word. He is excessively trustful, and being deficient in discernment, often falls into trouble (Ralbag).

looketh well to. lit. 'brings understanding to.' He looks before he leaps (Ralbag).

16 OVERCONFIDENCE OF THE FOOL

feareth. The parallelism is against the interpretation 'feareth the Lord' and favours 'is fearful, cautious' (Metsudath David).

17 He that is soon angry dealeth foolishly;
And a man of wicked devices is hated.

18 The thoughtless come into possession of folly;
But the prudent are crowned with knowledge.

19 The evil bow before the good,
And the wicked at the gates of the righteous.

20 The poor is hated even of his own neighbour;
But the rich hath many friends.

קְצַר־אַפַּיִם יַעֲשֶׂה אִוֶּלֶת 17
וְאִישׁ מְזִמּוֹת יִשָּׂנֵא׃
נָחֲלוּ פְתָאיִם אִוֶּלֶת 18
וַעֲרוּמִים יַכְתִּרוּ דָעַת׃
שַׁחוּ רָעִים לִפְנֵי טוֹבִים 19
וּרְשָׁעִים עַל־שַׁעֲרֵי צַדִּיק׃
גַּם־לְרֵעֵהוּ יִשָּׂנֵא רָשׁ 20
וְאֹהֲבֵי עָשִׁיר רַבִּים׃

17 FOLLY OF ANGER, MISCHIEF-MAKER HATED

dealeth foolishly. Because he harms himself. Rabbinic proverbs on this fault are: 'When the kettle boils over, it overflows its own sides,' 'Who gives vent to his wrath destroys his house.'

wicked devices. See on xii. 2. One who devises plots to harm others. Although he is slow to anger, this is only so that he can trap people in his net (Malbim).

is hated. One who plots people's downfall is hated by all (Malbim).

18 ACQUISITION OF SIMPLETON AND PRUDENT

come into . . . folly. Or, 'have folly as their possession.' [In their lack of sagacity they give preference to what is foolish] and so *folly* is their portion in life (Ibn Ezra).

are crowned with. The verb is active in Hebrew and should be understood as denominative, 'have wisdom as their crown.' Like the simpleton, prudent men also have a possession, but in their case it is a 'crown,' something that adorns and honours them (Metsudath David).

19 THE GOOD EVENTUALLY TRIUMPH

bow. In acknowledgement of their defeat. The verb is in the perfect tense, 'have bowed.' According to a common Hebrew idiom, what is yet to take place is pictured as having happened, an expression of certainty that it will be so. The conviction that in the end goodness prevails over evil is deep-rooted in Hebraic thought (so Rashi).

the wicked at the gates. A verb has to be supplied: 'the wicked (bow) at the gates' (Ibn Nachmiash, Isaiah da Trani).

20 THE POOR ARE FRIENDLESS

hated. The force is only 'unpopular with,' in contrast to *friends* in the second clause which is lit. 'lovers' (see on xiii. 24).

neighbour. Hebrew *rea,* his friends and intimates (Rashi).

the rich hath many friends. More lit. 'the friends of a rich man are many.' A corresponding Talmudic proverb runs, 'At the door of shops brothers and friends are numerous; at the door of misery there are no brothers and no friends.'

21 He that despiseth his neighbour sinneth;
But he that is gracious unto the humble, happy is he.

22 Shall they not go astray that devise evil?
But mercy and truth shall be for them that devise good.

23 In all labour there is profit;
But the talk of the lips tendeth only to penury.

24 The crown of the wise is their riches;
But the folly of fools remaineth folly.

21 בָּז־לְרֵעֵהוּ חוֹטֵא
וּמְחוֹנֵן עֲנָיִים אַשְׁרָיו׃
22 הֲלוֹא־יִתְעוּ חֹרְשֵׁי רָע
וְחֶסֶד וֶאֱמֶת חֹרְשֵׁי טוֹב׃
23 בְּכָל־עֶצֶב יִהְיֶה מוֹתָר
וּדְבַר־שְׂפָתַיִם אַךְ־לְמַחְסוֹר׃
24 עֲטֶרֶת חֲכָמִים עָשְׁרָם
אִוֶּלֶת כְּסִילִים אִוֶּלֶת׃

v. 21. ענוים ק׳

21 BE AFFABLE

neighbour. Has the same meaning as in the last verse. The advice is not to assume superior airs and look with contempt upon one's fellow (Gerondi).

sinneth. Because the Torah ordained, *Thou shalt love thy neighbour as thyself* (Lev. xix. 18).

gracious unto the humble. So the *kethib*, the *kerë* signifying 'the poor.' With this exhortation cf. the aphorism, 'Receive all men with a friendly countenance' (Aboth 1.15).

22 CONSEQUENCE OF PLANNING EVIL AND GOOD

shall they not go astray? An emphatic way of saying 'they assuredly go astray,' because they earn for themselves the harm they intended for their victims (Metsudath David).

mercy and truth. See on iii. 3 where the first word is translated *kindness*.

23 WORK IS PROFITABLE, TALK PROFITLESS

labour. Better, 'toil,' since the Hebrew includes the idea of what is painful (so Metsudath David).

there is profit. However laborious the work and small the wage, some advantage is derived (Metsudath David).

24 THE WISE AND FOOLISH

crown of the wise is their riches. So A.V. and R.V. This means that the wisdom which crowns them who possess it constitutes the wealth for which they long for and strive. On the other hand, the folly which distinguishes fools gains for them nothing else than folly (Saadiah Gaon). Another possible translation is R.V. margin: 'their riches is a crown unto the wise,' i.e. when the wise own wealth they use it in a manner which brings them honour; but when fools have riches their use of it reveals their folly (so Ibn Ezra).

the folly of fools remaineth folly. lit. 'is folly.' Sometimes the prudent commit folly. It is, however, always possible to find some redeeming factor in that act of folly. The act of the fools, however, is completely folly, devoid of any redeeming factor (Ibn Nachmiash).

25 A true witness delivereth souls;
But he that breatheth forth lies is all deceit.

25 מַצִּיל נְפָשׁוֹת עֵד אֱמֶת
וְיָפִחַ כְּזָבִים מִרְמָה׃

26 In the fear of the LORD a man hath strong confidence;
And his children shall have a place of refuge.

26 בְּיִרְאַת יְהוָה מִבְטַח־עֹז
וּלְבָנָיו יִהְיֶה מַחְסֶה׃

27 The fear of the LORD is a fountain of life,
To depart from the snares of death.

27 יִרְאַת יְהוָה מְקוֹר חַיִּים
לָסוּר מִמֹּקְשֵׁי מָוֶת׃

28 In the multitude of people is the king's glory;
But in the want of people is the ruin of the prince.

28 בְּרָב־עָם הַדְרַת־מֶלֶךְ
וּבְאֶפֶס לְאֹם מְחִתַּת רָזוֹן׃

29 He that is slow to anger is of great understanding;
But he that is hasty of spirit exalteth folly.

29 אֶרֶךְ אַפַּיִם רַב־תְּבוּנָה
וּקְצַר־רוּחַ מֵרִים אִוֶּלֶת׃

30 A tranquil heart is the life of the flesh;
But envy is the rottenness of the bones.

30 חַיֵּי בְשָׂרִים לֵב מַרְפֵּא
וּרְקַב עֲצָמוֹת קִנְאָה׃

25 TRUE AND FALSE EVIDENCE

delivereth souls. Or, 'lives,' by clearing the innocent of a false charge (Ibn Ezra).

26–27 SAVING POWER OF PIETY

26. The more correct translation is: 'In the reverence of the Lord is a strong confidence, and to his children (viz. of the man who has this reverence) it will be a refuge.' The merit of the pious father passes on to his offspring (cf. xx. 7) (Rashi).

28 POPULATION AND THE STATE

the king's glory. *King* and *prince* (or ruler) are symbolic of the State whose political standing with its neighbours depends upon the numerical strength of the population. When it is large, the king wins glory for himself; when it is small, the country is liable to attack and conquest (after Targum, Daath Mikra from Ibn Ezra, Isaiah da Trani).

29 FOLLY OF A VIOLENT TEMPER

is of great understanding. [In not giving way to his anger, he saves himself worry of mind and perhaps injury of body. He also helps to maintain a peaceful atmosphere in the community from which he benefits.]

30 INFLUENCE OF MIND ON BODY

a tranquil heart. In Eccles. x. 4 the word *marpë* is translated *gentleness.* The English equivalent of the phrase here is 'an even temperament' which takes things calmly (Ralbag, Metsudath David).

envy. While it is true that envy corrodes the mind and so has a harmful effect upon the body, the context suggests that the other sense of the word, 'passion, hot-headedness,' is required, the opposite of an even temperament (so Rashi).

31 He that oppresseth the poor blasphemeth his Maker;
But he that is gracious unto the needy honoureth Him.

עֹשֵׁק דָּל חֵרֵף עֹשֵׂהוּ 31
וּמְכַבְּדוֹ חֹנֵן אֶבְיוֹן׃

32 The wicked is thrust down in his misfortune;
But the righteous, even when he is brought to death, hath hope.

בְּרָעָתוֹ יִדָּחֶה רָשָׁע 32
וְחֹסֶה בְמוֹתוֹ צַדִּיק׃

33 In the heart of him that hath discernment wisdom resteth;
But in the inward part of fools it maketh itself known.

בְּלֵב נָבוֹן תָּנוּחַ חָכְמָה 33
וּבְקֶרֶב כְּסִילִים תִּוָּדֵעַ׃

31 GOD'S HONOUR INVOLVED IN HUMAN RELATIONSHIP

he that oppresseth. By depriving him of his due, e.g. the gleanings, the forgotten sheaves, and the grain growing at the end of the field, as well as the tithe of the poor (Daath Mikra). Or, as Saadiah Gaon explains it, he mistreats him by being unfriendly and harsh to him.

his Maker. The pronoun may refer to *he that oppresseth.* By his callous behaviour he defies the will of God Who had commanded that the poor should be assisted. A much deeper thought is obtained if *his* is related to *the poor* (so Ibn Ezra). God had made this man. By oppressing him, his oppressor demonstrates his belief that God is unable to protect the poor, thereby blaspheming his Maker by denying His power (Ibn Ezra, Ibn Nachmiash).

32 HOPEFULNESS OF THE RIGHTEOUS

The teaching of the verse is elaborated in Ps. lxxiii. With the first clause, cf. verse 19 of the Psalm, and with the second clause, verse 24.

even when he is brought to death. lit. 'in his death' or 'when he is dying.' Even if, as modern exegetes assert, there is no expectation of immorality in the verse, emendation of the text is unnecessary. The thought is that the righteous man, imbued with trust in God, does not abandon hope though he be in so desperate a plight that he imagines himself to be at the point of death (Ibn Ezra, Ibn Nachmiash).

33 WISDOM ASSERTS ITSELF WITH FOOLS

maketh itself known. The little wisdom that he possesses announces itself (Rashi). Ibn Nachmiash elaborates that the fool announces his wisdom at inappropriate occasions. They both quote a Talmudic adage that expresses the same idea as the English 'Empty barrels make the most noise.' Gerondi suggests that, although 'in the heart of him that hath discernment wisdom rests quietly,' i.e. he does not disclose his wisdom, 'among fools it maketh itself known.' The most intelligent of the fools recognizes from the behaviour of the wise man, from the fact that he does not jest with the fools, that he is indeed a wise man.

34 Righteousness exalteth a nation;
But sin is a reproach to any people.

35 The king's favour is toward a servant that dealeth wisely;
But his wrath striketh him that dealeth shamefully.

צְדָקָה תְרוֹמֵם־גּוֹי 34
וְחֶסֶד לְאֻמִּים חַטָּאת׃
רְצוֹן־מֶלֶךְ לְעֶבֶד מַשְׂכִּיל 35
וְעֶבְרָתוֹ תִּהְיֶה מֵבִישׁ׃

34 RIGHTEOUSNESS IN NATIONAL LIFE

righteousness. A characteristic doctrine of the Bible; the true greatness of a nation rests upon the exercise of justice and the pursuit of worthy aims, not upon military strength and imperial expansion. The question arises whether *nation* and *people* are general terms or whether they specifically denote Israel. Rashi explains: *Righteousness exalteth a nation*; this refers to Israel. *But the kindness of peoples is sin*; this refers to the heathens who steal from one and give to the other. Ibn Ezra, according to one interpretation, takes the same view. This is the unanimous view of the Rabbis of the Talmud and Midrash.

reproach. Although identical in form with *chesed,* 'love,' it is in reality of different origin. It occurs again in Lev. xx. 17, *a shameful thing,* and the verb in Prov. xxv. 10, *revile*. This translation follows Targum (Ibn Nachmiash). Many of the Rabbis understand it, however, in the usual sense of 'kindness.' They explain that the kindness of the heathen nations is sin, because their sole intention is to aggrandize themselves, to show arrogance, or to extend their rule. R. Nechuniah ben Hakanah found a different and a beautiful explanation of the obscure passage. He held that 'the love and merciful deeds of the heathen are elements of atonement and expiation, as the sin-offering has previously been for Israel. (The word for *sin* is the usual term for an expiatory sacrifice.)

35. As translated and interpreted, the saying is trite and pointless. Ibn Ezra and Ibn Nachmiash connect this verse to the following one: 'The king's favour is toward a servant that dealeth wisely; But his wrath striketh him that dealeth shamefully; (For) a soft answer turneth away wrath.' This is the behaviour of the servant that dealeth wisely; he answers him softly and thereby turns away his wrath. 'But a grievous word stirreth up anger.' This is the behaviour of the servant who dealeth shamefully; he displeases the king with his statements.

1 מַֽעֲנֶה־רַּךְ יָשִׁיב חֵמָה
וּדְבַר־עֶצֶב יַעֲלֶה־אָף׃
2 לְשׁוֹן חֲכָמִים תֵּיטִיב דָּעַת
וּפִי כְסִילִים יַבִּיעַ אִוֶּלֶת׃
3 בְּכָל־מָקוֹם עֵינֵי יְהוָה
צֹפוֹת רָעִים וְטוֹבִים׃
4 מַרְפֵּא לָשׁוֹן עֵץ חַיִּים
וְסֶלֶף בָּהּ שֶׁבֶר בְּרוּחַ׃

1 A soft answer turneth away wrath;
But a grievous word stirreth up anger.

2 The tongue of the wise useth knowledge aright;
But the mouth of fools poureth out foolishness.

3 The eyes of the LORD are in every place,
Keeping watch upon the evil and the good.

4 A soothing tongue is a tree of life;
But perverseness therein is a wound to the spirit.

CHAPTER XV

1 PEACEFUL RELATIONSHIP

a soft answer. The verse states a fact, but also urges an ideal of conduct. For the purpose of maintaining peace, check the hot retort and give a pacifying reply (Gerondi).

2 SPEECH OF THE WISE AND FOOLS

useth knowledge aright. Rather, 'adorneth knowledge.' For this sense of the verb, cf. 2 Kings ix. 30, *attired* (lit. adorned) *her head.* A wise man talks sense couched in well-phrased language (Meiri, Saadiah Gaon).

3 THE DIVINE SCRUTINY

in every place. The traditional interpretation is that no part of the world is hidden from 'the all-seeing Eye.' Alshich explains this verse as the statement of the fools out of whose mouth poureth foolishness. They ask the philosophic question posed by Maimonides in the Guide to the Perplexed and in Mishneh Torah, viz. since God knows the future, He knows what everyone is destined to do. He knows too what precepts a person will fulfill and what sins he will commit. Consequently, everyone is compelled to fulfill those precepts and commit those sins. How, then, can there be retribution or reward for a compelled action? He replies that God's knowledge is beyond our comprehension. The fools, who wish to free themselves from the yoke of the commandments, argue that the eyes of the Lord are in every place, seeing the evil and the good. God sees now the evil and the good every person will do. They are therefore not liable to any punishment.

4 TONGUE'S EFFECT UPON THE ONE WHO IS REPROVED

The difference between this verse and verse 1 is that the latter tells the results of a *soft answer* in appeasing anger, whereas here he tells of a soothing tongue that gives instruction and reproves the foolish.

wound to the spirit. lit. 'a breaking in spirit'; it produces injury for the man who so misuses his tongue, the harm recoiling upon himself (Ibn Ezra).

Alshich explains: 'The tongue (of the wise) heals the Tree of Life.' The reply of the wise rectifies the difficulty concerning the exalted state of God, the Tree of Life, and he who finds perverseness in their reply,' it is in reality a fault in his spirit.

5 A fool despiseth his father's correction;
But he that regardeth reproof is prudent.

6 In the house of the righteous is much treasure;
But in the revenues of the wicked is trouble.

7 The lips of the wise disperse knowledge;
But the heart of the foolish is not stedfast.

8 The sacrifice of the wicked is an abomination to the LORD;
But the prayer of the upright is His delight.

אֱוִיל יִנְאַץ מוּסַר אָבִיו 5
וְשֹׁמֵר תֹּכַחַת יַעְרִם׃
בֵּית צַדִּיק חֹסֶן רָב 6
וּבִתְבוּאַת רָשָׁע נֶעְכָּרֶת׃
שִׂפְתֵי חֲכָמִים יְזָרוּ דָעַת 7
וְלֵב כְּסִילִים לֹא־כֵן׃
זֶבַח רְשָׁעִים תּוֹעֲבַת יְהוָה 8
וּתְפִלַּת יְשָׁרִים רְצוֹנוֹ׃

5 CORRECTION IS SALUTARY

a fool despiseth. The same thought occurred in positive form in xiii. 1.

regardeth reproof. See on xiii. 18. [The words may be general, or refer to a father's reproof.]

is prudent. Or, 'acts prudently.' A parent's correction is always given in the best interests of a child (Ibn Ezra).

6 REWARD OF RIGHTEOUSNESS

in the house . . . treasure. More lit. 'the house of the righteous is a great store,' full of good things which God's protection allows him to enjoy (Gerondi).

revenues. The Hebrew is singular, and the word is usually employed in this Book for what the wicked acquire (see on x. 16).

trouble. lit. 'is troubled.' It will be beset by curse and blight (Meiri).

7 SPEECH OF THE WISE

disperse. The verb has the same force as in i. 17 (see note) lit. 'sprinkle.' From *the lips of the wise* a trail of *knowledge* issues; their words are enlightenment to those who hear them or hear of them (see Metsudath David).

heart. [A parallel to *lips,* because as the seat of intelligence it directs speech.]

is not stedfast. Better, 'is not so,' and the phrase is used exactly as in Ps. i. 4 (so Metsudath David).

8–9 TWO ABOMINATIONS OF GOD

8. *the sacrifice* . . . LORD. [An accurate summary of Biblical teaching with respect to sacrifices. The view that there were two schools of thought in Israel, one favourable and the other antagonistic to the Temple-offerings, is not borne out by the evidence. All the passages which are apparently against the system in fact denounce *the sacrifice of the wicked* (cf. 1 Sam. xv. 22; Isa. i. 11ff.; Amos v. 22ff.).]

prayer of the upright. [*Prayer* is not to be thought of here as implying a different and superior expression of worship than *sacrifice.*] The act of prayer was made more realistic by the simultaneous act of bringing an offering to the Temple, and there can be no question that *the upright* were then loyal to the service of the Sanctuary (see Metsudath David).

The way of the wicked is an abomination to the LORD;
But He loveth him that followeth after righteousness.

0 There is grievous correction for him that forsaketh the way;
And he that hateth reproof shall die.

1 The nether-world and Destruction are before the LORD;
How much more then the hearts of the children of men!

2 A scorner loveth not to be reproved;
He will not go unto the wise.

9 תּוֹעֲבַת יְהוָה דֶּרֶךְ רָשָׁע
וּמְרַדֵּף צְדָקָה יֶאֱהָב׃
10 מוּסָר רָע לְעֹזֵב אֹרַח
שׂוֹנֵא תוֹכַחַת יָמוּת׃
11 שְׁאוֹל וַאֲבַדּוֹן נֶגֶד יְהוָה
אַף כִּי־לִבּוֹת בְּנֵי־אָדָם׃
12 לֹא־יֶאֱהַב לֵץ הוֹכֵחַ לוֹ
אֶל־חֲכָמִים לֹא יֵלֵךְ׃

9. As a pendant to what precedes, this verse is of the highest importance, because it clearly defines the final test of a man's religion. The criterion is not his scrupulous performance of rites such as sacrifice and prayer, but the *way* of life he treads and his ardent (the form of the verb is intensive) pursuit of *righteousness*.

10 PUNISHMENT OF EVIL

grievous correction. Stern punishment, viz. torments (Rashi).

the way. A different noun from that in the last verse, but occurring in xii. 28 which well defines it, *in the way of righteousness is life*.

hateth reproof. A sign that the wrongdoer has no wish to repent and persists in his evil (Ralbag).

shall die. Hating reproof is one of the twenty-four deterrents to repentance enumerated by the Sages. Therefore, he will die because of his sins (Ibn Nachmiash).

11 HUMAN HEART OPEN TO GOD

nether-world. Hebrew *sheol* (see on i. 12).

destruction. Hebrew *abaddon,* which R.V. retains. Its literal meaning is 'place of perishing,' and may be a synonym of sheol with which it is again combined in xxvii. 20. Ibn Nachmiash explains both terms as referring to the depths of the earth where the dead are buried. Meiri asserts that *abaddon* is deeper than *sheol*. Metsudath David defines *sheol* as the grave and *abaddon* as Gehinnom.

are before the LORD. To man these regions are a mystery, but to God all about them is known (Saadia Gaon).

how much more. If those remote parts of the universe are open to His inspection, surely that must be even more so with something like the human heart which is readily accessible for His scrutiny (Ralbag).

the hearts. These may be unreadable by man, but to God they are an open book (Jer. xvii. 10).

12 A SCORNER IS INCORRIGIBLE

to be reproved. lit. '(one) to reprove him.'

go unto. For the purpose of receiving instruction (cf. *go to the ant,* vi. 6). On the nature of the *scorner,* see on i. 22, xiii. 1.

13 A merry heart maketh a cheerful countenance;
But by sorrow of heart the spirit is broken.

14 The heart of him that hath discernment seeketh knowledge;
But the mouth of fools feedeth on folly.

15 All the days of the poor are evil;
But he that is of a merry heart hath a continual feast.

16 Better is little with the fear of the LORD,
Than great treasure and turmoil therewith.

לֵב שָׂמֵחַ יֵיטִב פָּנִים 1
וּבְעַצְּבַת־לֵב רוּחַ נְכֵאָה׃
לֵב נָבוֹן יְבַקֶּשׁ־דָּעַת 1
וּפְנֵי כְסִילִים יִרְעֶה אִוֶּלֶת׃
כָּל־יְמֵי עָנִי רָעִים 1
וְטוֹב־לֵב מִשְׁתֶּה תָמִיד׃
טוֹב־מְעַט בְּיִרְאַת יְהוָה 1
מֵאוֹצָר רָב וּמְהוּמָה בוֹ׃

v. 14. ופי ק׳

13 EFFECT OF JOY AND SORROW

merry heart. Again verse 15, xvii. 22. *Merry* must be understood simply as 'happy.' For the thought of the verse, cf. 'The heart of a man changeth his countenance, whether it be for good or for evil. A cheerful countenance is a token of a heart that is in prosperity' (Ecclus. xiii. 25f.) (see Ibn Nachmiash).

14 MENTAL FOOD OF THE WISE AND FOOLS

mouth. So the *kerë* in agreement with the ancient versions. The *kethib* means 'face,' which does not suit the verb. Isaiah da Trani, however, rectifies this by explaining: 'the face of fools, each one directs his face toward folly.'

feedeth on. This translation does not follow any of the classical Jewish commentaries. Some render: 'desireth,' after the cognate Aramaic (Meiri). Others render 'thinketh,' after another cognate Aramaic (Ibn Ganah). Still others render: 'befriend' (Metsudath David).

15 EXPERIENCE OF THE POOR

The verse is usually explained as an antithesis between the hard lot of the needy and the happy life of the well-to-do; but if that were so, *merry heart* is not a true contrast to *poor,* and a word for 'rich' would be expected. A different interpretation is accordingly offered, which is suggested by the Jewish commentary, Metsudath David and before him by Meiri.

are evil. His plight is not only unenviable by reason of the hardships he suffers, but even when he has a sufficiency for the bare necessities of life he does not enjoy it, because he is jealous of the more fortunate.

but . . . feast. Render: 'but if he be of happy mind he hath a constant feast.' Though poor, he can always find his life enjoyable, if he has a cheerful disposition. In this sense the verse is analogous to the Rabbinic maxim: 'Who is rich? He who rejoices in his portion' (Aboth 4.1).

16–17 TRUE WEALTH

turmoil. The import of the word here is illustrated by Amos iii. 9 where it is used of outcries from the sufferers of oppression who have been plundered to enrich their despoilers (Rashi).

17 Better is a dinner of herbs where love is,
Than a stalled ox and hatred therewith.

18 A wrathful man stirreth up discord;
But he that is slow to anger appeaseth strife.

19 The way of the sluggard is as though hedged by thorns;
But the path of the upright is even.

20 A wise son maketh a glad father;
But a foolish man despiseth his mother.

21 Folly is joy to him that lacketh understanding;
But a man of discernment walketh straightforwards.

17 טוֹב אֲרֻחַת יָרָק וְאַהֲבָה־שָׁם
מִשּׁוֹר אָבוּס וְשִׂנְאָה־בוֹ׃
18 אִישׁ חֵמָה יְגָרֶה מָדוֹן
וְאֶרֶךְ אַפַּיִם יַשְׁקִיט רִיב׃
19 דֶּרֶךְ עָצֵל כִּמְשֻׂכַת חָדֶק
וְאֹרַח יְשָׁרִים סְלֻלָה׃
20 בֵּן חָכָם יְשַׂמַּח־אָב
וּכְסִיל אָדָם בּוֹזֶה אִמּוֹ׃
21 אִוֶּלֶת שִׂמְחָה לַחֲסַר־לֵב
וְאִישׁ תְּבוּנָה יְיַשֶּׁר־לָכֶת׃

17. *dinner.* The literal meaning is 'portion of food assigned to a wayfarer' (Ibn Ezra).

of herbs. Signifying a humble and frugal meal (Daath Mikra).

stalled ox. i.e. a fatted ox, symbol of a luxurious repast (Daath Mikra).

18 A COOL TEMPER LESSENS CONTENTION

wrathful man. lit. 'a man of heat,' hot-tempered and quick to quarrel (Rashi).

appeaseth strife. lit. 'causeth strife to be quiet.'

19 PENALTY OF SLOTH

as though hedged by thorns. The idle man imagines himself walking on a road hedged by thorns; as he walks along his path, the thorns catch his clothes, and his progress is impeded (Rashi).

the upright. Men of this class are free of the vice of laziness, attend to their duties, and so they proceed along a properly constructed road and make good progress (Rashi).

even. lit. 'cast up' with earth and then flattened evenly (cf. Isa. lvii. 14; Jer. xviii. 15) (Rashi).

20 WISDOM AND FILIAL BEHAVIOUR

a wise . . . father. Identical with the first clause of x. 1.

despiseth his mother. [An attitude which must cause her the deepest grief, hence the contrast to *glad*.]

21 WISDOM AND CONDUCT

folly. [Having both an intellectual and ethical connotation, the word indicates that without the ability to discern between the good and the bad, the natural tendency is for a man to give preference to, and take delight in, the latter.]

walketh straightforwards. lit. 'maketh his going straight'; he consciously and deliberately chooses the path which is morally right (Ibn Ezra).

22 For want of counsel purposes are frustrated;
But in the multitude of counsellors they are established.

23 A man hath joy in the answer of his mouth;
And a word in due season, how good is it!

24 The path of life goeth upward for the wise,
That he may depart from the nether-world beneath.

25 The LORD will pluck up the house of the proud;
But He will establish the border of the widow.

הָפֵר מַחֲשָׁבוֹת בְּאֵין ס֑וֹד 22
וּבְרֹ֖ב יוֹעֲצִ֣ים תָּקֽוּם׃
שִׂמְחָ֣ה לָ֭אִישׁ בְּמַעֲנֵה־פִ֑יו 23
וְדָבָ֖ר בְּעִתּ֣וֹ מַה־טּֽוֹב׃
אֹ֣רַח חַ֭יִּים לְמַ֣עְלָה לְמַשְׂכִּ֑יל 24
לְמַ֥עַן ס֝֗וּר מִשְּׁא֥וֹל מָֽטָּה׃
בֵּ֣ית גֵּ֭אִים יִסַּ֥ח ׀ יְהוָ֑ה 25
וְ֝יַצֵּ֗ב גְּב֣וּל אַלְמָנָֽה׃

22–23 BENEFIT OF CONSULTATION

22. A variant of xi. 14.

for want of counsel. Or, 'where there is no counsel.'

purposes are frustrated. lit. 'there is frustrating of plans.' The deviser of a scheme may achieve success by acting entirely on his own, but more usually he courts failure by refusing to discuss it with others and hear their criticisms (after Rashi, Meiri).

they are established. The verb is singular, referring to each of the *purposes* (Meiri).

23. *in the answer of his mouth.* Better, 'in the utterances of his mouth,' the verb *anah* being sometimes used to indicate 'speak,' not 'answer.' A man naturally approves his own expression of opinion and regards it as sound (Metsudath David).

a word in due season. If this verse is a pendant to the preceding, then *word* is a timely word of advice from others, not necessarily in agreement with his own views. Criticism can be most helpful (Metsudath David).

24 WISDOM LEADS TO LIFE

goeth upward. The phrase is nothing more than the opposite of *beneath.* The way which the wise man adopts is one of life, leading in a direction the reverse of the fool's which is the road to death (Malbim).

beneath. See on i. 12.

25–26 GOD IS AGAINST EVIL

25. *house of the proud.* Men of power which they use arrogantly and unscrupulously. In particular they take advantage of their authority to rob the unprotected to make themselves richer (cf. xvi. 19). The conduct of this class is often denounced in the Psalms and by the prophets (Daath Mikra from Ibn Ezra).

He will establish. As the Champion of the defenceless He will secure the lawful owner's possession of the *border,* the family allotment (Meiri).

widow. Typical of the person without a protector, and so most liable to be harmed by the *proud* (Metsudath David).

26 The thoughts of wickedness are an abomination to the LORD;
But words of pleasantness are pure.

27 He that is greedy of gain troubleth his own house;
But he that hateth gifts shall live.

28 The heart of the righteous studieth to answer;
But the mouth of the wicked poureth out evil things.

29 The LORD is far from the wicked;
But He heareth the prayer of the righteous.

26 תּוֹעֲבַת יְהוָה מַחְשְׁבוֹת רָע
וּטְהֹרִים אִמְרֵי־נֹעַם׃
27 עֹכֵר בֵּיתוֹ בּוֹצֵעַ בָּצַע
וְשׂוֹנֵא מַתָּנֹת יִחְיֶה׃
28 לֵב צַדִּיק יֶהְגֶּה לַעֲנוֹת
וּפִי רְשָׁעִים יַבִּיעַ רָעוֹת׃
29 רָחוֹק יְהוָה מֵרְשָׁעִים
וּתְפִלַּת צַדִּיקִים יִשְׁמָע׃

26. *thoughts of wickedness.* Or, 'schemes of evil,' designed to injure (after Targum).

words of pleasantness. Actuated by good motives and intended to be friendly and helpful (see Elijah of Wilna).

pure. In the sight of God (Isaiah da Trani). [In contrast to what is an *abomination.* The word seems to be employed in its technical sense as applied to 'pure animals' which are acceptable as sacrifices.]

27 AGAINST AVARICE

greedy of gain. See on i. 19.

troubleth . . . house. Again in xi. 29. Money so obtained does not benefit a man's household as when it is honestly earned. In due course he is punished for his offence, and in his downfall his family experiences trouble and hardship (Daath Mikra).

hateth. [In contrast to the idea of inordinate love of money implied in *greedy of gain,* the word *hateth* merely signifies the absence of such eager desire (see on xiii. 24).]

gifts. Bribes (Daath Mikra from Ibn Ezra).

28 SPEECH OF RIGHTEOUS AND WICKED

heart. [Mind.]

studieth. lit. 'meditates,' reflects before speaking so that the words which he utters are sympathetic and beneficial (Rashi).

poureth out. Without reflection by the *heart,* as happens with the righteous man (Metsudath David).

29 WHOSE PRAYER GOD HEARS

far from. In the event of their praying. The writer may have had in mind and adapted Ps. cxlv. 18 (Metsudath David).

30 The light of the eyes rejoiceth the heart;
And a good report maketh the bones fat.

31 The ear that hearkeneth to the reproof of life
Abideth among the wise.

32 He that refuseth correction despiseth his own soul;
But he that hearkeneth to reproof getteth understanding.

33 The fear of the LORD is the instruction of wisdom;
And before honour goeth humility.

30 מְאֽוֹר־עֵינַיִם יְשַׂמַּֽח־לֵב
שְׁמוּעָה טוֹבָה תְּדַשֶּׁן־עָֽצֶם׃
31 אֹזֶן שֹׁמַעַת תּוֹכַחַת חַיִּים
בְּקֶרֶב חֲכָמִים תָּלִֽין׃
32 פּוֹרֵעַ מוּסָר מוֹאֵס נַפְשׁוֹ
וְשׁוֹמֵעַ תּוֹכַחַת קֽוֹנֶה לֵּֽב׃
33 יִרְאַת יְהוָה מוּסַר חָכְמָה
וְלִפְנֵי כָבוֹד עֲנָוָֽה׃

30 EFFECT OF GOOD NEWS

the light of the eyes. [From the context it is to be deduced that the phrase describes the brightness which shines in the eyes when one is brought good news.]

good report. R.V. 'good tidings.'

maketh the bones fat. Invigorates the body. *Fat* means 'full of marrow.' For the opposite, cf. *a broken spirit drieth the bones* (xvii. 22) (Malbim).

31-33 HUMBLE ACCEPTANCE OF DISCIPLINE

31. *the ear.* [i.e. the man who possesses an ear, etc.]

reproof of life. Reproof which, if hearkened to, prolongs life (Metsudath David).

abideth among the wise. Associates with this class of man in order to have the opportunity of receiving the life-giving *reproof* (Metsudath David).

32. *despiseth his own soul.* Ibn Ezra understands the phrase as 'despiseth his life'; he throws it away by rejecting correction of his evil ways.

understanding. lit. 'heart.' Ibn Ezra explains, knowledge and fear or God. This type of person learns to appreciate that as evil shortens life, virtue prolongs it.

33. *the instruction of wisdom.* Perhaps, 'instruction in wisdom.' The clause is a variant of i. 7 and ix. 10. It identifies the tenets of wisdom which are taught by the sages with the revealed will of God. Although they express the thoughts of mortal men, yet they are derived from, and accord with, Divine teaching (see Ibn Nachmiash).

before honour goeth humility. Repeated in xviii. 12. Rashi explains that humility causes honour to follow it. Ibn Nachmiash elaborates and explains this verse in the light of xvi. 18, 'Pride goeth before destruction.' If one is proud, he meets destruction. Therefore, in order to attain honour, one must possess humility.

1 The preparations of the heart are man's,
But the answer of the tongue is from the LORD.

2 All the ways of a man are clean in his own eyes;
But the LORD weigheth the spirits.

3 Commit thy works unto the LORD,
And thy thoughts shall be established.

4 The LORD hath made every thing for His own purpose,
Yea, even the wicked for the day of evil.

1 לְאָדָם מַעַרְכֵי־לֵב
וּמֵיְהוָה מַעֲנֵה לָשׁוֹן׃
2 כָּל־דַּרְכֵי־אִישׁ זַךְ בְּעֵינָיו
וְתֹכֵן רוּחוֹת יְהוָה׃
3 גֹּל אֶל־יְהוָה מַעֲשֶׂיךָ
וְיִכֹּנוּ מַחְשְׁבֹתֶיךָ׃
4 כֹּל פָּעַל יְהוָה לַמַּעֲנֵהוּ
וְגַם־רָשָׁע לְיוֹם רָעָה׃

CHAPTER XVI

1–9 GOD AND HUMAN ACTIVITY

1. *preparations of the heart.* Processes of thought. Endowed with intellect, man has the power of connecting ideas, drawing conclusions, and arranging in his mind a logical presentation of his case (Rashi, Ibn Ezra, Metsudath David).

answer of the tongue. Better, 'utterance of the tongue' (see on xv. 23). The ability to phrase one's ideas in convincing language is a special gift from God (cf. Isa. l. 4), without which the careful preparatory thinking is abortive (Rashi, Metsudath David).

2. *all the ways . . . eyes.* A normal man always tries to justify his actions and prove them right. In so doing he may, consciously or unconsciously, practise self-deception. His judgment is not always objective and may be coloured by his predilections (Isaiah da Trani).

weigheth the spirits. God holds an even balance and critically tests the genuineness of the impulses which motivated the deed. Accordingly, man should not be guided by his own judgment but apply the criterion, how will it be judged by God? (Isaiah da Trani).

3. *commit.* lit. 'roll on to.' The verse repeats the thought of the preceding in more precise language: refer your deeds to God for His appraisement (Meiri).

and thy thoughts . . . established. Better, 'then shall thy plans (or, thoughts) be sincere.' For this meaning of the last word, cf. *there is no sincerity in their mouth* (Ps. v. 10) (Meiri).

4. *for His own purpose.* As the absolute Creator and Controller of the universe, He determined for which purpose everything that exists was made. There is nothing aimless in the world, even if it appear so to man's finite intelligence (see Ibn Nachmiash).

even the wicked. The intention cannot be that God designed that a person should be wicked, because it would conflict with the doctrine of the Wisdom literature, *God made man upright, but they have sought out many inventions* (Eccles. vii. 29). Knowing that some men would be wicked, God arranged that the scheme of the universe should include a *day of evil,* a day of judgment and retribution, for them (after Saadia Gaon).

5 Every one that is proud in heart
is an abomination to the LORD;
My hand upon it! he shall not be
unpunished.

6 By mercy and truth iniquity is
expiated;
And by the fear of the LORD men
depart from evil.

7 When a man's ways please the
LORD,
He maketh even his enemies to be
at peace with him.

8 Better is a little with righteousness
Than great revenues with injustice.

תּוֹעֲבַת יְהוָה כָּל־גְּבַהּ־לֵב 5
יָד לְיָד לֹא יִנָּקֶה׃
בְּחֶסֶד וֶאֱמֶת יְכֻפַּר עָוֺן 6
וּבְיִרְאַת יְהוָה סוּר מֵרָע׃
בִּרְצוֹת יְהוָה דַּרְכֵי־אִישׁ 7
גַּם־אוֹיְבָיו יַשְׁלִם אִתּוֹ׃
טוֹב מְעַט בִּצְדָקָה 8
מֵרֹב תְּבוּאוֹת בְּלֹא מִשְׁפָּט׃

5. The writer seems to have had xi. 20f. in mind. The first clause is the same as in xi. 20, with the variant *perverse in heart,* and the second clause is almost a repetition of xi. 21 (see notes *ad loc.*).

an abomination. This expression is analogous to that mentioned in the Torah in regard to idolatry and immorality. The Rabbis, therefore, equated haughtiness with these serious sins.

6. *mercy and truth.* See on iii. 3. The Rabbis explained this to mean deeds of kindness and the study of the Torah.

iniquity is expiated. [If God made arrangements for the punishment of the wicked, He likewise ordained the means by which it could be averted. Should the sinner reform and mark his repentance by the practice of *mercy and truth,* whatever wrong he may have done becomes *expiated* (lit. 'covered over' and so hidden from God's sight).]

depart from evil. lit. 'is turning from evil,' the prevention which is better than the cure. Reverence of God gives man the strength to turn away from sin when tempted (after Saadia Gaon, Meiri, Ibn Nachmiash).

Many commentators explain the end of the verse to mean that, although the sinner perform acts of *mercy and truth,* he must *depart from evil,* repent of his evil ways *by the fear of the* LORD. Merely doing good without remorse for his sins is inadequate (Metsudath David, Isaiah da Trani). Ibn Nachmiash suggests: 'and by the fear of the LORD and by departing from evil.' One's sins will be expiated by performing deeds of mercy and truth and by. . .

7. *He maketh . . . him.* According to most exegetes, the subject is *God,* not man. The intention is that God inspires his enemies to make peace with him. Examples of this are the narratives of the patriarchs (Gen. xx. 15, xxvi. 27ff., xxxiii. 4) (Ibn Nachmiash, also implied by others). He suggests further that the subject may be *man.* In that case, we render: 'He shall make his enemies to be at peace with him.' The intention is that if a man sins against his fellowman and repents, he must, in addition to his repentance, appease the one against whom he sinned.

8. Repeats the thought of xv. 16, and a comparison shows that *righteousness* is the equivalent of *the fear of the* LORD.

A man's heart deviseth his way;
But the LORD directeth his steps.

A divine sentence is in the lips of the king;
His mouth trespasseth not in judgment.

A just balance and scales are the LORD's;
All the weights of the bag are His work.

9 לֵב אָדָם יְחַשֵּׁב דַּרְכּוֹ
וַיהוָה יָכִין צַעֲדוֹ׃
10 קֶסֶם ׀ עַל־שִׂפְתֵי־מֶלֶךְ
בְּמִשְׁפָּט לֹא יִמְעַל־פִּיו׃
11 פֶּלֶס ׀ וּמֹאזְנֵי מִשְׁפָּט לַיהוָה
מַעֲשֵׂהוּ כָּל־אַבְנֵי־כִיס׃

9. The interpretation which makes the verse a form of the proverb, 'Man proposes, God disposes,' is out of accord with the context. It illustrates a doctrine of the Rabbis, 'God helps him who aims at self-purification.' Man chooses the path of his life and, if it meets with His approval, God directs his steps to the desired goal (after Rashi).

10–15 A KING'S RESPONSIBILITY

The theory of kingship held by the Scriptural writers was diametrically opposite to the autocratic despotism which held sway in the East. The essential point of difference is that, in the Hebrew doctrine, the king was not above the law but, like everybody else, subject to it (cf. especially Deut. xvii. 14ff.; Ps. lxxii).

10. *divine sentence.* Normally the term signifies an act of divination which is forbidden by the Torah (Deut. xviii. 10), but here it is employed in a good sense. The king was anointed with the consecrating oil on his enthronement; his office was sacred and consequently he must think of his official pronouncements as something holy (after Meiri's second interpretation).

his mouth. [When he gave judgment, the king being the highest judge in the land.]

trespasseth. [The verse has the technical meaning (cf. Lev. v. 15) of putting to improper use anything which had been dedicated to the Sanctuary. *Judgment is God's* (Deut. i. 17), and therefore in the category of the holy; consequently the violation of justice is sacrilege.]

11. This verse is misunderstood by the modern expositors who hold it to refer to honest weights and measures. If so interpreted, it is out of place and has no connection with the group which deals with the subject of a king's obligations, and preference should be given to the Jewish commentaries which relate the verse to the Divine origin of justice.

a just balance and scales. An improbable translation, since *tsedek* would have been used instead of *mishpat* if the meaning were *just balance* (cf. Lev. xix. 36). The correct rendering is: 'the balance and scales of justice are the Lord's,' i.e. they are not something arbitrary which each king can manufacture to suit his convenience. They are fixed by God and delivered into the king's keeping to administer fairly (Alshich).

weights of the bag. Cf. Deut. xxv. 13. The imagery of scales is continued in detail. The weights to be used on the scales, like the scales themselves, are made by God; the king may not provide his own (Alshich).

12 תּוֹעֲבַת מְלָכִים עֲשׂוֹת רֶשַׁע
כִּי בִצְדָקָה יִכּוֹן כִּסֵּא׃
13 רְצוֹן מְלָכִים שִׂפְתֵי־צֶדֶק
וְדֹבֵר יְשָׁרִים יֶאֱהָב׃
14 חֲמַת־מֶלֶךְ מַלְאֲכֵי־מָוֶת
וְאִישׁ חָכָם יְכַפְּרֶנָּה׃
15 בְּאוֹר־פְּנֵי־מֶלֶךְ חַיִּים
וּרְצוֹנוֹ כְּעָב מַלְקוֹשׁ׃
16 קְנֹה־חָכְמָה מַה־טּוֹב מֵחָרוּץ
וּקְנוֹת בִּינָה נִבְחָר מִכָּסֶף׃
17 מְסִלַּת יְשָׁרִים סוּר מֵרָע

12 It is an abomination to kings to commit wickedness;
For the throne is established by righteousness.

13 Righteous lips are the delight of kings;
And they love him that speaketh right.

14 The wrath of a king is as messengers of death;
But a wise man will pacify it.

15 In the light of the king's countenance is life;
And his favour is as a cloud of the latter rain.

16 How much better is it to get wisdom than gold!
Yea, to get understanding is rather to be chosen than silver.

17 The highway of the upright is to depart from evil;

12. *to commit.* i.e. if they commit (Rashi).

throne . . . righteousness. Cf. xxv. 5, xxix. 14.

14. *wrath of a king.* Likened to *the roaring of a lion* (xix. 12).

as messengers of death. Omit *as.* For historical illustrations, cf. 1 Sam. xxii. 16ff. (Saul); Esther vii. 8ff. (Ahasuerus); Dan. ii. 5 (Nebuchadnezzar).

will pacify. i.e. is able to pacify the king's wrath (Metsudath David).

15. *in the light . . . life.* i.e. when the king looks upon someone in a friendly manner (Metsudath David). The moral is that we must avoid provoking the king's anger (Ibn Nachmiash). Midrashically, this is explained as referring to God, the King of the world (Rashi).

Life. May be the antithesis of *messengers of death* or imply a state of happiness and prosperity (Daath Mikra).

latter rain. Which fell in the Spring and assured the ripening of the crops (Metsudath David).

17 WAY OF THE UPRIGHT

highway. The way trodden by the *upright* is described by a word which indicates a properly constructed path, levelled and freed from obstructions (see on xv. 19).

is to depart from evil. This is to be explained in its ethical sense, the usual meaning of the phrase. The thought which the verse conveys is: if one wishes to proceed along *the highway of the upright,* what he has to do *is to depart from evil* (Metsudath David).

he that keepeth . . . soul. Better, 'he that guardeth his soul (life) taketh heed to his way,' i.e. does not walk aimlessly but carefully chooses the *highway* (Metsudath David).

He that keepeth his way preserveth his soul.

18 Pride goeth before destruction,
And a haughty spirit before a fall.

19 Better it is to be of a lowly spirit with the humble,
Than to divide the spoil with the proud.

20 He that giveth heed unto the word shall find good;
And whoso trusteth in the LORD, happy is he.

21 The wise in heart is called a man of discernment;
And the sweetness of the lips increaseth learning.

שֹׁמֵר נַפְשׁוֹ נֹצֵר דַּרְכּוֹ׃
18 לִפְנֵי־שֶׁבֶר גָּאוֹן
וְלִפְנֵי כִשָּׁלוֹן גֹּבַהּ רוּחַ׃
19 טוֹב שְׁפַל־רוּחַ אֶת־עֲנִיִּים
מֵחַלֵּק שָׁלָל אֶת־גֵּאִים׃
20 מַשְׂכִּיל עַל־דָּבָר יִמְצָא־טוֹב
וּבוֹטֵחַ בַּיהוָה אַשְׁרָיו׃
21 לַחֲכַם־לֵב יִקָּרֵא נָבוֹן
וּמֶתֶק שְׂפָתַיִם יֹסִיף לֶקַח׃

v. 19 ענוים ק'

18 PRIDE LEADS TO FALL

In Rabbinical literature, as well as in the Prophets, pride is looked upon as a serious offence. Nachmanides writes to his son: And now, my son, know and see that one who feels proud over his fellowmen rebels against the Kingdom of Heaven, for he usurps the royal robes of the Kingdom of Heaven, as the Psalmist states: *The Lord reigneth; He is clothed in majesty* (xciii. 1). It follows, therefore, that he who rebels against God is to be punished.

19 PRAISE OF HUMILITY

of a lowly spirit. The opposite of the feeling of self-importance, a vice which urges a person to keep in with the 'upper class' whatever be its true moral character (Metsudath David).

humble. The *kethib* is 'poor'; the *kerë* indicates the oppressed class. Associate rather with these despised people who earn a scanty living by honest labour (see Daath Mikra).

divide the spoil. [A phrase taken from military life (Gen. xlix. 27; Exod. xv. 9), and then applied to the enrichment of the strong at the expense of the weak.]

20–24 VIRTUE OF WISDOM

20. *he that giveth heed.* lit. 'he that acteth wisely,' by foresight (Rashi).

good. Happiness and prosperity (Metsudath David).

happy is he. In his good fortune which God sends to him (Ibn Ezra).

21. *is called.* Will eventually become known as a man of discernment (Rashi).

a man of discernment. He will learn to derive new ideas from the instruction he received from his mentors (Rashi).

sweetness of the lips. This is a desirable possession of *the man of discernment* if he is to exercise his influence to its full extent. When questioned, the answers he gives should be choicely worded and spoken in pleasant tones, so that his replies find ready acceptance (Isaiah da Trani).

increaseth learning. As in i. 5, 'enlarges (his) teaching,' spreads his knowledge among a large number of people (Isaiah da Trani).

22 Understanding is a fountain of life unto him that hath it;
But folly is the chastisement of fools.

23 The heart of the wise teacheth his mouth,
And addeth learning to his lips.

24 Pleasant words are as a honeycomb,
Sweet to the soul, and health to the bones.

25 There is a way which seemeth right unto a man,
But the end thereof are the ways of death.

26 The hunger of the labouring man laboureth for him;
For his mouth compelleth him.

מְקוֹר חַיִּים שֵׂכֶל בְּעָלָיו 22
וּמוּסַר אֱוִלִים אִוֶּלֶת׃
לֵב חָכָם יַשְׂכִּיל פִּיהוּ 23
וְעַל־שְׂפָתָיו יֹסִיף לֶקַח׃
צוּף־דְּבַשׁ אִמְרֵי־נֹעַם 24
מָתוֹק לַנֶּפֶשׁ וּמַרְפֵּא לָעָצֶם׃
יֵשׁ דֶּרֶךְ יָשָׁר לִפְנֵי־אִישׁ 25
וְאַחֲרִיתָהּ דַּרְכֵי־מָוֶת׃
נֶפֶשׁ עָמֵל עָמְלָה לּוֹ
כִּי־אָכַף עָלָיו פִּיהוּ׃

22. *understanding.* Hebrew *sechel,* the equivalent of *haskel* (see on i. 3).

chastisement. Because it deprives the foolish of the *fountain of life* which is enjoyed by the wise (see Isaiah da Trani).

23. *teacheth his mouth.* Or, 'giveth discernment to his mouth,' invests his words with insight and sagacity (Isaiah da Trani).

and addeth . . . lips. Better, 'and increaseth teaching upon his lips,' adds to the instruction he is able to impart to others (Isaiah da Trani).

24. *pleasant words.* Wisdom adorns words with graciousness, just as its *ways* are pleasant (iii. 17).

as a honeycomb. Cf. *sweeter also than honey and the honeycomb* (Ps. xix. 11), of God's ordinances.

soul. Here the non-physical nature of the human being, the mind and spirit (Malbim).

26 HUNGER THE URGE TO WORK

laboureth for him. i.e. compels him to labour, giving him no rest (Isaiah da Trani). Other commentators explain *nefesh* in its literal sense, here meaning 'the body,' Rashi explains the verse to mean that the labourer labours for himself when his mouth compels him and demand food; then his toil stands him in good stead, for he eats what was earned by his toil . Gernodi explains *nefesh* in its very literal, spiritual sense. He renders: Sometimes the soul of the labourer labours for the labourer, viz. for his body instead of for the soul itself, the opposite of the wise man, who labours for his soul, 'for his mouth compels him,' the food for his mouth is extremely necessary for him, since he seeks luxuries and rich foods. Therefore, he must toil and labour in order to fill his mouth with these desires. This follows verse 25, since this way 'seemeth right to a man. But the end thereof are the ways of death.' He wastes his days with vanity and forgets his Maker, thinking only of the wants of his body.

27 An ungodly man diggeth up evil,
And in his lips there is as a burning fire.

28 A froward man soweth strife;
And a whisperer separateth familiar friends.

29 A man of violence enticeth his neighbour,
And leadeth him into a way that is not good.

30 He that shutteth his eyes, it is to devise froward things;
He that biteth his lips bringeth evil to pass.

27 אִישׁ בְּלִיַּעַל כֹּרֶה רָעָה
וְעַל־שְׂפָתָיו כְּאֵשׁ צָרָבֶת׃
28 אִישׁ תַּהְפֻּכוֹת יְשַׁלַּח מָדוֹן
וְנִרְגָּן מַפְרִיד אַלּוּף׃
29 אִישׁ חָמָס יְפַתֶּה רֵעֵהוּ
וְהוֹלִיכוֹ בְּדֶרֶךְ לֹא־טוֹב׃
30 עֹצֶה עֵינָיו לַחְשֹׁב תַּהְפֻּכוֹת
קֹרֵץ שְׂפָתָיו כִּלָּה רָעָה׃

v. 27. שפתו ק׳

27–30 MISCHIEVOUS SPEECH

The moral evil of mischief-making by slanderous talk was dealt with in vi. 12ff., and this group resumes the subject.

27. *ungodly man.* The Hebrew word in vi. 12 is translated *base* (see *ad loc.*).

diggeth up evil. The verb is especially used in Psalms for 'digging a pit' in the metaphorical sense, to trap the innocent. R.V. 'deviseth mischief' is a good equivalent (after Metsudoth).

in his lips. More lit. 'on his lips.'

burning. Better, 'scorching.' The root occurs again in Lev. xiii. 23, 28 for a skin inflammation, and in Ezek. xxi. 3, *all faces shall be seared* in a forest fire. The words on the lips of a mischiefmaker have a scorching effect upon the object of his malice (after Isaiah da Trani).

28. *a froward man.* lit. 'a man of upside down (utterances),' who speaks lies (Metsudath David).

soweth strife. Cf. vi. 14.

whisperer. Elsewhere the root signifies 'murmur, complain' (Metsudath Zion).

familiar friends. Hebrew *alluf.* It is found in ii. 17, *the lord of her youth,* a husband. As there remarked, 'the phrase is applied by Israel to God in Jer. iii. 4.' Rashi, accordingly, explains it here as 'separates from himself the Chief of the universe'; but more naturally its meaning is that given in A.J., the word being used collectively, as in xvii. 9 (Targum, Isaiah da Trani).

29. *a man of violence.* [One who enters upon a career of crime.]

enticeth his neighbour. To become a confederate (cf. the illustration in i. 10ff.) (Ibn Ezra).

a way that is not good. Again Isa. lxv. 2; Ps. xxxvi. 5.

30. *shutteth his eyes.* The corresponding English idiom is 'winks knowingly,' to convey the insinuation that he could say much about a certain person if he so wished. A slanderer's mode of operation is more fully described in vi. 13f. (after Rashi).

biteth. Rather, 'compresseth'; the verb is employed in connection with the eyes in vi. 13, x. 10, a silent expression which, however, speaks more than words (after Metsudath David).

31 The hoary head is a crown of glory,
It is found in the way of righteousness.

32 He that is slow to anger is better than the mighty;
And he that ruleth his spirit than he that taketh a city.

33 The lot is cast into the lap;
But the whole disposing thereof is of the LORD.

31 עֲטֶרֶת תִּפְאֶרֶת שֵׂיבָה
בְּדֶרֶךְ צְדָקָה תִּמָּצֵא׃
32 טוֹב אֶרֶךְ אַפַּיִם מִגִּבּוֹר
וּמשֵׁל בְּרוּחוֹ מִלֹּכֵד עִיר׃
33 בַּחֵיק יוּטַל אֶת־הַגּוֹרָל
וּמֵיְהוָה כָּל־מִשְׁפָּטוֹ׃

bringeth evil to pass. Closer to the Hebrew would be the translation, consummates mischief.'

31 RIGHTEOUSNESS PROLONGS LIFE

a crown of glory. Length of days was a gift from God, bestowed as a reward for a life well spent. This is a cardinal doctrine of Proverbs. Also to be noted is the implied respect of the aged which was characteristic of the Hebrews in the Biblical era and which persisted later in Jewry. It is in striking contrast to the view which prevailed in early times when a man, whose prowess as a fighter or hunter waned with advancing years, was looked upon as an encumbrance and, by some tribes, removed by death. Scripture taught, *Thou shalt rise up before the hoary head, and honour the face of the old man* (Lev. xix. 32); and the Talmud (Nedarim 40a) has the aphorism, 'The building of the young is destruction, the destruction of the aged is building,' to teach that the opinion of the latter, based upon long experience of life, deserves the fullest consideration. A fine tribute to the wisdom of the old is paid in Ecclus. xxv. 4ff.

in the way of righteousness. Cf. xii. 28. Through righteousness, longevity is achieved (Rashi). Meiri explains: 'The hoary head is a crown of glory, *if* it is found in the way of righteousness.' The hoary head is a crown of glory only if it is found on one who demeans himself with righteousness and admirable character traits.

32 PRAISE OF SELF-CONTROL

The verse is quoted by a Rabbi of the first century, as the basis of his aphorism: 'Who is mighty? He who subdues his nature' (Aboth), exercises self-control.

better. i.e. superior, in that he possesses a quality which is superior to physical strength for the ultimate success of his endeavour (Gerondi).

ruleth his spirit. He is able to master himself, *spirit* denoting his temperament. Contrast xxv. 28 (Meiri).

33 GOD'S DIRECTION IN HUMAN AFFAIRS

lot. A method usually adopted in ancient Israel when in doubt to take a decision which, it was believed, would be directed by God (Daath Mikra).

lap. Fold in the garment (see on vi. 27), in which were deposited the two lots from which the selection was made (Daath Mikra).

disposing thereof. lit. its judgment,' decision as to which of the lots was chosen (Ralbag).

Better is a dry morsel and quietness therewith,
Than a house full of feasting with strife.

A servant that dealeth wisely shall have rule over a son that dealeth shamefully,
And shall have part of the inheritance among the brethren.

The refining pot is for silver, and the furnace for gold;
But the LORD trieth the hearts.

An evil-doer giveth heed to wicked lips;
And a liar giveth ear to a mischievous tongue.

1 טוֹב פַּת חֲרֵבָה וְשַׁלְוָה־בָהּ
מִבַּיִת מָלֵא זִבְחֵי־רִיב׃
2 עֶבֶד מַשְׂכִּיל יִמְשֹׁל בְּבֵן מֵבִישׁ
וּבְתוֹךְ אַחִים יַחֲלֹק נַחֲלָה׃
3 מַצְרֵף לַכֶּסֶף וְכוּר לַזָּהָב
וּבֹחֵן לִבּוֹת יְהוָה׃
4 מֵרַע מַקְשִׁיב עַל־שְׂפַת־אָוֶן
שֶׁקֶר מֵזִין עַל־לְשׁוֹן הַוֺּת׃

CHAPTER XVII

1 BLESSING OF A PEACEFUL HOMELIFE

A PARALLEL to xv. 16f. teaching the truth that a loveless home, however luxurious, is a place of misery.

feasting with strife. lit. 'sacrifices of strife.' Among the ancient Hebrews meat was not a customary article of diet; and when an animal was slain for a sacrifice and the flesh eaten by a family, it was thought of as a festive occasion (cf. Deut. xii. 7; 1 Sam. ix. 12f. and see above vii. 14). For a house to be abundantly supplied with meat was therefore a sign of wealth; but of what use was it when the feasting was marred by an atmosphere of contention? (see Daath Mikra).

2 ABILITY WINS APPRECIATION

servant. Better, 'slave.' An appreciative master might grant him freedom and include him among his heirs. During his lifetime he could show preference to a loyal and able slave, so that the latter was in a superior position to the sons (cf. the status of Eliezer in Abraham's house, Gen. xv. 2, xxiv. 2; of Ziba who became heir to Mephibosheth, 2 Sam. xvi. 4; and of Jarha who married his master's daughter, 1 Chron. ii. 34f.). That slaves had the opportunity of rising to affluence is noted in Eccles. x. 7, *I have seen servants* (slaves) *upon horses.*

have part of the inheritance. Only if the master so designates it, otherwise a slave was not entitled to inherit. Saadia Gaon writes. 'According to our tradition, one who has a bad son and wishes to transfer his property to a stranger, is permitted to do so.'

3 GOD TESTS CHARACTER

the refining . . . gold. Again xxvii. 21. Man possesses the ability to test silver and gold. So far as the human heart is concerned, the analogous power is possessed by God alone (Ralbag).

4 LISTENING TO SCANDAL DENOUNCED

and a liar . . . tongue. There is no *and* in the Hebrew and *liar* is 'falsehood.' The text should be translated: 'giving ear to falsehood upon a tongue of (i.e. working) destruction.' A Talmudic proverb declared, 'The third tongue (an idiom for 'slander') slays three: the speaker, the spoken to and the spoken of' (Arachin 15b). Most commentators, however, render as A.J.

5 **Whoso mocketh the poor blasphemeth his Maker;**
And he that is glad at calamity shall not be unpunished.

6 **Children's children are the crown of old men;**
And the glory of children are their fathers.

7 **Overbearing speech becometh not a churl;**
Much less do lying lips a prince.

8 **A gift is as a precious stone in the eyes of him that hath it:**
Whithersoever he turneth, he prospereth.

ה לֹעֵג לָרָשׁ חֵרֵף עֹשֵׂהוּ
שָׂמֵחַ לְאֵיד לֹא יִנָּקֶה׃
ו עֲטֶרֶת זְקֵנִים בְּנֵי בָנִים
וְתִפְאֶרֶת בָּנִים אֲבוֹתָם׃
ז לֹא־נָאוָה לְנָבָל שְׂפַת־יֶתֶר
אַף כִּי־לְנָדִיב שְׂפַת־שָׁקֶר׃
ח אֶבֶן־חֵן הַשֹּׁחַד בְּעֵינֵי בְעָלָיו
אֶל־כָּל־אֲשֶׁר יִפְנֶה יַשְׂכִּיל׃

5 REJOICE NOT AT ANOTHER'S MISFORTUNE

whoso mocketh . . . Maker. The underlying principle is similar to that expressed in the first clause of xiv. 31, but goes deeper since *the* LORD *maketh poor and maketh rich* (1 Sam. ii. 7), mocking at a man's poverty is in fact blasphemy (see Daath Mikra).

at calamity. At another's misfortune, similarly ordained by God (Metsudath David).

6 THE FAMILY CHAIN

The greatest blessing to the observant Jew is to see his children and grandchildren following the teachings of the Torah and adhering to his lifestyle. Similarly, children are proud of their fathers if they, too, observe the same rules the children were taught to observe. Rabbi Joseph Kimchi notes that Hezekiah did not pride himself in his father Ahaz, neither did he pride himself in his son Manasseh.

glory of children. [How eagerly a child boasts of his father if he has cause to! No words could present a more powerful incentive for a man to live honourably, that his children should have reason to be proud of him. While it is true that the Hebrew words are masculine in form, mother and daughter are probably included.]

7 WORDS ILL BEFITTING A SPEAKER

overbearing speech. lit. 'lips of excellence, superiority,' hence 'superior talk' (Rashi).

churl. The same Hebrew word as in *The fool hath said in his heart: There is no God* (Ps. xiv. 1). It denotes a person of depraved character (Metsudath Zion).

prince. Better, 'man of noble character' (Isaiah da Trani).

8 EFFICACY OF A BRIBE

While the general meaning of the verse is clear, there are ambiguities resulting from the laconic wording of the text. *Him that hath it* may imply the receiver or the giver, and the subject of the verbs can be the bribe or the person. One interpretation is: 'To the giver a bribe is the means whereby he gains his end' (Ibn Ezra). The best translation is: 'The bribe is a gem (which has) favour in the eyes of its receiver; it succeeds in all that it undertakes (lit. to all that it turns it succeeds)' (Ralbag). To give or receive a bribe is explicitly forbidden (Exod. xxiii. 8; Deut. xvi. 19), and, of course, the proverb does not commend it.

9 He that covereth a transgression seeketh love;
But he that harpeth on a matter estrangeth a familiar friend.

10 A rebuke entereth deeper into a man of understanding
Than a hundred stripes into a fool.

11 A rebellious man seeketh only evil;
Therefore a cruel messenger shall be sent against him.

12 Let a bear robbed of her whelps meet a man,
Rather than a fool in his folly.

9 מְכַסֶּה־פֶּשַׁע מְבַקֵּשׁ אַהֲבָה
וְשֹׁנֶה בְדָבָר מַפְרִיד אַלּוּף׃
10 תֵּחַת גְּעָרָה בְמֵבִין
מֵהַכּוֹת כְּסִיל מֵאָה׃
11 אַךְ־מְרִי יְבַקֶּשׁ־רָע
וּמַלְאָךְ אַכְזָרִי יְשֻׁלַּח־בּוֹ׃
12 פָּגוֹשׁ דֹּב שַׁכּוּל בְּאִישׁ
וְאַל־כְּסִיל בְּאִוַּלְתּוֹ׃

9 OVERLOOK A FAULT AND RETAIN A FRIEND

covereth. Keeps silent about and does not indulge in recrimination (Rashi).

seeketh love. Promotes friendship. The guilty party will be well disposed towards him because of his forbearance (Rashi).

harpeth on a matter. i.e. repeatedly talks about the wrong which had been done (Rashi and most modern expositers). An alternative is: 'and repeateth the matter' (Ibn Ezra). If the wrongdoer takes advantage of the other man's silence and repeats the offence, he is responsible for the severing of friendship because the repetition will be resented.

10 THE WISE HEED CORRECTION

a man of understanding. This expression denotes a man who is both willing and able to understand, not to be confused with *nabon,* a man of discernment, which denotes a man who possesses a high degree of wisdom to the extent that he is able to make deductions from what he has learned. Such a person does not require a rebuke (Gerondi).

than . . . fool. lit. 'than striking a fool a hundred (strokes)'; *hundred* stands for a large number (Ibn Nachmiash). The fool is not interested in words of wisdom, only in gratifying his lusts (cf. xviii. 2), just the opposite of the man of understanding. Consequently, the only remedy for him is stripes (Gerondi).

11 REBELLION PUNISHED

a rebellious man. Hebrew 'rebellion,' but the abstract noun is so interpreted by most commentators. Saadia Gaon also refers the verse to a revolt against civil authority, but most commentators interpret it as rebellion against God, for sin is open defiance of the Divine Kingship (see on xiv. 2). Gerondi refers: 'Only rebellion (against God) doth a wicked man seek, but a stern messenger shall be sent against him.' Such a revolt does not go unpunished. For *messenger* as a symbol of the medium of retribution, cf. xvi. 14; Ps. lxxviii. 49.

12 A FOOL IS DANGEROUS

bear. Whereas this animal is now a rarity in Palestine, it must have been common in ancient times. From such passages as 2 Sam. xvii. 8; Hoea xiii. 8; Amos v. 19 it is seen that the bear's dangerous character, particularly when bereft of its young, had become proverbial (Ibn Nachmiash, Metsudath David, Daath Mikra).

13 Whoso rewardeth evil for good,
Evil shall not depart from his house.

14 The beginning of strife is as when one letteth out water;
Therefore leave off contention, before the quarrel break out.

15 He that justifieth the wicked, and he that condemneth the righteous,
Even they both are an abomination to the LORD.

16 Wherefore is there a price in the hand of a fool
To buy wisdom, seeing he hath no understanding?

13 מֵשִׁיב רָעָה תַּחַת טוֹבָה
לֹא־תָמִישׁ רָעָה מִבֵּיתוֹ׃
14 פּוֹטֵר מַיִם רֵאשִׁית מָדוֹן
וְלִפְנֵי הִתְגַּלַּע הָרִיב נְטוֹשׁ׃
15 מַצְדִּיק רָשָׁע וּמַרְשִׁיעַ צַדִּיק
תּוֹעֲבַת יְהוָה גַּם־שְׁנֵיהֶם׃
16 לָמָּה־זֶּה מְחִיר בְּיַד־כְּסִיל
לִקְנוֹת חָכְמָה וְלֶב־אָיִן׃

v. 13. תמוש ק׳

13 INGRATITUDE MEETS WITH PUNISHMENT

evil shall not depart. The cause may be God's visitation; but Ralbag and Metsudath David see in the clause the natural consequence of such base conduct, viz. he arouses the contempt of his fellows so that when he is in trouble nobody will come to his aid. For the admonition to return good for evil, cf. xx. 22, xxv. 21.

14 STOP A QUARREL IN ITS EARLY STAGE

While the general import and imagery of the verse are clear, the exact translation of the text is not certain. A quarrel begins like a small hole in a reservoir, letting out a tiny trickle. But if it is not stopped, the hole is enlarged and a flood pours through. A corresponding Talmudic proverb is, 'Strife is like the aperture of a leakage; as the aperture widens so the stream of water increases.'

the beginning . . . water. lit. 'he who lets out water (so is) the beginning of strife.'

leave off . . . break out. lit. 'before it bursts forth, abandon the contention,' or, 'before the contention bursts forth, desist.'

15 GOD ABHORS UNJUST JUDGES

Based on Exod. xxiii. 6f. (see on xvi. 11).

16 WISDOM INACCESSIBLE TO A FOOL

a price. [No deduction is to be drawn that fees were then paid for instruction. Such a practice is unknown in Jewry down to the Middle Ages; and when owing to economic necessity, some teachers began to charge a fee, the innovation was frowned upon by the majority. Ben Sira exhorted, 'Get her (instruction) for yourselves without money' (Ecclus. li. 25), and the Talmudic principle was 'As I (God) taught you gratuitously, so must you teach gratuitously.' Therefore the language of the verse has to be taken figuratively. A person evidences keen desire for an object by his willingness to pay in full the price demanded.] So, should a fool, as it were, hold out his hand containing the money, i.e. display an eager longing, to acquire wisdom, it would be useless. He does not possess the qualities of mind and character without which instruction cannot be gained (Gerondi).

A friend loveth at all times,
And a brother is born for adversity.

17 בְּכָל־עֵת אֹהֵב הָרֵעַ
וְאָח לְצָרָה יִוָּלֵד׃

A man void of understanding is he that striketh hands,
And becometh surety in the presence of his neighbour.

18 אָדָם חֲסַר־לֵב תֹּקֵעַ כָּף
עֹרֵב עֲרֻבָּה לִפְנֵי רֵעֵהוּ׃

He loveth transgression that loveth strife;
He that exalteth his gate seeketh destruction.

19 אֹהֵב פֶּשַׁע אֹהֵב מַצָּה
מַגְבִּיהַּ פִּתְחוֹ מְבַקֶּשׁ־שָׁבֶר׃

He that hath a froward heart findeth no good;
And he that hath a perverse tongue falleth into evil.

20 עִקֶּשׁ־לֵב לֹא יִמְצָא־טוֹב
וְנֶהְפָּךְ בִּלְשׁוֹנוֹ יִפּוֹל בְּרָעָה׃

17 TRUE FRIENDSHIP

a friend. i.e. a genuine friend (Meiri).

loveth. This follows Meiri. Rashi, however, renders: 'Always love (to acquire) friends. And he is born as a brother in time of adversity.' Ibn Ezra renders: 'At all times one loves his friend, but a brother loves only when adversity develops.' Ralbag elaborates on this interpretation. A friend will join his friend at all times, even in times of adversity in order to join him in times of joy. A brother, however, does not care to join his brother in times of joy, but in times of adversity, his nature compels him to join him to assist him in his straits.

at all times. In adversity as well as prosperity (Meiri).

a brother. Synonym for a true friend. David called Jonathan *my brother* (2 Sam. i. 26), and Solomon used the word in connection with his friend Hiram of Tyre (1 Kings ix. 13) (after R.J. Kimchi).

18 FOLLY OF STANDING SURETY

striketh hands. Cf. vi. 1, xi. 15.

becometh surety. lit. 'guaranteeing a guarantee.'

19 EVILS OF QUARRELSOMENESS AND OSTENTATION

transgression. Not a sin against God but a wrong to a neighbour (Rashi). For this use of the word, cf. verse 9. A quarrelsome man is a person who finds pleasure in offending his neighbour (Malbim).

his gate. lit. 'his opening' which the Jewish commentators apply to the mouth (cf. Ps. cxix. 130), understanding the phrase as 'talking big, in loud and arrogant language.' Another explanation is: living in an ostentatious manner which attracts envious attention and can easily be the cause of ruin (Ibn Caspi). The LXX renders: 'who makes his house high,' i.e. conspicuous.

20 EVILS OF A WICKED MIND AND TONGUE

he that hath a froward heart. lit. 'he who is crooked of heart,' has a warped mind and cannot think straight (Gerondi).

findeth no good. [Experiences hardship and misfortune, because he creates antagonism.]

he that hath a perverse tongue. lit. 'he who is turned (perverse) in his tongue,' who speaks lies (Ibn Nachmiash).

21 He that begetteth a fool doeth it to his sorrow;
And the father of a churl hath no joy.

22 A merry heart is a good medicine;
But a broken spirit drieth the bones.

23 A wicked man taketh a gift out of the bosom,
To pervert the ways of justice.

24 Wisdom is before him that hath understanding;
But the eyes of a fool are in the ends of the earth.

25 A foolish son is vexation to his father,
And bitterness to her that bore him.

יֹלֵד כְּסִיל לְתוּגָה לוֹ
וְלֹא יִשְׂמַח אֲבִי נָבָל׃
לֵב שָׂמֵחַ יֵיטִב גֵּהָה
וְרוּחַ נְכֵאָה תְּיַבֶּשׁ־גָּרֶם׃
שֹׁחַד מֵחֵיק רָשָׁע יִקָּח
לְהַטּוֹת אָרְחוֹת מִשְׁפָּט׃
אֶת־פְּנֵי מֵבִין חָכְמָה
וְעֵינֵי כְסִיל בִּקְצֵה־אָרֶץ׃
כַּעַס לְאָבִיו בֵּן כְּסִיל
וּמֶמֶר לְיוֹלַדְתּוֹ׃

21 PARENTS' DISTRESS OVER BAD CHILDREN

a fool. A child backward in character (Gerondi).

sorrow. Translated *grief* in x. 1.

22 BENEFICIAL EFFECT OF CHEERFULNESS

a merry heart. Cf. xv. 13.

is a good medicine. The noun occurs nowhere else, and the translation is based on the use of the verb in Hosea v. 13, *neither shall he cure you of your wound* (so Ibn Ezra). Rashi gives it the meaning, 'face,' which some modern commentators defend by connecting it with a similar word in Arabic. In that case, it is synonymous with the common word, *panim,* as in xv. 13. Saadia Gaon and Ibn Ganah, too, interpret in this manner.

broken spirit. Depression.

drieth. Converse of *maketh the bones fat* (xv. 30) (Daath Mikra).

bones. The body. The verse deals with the physical effects of a cheerful disposition and its opposite (Ralbag).

23 BRIBERY

wicked man. The commentators explain this as a venal judge. [It may also be a man who is prepared to commit perjury if paid to do so.]

gift. Bribe.

out of the bosom. See on vi. 27. The perverter of justice accepts a bribe from the pocket of one of the men involved in a lawsuit. We may read into the phrase the furtive manner in which the bribe is given and received; it is handed over secretly (Rashi, Meiri).

24 CONCENTRATION OF THE WISE

is before him. He has the gaining of wisdom as his constant purpose; he learns from everyone (Ibn Ezra, Metsudath David), or, he sees wisdom in everything around him (Ralbag).

in the ends of the earth. Only there will he find wisdom, and he is too lazy to seek it (Ralbag). Ibn Ezra explains that he wishes to travel far away to seek wisdom, thereby angering his father, as in the following verse.

26 To punish also the righteous is not good,
Nor to strike the noble for their uprightness.

27 He that spareth his words hath knowledge;
And he that husbandeth his spirit is a man of discernment.

28 Even a fool, when he holdeth his peace, is counted wise;
And he that shutteth his lips is esteemed as a man of understanding.

26 גַּם עֲנוֹשׁ לַצַּדִּיק לֹא־טוֹב
לְהַכּוֹת נְדִיבִים עַל־יֹשֶׁר׃
27 חוֹשֵׂךְ אֲמָרָיו יוֹדֵעַ דָּעַת
וְקַר־רוּחַ אִישׁ תְּבוּנָה׃
28 גַּם אֱוִיל מַחֲרִישׁ חָכָם יֵחָשֵׁב
אֹטֵם שְׂפָתָיו נָבוֹן׃

v. 27. יקר ק׳

26 INJUSTICE

In this verse the difficulty for the commentators has been the initial conjunction *gam,* 'also,' which they find difficult to explain. Saadia Gaon explains: 'Not only is slaying a righteous man evil, but even punishing him with fines or stripes is also not good.' This is suggested also by Ibn Nachmiash. Others explain: 'One who is not good punishes even the righteous and will also strike the noble for their uprightness' (Ralbag, Metsudath David). The Rabbis (Ber. 7a) explain: 'It is not good even for a righteous man to punish, nor for nobles, although it is for uprightness.' Should one sin against a righteous man, it is not proper for him to pray to God to avenge him, neither is it proper for the nobles to pray that their offenders be punished although it is justified. They should instead forgive them and forbear to retaliate (Ibn Nachmiash).

punish. The verb specifically has the meaning 'to fine' in Deut. xxii. 19 (Saadia Gaon).

not good. An improper procedure (Ibn Nachmiash).

strike. A more severe form of judicial punishment than a fine (Saadia Gaon).

27–28 VIRTUE OF RIGHT SPEECH AND SILENCE

27. *spareth his words.* Same verb as in *refraineth his lips* (x. 19), and a better rendering is: 'restraineth his words,' not to offend. The admonition is against loquacity (all commentaries).

hath knowledge. [lit. 'knows knowledge,' displays a possession of knowledge, good sense.]

and he that husbandeth his spirit. The *kethib* means, 'and he who is cool of spirit,' self-controlled and cautious in his speech (Daath Mikra). The *kerë* is literally 'he who is rare of spirit,' of dignified bearing, which enables him to keep a curb on his tongue (Metsudath David).

28. *is counted wise.* More lit. 'may be thought to be a wise man,' his silence being taken as evidence of a profound man. Saadia Gaon notes that if one is silent, he should be judged as a wise man until his foolishness is proven. The Rabbis state: 'Silence is good for the wise, surely for the foolish' (Yerushalmi Pesahim ch. 9). Gerondi sees this verse as advice to the foolish to keep their peace and listen to the wise. Eventually, they too will gain wisdom.

1 He that separateth himself seeketh his own desire,
And snarleth against all sound wisdom.

2 A fool hath no delight in understanding,
But only that his heart may lay itself bare.

3 When the wicked cometh, there cometh also contempt,
And with ignominy reproach.

4 The words of a man's mouth are as deep waters;
A flowing brook, a fountain of wisdom.

1 לְתַאֲוָה יְבַקֵּשׁ נִפְרָד
בְּכָל־תּוּשִׁיָּה יִתְגַּלָּע׃
2 לֹא־יַחְפֹּץ כְּסִיל בִּתְבוּנָה
כִּי אִם־בְּהִתְגַּלּוֹת לִבּוֹ׃
3 בְּבוֹא־רָשָׁע בָּא גַם־בּוּז
וְעִם־קָלוֹן חֶרְפָּה׃
4 מַיִם עֲמֻקִּים דִּבְרֵי פִי־אִישׁ
נַחַל נֹבֵעַ מְקוֹר חָכְמָה׃

CHAPTER XVIII

1 CENSURE OF SEPARATISM

THE moral of the verse is not certain. Rashi applies it to a man who separates himself from God to rebel against the laws of wisdom; Ibn Ezra to one who leaves his family in search of wisdom. It is best to interpret the sentence as an anticipation of Hillel's aphorism, 'Separate not thyself from the community' (Aboth 2.5).

separateth himself. From adopting the will of the majority among whom he lives (Saadia Gaon, Ibn Nachmiash).

his own desire. Which may well be contrary to the common good. He refuses to subordinate his own purposes to civic or national ends (Saadia Gaon, Ibn Nachmiash).

and snarleth against. Better 'he breaketh out'; the same verb as in xvii. 14 (Daath Mikra).

2 THE FOOL'S EGOTISM

a fool . . . understanding. He has no wish to possess the faculty of distinguishing between the true and the false (Metsudath David).

his heart . . . bare. i.e. to disclose his own mind and air his personal opinions, although these are based on nothing else than his stupidity. To him the views he holds are unquestionably right (Metsudath David).

3 DISTURBING EFFECT OF THE WICKED

and with ignominy reproach. Better, 'and with disdain (cometh) provocation.' The disdainful way in which he treats his neighbours provokes resentment. The Hebrew *cherpah* signifies a 'reproach' directed to a person, 'disgrace,' or directed by a person, 'provocation' (see Ibn Nachmiash).

4 COMMON AND WISE SPEECH

Most expositors assume that the man referred to is a sage and the verse describes his talk in a series of similes. But his qualification as a wise person would certainly have been explicitly mentioned if his characteristic were the subject of the proverb. Without specification, *ish* must be taken to mean an ordinary, average, man.

It is not good to respect the person of the wicked,
So as to turn aside the righteous in judgment.

5 שְׂאֵת פְּנֵי־רָשָׁע לֹא־טוֹב
לְהַטּוֹת צַדִּיק בַּמִּשְׁפָּט׃

A fool's lips enter into contention,
And his mouth calleth for strokes.

6 שִׂפְתֵי כְסִיל יָבֹאוּ בְרִיב
וּפִיו לְמַהֲלֻמוֹת יִקְרָא׃

A fool's mouth is his ruin,
And his lips are the snare of his soul.

7 פִּי־כְסִיל מְחִתָּה־לוֹ
וּשְׂפָתָיו מוֹקֵשׁ נַפְשׁוֹ׃

The words of a whisperer are as dainty morsels,
And they go down into the innermost parts of the belly.

8 דִּבְרֵי נִרְגָּן כְּמִתְלַהֲמִים
וְהֵם יָרְדוּ חַדְרֵי־בָטֶן׃

are as deep waters. As water lying far underground is only reached and drawn up with much effort, so the words of an ordinary man are normally expressed in obscure and incoherent language which can only be understood with difficulty.

a flowing . . . wisdom. Translate: '(but) a fountain of wisdom is a flowing brook.' With the greatest ease one is able to drink from a stream, and as easily understood is the flow of language from a man who is *a fountain of wisdom* (Daath Mikra, footnote).

5 PERVERSION OF JUSTICE

not good. Cf. xvii. 26.

respect the person. lit. 'lift up the face,' an idiom for 'show favour to.'

wicked. The guilty party in a suit (Ibn Ezra).

righteous. The innocent party (Ibn Ezra).

6–8 FOOLISH AND SLANDEROUS TALK

6. *enter into contention.* Lead him to strife, i.e. a personal quarrel (Metsudath David).

calleth for. Invites, brings upon the speaker (Metsudath David).

strokes. Only again xix. 29, *stripes.* From the same root the word for 'hammer' is derived. It can denote blows from the offended person or scourging by order of the court. However, all commentators, adopt the former interpretation.

7. The same thought as in the preceding verse.

the snare of his soul. [A snare to himself, involving him in trouble.]

8. Repeated in xxvi. 22.

whisperer. Slanderer, as in xvi. 28.

dainty morsels. From a root meaning 'to swallow greedily.' Slander is eagerly gulped down by a person disposed to listen to it, as a glutton helps himself freely to tempting food (see Ibn Ganah).

go down . . . belly. The slanderous words do not make a superficial impression, but penetrate into the innermost recesses of the listener where they are thoroughly digested (Ibn Ganah).

9 Even one that is slack in his work
Is brother to him that is a destroyer.

10 The name of the LORD is a strong tower:
The righteous runneth into it, and is set up on high.

11 The rich man's wealth is his strong city,
And as a high wall in his own conceit.

12 Before destruction the heart of a man is haughty,
And before honour goeth humility.

13 He that giveth answer before he heareth,
It is folly and confusion unto him.

9 גַּם מִתְרַפֶּה בִמְלַאכְתּוֹ
אָח הוּא לְבַעַל מַשְׁחִית׃
10 מִגְדַּל־עֹז שֵׁם יְהוָה
בּוֹ־יָרוּץ צַדִּיק וְנִשְׂגָּב׃
11 הוֹן עָשִׁיר קִרְיַת עֻזּוֹ
וּכְחוֹמָה נִשְׂגָּבָה בְּמַשְׂכִּתוֹ׃
12 לִפְנֵי־שֶׁבֶר יִגְבַּהּ לֵב־אִישׁ
וְלִפְנֵי כָבוֹד עֲנָוָה׃
13 מֵשִׁיב דָּבָר בְּטֶרֶם יִשְׁמָע
אִוֶּלֶת הִיא־לוֹ וּכְלִמָּה׃

9 DESTRUCTIVE POWER OF IDLENESS

brother. Is similar to, in the same class as. In xxviii. 24 *companion* is employed in this sense (Targum, Malbim).

him that is a destroyer. lit. 'an owner destroying (his property).' A workman who is slack in his work ruins his livelihood exactly as a landowner reduces himself to poverty if he neglects his land (Isaiah da Trani).

10 GOD A SURE REFUGE

name of the LORD. Mention of God's name in prayer (Gerondi). For the Divine name as a protection, cf. Ps. xx. 8.

set up on high. So as to be inaccessible to the dangers that threaten below (after Kimchi).

11 PROTECTION AFFORDED BY WEALTH

and as a high . . . conceit. Translate: 'but it is like a high wall in his imagination.' The first clause has a different intention here. In the other passage it stated the fact of the advantages which the wealthy enjoyed; in this verse, which should be linked to the preceding, it receives a qualification. The advantages may be illusory if riches are put to a bad use. The protection they afford the wrongdoer is only like *a high wall* in his own estimation. It can be readily demolished by God Who alone is the sure refuge (Ralbag).

12 PRIDE PRECEDES A FALL

before destruction. Cf. the first clause of xvi. 18.

13 LISTEN BEFORE ANSWERING

heareth. i.e. hears the complete statement and understands its import (Gerondi, Ibn Nachmiash).

confusion. Or, 'shame.' His action exposes his want of wisdom. With the moral, cf. 'Answer not before thou hast heard, and interrupt not in the midst of speech' (Ecclus. xi. 8). A characteristic of the wise man is, he 'does not break in upon the speech of his fellow, and is not hasty to answer' (Aboth 5.9).

14 The spirit of a man will sustain his infirmity;
But a broken spirit who can bear?

14 רוּחַ־אִישׁ יְכַלְכֵּל מַחֲלֵהוּ
וְרוּחַ נְכֵאָה מִי יִשָּׂאֶנָּה׃

15 The heart of the prudent getteth knowledge;
And the ear of the wise seeketh knowledge.

15 לֵב נָבוֹן יִקְנֶה־דָּעַת
וְאֹזֶן חֲכָמִים תְּבַקֶּשׁ־דָּעַת׃

16 A man's gift maketh room for him,
And bringeth him before great men.

16 מַתָּן אָדָם יַרְחִיב לוֹ
וְלִפְנֵי גְדֹלִים יַנְחֶנּוּ׃

17 He that pleadeth his cause first seemeth just;
But his neighbour cometh and searcheth him out.

17 צַדִּיק הָרִאשׁוֹן בְּרִיבוֹ
יָבֹא רֵעֵהוּ וַחֲקָרוֹ׃

v. 17. ובא ק׳

14 POWER OF THE WILL TO SUSTAIN

spirit. Will-power and determination can counterbalance physical weakness and enable a man to win through (Rashi).

broken spirit. But when the will-power is undermined, a man cannot endure. He must succumb and suffer defeat (Metsudath David).

15 TWO TYPES OF STUDENT

heart of the prudent. The Hebrew is the same as in *the heart of him that hath discernment seeketh knowledge* (xv. 14). This clause refers to the person with a keen intellect who has the capacity to pursue his studies independently and make his own deductions (Metsudath David).

wise. He is the learner who gains knowledge by listening to teachers. Hence in his case the *ear* is mentioned. This is the explanation of Metsudath David which is more probable than the one accepted by most moderns, viz. both the inner and outer organs of perception (heart and ear) are to be utilized by searchers after wisdom.

16 MONEY SMOOTHES THE WAY

gift. Not necessarily a bribe (Ibn Ezra); it might be a present in cash or kind given to persons of influence by a man who needs their help to achieve his purpose (Metsudath David, Ralbag).

maketh room for him. lit. 'enlarges (the path) for him,' so that it is easier for him to walk along it and reach his goal (Metsudath David, Ralbag).

before great men. Whose patronage is desired. This may be interpreted as general advice to people who need patronage of dignitaries, or an allusion to the benefit of giving charity (Meiri).

17 HEAR BOTH SIDES

seemeth just. The plaintiff who states his case first puts forward every point which tells in his favour. When he finishes, it looks as though he must be in the right (Metsudath David).

neighbour. The defendant (Meiri).

searcheth him out. Or, 'searcheth it out,' viz. the other's case. He brings evidence which casts doubts upon the first statement. The judges must therefore not come to a conclusion until both sides are heard (Meiri, Isaiah da Trani).

18 The lot causeth strife to cease,
And parteth asunder the contentious.

19 A brother offended is harder to be won than a strong city;
And their contentions are like the bars of a castle.

20 A man's belly shall be filled with the fruit of his mouth;
With the increase of his lips shall he be satisfied.

21 Death and life are in the power of the tongue;
And they that indulge it shall eat the fruit thereof.

18 מִדְיָנִים יַשְׁבִּית הַגּוֹרָל
וּבֵין עֲצוּמִים יַפְרִיד׃
19 אָח נִפְשָׁע מִקִּרְיַת־עֹז
וּמִדוֹנִים כִּבְרִיחַ אַרְמוֹן׃
20 מִפְּרִי פִי־אִישׁ תִּשְׂבַּע בִּטְנוֹ
תְּבוּאַת שְׂפָתָיו יִשְׂבָּע׃
21 מָוֶת וְחַיִּים בְּיַד־לָשׁוֹן
וְאֹהֲבֶיהָ יֹאכַל פִּרְיָהּ׃

v. 19. ומדינים ק'

18 DECISION BY LOT

lot. In cases of contention over the division of estates or partnerships, dividing by lot can cause the strife to cease (Ralbag, Metsudath David).

parteth asunder. So that harmony is restored between them (Metsudath David).

the contentious. lit. 'the strong,' those who stand firm with their claims (Metsudath David).

parteth asunder. So that harmony is restored between them (Metsudath David).

19 WHEN BROTHERS FALL OUT

The Hebrew is lit. 'a brother transgressed against than a strong city, and contentions like the bar of a castle.' A.J., which adopts A.V. and R.V., gives the general sense. The closer the kinship the more bitter the enmity between them if it occurs and the harder to reconcile them. It is more difficult to assuage their mutual animosity than to storm a citadel, and their quarrel creates a barrier to the restoration of friendly relations as formidable as the iron bars to be found in a fortress (Ibn Caspi, J. Kimchi, Isaiah da Trani).

20–21 CONSEQUENCES OF SPEECH

20. Cf. xii. 14, xiii. 2.

a man's . . . mouth. A figurative way of saying that a man has to bear the responsibility for what his mouth utters (Metsudath David).

shall he be satisfied. Rather, 'shall he be filled,' the verb being the same as in the first clause.

21. *death and life.* Cf. 'Good and evil, life and death; and that which ruleth over them continually is the tongue' (Ecclus. xxxvii. 18). Cautious speech may preserve life as rash talk can imperil it (Ibn Ezra).

they that indulge it. lit. 'they that love it,' are prone to make use of this delicate instrument (Metsudath David).

shall eat the fruit thereof. Must take the consequences of the way in which they employ the tongue (Metsudath David).

Whoso findeth a wife findeth a great good,
And obtaineth favour of the LORD.

22 מָצָא אִשָּׁה מָצָא טוֹב
וַיָּפֶק רָצוֹן מֵיְהוָה׃

The poor useth entreaties,
But the rich answereth impudently.

23 תַּחֲנוּנִים יְדַבֶּר־רָשׁ
וְעָשִׁיר יַעֲנֶה עַזּוֹת׃

There are friends that one hath to his own hurt;
But there is a friend that sticketh closer than a brother.

24 אִישׁ רֵעִים לְהִתְרוֹעֵעַ
וְיֵשׁ אֹהֵב דָּבֵק מֵאָח׃

22 A GOOD WIFE

findeth. lit. 'hath found.'

a wife. The context makes it clear that a *good* wife is meant (Rashi and others), and the adjective is included in the ancient Versions but not in M.T. or Targum.

a great good. Hebrew 'good,' an asset, an aid to his material and moral advancement (cf. 'Happy is the husband of a good wife; the number of his days shall be twofold' Ecclus. xxvi. 1).

obtaineth favour of the LORD. The same phrase as used of acquiring wisdom (viii. 35; cf. 'A good wife is a good portion; she shall be given in the portion of such as fear the Lord,' Ecclus. xxvi. 3). The Talmud (Berachoth 8a) records, 'In the West (i.e. Palestine) when a man took to himsef a wife, people used to ask him *matsa* or *motsë?*' The key to the question is the two Biblical passages, 'Whoso hath found *(matsa)* a wife hath found good' and 'I find *(motsë)* woman more bitter than death' (Eccles. vii. 26).

23 TONE OF THE POOR AND RICH

impudently. Or, 'roughly.' The writer decries the fact that both poverty and wealth have grave drawbacks. Poverty gives one excessive humility, so that he speaks with entreaties. Wealth too is likely to bring a person to speak roughly (Ibn Nachmiash). Rashi explains that the verse teaches manners, that although the rich answer impudently, the poor man must use entreaties.

24 TWO TYPES OF FRIENDS

there are friends. The first word, *ish,* means 'a man,' and the phrase 'a man of friends' signifies one who indiscriminately multiplies his friends. A.J. is based on the supposition that, as in 2 Sam. xiv. 19 and Micah vi. 10, *ish* is a variant of *yesh,* 'there is (are),' and it is so construed by the Targum.

that one hath to his own hurt. The verb may be derived from two roots: (1) 'to associate with,' and then the sense is 'to act as companions one to another.' This type of friendship is referred to in the passage, 'There is a friend that is a companion at the table, and he will not continue in the day of thy affliction' (Ecclus. vi. 10). (2) 'to break,' which gives to the text the meaning 'to break one another,' i.e. they pretend a friendship but do not scruple to do harm to one another if it is to their personal advantage. Classical commentators adopt the first alternative, which is to be preferred.

friend. Hebrew 'lover,' a genuine friend.

1 Better is the poor that walketh
in his integrity
Than he that is perverse in his lips
and a fool at the same time.

2 Also, that the soul be without
knowledge is not good;
And he that hasteth with his feet
sinneth.

3 The foolishness of man perverteth
his way;
And his heart fretteth against the
Lord.

4 Wealth addeth many friends;
But as for the poor, his friend
separateth himself from him.

1 טוֹב רָשׁ הוֹלֵךְ בְּתֻמּוֹ
מֵעִקֵּשׁ שְׂפָתָיו וְהוּא כְסִיל׃
2 גַּם בְּלֹא־דַעַת נֶפֶשׁ לֹא־טוֹב
וְאָץ בְּרַגְלַיִם חוֹטֵא׃
3 אִוֶּלֶת אָדָם תְּסַלֵּף דַּרְכּוֹ
וְעַל־יְהוָה יִזְעַף לִבּוֹ׃
4 הוֹן יֹסִיף רֵעִים רַבִּים
וְדָל מֵרֵעֵהוּ יִפָּרֵד׃

CHAPTER XIX

1 HONESTY IN POVERTY

The first clause reappears in xxviii. 6 where it is followed by, *than he that is perverse in his ways, though he be rich.* All modern expositors assume that in this verse *fool* means 'a rich fool,' and some alter the word to 'rich' to obtain the required contrast. But the two verses teach different lessons. Here the point is: better is a poor man who is contented to remain poor and retain his integrity, than a person who tries to escape from poverty by resorting to a dishonest life; because the latter is a fool to imagine that by evil methods he can truly prosper. Either he will be found out and suffer punishment, or God will thwart his plans. Translate: 'than he who is perverse in his lips, since he is a fool.' This follows Metsudath David.

2 AIMLESS AND PRECIPITOUS ACTION

The conjunction *gam,* 'also,' has the same purpose as in xvii. 26, to introduce an argument from the less to the greater. Translate: 'If (to act) without knowledge of desire (lit. soul) is not good, (how much more) does one who hastens with his feet miss the mark!' A comparison is drawn between two reprehensible lines of action. The first has no definite purpose in view, and the second illustrates the saying 'more haste, less speed.' The verb *chata,* 'to sin,' has here the original meaning of shooting at a target and missing it (cf. viii. 36) (Gerondi).

3 BLAMING GOD FOR ONE'S FAILURE

fretteth. Better, 'is sullen.' He has a grievance against God for his failure, whereas the cause lies in his own folly (Metsudath David). Ecclus. xv. 11f. similarly exhorts, 'Say not thou, It is through the Lord that I fell away,' ascribing to Him the cause of a man's lapse into sin.

4 FRIENDS IN WEALTH AND POVERTY

his friend. The singular is to be noted as compared with the *friends* of the rich: the poor man's only friend cools towards him. A.V. 'but the poor is separated from his friend' is a possible translation.

A false witness shall not be unpunished;
And he that breatheth forth lies shall not escape.

5 עֵד שְׁקָרִים לֹא יִנָּקֶה
וְיָפִיחַ כְּזָבִים לֹא יִמָּלֵט׃

Many will entreat the favour of the liberal man;
And every man is a friend to him that giveth gifts.

6 רַבִּים יְחַלּוּ פְנֵי־נָדִיב
וְכָל־הָרֵעַ לְאִישׁ מַתָּן׃

All the brethren of the poor do hate him;
How much more do his friends go far from him!
He that pursueth words, they turn against him.

7 כָּל אֲחֵי־רָשׁ ׀ שְׂנֵאֻהוּ
אַף כִּי מְרֵעֵהוּ רָחֲקוּ מִמֶּנּוּ
מְרַדֵּף אֲמָרִים לֹא־הֵמָּה׃

He that getteth wisdom loveth his own soul;
He that keepeth understanding shall find good.

8 קֹנֶה־לֵּב אֹהֵב נַפְשׁוֹ
שֹׁמֵר תְּבוּנָה לִמְצֹא־טוֹב׃

לו ק׳ v. 7.

5 A PERJURER DOES NOT ESCAPE

Almost identical with verse 9.

6 GIFTS SECURE ADHERENTS

entreat the favour. lit. 'smooth the face,' ingratiate themselves with.

him that giveth gifts. lit. 'a man of gift.' This is the advantage of wealth over poverty (Ralbag). The Rabbis interpret this verse as referring to a charitable man (Rashi).

7 ESTRANGEMENT CAUSED BY POVERTY

brethren. They who are connected with him by ties of blood-relationship (Rashi).

hate him. Because of his repeated requests for help (Ibn Nachmiash).

friends. Who have not the blood-tie with its normally strong appeal (Ibn Nachmiash).

he . . . against him. This is the only verse in the central section of Proverbs which has three clauses and the sentence is complete without these words. The problem of translation is complicated by the variant which occurs. The *kerē* is literally 'he pursues (them with) sayings, they are his'; although kinsmen and friends desert him, he persists in advancing claims upon them on the ground of relationship or friendship (Malbim). The *kethib* means, 'he pursues (them with) sayings, they are not'; he urges his demands, but they are no longer there to listen, having abandoned him (Isaiah da Trani, Ibn Nachmiash, Ibn Ezra).

8 ADVANTAGE OF INTELLIGENCE

loveth his own soul. Best explained as: has the desire to make the most of his capabilities and get the best out of life (Ralbag).

keepeth understanding. Lest he forget it (Metsudath David, Gerondi).

shall find good. lit. 'to find good'; [the phrase may be governed by *loveth* in the first clause,] or it equals 'is the way to find good' (Metsudath David). *Good* is here employed with a material, not ethical, connotation, but it may also include the reward in the hereafter (Ibn Ezra).

9 A false witness shall not be unpunished;
And he that breatheth forth lies shall perish.

עֵד שְׁקָרִים לֹא יִנָּקֶה 9
וְיָפִיחַ כְּזָבִים יֹאבֵד׃

10 Luxury is not seemly for a fool;
Much less for a servant to have rule over princes.

לֹא־נָאוֶה לִכְסִיל תַּעֲנוּג 10
אַף כִּי־לְעֶבֶד ׀ מְשֹׁל בְּשָׂרִים׃

11 It is the discretion of a man to be slow to anger,
And it is his glory to pass over a transgression.

שֵׂכֶל אָדָם הֶאֱרִיךְ אַפּוֹ 11
וְתִפְאַרְתּוֹ עֲבֹר עַל־פָּשַׁע׃

12 The king's wrath is as the roaring of a lion;
But his favour is as dew upon the grass.

נַהַם כַּכְּפִיר זַעַף מֶלֶךְ 12
וּכְטַל עַל־עֵשֶׂב רְצוֹנוֹ׃

13 A foolish son is the calamity of his father;
And the contentions of a wife are a continual dropping.

הַוֺּת לְאָבִיו בֵּן כְּסִיל 13
וְדֶלֶף טֹרֵד מִדְיְנֵי אִשָּׁה׃

9 A PERJURER IS PUNISHED

Same as verse 5 with the substitution of the stronger verb *shall perish* for *shall not escape*.

10 LUXURY ILL BECOMES A FOOL

is not seemly. Rather, 'is not befitting.' The effect of luxurious living would be to confirm the fool in his folly and make him brutish in his habits (Metsudath David).

for a servant . . . princes. Because it usually happened that he proceeds from one extreme to the opposite. Having been kept in subjection, when he is invested with power, he abuses it and becomes tyrannical (Saadia Gaon).

11 RESTRAINT A SIGN OF INTELLIGENCE

it is . . . anger. lit. 'intelligence of a man (it is when) he restrains his anger' (cf. xiv. 27, 29).

12 ROYAL ANGER AND FAVOUR

grass. Better, 'herbage, vegetation.' For the imagery, applied to God, cf. Hosea xiv. 6, and for the thought, in connection with a king, xvi. 15.

13 BAD SON AND WIFE

calamity of his father. [The Hebrew is stronger, 'ruin of his father,' and the plural of the original may signify many and severe blows.]

a continual dropping. The phrase recurs in xxvii. 15, and cf. the use of the verb in Eccles. x. 18, *through idleness of the hands the house leaketh.* This translation follows Ibn Ezra. A more probable translation is 'a dripping which drives out' those who reside in the house (Metsudath David). A wife's nagging similarly drives the husband away. Although a foolish son is the calamity of his father, his annoyance does not drive him out of the house. A wife's nagging, however, drives a husband out of the house (Gerondi).

14 House and riches are the inheritance of fathers;
But a prudent wife is from the LORD.

15 Slothfulness casteth into a deep sleep;
And the idle soul shall suffer hunger.

16 He that keepeth the commandment keepeth his soul;
But he that despiseth His ways shall die.

17 He that is gracious unto the poor lendeth unto the LORD,
And his good deed will He repay unto him.

14 בַּיִת וָהוֹן נַחֲלַת אָבוֹת
וּמֵיְהוָה אִשָּׁה מַשְׂכָּלֶת׃
15 עַצְלָה תַּפִּיל תַּרְדֵּמָה
וְנֶפֶשׁ רְמִיָּה תִרְעָב׃
16 שֹׁמֵר מִצְוָה שֹׁמֵר נַפְשׁוֹ
בּוֹזֵה דְרָכָיו יוּמָת׃
17 מַלְוֵה יְהוָה חוֹנֵן דָּל
וּגְמֻלוֹ יְשַׁלֶּם־לוֹ׃

ימות ק׳ v. 16.

14 A GOOD WIFE IS A DIVINE GIFT

inheritance of fathers. An ancestral heritage which comes to the sons as a matter of course (Gerondi).

prudent. Or, 'intelligent.'

from the LORD. Cf. xviii. 22; Gen. xxiv. 14. To possess a wife of merit is not a matter of course, but a gift from God (Gerondi).

15 CONSEQUENCE OF IDLENESS

casteth into a deep sleep. With the result that the man is inactive when he should be working (Gerondi).

the idle soul. lit. 'a soul of idleness,' i.e. an idle person.

16 OBEDIENCE TO THE TORAH PROLONGS LIFE

the commandment. lit. 'a commandment.' The commandments of God are definitely meant. Cf. above vi. 23. The expression is used in the Torah (Deut. xxviii. 1) (Daath Mikra).

keepeth his soul. Preserves his life (Ibn Ezra).

despiseth His ways. It is not certain that God's ways are referred to, and the phrase may imply: he who despises the ways in which he should properly go (Metsudath David).

shall die. Prematurely as the effect of his misbehaviour. So the *kerê,* whereas the *kethib* is 'shall be put to death,' by sentence of a court if he despised the way of the commandments in public (Ibn Ezra).

17 BLESSEDNESS OF PHILANTHROPY

the poor. Not the ordinary Hebrew term for a pauper, but a word signifying 'feeble'; a man in need of help, not necessarily in the form of money (Chotam Tochnit).

lendeth unto the LORD. Whether the assistance was financial or otherwise, God becomes the debtor because He must sustain the poor man (Ralbag).

will He repay. Cf. Ps. xli. 2ff.

18 **Chasten thy son, for there is hope;**
But set not thy heart on his destruction.

19 **A man of great wrath shall suffer punishment;**
For if thou interpose, thou wilt add thereto.

20 **Hear counsel, and receive instruction,**
That thou mayest be wise in thy latter end.

21 **There are many devices in a man's heart;**
But the counsel of the LORD, that shall stand.

18 יַסֵּר בִּנְךָ כִּי־יֵשׁ תִּקְוָה
וְאֶל־הֲמִיתוֹ אַל־תִּשָּׂא נַפְשֶׁךָ׃
19 גְּרָל־חֵמָה נֹשֵׂא עֹנֶשׁ
כִּי אִם־תַּצִּיל וְעוֹד תּוֹסִף׃
20 שְׁמַע עֵצָה וְקַבֵּל מוּסָר
לְמַעַן תֶּחְכַּם בְּאַחֲרִיתֶךָ׃
21 רַבּוֹת מַחֲשָׁבוֹת בְּלֶב־אִישׁ
וַעֲצַת יְהוָה הִיא תָקוּם׃

v. 19. גדל ק׳

18–19 CORRECTION OF A CHILD

18. *chasten.* With corporal punishment (Targum).

set not . . . destruction. lit. 'and to the killing of him lift not up thy soul.' This may mean, as Rashi comments, that the father was not to make the punishment so severe that the son died under it. The phrase 'lift up thy soul unto' is translated *set the heart upon* in Deut. xxiv. 15, and the intention here is: 'but set not thy heart on his being put to death.' It may also mean that however depraved a son may be, keep on correcting him and do not say in despair, 'I can do nothing more with him; sooner or later he will be put to death for his crime and then I shall be rid of him' (Ibn Ezra). Included in this verse is the obligation of the teacher to chasten his pupils (Ibn Nachmiash).

19. Ibn Ezra suggests that this verse is a continuation of the preceding: 'Who is great of anger (so the *kerë*) must bear the penalty' — that lays down a general principle which is applied to the case in question. If the son is excessively angry; i.e. if he has an uncontrollable temper, let him suffer his punishment; i.e. do not chasten him; for if you rescue him once, you will have to rescue him many more times. Ibn Nachmiash explains. 'If you are excessively angry, do not chasten him but bear his sin; for if you spare him, you will be able to continue to chasten him later.'

20–21 MAN'S SCHEMES AND GOD'S

20. *counsel.* Until now, he instructed the father to chasten his son. Now he admonishes the son to take his father's advice and accept his instruction (Gerondi).

in thy latter end. In other Biblical Books the term usually indicates the end of life, but in Proverbs the meaning is 'the future, the rest of one's life' (after Gerondi, Ibn Nachmiash).

21. *there are many devices.* Better, 'many are the plans.'

counsel. As in Ps. xxxiii. 11 the word signifies 'decision.' Let not the youth think that he will become serious and accept instruction in his later years, for no one knows God's plans, and he may not live much longer (Gerondi).

2 The lust of a man is his shame;
And a poor man is better than a liar.

22 תַּאֲוַת אָדָם חַסְדּוֹ
וְטוֹב רָשׁ מֵאִישׁ כָּזָב׃

3 The fear of the LORD tendeth to life;
And he that hath it shall abide satisfied,
He shall not be visited with evil.

23 יִרְאַת יְהוָה לְחַיִּים
וְשָׂבֵעַ יָלִין בַּל־יִפָּקֶד רָע׃

4 The sluggard burieth his hand in the dish,
And will not so much as bring it back to his mouth.

24 טָמַן עָצֵל יָדוֹ בַּצַּלָּחַת
גַּם־אֶל־פִּיהוּ לֹא יְשִׁיבֶנָּה׃

5 When thou smitest a scorner, the simple will become prudent;
And when one that hath understanding is reproved, he will understand knowledge.

25 לֵץ תַּכֶּה וּפֶתִי יַעְרִם
וְהוֹכִיחַ לְנָבוֹן יָבִין דָּעַת׃

22 DISAPPOINTED EXPECTATIONS

'A riddle to the interpreter' is a description given of this verse. The rendering of A.J. is unacceptable and fails to provide a connection between the two clauses. Rashi offers a simple interpretation. In *the lust of a man* the construct state has an objective force, and *lust* is employed as in Gen. iii. 6, *a delight to the eyes,* i.e. attractive to the sight. *Shame* is a sense the Hebrew *chesed* sometimes has (cf. xiv. 34), but there is no reason to depart from its usual meaning. The first clause should be translated: 'A man's attraction is his kindness,' i.e. his ability to practise benevolence invests him with attractiveness to his fellows.

and a poor man. Better, 'but a poor man,' who has not the means to do a kindness, is preferable as an associate to a rich man who gives a promise of help and fails to keep it (Rashi, Ibn Ezra).

23 BLESSING UPON THE GOD-FEARING

and he that hath . . . evil. Translate: 'and (the God-fearing) abides satisfied unvisited by calamity' (Rashi).

24 THE LAZY MAN SATIRIZED

in the dish. Orientals dispensed with spoons and forks, dipping their hand into the dish to take their portion. The older commentators translated, 'bosom, slit in a garment,' like our expression 'buries his hands in his pockets' (quoted by Rashi). A.J.'s translation is found in Meiri.

25 TWO METHODS OF INSTRUCTION

scorner . . . simple. See on i. 4, 22. The simpleton learns prudence when he has an object-lesson of how the mocker suffers for his wickedness. He needs the powerful deterrent of fear of punishment (Ralbag).

one that hath understanding. On the other hand, a man of intelligence only needs a word of reproof to put him right cf. the Rabbinic saying, 'To the wise man with a hint, to the fool with a fist' (Midrash Proverbs 22.15). Meiri renders: 'And when one is reproved, it will enable one that hath understanding to understand knowledge.' If the one who has understanding witnesses another person being reproved will cause him to understanding his shortcomings, and he will obey. Unlike the simple, who must see the scorner smitten before him, he who has understanding must merely see him receiving reproof.

26 A son that dealeth shamefully and reproachfully
Will despoil his father, and chase away his mother.

27 Cease, my son, to hear the instruction
That causeth to err from the words of knowledge.

28 An ungodly witness mocketh at right;
And the mouth of the wicked devoureth iniquity.

29 Judgments are prepared for scorners,
And stripes for the back of fools.

מְשַׁדֶּד־אָב יַבְרִיחַ אֵם 26
בֵּן מֵבִישׁ וּמַחְפִּיר׃
חֲדַל־בְּנִי לִשְׁמֹעַ מוּסָר 27
לִשְׁגוֹת מֵאִמְרֵי־דָעַת׃
עֵד בְּלִיַּעַל יָלִיץ מִשְׁפָּט 28
וּפִי רְשָׁעִים יְבַלַּע־אָוֶן׃
נָכוֹנוּ לַלֵּצִים שְׁפָטִים 29
וּמַהֲלֻמוֹת לְגֵו כְּסִילִים׃

26 SHAMEFUL TREATMENT OF PARENTS

will despoil. He gives robbers a plan to rob his father so that he can share the spoils with them. Consequently, his mother runs away from the house (Ibn Ezra). Ibn Nachmiash explains that he causes both his father and mother to be despoiled and run away from the house. However, since the money belongs to the father, the author states that he despoils his father, and since the mother is usually in the house, he states that he drives her from the house.

27 WARNING AGAINST LICENCE

The objection to the rendering of A.J. is that *instruction (musar)* is never used of a bad influence. Translate: 'Cease, my son, to obey discipline (i.e. if thou throwest it off), it is to stray from the sayings (principles) of knowledge.' The verse is an admonition that rebellion against the restraints imposed by wisdom is a desire to indulge in harmful licence (Ibn Ezra).

28 PERJURY DENOUNCED

ungodly. See on vi. 12, *a base person*; here 'a depraved witness' who knowingly gives false evidence.

right. Rather, 'justice.' He scorns his duty to see that strict equity is maintained and so has no scruples against giving lying testimony (after Ibn Ezra).

devoureth. This root denotes swallowing or devouring only when it appears in the 'kal' conjugation. In the 'pi'el' conjugation, however, it means either to conceal or to destroy. Ibn Ezra and Metsudath David adopt the former definition, explaining: 'conceals iniquity.' He conceals his intentions and testifies innocently as though he had no intention to falsify his testimony. Rashi adopts the latter definition, rendering: 'iniquity destroys the mouth. . .'

29 SCORNERS AND FOOLS SUFFER

judgments. i.e. punishments sent by God. *Scorners* may keep within the law and escape civil penalties, but God does not overlook their conduct (Ibn Ezra).

stripes. See on xviii. 6. This class suffers at the hands of their fellows (Ibn Ezra).

Wine is a mocker, strong drink is riotous;
And whosoever reeleth thereby is not wise.

The terror of a king is as the roaring of a lion:
He that provoketh him to anger forfeiteth his life.

It is an honour for a man to keep aloof from strife;
But every fool will be snarling.

The sluggard will not plow, when winter setteth in;
Therefore he shall beg in harvest, and have nothing.

1 לֵץ הַיַּיִן הֹמֶה שֵׁכָר
וְכָל־שֹׁגֶה בּוֹ לֹא יֶחְכָּם׃
2 נַהַם כַּכְּפִיר אֵימַת מֶלֶךְ
מִתְעַבְּרוֹ חוֹטֵא נַפְשׁוֹ׃
3 כָּבוֹד לָאִישׁ שֶׁבֶת מֵרִיב
וְכָל־אֱוִיל יִתְגַּלָּע׃
4 מֵחֹרֶף עָצֵל לֹא יַחֲרֹשׁ
יִשְׁאַל בַּקָּצִיר וָאָיִן׃

v. 4 ושאל ק'

CHAPTER XX

1 AGAINST DRUNKENNESS

is a mocker. Hebrew *lets,* 'scorner.' The effects produced upon the drinker are ascribed to the drink itself. An intoxicated person behaves like a 'scorner' because his senses are dulled (after Metsudath David).

strong drink. [Hebrew *shechar* which, through the cognate Arabic, appears in the English word 'sugar.' This beverage was more potent than wine, and was produced from the fermentation of certain fruit-juices, such as the pomegranate (Cant. viii. 2) and the date. It seems to have been freely indulged in by the people (Deut. xiv. 26), but was forbidden to the priests when officiating (Lev. x. 9).

riotous. R.V. *a brawler,* loud of voice and without self-control (Metsudath David).

2 A KING'S ANGER

terror of a king. The dread aroused in a subject by his king's wrath, against which he has no protection, is likened to the fear inspired by a lion's roar when about to spring upon its prey (Metsudath David) (cf. xvi. 14, xix. 12).

forfeiteth his life. A.V. more lit. *sinneth (against) his own soul* R.V. *life)*; not because he failed to pay the king the honour due to him (Ibn Ezra), but for jeopardizing his life (Metsudath David).

3 NOT TO QUARREL IS COMMENDABLE

it is an honour. To refuse to be drawn into a quarrel brings honour to a man in that he is spared the insults which he would probably have otherwise to endure (Malbim).

4 THE LAZY FARMER

when winter setteth in. lit. 'from winter.' A.V. *by reason of the cold* (R.V. *winter*) follows Rashi who supposes that the slothful farmer is deterred by the cold weather. Ibn Ezra comments 'in winter,' the preposition *min* denoting the point of time in which a task is undertaken. After the harvest in the autumn the work of ploughing should be done in winter; but in his laziness, the man is negligent with serious consequences in the following year.

5 Counsel in the heart of man is like deep water;
But a man of understanding will draw it out.

5 מַיִם עֲמֻקִּים עֵצָה בְלֶב־אִישׁ
וְאִישׁ תְּבוּנָה יִדְלֶנָּה׃

6 Most men will proclaim every one his own goodness;
But a faithful man who can find?

6 רָב־אָדָם יִקְרָא אִישׁ חַסְדּוֹ
וְאִישׁ אֱמוּנִים מִי יִמְצָא׃

7 He that walketh in his integrity as a just man,
Happy are his children after him.

7 מִתְהַלֵּךְ בְּתֻמּוֹ צַדִּיק
אַשְׁרֵי בָנָיו אַחֲרָיו׃

8 A king that sitteth on the throne of judgment
Scattereth away all evil with his eyes.

8 מֶלֶךְ יוֹשֵׁב עַל־כִּסֵּא־דִין
מְזָרֶה בְעֵינָיו כָּל־רָע׃

5 MAN'S DESIGN IS DEEP

counsel. A person's real intention as distinct from the words with which he conceals it (Metsudath David).

like deep water. See on xviii. 4.

draw it out. His cultivated mind enables him to penetrate beneath the verbal surface (Metsudath David).

6 A TRUE FRIEND IS RARE

The verse has been variously translated and explained. A.J. has adopted the translation of A.V. and R.V., the latter substituting 'kindness.' The meaning is: men commonly profess their willingness to do an act of kindness when an appeal is made to them, but few carry out their undertaking. This follows Ibn Ezra's second interpretation. Rashi explains: 'Many a man depends on his friend who promises him kindness and he appeals to him in time of need, but who can find a faithful person?' i.e., who can find a faithful person who will keep his promise. According to Ibn Ezra's first interpretation, the question is, 'who can find a faithful man who will not proclaim his own merits?'

7 GOODNESS REWARDED IN POSTERITY

he that walketh . . . man. Or, *a just man that walketh in his integrity* (R.V.). [The former translation denotes a man who is loyal to moral principles and the ordinances of God; the latter would seem to apply to a good man who persists in his goodness despite temptations and trials.]

happy are his children. On the principle, *Showing mercy unto the thousandth generation of them that love Me* (Exod. xx. 6). The merit of the good father is transmitted to his descendants (Metsudath David, Meiri).

8 A JUST KING JUDGES ARIGHT

king. [The chief judge in the land.]

throne of judgment. i.e. a throne distinguished by impartial justice (Meiri).

scattereth away. Better, 'winnoweth'; he sifts the true from the false in the evidence submitted to him (see Ralbag).

with his eyes. [As an anointed ruler he was endowed by God with acumen and discernment for the discharge of his judicial functions.]

Who can say: 'I have made my heart clean,
I am pure from my sin'?

Diverse weights, and diverse measures,
Both of them alike are an abomination to the LORD.

Even a child is known by his doings,
Whether his work be pure, and whether it be right.

The hearing ear, and the seeing eye,
The LORD hath made even both of them.

Love not sleep, lest thou come to poverty;
Open thine eyes, and thou shalt have bread in plenty.

'It is bad, it is bad,' saith the buyer;
But when he is gone his way, then he boasteth.

9 מִֽי־יֹאמַר זִכִּיתִי לִבִּי
טָהַרְתִּי מֵחַטָּאתִי׃
10 אֶבֶן וָאֶבֶן אֵיפָה וְאֵיפָה
תּוֹעֲבַת יְהוָה גַּם־שְׁנֵיהֶם׃
11 גַּם בְּמַעֲלָלָיו יִתְנַכֶּר־נָעַר
אִם־זַךְ וְאִם־יָשָׁר פָּעֳלוֹ׃
12 אֹזֶן שֹׁמַעַת וְעַיִן רֹאָה
יְהוָה עָשָׂה גַם־שְׁנֵיהֶם׃
13 אַל־תֶּאֱהַב שֵׁנָה פֶּן־תִּוָּרֵשׁ
פְּקַח עֵינֶיךָ שְׂבַע־לָחֶם׃
14 רַע רַע יֹאמַר הַקּוֹנֶה
וְאֹזֵל לוֹ אָז יִתְהַלָּל׃

10 FALSE WEIGHTS AND MEASURES

diverse weights, and diverse measures. lit. 'a stone (weight) and a stone, an ephah (measure) and an ephah,' i.e. one used when buying and another when selling (cf. xi. 1, xx. 23) (Elijah of Wilna).

11 CHILD FATHER OF THE MAN

is known. More lit. 'is recognizable (in character).' From his early years the human being reveals traits which remain with him throughout life (Isaiah da Trani).

12 MAN'S FACULTIES A DIVINE ENDOWMENT

the LORD *hath made.* The deduction to be drawn is that they should be employed in ways which are pleasing to their Maker, viz. an ear that listens to instruction and an eye that sees what will result from one's actions (Rashi). Or, to look at good deeds so as to emulate them (Isaiah da Trani). Or, to read books of wisdom (Ibn Nachmiash).

14 A BUYER DISPARAGES GOODS

it is bad. The remark is made to get the price reduced (Metsudath David).

but when he is gone his way. Better, 'but going his way,' after having made the purchase at a cheaper rate (Metsudath David).

boasteth. Of his bargain and his smartness (Metsudath David). This is interpreted allegorically to describe one who engages in the study of the Torah amidst poverty and hunger. At first, he complains of his lot, but later, when he has acquired much wisdom, he boasts of his accomplishments (Rashi, Metsudath David).

15 **There is gold, and a multitude of rubies;**
But the lips of knowledge are a precious jewel.

16 **Take his garment that is surety for a stranger;**
And hold him in pledge that is surety for an alien woman.

17 **Bread of falsehood is sweet to a man;**
But afterwards his mouth shall be filled with gravel.

יֵשׁ זָהָב וְרָב־פְּנִינִים
וּכְלִי יְקָר שִׂפְתֵי־דָעַת׃
לְקַח־בִּגְדוֹ כִּי־עָרַב זָר
וּבְעַד נָכְרִים חַבְלֵהוּ׃
עָרֵב לָאִישׁ לֶחֶם שָׁקֶר
וְאַחַר יִמָּלֵא־פִיהוּ חָצָץ׃

v. 16. נכריה ק׳

15 KNOWLEDGE IS MOST PRECIOUS

there is gold. i.e. a fool may possess gold (Ibn Nachmiash).

rubies. Better, 'corals' (see on iii. 15).

lips of knowledge. Lips uttering knowledge, as in xiv. 7. The intention is that a fool may possess gold and corals, but 'lips of knowledge are a precious jewel,' more precious than all of them (Ibn Nachmiash).

16 HOLD A FOOLISH MAN TO HIS OBLIGATIONS

garment. Commonly deposited as security for a debt (Exod. xxii. 25).

surety. See on vi. 1. The verse draws a distinction between misfortune which inadvertently befalls a man, who should then be treated with sympathetic consideration, and misfortune which comes from stupidity and wilful neglect of advice. The Book of Proverbs sounds many warnings against the folly of acting as surety; so if a person deliberately ignores the advice, keep him to the consequences (after Metsudath David).

hold him in pledge. A second evil which has been denounced in the Book is association with *an alien woman* (v. vii). If she impoverishes him and he is held in person as security for his debts (cf. Neh. v. 5), let it be so and have no pity on him (Ibn Nachmiash).

for. Better, 'on account of.'

an alien woman. This is the reading of the *kerë* which is corroborated by xxvii. 13, a verbal repetition of the verse. The *kethib* means 'alien men.'

17 DISHONESTY BRINGS NO LASTING SATISFACTION

bread of falsehood. Food derived from fraudulent transactions (Meiri).

sweet. At first he feels pride in his ability to overreach his fellow; but when his fraud is discovered, the consequences are most unpleasant for him (Metsudath David). Rashi interprets the phrase as a euphemism for illicit intercourse with a married woman.

filled with gravel. Figurative for a disagreeable experience (cf. Lam. iii. 16).

18 מַחֲשָׁבוֹת בְּעֵצָה תִכּוֹן
וּבְתַחְבֻּלוֹת עֲשֵׂה מִלְחָמָה׃

Every purpose is established by counsel;
And with good advice carry on war.

19 גּוֹלֶה סּוֹד הוֹלֵךְ רָכִיל
וּלְפֹתֶה שְׂפָתָיו לֹא תִתְעָרָב׃

He that goeth about as a talebearer revealeth secrets;
Therefore meddle not with him that openeth wide his lips.

20 מְקַלֵּל אָבִיו וְאִמּוֹ
יִדְעַךְ נֵרוֹ בֶּאֱישׁוּן חֹשֶׁךְ׃

Whoso curseth his father or his mother,
His lamp shall be put out in the blackest darkness.

21 נַחֲלָה מְבֻחֶלֶת בָּרִאשֹׁנָה
וְאַחֲרִיתָהּ לֹא תְבֹרָךְ׃

An estate may be gotten hastily at the beginning;
But the end thereof shall not be blessed.

22 אַל־תֹּאמַר אֲשַׁלְּמָה־רָע
קַוֵּה לַיהוָה וְיֹשַׁע לָךְ׃

Say not thou: 'I will requite evil';
Wait for the LORD, and He will save thee.

v. 21. מבהלת ק'

18 CONSULT OTHERS

purpose. Or, 'plan,' viz. of campaign, as defined by the second clause.

counsel. Consultation with men of experience (Metsudath David).

with good advice carry on war. Again xxiv. 6. For *good advice,* see on i. 5 *(wise counsels).* From the phrase *carry on war* it would appear that the verse is addressed to a king or governor.

19 BEWARE OF A TALEBEARER

openeth wide his lips. A gossiper who carries to others the confidential information given to him (Meiri).

20 MORTAL OFFENCE TO CURSE PARENTS

his lamp shall be put out. Classical commentators regard the phrase as figurative of the soul's extinction by death. Meiri suggests that the words signify the eclipse of all his honour and esteem until he becomes devoid of any recognition, much as a candle flickers and goes out in the blackest darkness. Saadia Gaon interprets the going out of the lamp in various allegorical meanings. When he requires plans and counsel, he will be blind and not discover it. When he prays to God, He will not answer him. He will not receive the reward of the righteous in the hereafter. All these are referred to as 'light.'

21 HASTY GAINS NOT BLESSED

gotten hastily. The translation of the *kerë,* the sense being the same as the English expression 'get rich quick' (cf. xxviii. 20, 22). The *kethib* means 'made abominable' by foul means (Ibn Ezra).

22 GOD WILL RIGHT A WRONG

I will requite evil. Defined in xxiv. 29. Do not say that you will requite evil to those who have done evil to you (Ibn Ezra).

wait for. Or, 'hope, trust.' Trust in the Lord and He will rescue you from the hands of those who wish to harm you (Ibn Ezra, Metsudath David).

23 Diverse weights are an abomination to the LORD;
And a false balance is not good.

24 A man's goings are of the LORD;
How then can man look to his way?

25 It is a snare to a man rashly to say: 'Holy,'
And after vows to make inquiry.

26 A wise king sifteth the wicked,
And turneth the wheel over them.

23 תּוֹעֲבַת יְהוָה אֶבֶן וָאָבֶן
וּמֹאזְנֵי מִרְמָה לֹא־טוֹב׃
24 מֵיְהוָה מִצְעֲדֵי־גָבֶר
וְאָדָם מַה־יָּבִין דַּרְכּוֹ׃
25 מוֹקֵשׁ אָדָם יָלַע קֹדֶשׁ
וְאַחַר נְדָרִים לְבַקֵּר׃
26 מְזָרֶה רְשָׁעִים מֶלֶךְ חָכָם
וַיָּשֶׁב עֲלֵיהֶם אוֹפָן׃

23 FALSE WEIGHTS AND SCALES

diverse weights. See on verse 10.

false balance. See on xi. 1.

is not good. In the eyes of the Lord (Metsudath David). You may not even use it to cheat one who cheated you. Thus, this verse is a continuation of the preceding verse (Ibn Nachmiash).

24 MAN'S DESTINY CONTROLLED BY GOD

a man's goings are of the LORD. Perhaps a quotation from Ps. xxxvii. 23 where the identical words occur. The meaning is that, although a person has the freedom to choose his way, since the power to walk is given him by God, God may withdraw that power from him if his way is improper (Malbim). Gerondi explains that when one embarks on a journey to engage in commerce, many times he incurs a loss instead of a gain. He must therefore trust only in God to bring him success in his ventures.

look to. More lit. 'understand.' The person is sometimes unaware of God's reason for hindering him on his journey (Malbim).

25 WARNING AGAINST RASH VOWS

snare. The first clause is translated by the LXX, 'It is a snare to a man to sanctify any of his possessions hastily,' which well explains the intention. Under the emotion of religious fervor a person feels the urge to express his love of God in practical form by dedicating some of his possessions to the Temple (cf. Lev. xxvii). Such an impulse is a *snare* since it may carry a man too far, and later he will regret his impulsive action (see Daath Mikra, Malbim).

rashly to say. The verb is found again only in Job vi. 3: *are my words broken*.

after vows to make inquiry. Both the Bible and the Rabbis warn against such vowing. Its fulfilment may involve one in great difficulties. He should therefore give fullest consideration to the matter before he utters a vow. *Better is it that thou shouldest not vow, than that thou shouldest vow and not pay* (Eccles. v. 4).

26 A WISE KING PUNISHES THE WICKED

sifteth. Better, 'winnoweth,' as in verse 8. Here the meaning is: he is careful to separate the wicked among his subjects lest they organize (Metsudath David).

wheel. The simile from agriculture is continued. The *wheel* is that of the cart used in threshing (cf. Isa. xxviii. 27f.). If wise, a king takes measures to suppress the evil elements in his kingdom (see Ibn Ezra).

The spirit of man is the lamp of the LORD,
Searching all the inward parts.

27 נֵר יְהוָה נִשְׁמַת אָדָם
חֹפֵשׂ כָּל־חַדְרֵי־בָטֶן׃

Mercy and truth preserve the king;
And his throne is upheld by mercy.

28 חֶסֶד וֶאֱמֶת יִצְּרוּ־מֶלֶךְ
וְסָעַד בַּחֶסֶד כִּסְאוֹ׃

The glory of young men is their strength;
And the beauty of old men is the hoary head.

29 תִּפְאֶרֶת בַּחוּרִים כֹּחָם
וַהֲדַר זְקֵנִים שֵׂיבָה׃

Sharp wounds cleanse away evil;
So do stripes that reach the inward parts.

30 חַבֻּרוֹת פֶּצַע תַּמְרִיק בְּרָע
וּמַכּוֹת חַדְרֵי־בָטֶן׃

v. 30. תמרוק ק׳

27 MAN'S DIVINE ENDOWMENT

spirit. Hebrew *neshamah,* a reference to *the breath of life* which God breathed into man's nostrils (Gen. ii. 7). It is the vital element in the human being, different from that of animals. Just as a lamp enables one to see in the dark, so is the soul the reason for God's scrutiny of man's thoughts. In this way, man's soul is like God's lamp (Gerondi). This may also be explained: 'The lamp of the Lord searches the soul of man, and also searches all the inward parts.' In this way, the word *chofes,* searches, serves for the beginning of the verse as well as for the end (Ibn Nachmiash). Rashi explains the verse literally, that the soul is God's lamp, and that searches all the inward parts. He, therefore, states that the soul that is within the person testifies against him in judgment.

28 MORALITY SUPPORTS KINGSHIP

mercy and truth. The Hebrew is rendered *kindness and truth* in iii. 3 (see note). These qualities *preserve the king* because their exercise makes his subjects happy and contented, so that the possibility of revolt is reduced (Ralbag).

his throne is upheld by mercy. Better, 'he upholds his throne by kindness.' A just and kind-hearted monarch stabilizes his throne (cf. Isa. xvi. 5 which may have been in the writer's mind) (Ralbag).

29 ADORNMENT OF YOUTH AND THE AGED

glory. That in which the young take pride is their physical powers. One does not expect from them the wisdom which comes from a long experience of life (Ralbag).

30 EVIL CLEANSED BY SUFFERINGS

sharp wounds. lit. 'stripes of a wound,' blows which cause a wound, and are not so light as to be ignored. Afflictions of this kind have the power of expiating the sins of a person who has adopted evil ways (Metsudath David).

so do . . . parts. lit. 'and blows of the innermost parts of the belly.' The intention appears to be: the purifying effect of blows which fall upon the exterior of the body is also produced when blows fall upon the inner man, e.g. a shattering grief or overwhelming misfortune. A Talmudic Rabbi taught, 'Should a man see sufferings come upon him, let him scrutinize his actions.' If interpreted and applied in this manner, the hard knocks of fate can be turned to a salutary purpose (cf. Ps. cxix. 71).

1 The king's heart is in the hand of the LORD as the watercourses:
He turneth it whithersoever He will.

2 Every way of a man is right in his own eyes;
But the LORD weigheth the hearts.

3 To do righteousness and justice
Is more acceptable to the LORD than sacrifice.

4 A haughty look, and a proud heart—
The tillage of the wicked is sin.

5 The thoughts of the diligent tend only to plenteousness;
But every one that is hasty hasteth only to want.

פַּלְגֵי־מַיִם לֶב־מֶלֶךְ בְּיַד־יְהוָה
עַל־כָּל־אֲשֶׁר יַחְפֹּץ יַטֶּנּוּ׃
כָּל־דֶּרֶךְ אִישׁ יָשָׁר בְּעֵינָיו
וְתֹכֵן לִבּוֹת יְהוָה׃
עֲשֹׂה צְדָקָה וּמִשְׁפָּט
נִבְחָר לַיהוָה מִזָּבַח׃
רוּם־עֵינַיִם וּרְחַב־לֵב
נִר רְשָׁעִים חַטָּאת׃
מַחְשְׁבוֹת חָרוּץ אַךְ־לְמוֹתָר
וְכָל־אָץ אַךְ־לְמַחְסוֹר׃

CHAPTER XXI

1–2 DIVINE CONTROL IN HUMAN LIFE

1. *the king's heart.* [In the Orient the king was an absolute autocrat, and to his subjects it must have appeared that he exercised unfettered control over his actions. The writer points out that even such a monarch is not free from God's jurisdiction; and in the same way that an irrigator can cut a watercourse in any direction he desires, so God sways the heart of a despot.]

2. Almost identical with xvi. 2 (see notes).

3 MORALITY PREFERABLE TO SACRIFICES

Reproduces the thought of 1 Sam. xv. 22 which occurs again in this Book in verse 27, xv. 8 and is frequent in the prophets and Psalms. No antagonism to the Service of the Temple is implied, but the simple truth that offerings cannot be acceptable to God from a person who indulges in wrong-doing and persists in evil ways.

4 PRIDE AND DESIRE LEAD TO SIN

a proud heart. lit. 'broad of heart.' The two phrases (with a change in the first Hebrew word) occur in combination in Ps. ci. 5. Here it signifies not pride, but inordinate longing for wealth and power (Rashi).

the tillage of the wicked is sin. A difficult and obscure clause. The meaning seems to be: the farmer tills his field preparatory to reaping a harvest. In like manner, pride and ambition lead metaphorically to the tilling of the ground for the wicked, their schemings, the purpose of which is sinful (Isaiah da Trani).

5 DILIGENCE BETTER THAN HASTE

plenteousness. The man who makes up his mind to work steadily in a logical manner will find his prosperity increasing (Ralbag).

but every . . . want. lit. 'but every one who hasteth (it is) only to want.' The get-rich-quick method ends in disaster (cf. xiii. 11, xxviii. 20) (Metsudath David).

The getting of treasures by a lying tongue
Is a vapour driven to and fro; they [that seek them] seek death.

6 פֹּעַל אֹצָרוֹת בִּלְשׁוֹן שָׁקֶר
הֶבֶל נִדָּף מְבַקְשֵׁי־מָוֶת׃

The violence of the wicked shall drag them away;
Because they refuse to do justly.

7 שֹׁד־רְשָׁעִים יְגוֹרֵם
כִּי מֵאֲנוּ לַעֲשׂוֹת מִשְׁפָּט׃

The way of man is froward and strange;
But as for the pure, his work is right.

8 הֲפַכְפַּךְ דֶּרֶךְ אִישׁ וָזָר
וְזַךְ יָשָׁר פָּעֳלוֹ׃

It is better to dwell in a corner of the housetop,
Than in a house in common with a contentious woman.

9 טוֹב לָשֶׁבֶת עַל־פִּנַּת־גָּג
מֵאֵשֶׁת מִדוֹנִים וּבֵית חָבֶר׃

v. 9. מדינים ק׳

6–10 WICKED WAYS DENOUNCED

6. *is a vapour . . . death.* lit. 'a vapour dispersed, seekers of death.' The treasures are a vapour driven to and fro, and those that seek them are seekers of death (Isaiah da Trani). [The wealth accumulated by deceit melts away, its possessors derive no profit from them, and instead of riches they in reality seek death which is the punishment of sin.] Or, 'the treasures seek his death' (Gerondi, Ibn Ezra).

seek death. Rashi apparently had a text which read 'snares of death,' deadly snares, and such is the reading of the LXX (Minchath Shai).

7. *violence.* i.e. deeds of violence (Daath Mikra).

drag them away. The verb is used in Hab. i. 15 of wicked men ensnaring the righteous, *they catch them in their net.* Accordingly, the verse states that men who resort to violence get caught in the net of their evil schemes so that they are unable to break free, even if they so wish (Meiri).

because . . . justly. Their deliberate choice of criminal methods saps their will-power to live honestly (Meiri).

8. *the way . . . strange.* The Hebrew word for *and strange (vazar)* is regarded by some scholars as connected with the Arabic *wazara,* 'to perpetrate a crime,' thus yielding the satisfactory translation: 'Crooked is the way of a criminal' (Daath Mikra, footnote).

9. This verse is repeated in xxv. 24; and with the thought, cf. verse 19 below, xix. 13, xxvii. 15.

a corner of the housetop. On the roof itself, exposed to the elements (Metsudath David), or in a small attic at the top of the house (Daath Mikra, footnote). For the former, cf. 1 Sam. ix. **25f.**, and for the latter, 2 Kings iv. 10. The sequel suggests the meaning: it is better to live alone, perhaps unmarried, and sleep on the flat roof of the house in discomfort.

than in a house . . . woman. lit. 'than a woman of contentions and a house of companionship,' i.e. than to have a quarrelsome wife and a commodious house in which friends are entertained. The joys of companionship are more than offset by the presence of such a wife in the home. A criticism of an undesirable type of woman is included in this group which treats of undesirable men (Metsudath David).

10 The soul of the wicked desireth evil;
His neighbour findeth no favour in his eyes.

נֶפֶשׁ רָשָׁע אִוְּתָה־רָע
לֹא־יֻחַן בְּעֵינָיו רֵעֵהוּ׃

11 When the scorner is punished, the thoughtless is made wise;
And when the wise is instructed, he receiveth knowledge.

בַּעְנָשׁ־לֵץ יֶחְכַּם־פֶּתִי
וּבְהַשְׂכִּיל לְחָכָם יִקַּח־דָּעַת׃

12 The Righteous One considereth the house of the wicked,
Overthrowing the wicked to their ruin.

מַשְׂכִּיל צַדִּיק לְבֵית רָשָׁע
מְסַלֵּף רְשָׁעִים לָרָע׃

13 Whoso stoppeth his ears at the cry of the poor,
He also shall cry himself, but shall not be answered.

אֹטֵם אָזְנוֹ מִזַּעֲקַת־דָּל
גַּם־הוּא יִקְרָא וְלֹא יֵעָנֶה׃

14 A gift in secret pacifieth anger,
And a present in the bosom strong wrath.

מַתָּן בַּסֵּתֶר יִכְפֶּה־אָף
וְשֹׁחַד בַּחֵק חֵמָה עַזָּה׃

10. *evil.* To work mischief [upon others, if it is to his own advantage] (Isaiah da Trani).

his neighbour . . . eyes. He experiences no act of kindness, because the wicked man is utterly self-centered (Isaiah da Trani).

11 INSTRUCTION OF SIMPLETON AND WISE

is made wise. By the fear of suffering which the *scorner* has to undergo (Metsudath David).

when the wise is instructed. Even if he is instructed by his own studies, *he receiveth knowledge* (Metsudath David). Or, *when the wise is instructed* by others, *he receiveth knowledge.* He is called *wise* because he receives intruction, unlike the fool who ignores it (Meiri).

12 CONSIDERATENESS ABUSED

the Righteous One. God is so described in Job xxxiv. 17, but there the context makes the allusion to Him clear. If the word is interpreted in this way here, *considereth* (the same verb as in the previous verse) must mean 'takes notice of for the purpose of punishing' (so Rashi), whereas it is normally used in a favourable sense. It is better to understand the terms *righteous* and *wicked* in their forensic connotation as the innocent and guilty parties. The verse then teaches: If an innocent man has consideration for the household (family) of a guilty man (and out of pity for his wife and children does not press his case), he *perverts* (so translate instead of *overthrowing*) wicked men to evil, because they will rely upon such clemency and be the more tempted to do wrong (see Ibn Caspi).

13 INDIFFERENCE TO THE WEAK

shall cry. Either to God (so Targum), or to a fellow-man (Ibn Ezra). [The callousness he displayed will be remembered against him when he is in need of help.]

14 A BRIBE COOLS ANGER

gift. [Of course the verse does not advocate resort to bribery since the Book frequently denounces it, but merely states a fact of experience.] Rashi explains it as referring to charity.

To do justly is joy to the righteous,
But ruin to the workers of iniquity.

The man that strayeth out of the way of understanding
Shall rest in the congregation of the shades.

He that loveth pleasure shall be a poor man;
He that loveth wine and oil shall not be rich.

The wicked is a ransom for the righteous;
And the faithless cometh in the stead of the upright.

It is better to dwell in a desert land,
Than with a contentious and fretful woman.

15 שִׂמְחָה לַצַּדִּיק עֲשׂוֹת מִשְׁפָּט
וּמְחִתָּה לְפֹעֲלֵי אָוֶן׃
16 אָדָם תּוֹעֶה מִדֶּרֶךְ הַשְׂכֵּל
בִּקְהַל רְפָאִים יָנוּחַ׃
17 אִישׁ מַחְסוֹר אֹהֵב שִׂמְחָה
אֹהֵב יַיִן־וָשֶׁמֶן לֹא יַעֲשִׁיר׃
18 כֹּפֶר לַצַּדִּיק רָשָׁע
וְתַחַת יְשָׁרִים בּוֹגֵד׃
19 טוֹב שֶׁבֶת בְּאֶרֶץ־מִדְבָּר
מֵאֵשֶׁת מְדוֹנִים וָכָעַס׃

v. 19. מדינים ק'

15 EFFECT OF JUSTICE

to do . . . righteous. Better, 'the doing of justice is a joy to the innocent.' The implication is that a stable society can only exist when justice is strictly administered (Daath Mikra).

16 FATE OF THE UNWISE

the shades. See on ii. 18. The meaning is not that he dies prematurely, and *rest* is not 'the poetic equivalent of *dwell.*' What the sage asserts is: the man who is not guided by the tenets of wisdom wanders aimlessly throughout his lifetime, and only when he is dead has he rest from his wandering (Metsudath David).

17 LUXURIOUS LIVING LEADS TO WANT

pleasure. lit. 'joy, rejoicing,' overindulgence in material comforts (Rashi).

wine and oil. Used in luxurious banquets, the oil for anointing, as was then customary (Daath Mikra). This may also refer to fat foods (Ibn Nachmiash).

18 THE INNOCENT VINDICATED

The moral of xi. 8 is repeated here, and the verse declares that finally the innocent man is justified (Ibn Nachmiash).

wicked . . . righteous. The guilty man in the end pays the penalty for the hardships which an innocent person has to undergo if wrongly convicted, e.g. Mordecai and Haman (Rashi).

and the faithless . . . upright. lit. 'and in the place of the upright is the treacherous man.' [Eventually the law-breaker will be in the same plight as the upright who suffer without cause.]

19 A QUARRELSOME WOMAN

a desert land. In an uninhabited spot, leading a solitary existence (Metsudath David).

than with . . . woman. Render 'than (to have) a contentious wife and vexation' (cf. verse 9) (Metsudath David).

20 There is desirable treasure and oil in the dwelling of the wise;
But a foolish man swalloweth it up.

21 He that followeth after righteousness and mercy
Findeth life, prosperity, and honour.

22 A wise man scaleth the city of the mighty,
And bringeth down the stronghold wherein it trusteth.

23 Whoso keepeth his mouth and his tongue
Keepeth his soul from troubles.

24 A proud and haughty man, scorner is his name,
Even he that dealeth in overbearing pride.

אוֹצָר ׀ נֶחְמָד וָשֶׁמֶן בִּנְוֵה חָכָם
וּכְסִיל אָדָם יְבַלְּעֶנּוּ׃
רֹדֵף צְדָקָה וָחָסֶד
יִמְצָא חַיִּים צְדָקָה וְכָבוֹד׃
עִיר גִּבֹּרִים עָלָה חָכָם
וַיֹּרֶד עֹז מִבְטֶחָה׃
שֹׁמֵר פִּיו וּלְשׁוֹנוֹ
שֹׁמֵר מִצָּרוֹת נַפְשׁוֹ׃
זֵד יָהִיר לֵץ שְׁמוֹ
עוֹשֶׂה בְּעֶבְרַת זָדוֹן׃

20 WISE ECONOMY

Some commentators find a difficulty in the verse because in Proverbs the sage is not depicted as rich in worldly goods (but cf. iii. 16), and therefore suggest that the *treasure* is figurative of wise doctrines. This is an improbable interpretation, and the thought becomes clear if by *wise* is understood a provident man who exercises good sense in the disposition of his property (Metsudath David).

desirable treasure. A store of desirable articles, *oil* being specified as a symbol of comfort (see Ibn Ezra).

foolish man. lit. 'fool of a man,' as in xv. 20. He destroys the amenities of his home by his improvidence (Metsudath David).

21 GOODNESS HAS ITS REWARD

followeth after. Better 'pursueth.' He hastens to perform righteousness and mercy (Ibn Ezra).

mercy. Hebrew *chesed,* brotherly love.

prosperity. In the Hebrew it is the same word as *righteousness* in the first clause, but its signification is illustrated by Ps. xxiv. 5 where it is parallel to *blessing,* viz. righteous treatment from God Who is faithful to reward (Daath Mikra).

22 WISDOM SUPERIOR TO MIGHT

a wise man . . . mighty. A concrete formulation of the teaching that intellectual and moral power overcomes physical strength (cf. xxiv. 5f.; Eccles. ix. 14f.).

the stronghold. viz. the strong walls which are the city's defence (Metsudath David).

24 DEFINITION OF 'SCORNER'

a proud and haughty man. lit. 'presumptuous, arrogant'; such are the characteristics of the person who is called a *scorner,* displayed in his contempt of the moral law. The word for *haughty* occurs again only in Hab. ii. 5 (see Metsudath David).

The desire of the slothful killeth him; For his hands refuse to labour.	25 תַּאֲוַת עָצֵל תְּמִיתֶנּוּ כִּי־מֵאֲנוּ יָדָיו לַעֲשׂוֹת׃
There is that coveteth greedily all the day long; But the righteous giveth and spareth not.	26 כָּל־הַיּוֹם הִתְאַוָּה תַאֲוָה וְצַדִּיק יִתֵּן וְלֹא יַחְשֹׂךְ׃
The sacrifice of the wicked is an abomination; How much more, when he bringeth it with the proceeds of wickedness!	27 זֶבַח רְשָׁעִים תּוֹעֵבָה אַף כִּי־בְזִמָּה יְבִיאֶנּוּ׃
A false witness shall perish; But the man that obeyeth shall speak unchallenged.	28 עֵד־כְּזָבִים יֹאבֵד וְאִישׁ שׁוֹמֵעַ לָנֶצַח יְדַבֵּר׃

even he that dealeth. Better, 'doing, acting,' i.e. behaving.

25–26 EFFECT OF IDLENESS

The correct interpretation of the two verses which form a continuous sentence is as most commentators explain it: *The desire of the slothful* (to rest all day) *killeth him, for his hands refuse to labour,* (and he therefore dies of hunger.) All day he desires a desire (to satisfy his appetite), and *the righteous giveth* (him) *and spareth not* (although he himself is at fault for his difficulties (Metsudath David). Other explain: *The desire of the slothful* (to become wealthy) *killeth; for his hands refuse to labour.* (It is as though he wishes to labour and his hands refuse to obey.)

27 ABOMINABLE OFFERINGS

The first clause is repeated from xv. 8, where *to the* LORD is added.

the wicked. Who persist in their wrongdoing and believe that their sacrifice will avert Divine punishment (Saadia Gaon).

with the proceeds of wickedness. This rendering is quoted by Saadia Gaon and Ibn Nachmiash. They suggest also, 'as atonement for crime.' A.V. and R.V. render *with a wicked mind.* The second clause deals with the worse case of a man who offers a sacrifice and uses it as a means of furthering his designs. He thereby aims at impressing others with his piety to win their confidence, the more easily to practise deceit upon them (Metsudath David).

28 TESTIMONY FALSE AND TRUE

a false witness shall perish. Cf. xix. 5, 9, but here the stronger verb *perish* is employed to provide a contrast to the second clause. In some circumstances a false witness may incur the death penalty by the court (Deut. xix. 19), otherwise God will condemn him; so it is here implied (Metsudath David).

the man that obeyeth. More lit. 'but a man who heareth,' the phrase describing a truthful witness. It means either that hearing statements which bear on the case, he faithfully communicates them to the judges (Saadia Gaon, Isaiah da Trani) or he obeys the duty to tell the whole truth (Rashi).

29 A wicked man hardeneth his face;
But as for the upright, he looketh well to his way.

30 There is no wisdom nor understanding
Nor counsel against the LORD.

31 The horse is prepared against the day of battle;
But victory is of the LORD.

29 הֵעֵז אִישׁ רָשָׁע בְּפָנָיו
וְיָשָׁר הוּא ׀ יָכִין דְּרָכָיו׃
30 אֵין חָכְמָה וְאֵין תְּבוּנָה
וְאֵין עֵצָה לְנֶגֶד יְהוָה׃
31 סוּס מוּכָן לְיוֹם מִלְחָמָה
וְלַיהוָה הַתְּשׁוּעָה׃

v. 29 יבין ק׳ v. 29. דרכו ק׳

shall speak unchallenged. The final Hebrew word has two significations: 'for victory' or 'for ever.' A.J. follows R.V. which indicates that he gives evidence that cannot be upset and carries conviction (Daath Mikra, footnote). A.V. has *speaketh constantly,* which means 'he will live on to speak, in contrast to the false witness who will perish' (Isaiah da Trani). The latter appears to follow more appropriately on the first clause.

29 IMPUDENT AND CORRECT DEMEANOUR

hardeneth his face. Acts impudently, regardless of right (cf. vii. 13). This fault was considered in a serious light. 'He who hardens his face is destined for Gehinnom' (Aboth 5.20). The liturgy includes the daily prayer, 'May it be Thy will, O Lord my God and God of my fathers, to deliver me this day, and every day, from them who are hard-faced and from hardness of face' (*P.B.*, p. 7). Upon this petition Dr. Hertz comments: 'Hardened or shameless people who trample on the rights and feelings of others. Throughout the Scriptures there is a positive horror of human insolence. "Where impudence is abundant, there is absence of all human dignity" is a Midrashic saying.'

he looketh well to his way. The *kethib* reads 'ordereth his ways,' the *kerë* 'understandeth his way,' i.e. he directs his conduct with an understanding of the difference between right and wrong. The former is an opportunist, the latter acts on principle (after Ibn Ezra).

30–31 GOD'S SUPREMACY

30. Cf. Job v. 12f. Man's wisdom and planning are of no avail when they are contrary to God's purposes. An example is the brothers' selling Joseph as a slave to prevent him from ruling over them (Ralbag). Also the episode of Absalom, who rejected Ahithopel's advice (Daath Mikra).

no wisdom nor understanding. These terms are not employed here with the ethical content which is usual in this Book (see on i. 2). In this verse they signify the intelligence possessed by the human being which enables him to think and scheme (Ralbag).

counsel. [Here the word means consultation with others for the devising and execution of a plan].

31. *the horse.* lit. 'a horse,' to be understood collectively.

prepared against. Better, 'arranged for,' harnessed and protected with armour. For the use of horses in battle, cf. Ps. xx. 8, and their powerlessness to ensure victory, Ps. xxxiii. 17, lxxvi. 7.

but victory is of the LORD. Cf. *for the battle is the* LORD's (1 Sam. xvii. 47).

. good name is rather to be chosen than great riches, .nd loving favour rather than silver and gold.	נִבְחָר שֵׁם מֵעֹשֶׁר רָב 1 מִכֶּסֶף וּמִזָּהָב חֵן טוֹב׃
'he rich and the poor meet together— 'he LORD is the maker of them all.	עָשִׁיר וָרָשׁ נִפְגָּשׁוּ 2 עֹשֵׂה כֻלָּם יְהוָה׃
. prudent man seeth the evil, and hideth himself; ;ut the thoughtless pass on, and are punished.	עָרוּם ׀ רָאָה רָעָה וְיִסָּתֵר 3 וּפְתָיִים עָבְרוּ וְנֶעֱנָשׁוּ׃

ונסתר ק׳ v. 3.

CHAPTER XXII

1 VALUE OF A GOOD NAME

a good name. The Hebrew is simply *name,* the adjective being obvious from the context. Similarly in Eccles. vii. 1, *A good name* (lit. name) *is better than precious oil.* A good reputation has always been commended in Jewish ethics as man's most valuable asset (cf. 'Have regard to thy name; for it continueth with thee longer than a thousand great treasures of gold. A good life hath its number of days; and a good name continueth for ever,' Ecclus. xli. **12f.**). Rabbinic literature (Aboth 4.17) speaks of 'the crown of a good name.'

than great riches. A good name is the result of a person's admirable traits. This will serve him as a shelter in time of trouble more than his financial assets. A popular adage says: 'A beloved person in the street is better than gold in a trunk' (Ralbag).

loving favour. The phrase is to be defined in the light of iii. 4, xiii. 15 (see notes), viz. a character which creates a favourable impression (Elijah of Wilna).

2 EQUALITY BEFORE GOD

meet together. More lit. 'have met together,' the writer describing an ideal state of affairs as against prevailing conditions (so again xxix. 13). In the Bible we detect the existence of class division based upon the possession or want of wealth, and teaching aimed at breaking down the barrier by the doctrine that all men share a common humanity as creatures of God (Daath Mikra).

maker of them all. See on xiv. 31. The rich must realize that it was God Who gave him his riches and that He can just as easily take them away from him. The poor must realize that it was God Who made him poor and accept his plight uncomplainingly. He must trust in God and not covet the rich man's property, neither should he hate him or envy him (Meiri).

3 PRUDENCE AVOIDS DANGER

the evil. The Hebrew is without the article and here denotes 'calamity, trouble,' and more generally 'dire results' (Meiri).

hideth himself. Keeps clear of it. He avoids the act that may lead him to disaster. This is analogous to the Rabbinic saying: 'Who is wise? Who sees what will result' (Talmud, Tamid 32a) (Meiri). Ibn Nachmiash compares it to Isa. xxvi. 2.

thoughtless. Simpletons who do not possess shrewdness (Isaiah da Trani).

pass on. Continue along the way in which danger lurks (Meiri).

are punished. lit. 'are fined,' i.e. have to pay the penalty (after Meiri).

4 The reward of humility is the fear of the LORD,
Even riches, and honour, and life.

5 Thorns and snares are in the way of the froward;
He that keepeth his soul holdeth himself far from them.

6 Train up a child in the way he should go,
And even when he is old, he will not depart from it.

7 The rich ruleth over the poor,
And the borrower is servant to the lender.

4 עֵקֶב עֲנָוָה יִרְאַת יְהוָה
עֹשֶׁר וְכָבוֹד וְחַיִּים׃
5 צִנִּים פַּחִים בְּדֶרֶךְ עִקֵּשׁ
שׁוֹמֵר נַפְשׁוֹ יִרְחַק מֵהֶם׃
6 חֲנֹךְ לַנַּעַר עַל־פִּי דַרְכּוֹ
גַּם כִּי־יַזְקִין לֹא־יָסוּר מִמֶּנָּה׃
7 עָשִׁיר בְּרָשִׁים יִמְשׁוֹל
וְעֶבֶד לֹוֶה לְאִישׁ מַלְוֶה׃

4 REWARD OF PIETY

R.V. following Ibn Ganah and Isaiah da Trani, translates: 'The reward of humility *and* the fear of the Lord *is* riches.' A.J. rejects this because *and* does not appear in the Hebrew, but the identification of material prosperity with the fear of the LORD is harsh. Ibn Nachmiash explains that the result of the fear of the Lord is riches, meaning that he will be satisfied with his lot, whom the Rabbis (Aboth 4.1) designate as 'rich.' He will learn to honour his fellowman, only to be honoured by him, and he will not be concerned with worldly acquisitions, thus giving him a satisfying life.

5 AVOID SNARES

thorns and snares. The Hebrew omits *and.* [Life is compared to a pathway, in places hedged by thorns, which hamper progress and harm the passer-by (see on xv. 19); more explicitly, they are *snares* which lie in the way of the unwary.]

6 YOUTHFUL TRAINING

in the way he should go. lit. 'according to his way.' The intention is 'the way of uprightness and good living,' but even this training must be according to the way suitable for the individual child (Malbim). Others render: 'If you train a child according to his way, even when he is old, he will not depart from it.' If you train a child in the way he is accustomed to behaving, even when he is old, he will not improve his ways, but retain his childish training (Ralbag, Isaiah da Trani).

7 POVERTY MEANS DEPENDENCE

ruleth over. As often in this Book, the author faithfully depicts the facts of life, whether he approves of them or not. In this verse he alludes to the power which is bred by wealth, and the loss of independence a man experiences when he is beholden to another for assistance (Daath Mikra).

servant. The Hebrew word also means 'slave'; and although a person was forced to sell himself into servitude when destitute of food and lodging, there is no reference to the practice in the verse. It merely remarks on the loss of freedom when a man becomes a debtor. Daath Mikra refers to 2 Kings iv. 1, Jer. xxxiv. 11, Neh. v. 4f.

He that soweth iniquity shall reap vanity;
And the rod of his wrath shall fail.

He that hath a bountiful eye shall be blessed;
For he giveth of his bread to the poor.

Cast out the scorner, and contention will go out;
Yea, strife and shame will cease.

He that loveth pureness of heart,
That hath grace in his lips, the king shall be his friend.

8 זוֹרֵעַ עַוְלָה יִקְצָור־אָוֶן
וְשֵׁבֶט עֶבְרָתוֹ יִכְלֶה׃
9 טוֹב־עַיִן הוּא יְבֹרָךְ
כִּי־נָתַן מִלַּחְמוֹ לַדָּל׃
10 גָּרֵשׁ לֵץ וְיֵצֵא מָדוֹן
וְיִשְׁבֹּת דִּין וְקָלוֹן׃
11 אֹהֵב טהור־לֵב
חֵן שְׂפָתָיו רֵעֵהוּ מֶלֶךְ׃

8 DOOM OF THE WICKED

rod of his wrath. Better, 'the rod of his arrogance,' a signification the noun has in Isa. xvi. 6. *Rod* is the symbol of power, and the verse declares that the evil-doer will not only be overtaken by misfortune, but also deprived of his ability to act lawlessly (see Metsudath David).

9 THE CHARITABLE MAN IS BLESSED

a bountiful eye. lit. 'good of eye,' well-disposed, the opposite being 'evil of eye' (xxiii. 6, xxviii. 22). [The *eye* is the window through which a person's character may be discerned.]

blessed. By God (cf. xi. 26). Charity has always been one of the cardinal virtues of Jewish life. A Midrashic proverb asserts, 'The door which is not opened for charitable purposes will be opened to the physician' (Cant. Rabbah 6.17). Among the many Rabbinic exhortations on the subject are the following: 'Let the poor be the members of thy household' (Aboth 1.5); 'When a beggar stands at thy door, the Holy One, blessed be He, stands at his right hand' (Lev. Rabbah 34.6); 'Greater is the alms-giver than the bringer of sacrifices' (Sukkah 49b).

10 EXPEL THE SCORNER

cast out. The verb suggests his banishment, and the LXX explains the intention: 'Cast the scorner out of the assembly, and strife will depart with him; for so long as he remains seated in a council he insults every one.' [A man who comes within the category of *scorner* has no moral or religious principles. Should he have any place in the communal organization, he will be the cause of friction; so for the harmony and welfare of the community, expel him from the governing body.]

11 TWO INGRATIATING QUALITIES

The verse mentions two essential qualifications which must be possessed by a man who wishes to make his way up the social ladder to the top, viz. the king's friendship. Some attempt to reach it by intrigue and insincere flattery, a method which succeeds only for a time because eventually the king obtains a true estimate of them.

pureness of heart. i.e. genuine motives, and *grace in his lips,* i.e. ability to express one's thought in graceful language, in due course secure the king's recognition and enduring friendship (cf. xvi. 13) (see Isaiah da Trani).

12 The eyes of the LORD preserve him that hath knowledge,
But He overthroweth the words of the faithless man.

13 The sluggard saith: 'There is a lion without;
I shall be slain in the streets.'

14 The mouth of strange women is a deep pit:
He that is abhorred of the LORD shall fall therein.

15 Foolishness is bound up in the heart of a child;
But the rod of correction shall drive it far from him.

16 One may oppress the poor, yet will their gain increase;
One may give to the rich, yet will want come.

עֵינֵי יְהוָה נָצְרוּ דָעַת
וַיְסַלֵּף דִּבְרֵי בֹגֵד׃
אָמַר עָצֵל אֲרִי בַחוּץ
בְּתוֹךְ רְחֹבוֹת אֵרָצֵחַ׃
שׁוּחָה עֲמֻקָּה פִּי זָרוֹת
זְעוּם יְהוָה יִפּוֹל־שָׁם׃
אִוֶּלֶת קְשׁוּרָה בְלֶב־נָעַר
שֵׁבֶט מוּסָר יַרְחִיקֶנָּה מִמֶּנּוּ׃
עֹשֵׁק דָּל לְהַרְבּוֹת לוֹ
נֹתֵן לְעָשִׁיר אַךְ־לְמַחְסוֹר׃

12 GOD GUARDS THE TRUTH

preserve him that hath knowledge. lit. 'preserve knowledge.' It is doubtful whether the English version can be supported by the Hebrew. The sense becomes clear when it is remembered that in Proverbs *knowledge* has a moral rather than an intellectual content. It is the philosophy of the ethically wise man, and is therefore the equivalent of 'true doctrine.' This has the Divine guardianship, so that all attacks fail to upset it. (see Ralbag)

overthroweth. lit. 'perverteth.' The speech of a *faithless man* does not express the truth, and God turns it aside from reaching its target, viz. the acceptance of him to whom it is addressed (Ralbag).

13 THE SLUGGARD'S EXCUSE

Cf. xxvi. 13 for a different form of the saying, one of several humorous jibes at the lazy person (cf. xix. 24). He invents a fantastic reason for not going about his business.

15 NECESSITY OF CORPORAL PUNISHMENT

foolishness. The Hebrew refers to delinquency which is here said to be *bound up* in a child, i.e. a natural state in the early period of life. Let not the father say that it is bound up in his heart, I will therefore no longer chastise him, but the rod of instruction shall drive it far from him (Ibn Nachmiash).

16 GAIN AND LOSS THROUGH DISHONESTY

The Hebrew is ambiguous and open to a variety of interpretations. The first clause is literally 'who defrauds a poor man, to bring increase to him.' A.J. takes 'to him' to mean *the poor* in a collective sense, implying that such oppression may paradoxically have the opposite effect of that expected; as the result of exploitation, the poor man puts forward redoubled efforts, and not only makes good the loss but even prospers. This is not a feasible explanation, and it is better to translate more simply: 'A man defrauds a poor man to his own enrichment.'

XXII. 17—XXIV. 34. SECOND COLLECTION

17 Incline thine ear, and hear the words of the wise,
And apply thy heart unto my knowledge.

18 For it is a pleasant thing if thou keep them within thee;
Let them be established altogether upon thy lips.

19 That thy trust may be in the LORD,
I have made them known to thee this day, even to thee.

20 Have not I written unto thee excellent things
Of counsels and knowledge;

17 הַ֥ט אָזְנְךָ֮ וּשְׁמַ֗ע דִּבְרֵ֥י חֲכָמִ֑ים
וְ֝לִבְּךָ֗ תָּשִׁ֥ית לְדַעְתִּֽי׃
18 כִּֽי־נָ֭עִים כִּֽי־תִשְׁמְרֵ֣ם בְּבִטְנֶ֑ךָ
יִכֹּ֥נוּ יַ֝חְדָּ֗ו עַל־שְׂפָתֶֽיךָ׃
19 לִהְי֣וֹת בַּ֭יהוָה מִבְטַחֶ֑ךָ
הוֹדַעְתִּ֖יךָ הַיּ֣וֹם אַף־אָֽתָּה׃
20 הֲלֹ֤א כָתַ֣בְתִּי לְ֭ךָ שָׁלִשׁ֑וֹם
בְּמֹעֵצ֥וֹת וָדָֽעַת׃

v. 20. שלשים ק'

yet will want come. Here too there is ambiguity in the concise Hebrew statement. Is it the giver's or the recipient's *want* that is meant? A.J. accepts the former: a person gives a rich man a present of money to secure his patronage, but the gift fails in its purpose and the donor becomes poorer. A true point is made here, but it does not follow logically on the first clause. A better contrast is obtained by the alternative explanation. As the first clause declared that it is possible to increase wealth by dishonest means, the second asserts that it is also posible to decrease it by wrong methods. One bribes a rich man to abet him in a dubious project, but the receiver may become thereby involved and in the end lose much more than the amount of the bribe. Jewish exegetes, however, render the entire verse as one clause: 'One who oppresses the poor so that his gain shall increase, and one who gives to the rich, are but for want.' Just as one who oppresses the poor for his own gain will not profit by his oppression, so will one who gives a gift to the rich only lose by it since he cannot satisfy the greed of the rich (Isaiah da Trani).

XXII. 17–XXIV. 34 SECOND COLLECTION OF PROVERBS

An obvious break occurs at this point, and a new section is commenced with an introductory exhortation (verses 17–21).

17–21 INTRODUCTION

17. *words of the wise.* [If the phrase means 'more advanced instruction' as in i. 6, this section of Proverbs may be a continuation of what has gone before, and not a separate composition incorporated in the Book.]

18. *it is a pleasant thing.* The consequence will be pleasant, in agreement with the earlier assertion, *her ways are ways of pleasantness* (iii. 17).

19. *thy trust may be in the* LORD. Such is the aim and purpose of the instruction (Ibn Nachmiash).

even to thee. Just as they were a benefit to me, so shall they be a benefit to thee (Ibn Nachmiash).

20. *have not I written?* They who hold this section to be only a continuation find in the question an allusion to the teachings which precede. That a practice existed of writing treatises is attested by Eccles. xii. 10, 12.

21 That I might make thee know
the certainty of the words of
truth,
That thou mightest bring back
words of truth to them that
send thee?

22 Rob not the weak, because he is
weak,
Neither crush the poor in the
gate;

23 For the LORD will plead their
cause,
And despoil of life those that
despoil them.

24 Make no friendship with a man
that is given to anger;
And with a wrathful man thou
shalt not go;

21 לְהוֹדִיעֲךָ קֹשְׁטְ אִמְרֵי אֱמֶת
לְהָשִׁיב אֲמָרִים אֱמֶת לְשֹׁלְחֶךָ׃
22 אַל־תִּגְזָל־דָּל כִּי דַל־הוּא
וְאַל־תְּדַכֵּא עָנִי בַשָּׁעַר׃
23 כִּי־יְהוָה יָרִיב רִיבָם
וְקָבַע אֶת־קֹבְעֵיהֶם נָפֶשׁ׃
24 אַל־תִּתְרַע אֶת־בַּעַל אָף
וְאֶת־אִישׁ חֵמוֹת לֹא תָבוֹא׃

excellent things. A variant is found in the Hebrew text. The *kethib* means 'formerly' which Ibn Ezra adopts, and it implies that instruction had been previously given. The *kerė (shalishim)* signifies 'officers,' and on the analogy of viii. 6 (see note) is taken to denote 'superior admonitions' (Ralbag, Metsudath Zion).

21. *certainty.* Hebrew *kosht* which occurs only here, but is the common word for 'truth' in Aramaic. [It appears to be used as a technical term which is defined by the editor as *the words of truth.*]

thou mightest . . . send thee. Some explain this as an allusion to God. Thou wilt be able to give an account to God Who sent thee to this world (Isaiah da Trani). Others, 'those who send thee questions of law' (Saadia Gaon, Rashi).

22–23 DO NOT WRONG THE POOR

22. *weak.* Hebrew *dal,* a man who is defenceless through poverty or physical disability (Daath Mikra).

because he is weak. The phrase is capable of two interpretations: do not take advantage of his weakness and inability to resist (Rashi); or, have consideration for his weakness and refrain from exploiting it (Ibn Ezra).

in the gate. Where justice is dispensed (see on i. 21) (Metsudath David).

23. *will plead their cause.* To protect them (cf. xxiii. 11 and the petition in Ps. cxix. 154).

despoil. The verb is used again only in Mal. iii. 8f. For God's championship of the cause of the weak, cf. Exod. xxii. 20ff.

24–25 DO NOT ASSOCIATE WITH THE HOT-TEMPERED

24. *make no friendship with.* Better, 'do not associate with.'

a wrathful man. lit. 'a man of wraths,' a passionate man who readily loses his temper (Daath Mikra).

25 Lest thou learn his ways,
And get a snare to thy soul.

26 Be thou not of them that strike hands,
Or of them that are sureties for debts;

27 If thou hast not wherewith to pay,
Why should he take away thy bed from under thee?

28 Remove not the ancient landmark,
Which thy fathers have set.

29 Seest thou a man diligent in his business? he shall stand before kings;
He shall not stand before mean men.

25 פֶּן־תֶּאֱלַף אֹרְחֹתָו
וְלָקַחְתָּ מוֹקֵשׁ לְנַפְשֶׁךָ׃
26 אַל־תְּהִי בְתֹקְעֵי־כָף
בַּעֹרְבִים מַשָּׁאוֹת׃
27 אִם־אֵין־לְךָ לְשַׁלֵּם
לָמָּה יִקַּח מִשְׁכָּבְךָ מִתַּחְתֶּיךָ׃
28 אַל־תַּסֵּג גְּבוּל עוֹלָם
אֲשֶׁר עָשׂוּ אֲבוֹתֶיךָ׃
29 חָזִיתָ אִישׁ ׀ מָהִיר בִּמְלַאכְתּוֹ
לִפְנֵי־מְלָכִים יִתְיַצָּב
בַּל־יִתְיַצֵּב לִפְנֵי חֲשֻׁכִּים׃

v. 25 ארחתיו ק׳

25. *ways.* The translation of the *kerë*, the *kethib* being singular.

a snare to thy soul. A danger to thy life. A person of this temperament may become embroiled in a quarrel with fatal consequences (Ralbag).

26–27 AGAINST SURETY

26. *strike hands.* See on vi. 1.

for debts. lit. 'for (other men's) loans.'

27. *he.* The creditor.

take away thy bed. A harsh creditor might ignore the humane regulations of Deut. xxiv. 10ff., which, legally, apply only to the debtor, not to the guarantor (Ibn Nachmiash).

28 RESPECT A LANDMARK

remove not the ancient landmark. Repeated in xxiii. 10. The verse is a reminiscence of Deut. xix. 14. Rashi explains the verse as referring to traditional customs which have come down from the past; but it is better understood of the mark which divides off neighbours' property (Metsudath David).

29 SKILL EARNS ADVANCEMENT

diligent. Better, 'skilful,' as in Ps. xlv. 2; Ezra vii. 6 *(a ready writer)*.

business. Rather, 'work'; [whatever his occupation may be, his proficiency will receive recognition and secure his promotion.]

stand before. Enter into the service of (Metsudath David).

mean. More lit. 'obscure,' employers of lowly station (Metsudath David).

1 When thou sittest to eat with a ruler,
Consider well him that is before thee;

2 And put a knife to thy throat,
If thou be a man given to appetite.

3 Be not desirous of his dainties;
Seeing they are deceitful food.

4 Weary not thyself to be rich;
Cease from thine own wisdom.

כִּֽי־תֵשֵׁב לִלְחוֹם אֶת־מוֹשֵׁל
בִּין תָּבִין אֶת־אֲשֶׁר לְפָנֶֽיךָ׃
וְשַׂמְתָּ שַׂכִּין בְּלֹעֶךָ
אִם־בַּעַל נֶפֶשׁ אָֽתָּה׃
אַל־תִּתְאָו לְמַטְעַמּוֹתָיו
וְהוּא לֶחֶם כְּזָבִֽים׃
אַל־תִּיגַע לְהַעֲשִׁיר
מִֽבִּינָתְךָ חֲדָֽל׃

CHAPTER XXIII

1–3 BE CIRCUMSPECT IN A RULER'S PRESENCE

THIS group of verses is explained by some as rules of etiquette, such as avoiding overindulgence, to be meticulously observed especially in the presence of royalty (Ibn Nachmiash). Others explain it as a guide to avoid eating the food of a host who has an evil eye and is insincere in offering food to his guests. This is again discussed in verses 6ff. (Rashi). Others see it as advice to avoid accustoming oneself to luxuries one may not be able to enjoy in the future (Saadia Gaon).

1. *him that is before thee.* So R.V. in agreement with Rashi. A.V. *what is before thee* fits the Hebrew better, otherwise the text would have read, 'before whom thou sittest.' The writer seems to imply that at a governor's table a large variety of dishes is set before the guests; so be careful in making a polite selection and do not indulge in over-eating (J. Kimchi).

2. *put a knife to thy throat.* Said to be an Oriental idiom for 'practise self-restraint.' Another possible rendering is 'for thou wilt put a knife to thy throat,' i.e. endanger thy life by incurring the host's displeasure (Daath Mikra).

a man given to appetite. lit. 'owner of a soul'; for the sense of *appetite,* see on xiii. 4. With this advice, cf. Ecclus. ix. 13 'Keep thee far from the man that hath power to fill . . . and if thou come unto him, commit no fault, lest he take away thy life.'

3. *be not desirous of his dainties.* Repeated as the second clause of verse 6. Do not be attracted to close association with a ruler because it provides occasions for sumptuous feasting (Gerondi).

deceitful food. lit. 'bread of lies'; his hospitality may have a sinister purpose behind it. A Rabbi uttered the caution, 'Be on your guard against the ruling power; for they who exercise it draw no man near to them except for their own interests' (Aboth 2.3).

4–5 DO NOT COVET RICHES

4. *weary not thyself.* No depreciation of wealth as such is to be read into the words; the advice is only not to make its acquisition the chief aim of one's life and so concentrate all one's efforts upon gaining it (Isaiah da Trani).

cease from thine own wisdom. Desist from wearying thyself in such a pursuit at the dictation of thy 'understanding' (so the Hebrew lit.) which teaches a correct estimate of the value of riches (Ibn Nachmiash, Metsudath David).

5 התעוף עיניך בו ואיננו
כי עשה יעשה־לו כנפים
כנשר ועיף השמים:

Wilt thou set thine eyes upon it? it is gone;
For riches certainly make themselves wings,
Like an eagle that flieth toward heaven.

6 אל־תלחם את־לחם רע עין
ואל־תתאו למטעמתיו:

Eat thou not the bread of him that hath an evil eye,
Neither desire thou his dainties;

7 כי | כמו־שער בנפשו כן־הוא
אכול ושתה יאמר לך
ולבו בל־עמך:

For as one that hath reckoned within himself, so is he:
'Eat and drink,' saith he to thee;
But his heart is not with thee.

8 פתך־אכלת תקיאנה
ושחת דבריך הנעימים:

8 The morsel which thou hast eaten shalt thou vomit up,
And lose thy sweet words.

9 באזני כסיל אל־תדבר
כי־יבוז לשכל מליך:

9 Speak not in the ears of a fool;
For he will despise the wisdom of thy words.

10 אל־תסג גבול עולם
ובשדי יתומים אל־תבא:

10 Remove not the ancient landmark;
And enter not into the fields of the fatherless;

v. 5. התעיף ק׳ v. 5. יעוף ק׳

5. *will thou set thine eyes upon it?* The *kethib* means, 'will thine eyes fly at it?' and the *kerë*, 'wilt thou make thine eyes to fly at it?' Some render: 'If thou movest thine eyes to glance at it, it is gone' (Metsudath David, Ibn Ezra, Ralbag). Others, 'If thou liftest thine eyes from it, it is gone (Isaiah da Trani).

6–8 SHUN A NIGGARDLY HOST

7. *as one that hath reckoned within himself.* A generous host gives unstintingly to his guest and does not calculate what it costs him; but a miserly host resembles a man who estimates the amount involved in a transaction. Although he extends a cordial invitation to his guest to eat and drink, his heart is not in his words because he is worrying over the outlay (Daath Mikra).

8. *the morsel . . . vomit up.* As the meal proceeds, the guest senses the true attitude of the host and the food grows nauseating (Gerondi).

and lose thy sweet words. lit. 'and spoil thy pleasant words.' The probable meaning is: waste the pleasant compliments and thanks which courtesy demands should be expressed to a host (Rashi).

9 WASTE NO WORDS ON A FOOL

Ibn Ezra appears to attach this verse to the preceding: do not attempt to correct a man of this disposition; he will only treat your words with contempt. It rather appears to be a separate saying which advises that one should not take pains to make a statement clear to a fool; even if he grasps what you tell him, he will not appreciate its wisdom (Ralbag, Metsudath David).

10–11 RESPECT THE RIGHTS OF THE DEFENCELESS

10. *enter not.* Committing trespass for the purpose of damaging their property or stealing some produce (Metsudath David).

11 For their Redeemer is strong;
He will plead their cause with thee.

12 Apply thy heart unto instruction,
And thine ears to the words of knowledge.

13 Withhold not correction from the child;
For though thou beat him with the rod, he will not die.

14 Thou beatest him with the rod,
And wilt deliver his soul from the nether-world.

15 My son, if thy heart be wise,
My heart will be glad, even mine;

16 Yea, my reins will rejoice,
When thy lips speak right things.

11 כִּי־גֹאֲלָם חָזָק
הוּא־יָרִיב אֶת־רִיבָם אִתָּךְ׃
12 הָבִיאָה לַמּוּסָר לִבֶּךָ
וְאָזְנֶךָ לְאִמְרֵי־דָעַת׃
13 אַל־תִּמְנַע מִנַּעַר מוּסָר
כִּי־תַכֶּנּוּ בַשֵּׁבֶט לֹא יָמוּת׃
14 אַתָּה בַּשֵּׁבֶט תַּכֶּנּוּ
וְנַפְשׁוֹ מִשְּׁאוֹל תַּצִּיל׃
15 בְּנִי אִם־חָכַם לִבֶּךָ
יִשְׂמַח לִבִּי גַם־אָנִי׃
16 וְתַעְלֹזְנָה כִלְיוֹתָי
בְּדַבֵּר שְׂפָתֶיךָ מֵישָׁרִים׃

11. *Redeemer.* The Hebrew *goël* is a technical term for the next of kin who has the duty of repurchasing a family estate which had become alienated (Lev. xxv. 25). The *fatherless* are typical of persons who lack a protector. God will act on their behalf, since He is *father of the fatherless* (Ps. lxviii. 6) (Elijah of Wilna).

12 AN INTRODUCTORY EXHORTATION

The verse is a preface to the admonitions that follow. It may mark the beginning of a separate collection of sayings.

13–14 CORPORAL PUNISHMENT IN EDUCATION

13. *withhold not correction.* Cf. xiii. 24, xix. 18. Do not overlook the waywardness of a child, on the plea that it is a matter of little importance at that age and he will grow out of it when older (after Ralbag).

for though . . . die. This translation reads into the text an assurance that corporal punishment in such circumstances will not prove fatal. This follows Metsudath David and most other exegetes. More fitting to the next verse is the rendering of A.V. and R.V., *for if thou beatest him,* i.e. the effect of a flogging will be to eradicate the fault, and he will not die in manhood as a penalty for a crime (Ralbag).

14. *thou beatest him.* The pronoun *thou* is stressed in the text, as though to say, 'It is obligatory upon thee to beat him' (Metsudath David).

deliver his soul. Save him from the untimely fate of an evil-doer (Ibn Ezra).

15–16 EXHORTATION TO THE DISCIPLE

if thy heart be wise. To learn my instruction and put it into practice (Metsudath David).

15. *if thy heart be wise.* To learn my instruction and put it into practice (Metsudath David).
David).

16. *reins.* The seat of emotion (Metsudath Zion).

7 Let not thy heart envy sinners,
But be in the fear of the LORD
all the day;

8 For surely there is a future;
And thy hope shall not be cut off.

9 Hear thou, my son, and be wise,
And guide thy heart in the way.

0 Be not among winebibbers;
Among gluttonous eaters of flesh;

1 For the drunkard and the glutton
shall come to poverty;
And drowsiness shall clothe a
man with rags.

2 Hearken unto thy father that
begot thee,
And despise not thy mother when
she is old.

17 אַל־יְקַנֵּא לִבְּךָ בַּחַטָּאִים
כִּי אִם־בְּיִרְאַת־יְהֹוָה כָּל־הַיּוֹם׃
18 כִּי אִם־יֵשׁ אַחֲרִית
וְתִקְוָתְךָ לֹא תִכָּרֵת׃
19 שְׁמַע־אַתָּה בְנִי וַחֲכָם
וְאַשֵּׁר בַּדֶּרֶךְ לִבֶּךָ׃
20 אַל־תְּהִי בְסֹבְאֵי־יָיִן
בְּזֹלְלֵי בָשָׂר לָמוֹ׃
21 כִּי־סֹבֵא וְזוֹלֵל יִוָּרֵשׁ
וּקְרָעִים תַּלְבִּישׁ נוּמָה׃
22 שְׁמַע לְאָבִיךָ זֶה יְלָדֶךָ
וְאַל־תָּבוּז כִּי־זָקְנָה אִמֶּךָ׃

17–18 LIVE IN THE FEAR OF GOD

17. *envy sinners.* Cf. Ps. xxxvii. 1, lxxiii. 3. If they are seen to prosper in their wickedness, do not be envious of their wealth gained by sin and be tempted to follow their example (Ralbag, Metsudath David).

but be in the fear of the LORD. This clause lacks a verb and *be* is supplied (after Metsudath David). An alternative is to regard the verb *envy* as applying to both clauses; hence 'but envy a person who has fear of the Lord' (Ibn Ezra).

18. *there is a future . . . cut off.* Repeated in xxiv. 14. The reason for the advice given in the last verse is explained: do not be carried away by contemplation of the present; it has a sequel in which the wrong-doer receives his punishment, and the hope of reward for steadfastness in right living is proved to be justified (Malbim).

19–21 WARNING AGAINST EXCESS

19. *thy heart.* [The organ of the body which is the seat of intellect and controls actions.]

in the way. The way of wisdom both in beliefs and character traits (Ralbag).

20. *winebibbers . . . gluttonous.* Cf. Deut. xxi. 20.

21. *drowsiness.* The after-effects of excessive indulgence which makes a man unfit for work (Tanna de be Eliyahu).

22 OBEDIENCE TO PARENTS

hearken. To his instruction and advice (cf. i. 8).

when she is old. When women become old they often grow garrulous; a son should not lose patience with her and ignore what she tells him. What she has to say is intended for his welfare (Metsudath David).

23 Buy the truth, and sell it not;
Also wisdom, and instruction, and understanding.

24 The father of the righteous will greatly rejoice;
And he that begetteth a wise child will have joy of him.

25 Let thy father and thy mother be glad,
And let her that bore thee rejoice.

26 My son, give me thy heart,
And let thine eyes observe my ways.

27 For a harlot is a deep ditch;
And an alien woman is a narrow pit.

28 She also lieth in wait as a robber,
And increaseth the faithless among men.

23 אֱמֶת קְנֵה וְאַל־תִּמְכֹּר
חָכְמָה וּמוּסָר וּבִינָה׃
24 גּוֹל יָגוֹל אֲבִי צַדִּיק
יוֹלֵד חָכָם וְיִשְׂמַח בּוֹ׃
25 יִשְׂמַח־אָבִיךָ וְאִמֶּךָ
וְתָגֵל יוֹלַדְתֶּךָ׃
26 תְּנָה־בְנִי לִבְּךָ לִי
וְעֵינֶיךָ דְּרָכַי תִּרְצֶנָה׃
27 כִּי־שׁוּחָה עֲמֻקָּה זוֹנָה
וּבְאֵר צָרָה נָכְרִיָּה׃
28 אַף־הִיא כְּחֶתֶף תֶּאֱרֹב
וּבוֹגְדִים בְּאָדָם תּוֹסִף׃

v. 24. גיל ק׳ v. 24. יגיל ק׳ v. 24. ויולד ק׳ v. 24. ישמח ק׳ v. 26. תצרנה ק׳

23–25 GIVE PARENTS CAUSE FOR PLEASURE

23. *buy.* See on iv. 5.

the truth. As delineated at the end of the verse (Meiri).

sell it not. Do not accept money for teaching (Rashi).

wisdom, etc. These terms refer to the Oral Law. For teaching the Written Law, however, one may take pay (Metsudath David).

24. Cf. x. 1, xxix. 3. A son will be *righteous* and *wise* when he obeys the admonition of the preceding verse.

25. The corollary of verse 24. Since a good-living child rejoices his father, give parents that pleasure.

26–28 WARNING AGAINST IMMORALITY

26. *my son.* The teacher addresses his pupil.

give me thy heart. Attend to my teaching (Ibn Ezra, Ibn Nachmiash).

27. *a deep ditch.* In xxii. 14 this phrase is used of *the mouth of strange women.* The present verse alludes to two types of immoral women: a *harlot,* and one who resorts to her may find himself in serious difficulties by reason of her monetary demands upon him. Then there is the *alien woman,* a heathen from another nation, association with whom is like being in a *narrow pit* where one is unable to turn to extricate himself (Ibn Ezra, Metsudath David).

28. *she also.* Although she is not a Jewish woman and is not so familiar with the Jews (Metsudath David).

as a robber. The verb occurs in Job ix. 12, 'to snatch.' Despite her strangeness to the Jews, when she can snatch one of them, she lies in wait for him, and through her seduction *increaseth the faithless among men* (Metsudath David).

29 Who crieth: 'Woe'? who: 'Alas'?
Who hath contentions? who hath raving?
Who hath wounds without cause?
Who hath redness of eyes?

30 They that tarry long at the wine;
They that go to try mixed wine.

31 Look not thou upon the wine when it is red,
When it giveth its colour in the cup,
When it glideth down smoothly;

32 At the last it biteth like a serpent,
And stingeth like a basilisk.

29 לְמִי אוֹי לְמִי אֲבוֹי לְמִי מִדְוָנִים
לְמִי־שִׂיחַ לְמִי פְּצָעִים חִנָּם
לְמִי חַכְלִלוּת עֵינָיִם׃
30 לַמְאַחֲרִים עַל־הַיָּיִן
לַבָּאִים לַחְקֹר מִמְסָךְ׃
31 אַל־תֵּרֶא יַיִן כִּי יִתְאַדָּם
כִּי־יִתֵּן בַּכִּיס עֵינוֹ
יִתְהַלֵּךְ בְּמֵישָׁרִים׃
32 אַחֲרִיתוֹ כְּנָחָשׁ יִשָּׁךְ
וּכְצִפְעֹנִי יַפְרִשׁ׃

v. 29. מדינים ק׳ v. 31. בכוס ק׳

29–35 WARNING AGAINST DRUNKENNESS

29. *who crieth . . . who hath.* lit. 'to whom is.'

woe . . . alas. Reason for lament (Metsudath David).

contentions. A drunken man is quarrelsome (Ibn Nachmiash).

raving. Rather, 'complaining' (Daath Mikra). [The drunkard's senses are dulled so that he is often under the delusion that he has been wronged.]

wounds without cause. His pugnacity is aroused, and he exchanges blows although no grounds for a quarrel exist (Metsudath David).

redness of eyes. Cf. Gen. xlix. 12. A description of the inflamed condition of the eyes after excessive drinking, bloodshot (after Rashi, Ibn Ezra). Others translate 'dullness of eyes' from alcoholic stupor (Daath Mikra).

30. *to try.* Whenever they hear of a supply being available, they go out of their way to sample it (see Metsudath David).

mixed wine. See on ix. 2.

31. *look not thou upon.* Longingly, attracted by its beautiful colour (Meiri).

when it glideth down smoothly. Perhaps a reminiscence of Cant. vii. 10 (Ibn Nachmiash).

32. The deadly nature of drink, when taken immoderately, is compared to the bite of a poisonous snake.

stingeth. This follows Rashi. An unusual verb in such a connection, and some scholars prefer the translation 'spurt forth (poison)' (Daath Mikra).

basilisk. A particularly harmful species of snake (cf. Jer. viii. 17).

33 Thine eyes shall behold strange things,
And thy heart shall utter confused things.

34 Yea, thou shalt be as he that lieth down in the midst of the sea,
Or as he that lieth upon the top of a mast.

35 'They have struck me, and I felt it not,
They have beaten me, and I knew it not;
When shall I awake? I will seek it yet again.'

33 עֵינֶיךָ יִרְאוּ זָרוֹת
וְלִבְּךָ יְדַבֵּר תַּהְפֻּכוֹת׃
34 וְהָיִיתָ כְּשֹׁכֵב בְּלֶב־יָם
וּכְשֹׁכֵב בְּרֹאשׁ חִבֵּל׃
35 הִכּוּנִי בַל־חָלִיתִי
הֲלָמוּנִי בַּל־יָדָעְתִּי
מָתַי אָקִיץ אוֹסִיף אֲבַקְשֶׁנּוּ עוֹד׃

33. *strange . . . confused.* Intoxication distorts the vision and renders speech incoherent (Metsudath David).

strange things. The distorted fancies of the drunkard (Ralbag, Meiri). Rashi and Ibn Ezra follow the Targum (so also the LXX) and render 'strange women' (as does R.V. margin). [While it is true that intoxication often leads to immorality, the translation does not suit the parallelism of the second clause.]

confused things. lit. 'things which are upside down.' The word is rendered *froward things* in ii. 12.

34. While the imagery of the verse is clear, its exact application is uncertain. Some commentators understand it as denoting the loss of the sense of danger which is characteristic of a drunkard. He is like one who settles down to sleep, as if it were in a bed, on the surface of the sea into which he will sink and be drowned, or on the top of a mast from which he will fall and be killed (Elijah of Wilna). Others take it to describe the man as unable to stand on his feet and so *lieth,* and the ground seems to heave up and down as though he were aboard a ship (Metsudath David).

in the midst of the sea. lit. 'in the heart of the sea,' which may mean 'the bottom of the ocean' (Exod. xv. 8), but also its surface (again xxx. 19).

mast. The Hebrew word occurs only here. The root is the same as in *wise counsels* (i. 5; see *ad loc.*) (Rashi). Some understand it as a 'corded basket' (from *chebel* 'cord') that floats on the water where the ship is anchored (Ibn Ganah).

35. The verse vividly reveals the state of the drunkard's mind as he begins to come out of his stupor.

they have struck me. He had been mixed up in a fracas (cf. verse 29), but thanks to his intoxication he had not felt the blows which had struck him (Ibn Ezra).

when shall I awake? His one desire is to throw off the effects of the last debauch which is hampering his freedom of movement, and be sufficiently recovered to start another bout of drinking (Ralbag). [The realism of the picture drawn in these verses is a measure of the disgust which the average Hebrew felt with the addict to strong drink who, under its influence, lost all semblance of man created in the image of God.]

1 Be not thou envious of evil men,
Neither desire to be with them;

2 For their heart studieth destruction,
And their lips talk of mischief.

3 Through wisdom is a house builded,
And by understanding it is established;

4 And by knowledge are the chambers filled
With all precious and pleasant riches.

5 A wise man is strong;
Yea, a man of knowledge increaseth strength.

6 For with wise advice thou shalt make thy war;
And in the multitude of counsellors there is victory.

1 אַל־תְּקַנֵּא בְּאַנְשֵׁי רָעָה
וְאַל־תִּתְאָו לִהְיוֹת אִתָּם׃
2 כִּי־שֹׁד יֶהְגֶּה לִבָּם
וְעָמָל שִׂפְתֵיהֶם תְּדַבֵּרְנָה׃
3 בְּחָכְמָה יִבָּנֶה בָּיִת
וּבִתְבוּנָה יִתְכּוֹנָן׃
4 וּבְדַעַת חֲדָרִים יִמָּלְאוּ
כָּל־הוֹן יָקָר וְנָעִים׃
5 גֶּבֶר־חָכָם בַּעוֹז
וְאִישׁ דַּעַת מְאַמֶּץ־כֹּחַ׃
6 כִּי בְתַחְבֻּלוֹת תַּעֲשֶׂה־לְּךָ מִלְחָמָה
וּתְשׁוּעָה בְּרֹב יוֹעֵץ׃

CHAPTER XXIV

1–2 SHUN EVIL-DOERS

1. *envious.* Of the wealth they gain by lawlessness and contemplate joining them (cf. iii. 31, xxiii. 17).

evil men. lit. 'men of evil,' men who adopt a career of crime (Ralbag).

2. *studieth destruction.* lit. 'meditateth violence,' acts of robbery (Ibn Ezra).

3–4 WISDOM REQUIRED IN DOMESTIC LIFE

Rabbenu Yonah Gerondi is of the opinion that these verses are to be connected with the preceding. Instead of resorting to crime for the means to live, one can build up a comfortable and stable home by applying wisdom to his affairs. It may, however, be an independent teaching comparable with xiv. 1 as other commentators explain it.

3. *wisdom.* [The term is employed here not in its moral connotation, but signifies mental shrewdness.]

a house. A home (Metsudath David).

established. On a firm basis (Metsudath David).

4. *with all . . . riches.* i.e. furnishings which are costly and comfortable (Daath Mikra).

5–6 USE OF WISDOM IN WAR

5. *strong.* lit. 'in strength' (cf. *the voice of the* LORD *is powerful,* lit. 'in power,' Ps. xxix. 4). Even in circumstances where physical strength is the deciding factor, the possession of wisdom is found to be helpful to overcome an opponent (Gerondi).

increaseth strength. lit. 'strengtheneth might,' in that it enables a man to use his strength to the fullest advantage (Ibn Nachmiash).

7 Wisdom is as unattainable to a fool as corals;
He openeth not his mouth in the gate.

8 He that deviseth to do evil,
Men shall call him a mischievous person.

9 The thought of the foolish is sin;
And the scorner is an abomination to men.

10 If thou faint in the day of adversity,
Thy strength is small indeed.

7 רָאמוֹת לֶאֱוִיל חָכְמוֹת
בַּשַּׁעַר לֹא יִפְתַּח־פִּיהוּ׃
8 מְחַשֵּׁב לְהָרֵעַ
לוֹ בַּעַל־מְזִמּוֹת יִקְרָאוּ׃
9 זִמַּת אִוֶּלֶת חַטָּאת
וְתוֹעֲבַת לְאָדָם לֵץ׃
10 הִתְרַפִּיתָ בְּיוֹם צָרָה
צַר כֹּחֶכָה׃

7 WISDOM BEYOND A FOOL'S REACH

wisdom. The Hebrew is plural (see on i. 20).

unattainable as corals. This is a doubtful paraphrase of one Hebrew word which can be either the name of a precious stone (*corals,* as in Ezek. xxvii. 16; Job xxviii. 18), or an unusual form of the adjective meaning 'high.' Rashi accepts the former, and Ibn Ezra the latter which is preferable because 'wisdom is corals to the fool' is hardly the way to express the idea of an excessive price. The text is best understood as 'high to the fool is wisdom,' beyond his means to purchase.

in the gate. This usually indicates the meeting-place of the elders and wise men of the city. Here too, that definition fits the context very well. This interpretation is unanimously accepted by classical Jewish exegetes.

8–9 INTRIGUER AND SCORNER CONDEMNED

8. *men shall call.* Although his plot is not immediately known, eventually men will discover his mischief and call him a *mischievous person* (Metsudath David).

a mischievous person. lit. 'master of mischiefs,' a plotter, a schemer (Rashi).

9. *the thought.* The Hebrew is connected with the word for *mischievous* in the preceding verse, and always expresses harmful planning, intrigue. Since the term for *foolish* denotes a low moral standard, it follows that such a person's schemes will be sinful. The intention is that the plan itself, although not executed, is regarded as a sin (Metsudath David).

scorner is an abomination. Because he stirs up strife (see on xxii. 10).

10–12 RESCUE THOSE IN MORTAL DANGER

10. *faint.* The verb is translated *is slack* in xviii. 9, and it is uncertain how the verse is to be construed. The translation of A.J., which follows A.V. and R.V., only expresses a truism. An improvement is obtained by rendering, 'thy strength shall be small,' i.e. a faint heart reduces strength in a time of emergency. Most probably this verse is to be connected with the following, as Ibn Ezra suggests, and is to be understood: 'If thou art slack (in coming to the help of another who is in deadly peril), in a day of adversity (which happens to thee) narrow shall thy strength be,' because God will withhold His aid (see on verse 12).

11 Deliver them that are drawn unto death;
And those that are ready to be slain wilt thou forbear to rescue?

11 הַצֵּל לְקֻחִים לַמָּוֶת
וּמָטִים לַהֶרֶג אִם־תַּחְשׂוֹךְ׃

12 If thou sayest: 'Behold, we knew not this,'
Doth not He that weigheth the hearts consider it?
And He that keepeth thy soul, doth not He know it?
And shall not He render to every man according to his work?

12 כִּי־תֹאמַר הֵן לֹא־יָדַעְנוּ זֶה
הֲלֹא־תֹכֵן לִבּוֹת ׀ הוּא־יָבִין
וְנֹצֵר נַפְשְׁךָ הוּא יֵדָע
וְהֵשִׁיב לְאָדָם כְּפָעֳלוֹ׃

13 My son, eat thou honey, for it is good,
And the honeycomb is sweet to thy taste;

13 אֱכָל־בְּנִי דְבַשׁ כִּי טוֹב
וְנֹפֶת מָתוֹק עַל־חִכֶּךָ׃

14 So know thou wisdom to be unto thy soul;
If thou hast found it, then shall there be a future,
And thy hope shall not be cut off.

14 כֵּן ׀ דְּעֶה חָכְמָה לְנַפְשֶׁךָ
אִם־מָצָאתָ וְיֵשׁ אַחֲרִית
וְתִקְוָתְךָ לֹא תִכָּרֵת׃

11. *drawn unto death.* lit. 'taken to death.' The circumstances are not specified, but from the context it is to be gathered that the reference is to men who are in peril of death at the hands of lawless persons, and rescue is possible either by forceful intervention or the payment of a ransom (Maimonides).

ready to be slain. Better, 'bent down for the slaughter,' the verb being descriptive of the position of men in such a plight.

forbear to rescue. lit. 'withhold thyself,' and do nothing to save human lives.

12. *we knew not this.* [The plural *we,* instead of 'I,' obviates the plea that one man by himself could not have accomplished a rescue, which would have been countered by the question why he did not call upon others to co-operate with him.] The excuse offered is ignorance of the perilous situation in which the men were placed (Ibn Ezra).

weigheth the hearts. Accurately estimates the motives of human beings (Ibn Ezra).

consider it. More lit. 'understand.' Does not God understand the thoughts of the heart as distinct from the words of the lips? He will therefore reject the excuse (Metsudath David).

He that keepeth thy soul. [Better, 'He Who observeth thy soul,' looks into its depths and judges its motives.]

shall not He render? The punishment is indicated in verse 10.

13–14 BENEFICIAL EFFECT OF WISDOM

13. *it is good.* Wholesome to the body. As honey is beneficial and pleasant, so is wisdom (Rashi). For the comparison, cf. xvi. 24; Ps. xix. 11, cxix. 103.

14. *then shall there . . . cut off.* Quoted from xxiii. 18 but in a different sense. The discovery of wisdom by a man gives him a confident outlook on life (Ibn Ezra).

15 Lie not in wait, O wicked man, against the dwelling of the righteous,
Spoil not his resting-place;

16 For a righteous man falleth seven times, and riseth up again,
But the wicked stumble under adversity.

17 Rejoice not when thine enemy falleth,
And let not thy heart be glad when he stumbleth;

18 Lest the LORD see it, and it displease Him,
And He turn away His wrath from him.

אַל־תֶּאֱרֹב רָשָׁע לִנְוֵה צַדִּיק
אַל־תְּשַׁדֵּד רִבְצוֹ׃
כִּי שֶׁבַע ׀ יִפּוֹל צַדִּיק וָקָם
וּרְשָׁעִים יִכָּשְׁלוּ בְרָעָה׃
בִּנְפֹל אוֹיִבְךָ אַל־תִּשְׂמָח
וּבִכָּשְׁלוֹ אַל־יָגֵל לִבֶּךָ׃
פֶּן־יִרְאֶה יְהוָה וְרַע בְּעֵינָיו
וְהֵשִׁיב מֵעָלָיו אַפּוֹ׃

v. 17. יתיר י׳ (אויבך)

15–16 ATTACKS UPON THE RIGHTEOUS INEFFECTIVE

15. *dwelling . . . resting-place.* [Both nouns have a pastoral association. Unless they are a rhetorical choice for 'house,' they may suggest that the admonition is addressed to city criminals who set out to attack righteous men living in agricultural settlements, because these were not defended.]

16. *seven times.* An idiom for 'often' (Ibn Ezra).
stumble. And fall without rising again (Metsudath David). One blow is sufficient to crush him for ever (Meiri).

17–18 REJOICE NOT AT AN ENEMY'S FALL

17. *rejoice not.* Do not gloat when retribution overtakes one who has done you a wrong. The spirit of the exhortation is well exemplified by the Rabbinic account (Sanhedrin 36b) that, when the Egyptians were overthrown in the Red Sea, the ministering angels wished to offer a pæan of praise; but God silenced them with the rebuke, 'The work of My hands is drowning in the waters, and ye would sing!'

falleth. This is a greater downfall than *stumbleth*; hence the expression of *rejoice* as opposed to the less intense joy of *thy heart be glad* (Ibn Nachmiash). Meiri renders: show not thyself rejoicing. This verse was the favourite quotation of the first century Rabbi, Samuel the Younger (Aboth 4.19).

18. *turn away His wrath from him.* And turn it upon thee (Metsudath David, Ralbag, Ibn Ezra). Saadia Gaon proceeds to expound on this point that it is impossible to explain the verse in its simple sense, viz. that one should not rejoice at the misfortune in order that his enemy should not be released from his trouble or raised from his downfall, for then the command would be to see that the enemy remain with his punishment. The intention is that God will see your cruelty and your vengeance and weigh your deeds against the deeds of your enemy. In this way, He will declare you more wicked than he, and visit his retribution upon you (Malbim). Alshich explains that the Lord will see whether the person rejoices because of the downfall of a wicked man who rebels against Him or because his personal enemy has fallen. Should the latter be true, God will *turn away His wrath from him,* and visit it upon thee.

19 Fret not thyself because of evil-doers,
Neither be thou envious at the wicked;

20 For there will be no future to the evil man,
The lamp of the wicked shall be put out.

21 My son, fear thou the LORD and the king,
And meddle not with them that are given to change;

22 For their calamity shall rise suddenly;
And who knoweth the ruin from them both?

23 These also are sayings of the wise.
To have respect of persons in judgment is not good.

19 אַל־תִּתְחַר בַּמְּרֵעִים
אַל־תְּקַנֵּא בָּרְשָׁעִים׃
20 כִּי ׀ לֹא־תִהְיֶה אַחֲרִית לָרָע
נֵר רְשָׁעִים יִדְעָךְ׃
21 יְרָא־אֶת־יְהוָה בְּנִי וָמֶלֶךְ
עִם־שׁוֹנִים אַל־תִּתְעָרָב׃
22 כִּי־פִתְאֹם יָקוּם אֵידָם
וּפִיד שְׁנֵיהֶם מִי יוֹדֵעַ׃
23 גַּם־אֵלֶּה לַחֲכָמִים
הַכֵּר־פָּנִים בְּמִשְׁפָּט בַּל־טוֹב׃

19–20 FATE OF THE WICKED

19. Cf. verse 1.

fret not thyself. lit. 'make not thyself hot' with vexation because of their temporary ascendancy. The first clause is taken from Ps. xxxvii. 1 (Meiri). The usual translation is: 'do not compete.' Do not try to emulate the evil deeds of evildoers (Rashi, Ibn Ezra, Metsudath Zion).

20. *future.* Cf. verse 14. He will have no future in the hereafter (Saadia Gaon). Alternatively, 'there will be no *good* future to the evil man (Ibn Nachmiash). He will leave over no posterity (Ibn Ezra).

21–22 BE OBEDIENT TO AUTHORITY

21. *fear thou the* LORD *and the king.* Be loyal to God's ordinances and the king's edicts. Noting that *the* LORD is mentioned first, Rashi comments that the royal commands are to be obeyed only if they conform to the Divine will.

them that are given to change. i.e. men of revolutionary tendencies who revolt against the laws of God and the king (Metsudath David).

22. *their calamity.* viz. the calamity arising from the anger of God and the king (Ibn Ezra); and similarly with *from them both.*

23–24 APPENDIX TO THE SECOND COLLECTION

This section is appended to the collection of proverbs which began at xxii. 17. Some of the sentences are in prose which suggests that we have a miscellany which had not been incorporated in the foregoing.

23. *these also are sayings of the wise.* A heading inserted by the editor; lit. 'these also (belong) to the wise,' viz. *the words of the wise* (xxii. 17) (Elijah of Wilna).

23b–26 STRICT JUSTICE ENJOINED

23b. *respect of persons.* lit. 'the recognition of faces.' Partiality of any kind in the administration of justice is stringently forbidden by the Torah (Lev. xix. 15; Deut. xvi. 19).

24 He that saith unto the wicked:
'Thou art righteous,'
Peoples shall curse him, nations shall execrate him;

25 But to them that decide justly shall be delight,
And a good blessing shall come upon them.

26 He kisseth the lips
That giveth a right answer.

27 Prepare thy work without,
And make it fit for thyself in the field;
And afterwards build thy house.

28 Be not a witness against thy neighbour without cause;
And deceive not with thy lips.

אֹמֵר ׀ לְרָשָׁע צַדִּיק אָתָּה
יִקְּבֻהוּ עַמִּים יִזְעָמוּהוּ לְאֻמִּים׃
וְלַמּוֹכִיחִים יִנְעָם
וַעֲלֵיהֶם תָּבוֹא בִרְכַּת־טוֹב׃
שְׂפָתַיִם יִשָּׁק
מֵשִׁיב דְּבָרִים נְכֹחִים׃
הָכֵן בַּחוּץ ׀ מְלַאכְתֶּךָ
וְעַתְּדָהּ בַּשָּׂדֶה לָךְ
אַחַר וּבָנִיתָ בֵיתֶךָ׃
אַל־תְּהִי עֵד־חִנָּם בְּרֵעֶךָ
וַהֲפִתִּיתָ בִּשְׂפָתֶיךָ׃

24. *wicked . . . righteous.* In the legal sense, guilty and innocent (Ralbag, Ibn Ezra).

peoples shall curse him. The verse is concerned with a governor who exercises his function as judge unfairly; such a person earns the execration of all over whom he rules because he undermines the laws of the land (Malbim).

25. *decide justly.* lit. 'reprove,' condemn and sentence the guilty (Meiri).

shall be delight. i.e. they shall fare well, blessed by God. This word is used in Ps. xc. 17 (Saadia Gaon).

a good blessing. lit. 'a blessing of good (fortune).' This is in contradistinction to 'peoples shall curse him' (Ibn Ezra).

26. *kisseth the lips.* i.e. it is proper to kiss the lips that giveth a right answer. Saadia Gaon quotes this interpretation, but objects to it on grammatical grounds. He renders: 'It is as though he who gives a right answer kisseth the lips' of the guilty defendant. Although he causes him pain, it is as though he kisses him with love. Rashi explains: 'All lips should kiss him that gives a right answer.' Isaiah da Trani explains: When one 'closeth his lips' and does not hasten to answer, when he does answer, we are certain that 'he giveth a right answer.' Metsudath David: 'The guilty party closeth his lips when the judge gives a right answer.' i.e. he has nothing to say.

27 BE ECONOMICALLY SOUND BEFORE MARRYING.

make it fit. lit. 'ready,' the object being *thy work.* Have the ground prepared with crops and livestock (Rashi).

build thy house. Marry and rear a family (cf. Ruth iv. 11). The Rabbis similarly recommended, 'A man should first build a house (literally), then plant a vineyard, and after that take a wife' (Rashi).

28 AGAINST FALSE TESTIMONY

without cause. Having no grounds on which to offer evidence (Metsudath David).

and deceive not. More lit. with R.V. margin, 'and wouldest thou deceive?' by being a false witness (Ibn Ezra).

29 אַל־תֹּאמַר כַּאֲשֶׁר עָשָׂה־לִי
כֵּן אֶעֱשֶׂה־לּוֹ
אָשִׁיב לָאִישׁ כְּפָעֳלוֹ׃

Say not: 'I will do so to him as he hath done to me;
I will render to the man according to his work.'

30 עַל־שְׂדֵה אִישׁ־עָצֵל עָבַרְתִּי
וְעַל־כֶּרֶם אָדָם חֲסַר־לֵב׃

I went by the field of the slothful,
And by the vineyard of the man void of understanding;

31 וְהִנֵּה עָלָה כֻלּוֹ ׀ קִמְּשֹׂנִים
כָּסּוּ פָנָיו חֲרֻלִּים
וְגֶדֶר אֲבָנָיו נֶהֱרָסָה׃

And, lo, it was all grown over with thistles,
The face thereof was covered with nettles,
And the stone wall thereof was broken down.

32 וָאֶחֱזֶה אָנֹכִי אָשִׁית לִבִּי
רָאִיתִי לָקַחְתִּי מוּסָר׃

Then I beheld, and considered well;
I saw, and received instruction.

33 מְעַט שֵׁנוֹת מְעַט תְּנוּמוֹת
מְעַט ׀ חִבֻּק יָדַיִם לִשְׁכָּב׃

Yet a little sleep, a little slumber,
A little folding of the hands to sleep'—

34 וּבָא־מִתְהַלֵּךְ רֵישֶׁךָ
וּמַחְסֹרֶיךָ כְּאִישׁ מָגֵן׃

So shall thy poverty come as a runner,
And thy want as an armed man.

29 BE NOT REVENGEFUL

Cf. xx. 22. Ibn Ezra and many other commentators connect this verse with the preceding: the other man gave misleading evidence against me, I will do so to him. It may also be taken as an independent exhortation (Daath Mikra).

30–34 WARNING AGAINST LAZINESS

30. *I went by.* And observed the condition of the field (Metsudath David).

void of understanding. [He lacked the sense to perceive that hard work is essential for an estate to flourish.]

31. A scene of utter neglect is realistically depicted.

thistles. The word is found again in a different form in Isa. xxxiv. 13 and Hosea ix. 6, both passages describing a devastated area.

nettles. This word occurs again only in Zeph. ii. 9 and Job xxx. 7. It denotes a kind of weed which grows in derelict places.

stone wall. Erected round a field to protect the crops from trespassers and straying cattle (cf. Isa. v. 5).

32. *considered well.* lit. 'I set my heart' to what I saw.

received instruction. I learnt a lesson.

33f. Quoted from vi **10f.**

34. *as a runner.* The Hebrew is not the same as in vi. 11 and means 'so shall thy poverty come marching,' the phrase being also connected with *as an armed man.*

want. Here the noun is plural.

XXV—XXIX
THIRD COLLECTION

25 CHAPTER XXV כה

1 These also are proverbs of Solomon, which the men of Hezekiah king of Judah copied out.

2 It is the glory of God to conceal a thing;
But the glory of kings is to search out a matter.

3 The heaven for height, and the earth for depth,
And the heart of kings is unsearchable.

אֵלֶּה מִשְׁלֵי שְׁלֹמֹה
שֶׁר הֶעְתִּיקוּ
נְשֵׁי | חִזְקִיָּה מֶלֶךְ־יְהוּדָה׃
בֹד אֱלֹהִים הַסְתֵּר דָּבָר
כְבֹד מְלָכִים חֲקֹר דָּבָר׃
שָׁמַיִם לָרוּם וָאָרֶץ לָעֹמֶק
לֵב מְלָכִים אֵין חֵקֶר׃

CHAPTER XXV

1 EDITORIAL HEADING

the men of Hezekiah. i.e men of literary ability employed by the king who was himself interested in literature. During his reign Shebna *the scribe* evidently occupied a prominent position (2 Kings xviii. 18, 37, xix. 2). In 2 Kings xix. 3 a message of Hezekiah to the prophet Isaiah is distinguished for fine literary style, and in Isa. xxxviii. 10–20 a poem composed by him on his recovery from illness is preserved.

copied out. An improbable translation which gives no clear idea of what Hezekiah's men were commanded to do. The verb means 'to remove' (e.g. one's dwelling and possessions, Gen. xii. 8); and Ibn Ezra correctly explains that, at the king's bidding, a small selection was extracted from the mass of Solomonic proverbs and produced as a separate compilation. Saadia Gaon explains that these proverbs were transmitted orally from generation to generation until the men of Hezekiah committed them to writing. Elijah of Wilna explains that, when the Men of the Great Assembly arranged the material to be canonized in the Prophets and the Hagiographa, they found these proverbs that were copied by the men of Hezekiah as proverbs of Solomon.

2–7 ON KINGS

the glory . . . thing. God's government of the universe is mysterious and baffles human understanding. This fact redounds to His *glory* in that it points to the working of a mind of infinite wisdom which is inscrutable by man (Metsudath David).

to search out a matter. i.e. make his method of government understandable. He is human like his subjects, and it is not to his credit if his ordinances and policies are unintelligible to the people (Meiri).

3. If the second clause of the previous verse states the ideal, the present verse describes the actual. As it is impossible for man to estimate the height of the sky above his head and the depth of the earth beneath his feet, so it is a task beyond his powers to comprehend the diplomatic manoeuverings of the royal mind.

Take away the dross from the silver,
And there cometh forth a vessel for the refiner;

Take away the wicked from before the king,
And his throne shall be established in righteousness.

Glorify not thyself in the presence of the king,
And stand not in the place of great men;

For better is it that it be said unto thee: 'Come up hither,'
Than that thou shouldest be put lower in the presence of the prince,
Whom thine eyes have seen.

Go not forth hastily to strive,
Lest thou know not what to do in the end thereof,
When thy neighbour hath put thee to shame.

4 הָגוֹ סִיגִים מִכָּסֶף
וַיֵּצֵא לַצֹּרֵף כֶּלִי׃
5 הָגוֹ רָשָׁע לִפְנֵי־מֶלֶךְ
וְיִכּוֹן בַּצֶּדֶק כִּסְאוֹ׃
6 אַל־תִּתְהַדַּר לִפְנֵי־מֶלֶךְ
וּבִמְקוֹם גְּדֹלִים אַל־תַּעֲמֹד׃
7 כִּי טוֹב אֲמָר־לְךָ עֲלֵה הֵנָּה
מֵהַשְׁפִּילְךָ לִפְנֵי נָדִיב
אֲשֶׁר רָאוּ עֵינֶיךָ׃
8 אַל־תֵּצֵא לָרִב מַהֵר
פֶּן מַה־תַּעֲשֶׂה בְּאַחֲרִיתָהּ
בְּהַכְלִים אֹתְךָ רֵעֶךָ׃

4. *there cometh forth.* The verb appears to be used in a technical sense in connection with the silversmith and goldsmith's work (cf. *I cast it* (viz. the gold) *into the fire, and there came out this calf,* Exod. xxxii. 24). What is meant is, only with refined metal can a vessel be fashioned according to a perfect design (Rashi, Ibn Ezra).

5. *the wicked before the king.* More lit. 'a wicked man before a king,' i.e. a king's minister who exercises an evil influence upon him (Metsudath David).

6. *glorify not thyself.* R.V. paraphrases, 'put not thyself forward.' The circumstance is a royal feast where the guests are seated according to rules of precedence. Do not take up a position higher than that to which you are entitled (Rashi).

stand not in. i.e. occupy, the *great men* being dignitaries who have a superior claim to a place nearer the king (Ibn Ezra, Metsudath David).

7. *come up hither.* To a higher place in closer proximity to the royal host (Metsudath David).

than . . . prince. Better, 'than that thou shouldest be graded before a nobleman,' whose seat he had usurped, and in this way his own inferiority be publicly exposed (Metsudath David).

8–10 BE NOT CONTENTIOUS

8. *to strive.* Bringing a suit against a neighbour to court before he has assured himself that he has a sound case (Metsudath David).

lest . . . thereof. lit. 'lest what wilt thou do in the end thereof?' An elliptic phrase for 'lest thou find thyself in difficulties when the verdict is against thee, and what wilt thou do then?' (Rashi, Metsudath David).

9 Debate thy cause with thy neighbour,
But reveal not the secret of another;

רִיבְךָ רִיב אֶת־רֵעֶךָ
וְסוֹד אַחֵר אַל־תְּגָל׃

10 Lest he that heareth it revile thee,
And thine infamy turn not away.

פֶּן־יְחַסֶּדְךָ שֹׁמֵעַ
וְדִבָּתְךָ לֹא תָשׁוּב׃

11 A word fitly spoken
Is like apples of gold in settings of silver.

תַּפּוּחֵי זָהָב בְּמַשְׂכִּיּוֹת כָּסֶף
דָּבָר דָּבֻר עַל־אָפְנָיו׃

12 As an ear-ring of gold, and an ornament of fine gold,
So is a wise reprover upon an obedient ear.

נֶזֶם זָהָב וַחֲלִי־כָתֶם
מוֹכִיחַ חָכָם עַל־אֹזֶן שֹׁמָעַת׃

13 As the cold of snow in the time of harvest,
So is a faithful messenger to him that sendeth him;
For he refresheth the soul of his master.

כְּצִנַּת־שֶׁלֶג ׀ בְּיוֹם קָצִיר
צִיר נֶאֱמָן לְשֹׁלְחָיו
וְנֶפֶשׁ אֲדֹנָיו יָשִׁיב׃

9. *debate thy cause.* If you feel you have a complaint, discuss the matter with your neighbour and do not hurry to court; and should the interview result in your gaining secret information about him, treat it in confidence (see Malbim).

10. *revile thee.* As a tale-bearer (Rashi).

thine infamy. This follows Isaiah da Trani. Better, 'thy ill report,' the bad reputation gained by him through the disclosure will cling to him (Ibn Nachmiash). An alternative interpretation is: 'the slander (cf. x. 18) will not return,' i.e. once the disclosure is made, it will pass from mouth to mouth and can never be recalled. Therefore be most careful to keep a secret to yourself (Ibn Ezra).

11 A TIMELY WORD IS BEAUTIFUL

a word fitly spoken. lit. 'a word spoken upon its revolvings,' i.e. revolution of time, seasonably. The phrase means the same as *a word in due season* (xv. 23).

apples of gold in settings of silver. The Jewish commentaries explain the words of carvings of apples overlaid with gold upon a silver background, and this interpretation is accepted by some moderns. Maimonides thinks of a silver net covering golden apples. From a distance, only the silver net is visible.

13 WORTH OF A FAITHFUL MESSENGER

cold of snow. Rashi's contention that a fall of snow is not to be thought of in this connection is supported by xxvi. 1, where *as snow in summer* is mentioned as an incongruous phenomenon. The intention is the thought of snow's coolness in the intense heat of the harvest season and its refreshing effect if it were available.

refresheth the soul. For the phrase, cf. Ps. xxiii. 3. lit. 'returneth the soul.' It is as though the soul of the sender goes along with the messenger, and when he returns, he brings it back with him. It may also be rendered, 'returneth the desire.' He brings back the object desired by the sender (Ibn Ezra).

s vapours and wind without
rain,
o is he that boasteth himself of
a false gift.

y long forbearing is a ruler persuaded,
nd a soft tongue breaketh the
bone.

ast thou found honey? eat so
much as is sufficient for thee,
est thou be filled therewith, and
vomit it.

et thy foot be seldom in thy
neighbour's house;
est he be sated with thee, and
hate thee.

14 נְשִׂיאִים וְרוּחַ וְגֶשֶׁם אָיִן
אִישׁ מִתְהַלֵּל בְּמַתַּת־שָׁקֶר׃
15 בְּאֹרֶךְ אַפַּיִם יְפֻתֶּה קָצִין
וְלָשׁוֹן רַכָּה תִּשְׁבָּר־גָּרֶם׃
16 דְּבַשׁ מָצָאתָ אֱכֹל דַּיֶּךָּ
פֶּן־תִּשְׂבָּעֶנּוּ וַהֲקֵאתוֹ׃
17 הֹקַר רַגְלְךָ מִבֵּית רֵעֶךָ
פֶּן־יִשְׂבָּעֲךָ וּשְׂנֵאֶךָ׃

14 UNFULFILLED PROMISE OF HELP

vapours and wind. Usually a sign of an oncoming downpour of rain (1 Kings xviii. 45).

a false gift. i.e. a gift which in fact does not compare with what was boastingly promised. Like the clouds which vanished in the sky, the expectations aroused by the braggart's words did not materialize (Rashi).

15 EFFECT OF FORBEARANCE AND GENTLENESS

by long forbearing . . . persuaded. Rulers possessing despotic power are normally of fickle character. They are quick-tempered but their anger soon subsides. If, then, a ruler's wrath has been aroused, do not prolong it by a display of resentment; patiently endeavour to restore him to a more equitable frame of mind (after Ralbag).

breaketh the bone. Better, 'will (or, can) break a bone.' *Bone* represents a hard substance. Gentle speech, rather than harsh words, will the more effectively overcome stubborn opposition (Ibn Ezra).

16 EXERCISE MODERATION

honey. In xxiv. 13 *honey* is symbolical of wisdom; here it typifies anything desirable and enjoyed. Over-indulgence will cause satiety and eventual loathing. The thought is expanded in Ecclus. xxxvii. 29f., 'Be not insatiable in any luxury, and be not greedy on the things that thou eatest. For in multitude of meats there shall be disease, and surfeiting shall come nigh unto colic.'

17 DO NOT VISIT TOO FREQUENTLY

let thy foot be seldom in. lit. 'make thy foot rare from.' As in the previous verse, though the application is different, the practice of moderation is advised (Rashi).

18 As a maul, and a sword, and a sharp arrow,
So is a man that beareth false witness against his neighbour.

19 Confidence in an unfaithful man in time of trouble
Is like a broken tooth, and a foot out of joint.

20 As one that taketh off a garment in cold weather, and as vinegar upon nitre,
So is he that singeth songs to a heavy heart.

21 If thine enemy be hungry, give him bread to eat,
And if he be thirsty, give him water to drink;

22 For thou wilt heap coals of fire upon his head,
And the LORD will reward thee.

מֵפִיץ וְחֶרֶב וְחֵץ שָׁנוּן 18
אִישׁ־עֹנֶה בְרֵעֵהוּ עֵד שָׁקֶר׃
שֵׁן רָעָה וְרֶגֶל מוּעָדֶת 19
מִבְטָח בּוֹגֵד בְּיוֹם צָרָה׃
מַעֲדֶה־בֶּגֶד ׀ בְּיוֹם קָרָה 20
חֹמֶץ עַל־נָתֶר
וְשָׁר בַּשִּׁרִים עַל לֶב־רָע׃
אִם־רָעֵב שֹׂנַאֲךָ הַאֲכִלֵהוּ לָחֶם 21
וְאִם־צָמֵא הַשְׁקֵהוּ מָיִם׃
כִּי גֶחָלִים אַתָּה חֹתֶה עַל־רֹאשׁוֹ 22
וַיהוָה יְשַׁלֶּם־לָךְ׃

18 HARMFUL CHARACTER OF A FALSE WITNESS

maul. lit. '(an instrument which) scatters,' either a heavy hammer or a club used as a weapon (Michlol Yofi).

a man . . . neighbour. lit. 'a man who testifies against his neighbour (as) a false witness.'

20 UNTIMELY CHEERFULNESS

taketh off. It is doubtful whether the Hebrew verb has this meaning, and a preferable translation is 'putteth on a garment as an adornment.' A man who does not dress according to the season of the year, but attires himself in a thin garment on a cold day because it looks smart, acts foolishly (Metsudath David).

as vinegar upon nitre. The Hebrew word *nether* occurs again in Jer. ii. 22 for a substance used in washing, soda. 'Singing songs to a heavy heart throws it into a sour, angry fermentation, as when *natron* is cast into a pot of vinegar' (Thomson).

21–22 REPAY EVIL WITH GOOD

21. *give him bread to eat.* And do not bear a grudge against him (Metsudath David). It is a very laudable trait to do good to all people, friend and foe alike (Ralbag). The Talmud (Meg. 15b) interprets this as an allusion to Esther's inviting Haman to her banquet. The Midrash interprets it homiletically to mean that if your evil inclination is hungry for sins, feed him rather the bread and water of Torah (Rashi).

22. *coals of fire.* Friendly action of this kind, so unexpected and unmerited, will have a painful effect upon him and arouse remorse for his enmity. He will no longer harm you (J. Kimchi, Meiri).

the LORD *will reward thee.* For the brotherly act by the bestowal of His blessing. Thus, you will be doubly rewarded (Meiri). If this strategy is ineffective, you will, nevertheless, be rewarded by the Lord (J. Kimchi).

The north wind bringeth forth rain,
And a backbiting tongue an angry countenance.

23 רוּחַ צָפוֹן תְּחוֹלֵל גָּשֶׁם
וּפָנִים נִזְעָמִים לְשׁוֹן סָתֶר׃

It is better to dwell in a corner of the housetop,
Than in a house in common with a contentious woman.

24 טוֹב שֶׁבֶת עַל־פִּנַּת־גָּג
מֵאֵשֶׁת מִדוֹנִים וּבֵית חָבֶר׃

As cold waters to a faint soul,
So is good news from a far country.

25 מַיִם קָרִים עַל־נֶפֶשׁ עֲיֵפָה
וּשְׁמוּעָה טוֹבָה מֵאֶרֶץ מֶרְחָק׃

As a troubled fountain, and a corrupted spring,
So is a righteous man that giveth way before the wicked.

26 מַעְיָן נִרְפָּשׂ וּמָקוֹר מָשְׁחָת
צַדִּיק מָט לִפְנֵי־רָשָׁע׃

v. 24. מדינים ק׳

Saadia Gaon stresses that the author does not instruct the hated one to feed his enemy in order to cause him anguish. He instructs him to forgive his enemy and therefore to feed him. The enemy, by dint of his choice, distorts it into pain to himself.

23 EVIL OF BACKBITING

The translation of A.J. agrees with nearly all modern commentators and follows Rashi's interpretation. An entirely different sense is read into the verse by Ibn Ezra: 'as the north wind withholdeth rain, so an angry countenance (putteth a stop to) a backbiting tongue.' A slanderer will be checked if, as soon as he begins to tell his tale, the hearer turns to him a frowning look and shows his disapproval. In favour of this interpretation is the mention of the *north wind* which is said to herald fine weather (Job xxxvii. 22), whereas it is the wind from the east and west which brings rain.

a backbiting tongue. lit. 'a tongue of secret' (cf. the Hebrew of Ps. ci. 5).

25 EFFECT OF GOOD NEWS

from a far country. Rashi aptly quotes as an illustration, *The spirit of Jacob their father revived* (Gen. xlv. 27), on receiving evidence from Egypt that Joseph was alive (cf. also xv. 30).

26 A GOOD MAN'S LAPSE

a troubled fountain. lit. 'a trampled fountain' (cf. *Seemeth it a small thing unto you . . . to have drunk of the settled waters, but ye must foul* (lit. 'trample') *the residue with your feet?* Ezek. xxxiv. 18). The allusion is to the practice of wading into a pool and so trampling the earth that the water becomes undrinkable (Metsudath David).

corrupted spring. The phrase can mean 'a polluted stream'; i.e. because of its being trampled, the water becomes polluted (Metsudath David). It may also be rendered: 'a ruined well,' i.e. a well ruined at the source (Meiri).

that giveth way. The verb is employed in two senses: to slip and fall in a literal

27 **It is not good to eat much honey;**
So for men to search out their own glory is not glory.

28 **Like a city broken down and without a wall,**
So is he whose spirit is without restraint.

אָכֹל דְּבַשׁ הַרְבּוֹת לֹא־טוֹב
וְחֵקֶר כְּבֹדָם כָּבוֹד׃
עִיר פְּרוּצָה אֵין חוֹמָה
אִישׁ אֲשֶׁר ׀ אֵין מַעְצָר לְרוּחוֹ׃

sense and thus to be overthrown, or to lapse morally (cf. Ps. xvii. 5). Metsudath David adopts the former, explaining that when the righteous man falls before the wicked, this deters people from seeking instruction from him. They argue that, since his Torah did not protect him from his foes, what can it do for them? Rashi adopts the latter, explaining that the righteous man subordinates himself to the wicked and fears to reprove him.

27 WHEN EXCESS IS BAD

it is not good . . . honey. Cf. verse 16.

so for men . . . glory. The R.V. margin truly remarks, 'The Hebrew text is obscure.' The literal rendering is, 'and the searching of their glory (is) glory.' By the application of the parallelism the words of the first clause *not* and *much* are read into this clause. Typical of the Jewish commentaries is the explanation of Metsudath David: to over-indulge in honey is bad, but to investigate the honour of righteous men as much as possible is to be accounted an honour. With a slight variation, Meiri renders: 'and the limit of their glory is (not) glory.' To limit the glory of the righteous and the sages is not glory. Saadia Gaon explains: Do not accept unlimited glory from your friends, for they will later demand glory in return for their glory, i.e. for the glory they bestowed upon you. If they do not receive it, their friendship will turn to hatred.

28 DANGER OF LACK OF SELF-CONTROL

broken down. Better, 'broken into, breached,' by an invading army (Ibn Ezra).

a wall. The city's defence against assault and capture (Metsudath David).

so is he. Man is also defenceless against the attacks of his impulses when he is not master of himself. The Rabbis uttered a warning against whatever might lead to a weakening of self-control. They relate that Elijah advised a Rabbi, 'Be not wrathful and thou wilt not sin; be not intoxicated and thou wilt not sin' (Berachoth 29b).

As snow in summer, and as rain
in harvest,
So honour is not seemly for a fool.

As the wandering sparrow, as the
flying swallow,
So the curse that is causeless shall
come home.

A whip for the horse, a bridle for
the ass,
And a rod for the back of fools.

Answer not a fool according to his
folly,
Lest thou also be like unto him.

1 כַּשֶּׁלֶג ׀ בַּקַּיִץ וְכַמָּטָר בַּקָּצִיר
כֵּן לֹא־נָאוֶה לִכְסִיל כָּבוֹד׃
2 כַּצִּפּוֹר לָנוּד כַּדְּרוֹר לָעוּף
כֵּן קִלְלַת חִנָּם לֹא תָבֹא׃
3 שׁוֹט לַסּוּס מֶתֶג לַחֲמוֹר
וְשֵׁבֶט לְגֵו כְּסִילִים׃
4 אַל־תַּעַן כְּסִיל כְּאִוַּלְתּוֹ
פֶּן־תִּשְׁוֶה־לּוֹ גַם־אָתָּה׃

v. 2. לו ק׳

CHAPTER XXVI

1–12 ON FOOLS

1. *snow in summer.* A snowfall at that period of the year would not only be unseasonable but, were it to happen, most harmful to the fruits and crops (Metsudath David).

2. *as the wandering . . . swallow.* lit. 'as the sparrow to wander, as the swallow to fly.' The point of the comparison varies with the reading of the last Hebrew word but one of the verse. The *kethib* is, 'will not come,' the *kerë* 'will come to him.' According to the former, the simile is based upon the aimless flying and wandering of the birds; according to the latter, the reference is to their return to the nest after flying about (Ibn Nachmiash).

curse that is causeless. A curse for which there is no justification. On the other hand there is a Talmudical teaching, 'The curse of a sage, though uttered without cause, takes effect,' (Makkoth 11a) and also a warning 'Let not the curse of an ordinary man be a light matter in thine eyes' (Ber. 7a); from which it would appear that the popular belief was that a curse, whether deserved or not, must be considered seriously.

shall come home. The *kethib* means that the curse will not fall upon the person for whom it was intended; but the *kerë* states that the curse 'will come to him' who utters it (Ibn Nachmiash). A point to be noted is that every verse in this group, with the exception of the present, specifically mentions the fool. The inclusion of this verse in the context must imply that 'to him' means to a fool, because only one in this category would be guilty of a *curse that is causeless* (Daath Mikra).

3. *whip for the horse.* To keep him going in the desired direction (Metsudath David).

bridle for the ass. A rhetorical variation of the first phrase; or the ass, being more wilful than a horse, requires the restraint of a bridle (Malbim).

rod for the back of fools. Cf. x. 13, xix. 29. Words of advice are insufficient to keep him on the right course and more forceful means have to be employed much like dumb animals (Malbim).

4. *answer not.* Do not degrade yourself by descending to his level in an exchange of recriminations (Rashi).

5 Answer a fool according to his folly,
Lest he be wise in his own eyes.

6 He that sendeth a message by the hand of a fool
Cutteth off his own feet, and drinketh damage.

7 The legs hang limp from the lame;
So is a parable in the mouth of fools.

8 As a small stone in a heap of stones,
So is he that giveth honour to a fool.

עֲנֵה כְסִיל כְּאִוַּלְתּוֹ
פֶּן־יִהְיֶה חָכָם בְּעֵינָיו׃
מְקַצֶּה רַגְלַיִם חָמָס שֹׁתֶה
שֹׁלֵחַ דְּבָרִים בְּיַד־כְּסִיל׃
דַּלְיוּ שֹׁקַיִם מִפִּסֵּחַ
וּמָשָׁל בְּפִי כְסִילִים׃
כִּצְרוֹר אֶבֶן בְּמַרְגֵּמָה
כֵּן־נוֹתֵן לִכְסִיל כָּבוֹד׃

5. *answer.* When a fool expresses a view which is clearly wrong, it is necessary to correct him because otherwise he will imagine that his opinions are right. The two verses are complementary and the practice of each proverb depends upon the circumstances. The Talmud (Shabbath 30b) removes the apparent contradiction by applying verse 4 to foolish opinions on secular subjects which can be ignored, and verse 5f to erroneous ideas in connection with 'learning,' i.e. religious matters, which should be refuted.

6. *sendeth a message.* lit. 'sendeth words,' a verbal message which a fool easily distorts and delivers an incorrect version.

cutteth off his own feet. If a messenger is considered to be the *feet* of the sender, the latter, as it were, disables himself by failing to accomplish his purpose (Ibn Caspi, Meiri).

drinketh damage. The noun is lit. 'violence.' A wrong message may incense the recipient who, assuming its correctness, harms the sender (Rashi).

7. *hang limp.* And do not support the body in the act of walking (Daath Mikra).

a parable . . . fools. The comparison indicates the high value placed upon the parable as an effective medium for the expression of an opinion or teaching; but one must be wise to employ it correctly. With a fool it is as useless as are the legs of a cripple (Metsudath David).

8. Two words in the verse are of uncertain meaning. The first is *tseror,* translated *small (stone)* on the basis of 2 Sam. xvii. 13 where it denotes 'a pebble.' It may also be the infinitive of the verb 'to wrap up' or a noun for 'bag.' The second doubtful word is *margemah* rendered *heap of stones,* understood by others as 'a sling' or 'act of stoning.' Various translations of the verse have accordingly been proposed. A.V. has *as he that bindeth a stone in a sling,* a senseless act because the stone should be loose, not bound, if it is to fly from the sling (following Metsudath David). R.V. has *as a bag of gems in a heap of stones,* expressing an incongruous juxtaposition (following Ibn Caspi). The Hebrew *eben* signifies 'gem' without a qualifying word like 'precious,' e.g. the stones of the breastplate worn by the High Priest. A Talmudic interpretation, reproduced in the Latin Version (Vulgate), is 'he who casts a stone on the heap of Mercury' (Hullin 133a) referring to a rite of idolatrous worship. Kimchi renders: 'as a stone wrapped in purple cloth.' The wrapper does not lend the stone any importance.

As a thorn that cometh into the hand of a drunkard,
So is a parable in the mouth of fools.

9 חוֹחַ עָלָה בְיַד־שִׁכּוֹר
וּמָשָׁל בְּפִי כְסִילִים׃

A master performeth all things;
But he that stoppeth a fool is as one that stoppeth a flood.

10 רַב מְחוֹלֵל־כֹּל
וְשֹׂכֵר כְּסִיל וְשֹׂכֵר עֹבְרִים׃

As a dog that returneth to his vomit,
So is a fool that repeateth his folly.

11 כְּכֶלֶב שָׁב עַל־קֵאוֹ
כְּסִיל שׁוֹנֶה בְאִוַּלְתּוֹ׃

Seest thou a man wise in his own eyes?
There is more hope of a fool than of him.

12 רָאִיתָ אִישׁ חָכָם בְּעֵינָיו
תִּקְוָה לִכְסִיל מִמֶּנּוּ׃

The sluggard saith: 'There is a lion in the way;
Yea, a lion is in the streets.'

13 אָמַר עָצֵל שַׁחַל בַּדָּרֶךְ
אֲרִי בֵּין הָרְחֹבוֹת׃

9. *thorn.* The branch of a thorn-bush used as a stick; it may be a harmful weapon if not properly handled (see Daath Mikra).

cometh into. The verb seems to have a meaning which is common in Rabbinic Hebrew, 'comes into the grasp of.'

so is . . . fools. Identical with the second clause of verse 7.

10. The R.V. margin has the remark, 'The Hebrew text is obscure,' and its justification is evident by comparing with A.J. the renderings of A.V. *The great (God) that formed all (things) both rewardeth the fool, and rewardeth transgressors* (after Meiri), and R.V. *As an archer that woundeth all, so is he that hireth the fool and he that hireth them that pass by* (Daath Mikra). The nearest to the Hebrew text is R.V. margin, 'A master-worker formeth all things; but he that hireth the fool is as one that hireth them that pass by' (Rashi, quoting R. Moshe). The thought would then be: if you want a task accomplished, select an expert for the work; to choose a fool is like calling upon a casual passer-by without regard to his competence.

11. *as a dog . . . vomit.* The food which is ejected from the stomach is indigestible; but a dog, being senseless, will eat it again and suffer for it. In like manner a fool repeats his mistakes although they had previously harmed him (Metsudath David).

12. *wise in his own eyes.* His folly appears to him as wisdom (Elijah of Wilna).

more hope of a fool. A fool has the possibility of learning; a conceited ignoramus is hopeless (Metsudath David).

13–16 ON SLUGGARDS

13. A variant of xxii. 13.

lion. [Two different Hebrew words are employed in the verse, the first being reserved for poetical usage.]

14 The door is turning upon its hinges,
And the sluggard is still upon his bed.

הַדֶּלֶת תִּסּוֹב עַל־צִירָהּ
וְעָצֵל עַל־מִטָּתוֹ׃

15 The sluggard burieth his hand in the dish;
It wearieth him to bring it back to his mouth.

טָמַן עָצֵל יָדוֹ בַּצַּלָּחַת
נִלְאָה לַהֲשִׁיבָהּ אֶל־פִּיו׃

16 The sluggard is wiser in his own eyes
Than seven men that give wise answer.

חָכָם עָצֵל בְּעֵינָיו
מִשִּׁבְעָה מְשִׁיבֵי טָעַם׃

17 He that passeth by, and meddleth with strife not his own,
Is like one that taketh a dog by the ears.

מַחֲזִיק בְּאָזְנֵי־כָלֶב
עֹבֵר מִתְעַבֵּר עַל־רִיב לֹּא־לוֹ׃

18 As a madman who casteth firebrands,
Arrows, and death;

כְּמִתְלַהְלֵהַּ הַיֹּרֶה זִקִּים
חִצִּים וָמָוֶת׃

14. The rendering of A.J. agrees with one interpretation given by Ibn Ezra: the door keeps opening and shutting to let people in and out who are engaged with their daily tasks, but the sluggard stops in bed. His alternative explanation agrees with A.V. and R.V., *As the door turneth upon its hinges, so doth the sluggard upon his bed,* the verb governing both clauses.

15. almost identical with xix. 24.

it wearieth him. [The effort required is too much for him.]

16. *seven.* A round number, equals 'several' (Ibn Nachmiash).

that give wise answer. Or, 'that answer with discretion.' [To be able to give an intelligent reply requires training in wisdom. The sluggard is too lazy to undergo this training, and yet considers himself competent to give a wiser opinion than several men together who have done so.]

17 INTERFERING IN ANOTHER'S QUARRELS

passeth by. This emphasizes the fact that he was not really concerned in the quarrel. He just chanced to be passing at the time (Ibn Nachmiash).

meddleth. lit. 'angers himself,' gets heated (Metsudath David).

taketh a dog. And is bitten (Metsudath David). In Palestine the dog was not a domestic pet but ran wild in the streets, and to touch it was dangerous.

18–19 DANGER OF A PRACTICAL JOKE

18. *madman.* His actions may have fatal consequences although such is not his intention (Meiri).

death. That is the consequence of the madman hurling lighted torches or shooting arrows (Ibn Caspi). Others render: 'weapons of death' (Metsudath David). Or, 'arrows of death' (Daath Mikra).

19. *deceiveth.* To mislead may likewise have serious consequences, and it is no excuse for the deceiver to plead that he was not in earnest (Meiri).

19 So is the man that deceiveth his neighbour,
And saith: 'Am not I in sport?'

20 Where no wood is, the fire goeth out;
And where there is no whisperer, contention ceaseth.

21 As coals are to burning coals, and wood to fire;
So is a contentious man to kindle strife.

22 The words of a whisperer are as dainty morsels,
And they go down into the innermost parts of the body.

23 Burning lips and a wicked heart
Are like an earthen vessel overlaid with silver dross.

24 He that hateth dissembleth with his lips,
But he layeth up deceit within him.

19 כֵּן־אִישׁ רִמָּה אֶת־רֵעֵהוּ
וְאָמַר הֲלֹא־מְשַׂחֵק אָנִי׃
20 בְּאֶפֶס עֵצִים תִּכְבֶּה־אֵשׁ
וּבְאֵין נִרְגָּן יִשְׁתֹּק מָדוֹן׃
21 פֶּחָם לְגֶחָלִים וְעֵצִים לְאֵשׁ
וְאִישׁ מְדוֹנִים לְחַרְחַר־רִיב׃
22 דִּבְרֵי נִרְגָּן כְּמִתְלַהֲמִים
וְהֵם יָרְדוּ חַדְרֵי־בָטֶן׃
23 כֶּסֶף סִיגִים מְצֻפֶּה עַל־חָרֶשׂ
שְׂפָתַיִם דֹּלְקִים וְלֶב־רָע׃
24 בִּשְׂפָתָו יִנָּכֵר שׂוֹנֵא
וּבְקִרְבּוֹ יָשִׁית מִרְמָה׃

v. 21. מדינים ק׳ v. 24. בשפתיו ק׳

am not I in sport? i.e. I was only joking.

20–22 MALICIOUS TALK

20. *no wood.* As a fire must have fresh fuel to continue burning, so contention is kept alive by slander (Rashi).

whisperer. See on xvi. 28.

21. *kindle.* R.V. *inflame,* keep the fire burning.

22. Repeated from xviii. 8.

23–26 FALSE SPEECH

23. *burning lips.* R.V. *fervent lips,* lips which hotly profess friendship (Malbim).

wicked heart. Scheming the ruin of the man who is lulled into a sense of security by the *burning lips* (following Malbim).

silver dross. lit. 'silver of dross,' the base metal which is left when the pure silver has been refined. This was used to overlay earthenware and gave the vessel the appearance of being made of silver. The point is the existence of a false exterior which hides the reality (Rashi).

24. *he that hateth . . . lips.* Cf. x. 18.

dissembleth. He conceals his hatred behind friendly words (Rashi).

layeth up. Until an opportunity occurs of venting his animosity (Ralbag).

25 When he speaketh fair, believe him not;
For there are seven abominations in his heart.

26 Though his hatred be concealed with deceit,
His wickedness shall be revealed before the congregation.

27 Whoso diggeth a pit shall fall therein;
And he that rolleth a stone, it shall return upon him.

28 A lying tongue hateth those that are crushed by it;
And a flattering mouth worketh ruin.

כִּֽי־יְחַנֵּן קוֹלוֹ אַל־תַּאֲמֶן־בּוֹ 25
כִּי שֶׁבַע תּוֹעֵבוֹת בְּלִבּוֹ׃
תִּכַּסֶּה שִׂנְאָה בְּמַשָּׁאוֹן 26
תִּגָּלֶה רָעָתוֹ בְקָהָל׃
כֹּֽרֶה שַׁחַת בָּהּ יִפּוֹל 27
וְגֹלֵל אֶבֶן אֵלָיו תָּשׁוּב׃
לְשׁוֹן־שֶׁקֶר יִשְׂנָא דַכָּיו 28
וּפֶה חָלָק יַעֲשֶׂה מִדְחֶה׃

25. *speaketh fair.* lit. 'maketh his voice gracious,' or 'sheweth graciousness with his voice.' He addresses you in friendly tones (see on verse 23) (Meiri).

believe him not. [Place no reliance upon his words and do not trust him.]

seven abominations. Countless wickednesses (Meiri).

26. *his hatred.* The Hebrew lacks *his.* Render: 'Hatred is covered with deceit, yet his (the man who hates) wickedness,' etc.

before the congregation. Whoever conceals his hatred, not because of ethics, but because of guile and cunning, his evil plot will eventually be discovered in public, when he executes his plot, and he will be punished by falling into his own trap (Meiri).

27 RETRIBUTION

diggeth a pit. For the injury of others (cf. Ps. vii. 16f.; Eccles. x. 8).

rolleth a stone. Upon another (Metsudath David). The verse is elaborated in Ecclus. xxvii. 26f., 'He that diggeth a pit shall fall into it; and he that setteth a snare shall be taken therein. He that doeth evil things, they shall roll upon him, and he shall not know whence they have come to him.'

28 THE MISCHIEVOUS TONGUE

lying tongue . . . by it. A liar selects as the objects of his slander men whom he hates; and although they did him no wrong, he imagines that they are his enemies since they were crushed by his lies (Metsudath David).

flattering mouth. lit. 'smooth mouth.' The intention of a person who resorts to smooth speech, which screens his real thoughts, is to bring about somebody's downfall. Some commentators connect this verse with the preceding, and therefore explain the second clause as meaning that the person with *a flattering mouth* brings *ruin* upon himself. The parallelism favours the first interpretation (so Ibn Ezra).

27 CHAPTER XXVII כז

1 Boast not thyself of to-morrow;
For thou knowest not what a day
may bring forth.

2 Let another man praise thee, and
not thine own mouth;
A stranger, and not thine own lips.

3 A stone is heavy, and the sand
weighty;
But a fool's vexation is heavier
than they both.

4 Wrath is cruel, and anger is overwhelming;
But who is able to stand before
jealousy?

5 Better is open rebuke
Than love that is hidden.

1 אַל־תִּתְהַלֵּל בְּיוֹם מָחָר
כִּי לֹא־תֵדַע מַה־יֵּלֶד יוֹם׃
2 יְהַלֶּלְךָ זָר וְלֹא־פִיךָ
נָכְרִי וְאַל־שְׂפָתֶיךָ׃
3 כֹּבֶד אֶבֶן וְנֵטֶל הַחוֹל
וְכַעַס אֱוִיל כָּבֵד מִשְּׁנֵיהֶם׃
4 אַכְזְרִיּוּת חֵמָה וְשֶׁטֶף אָף
וּמִי יַעֲמֹד לִפְנֵי קִנְאָה׃
5 טוֹבָה תּוֹכַחַת מְגֻלָּה
מֵאַהֲבָה מְסֻתָּרֶת׃

CHAPTER XXVII

1–2 BOASTFULNESS

1. *boast not thyself.* lit. 'praise not thyself,' speak in self-praise (Metsudath Zion).

of to-morrow. Of what you say is going to happen then (Rashi), or, of what you intend doing then (Ibn Ezra).

a day. i.e. the day before *to-morrow.* Ignorant of what to-day may bring, how much less can one know of the next day! (after Rashi, Ibn Nachmiash).

2. *praise thee.* The first verse deals with boastfulness about the future; this verse relates to the past and present. Do not sing your own praises for what you have accomplished; leave it to another to do this (Ralbag, Metsudath David). This is better than Ibn Ezra's comment: *let another man praise thee* after the event; *and not thine own lips* before the event.

3 A FOOL'S ANGER

a fool's vexation. The effect produced upon others when a fool loses his temper. It is particularly heavy because, being unrestrained by reason, it is immoderate (Metsudath David). The Hebrew word may also be translated 'provocation' (following Rashi).

4 FIERCENESS OF JEALOUSY

jealousy. That one harbours of his friend's good fortune (Isaiah da Trani).

5–6 RIGHTNESS OF REPROOF

5. *than love that is hidden.* Usually explained as a love which does not show itself by correcting a friend when it is necessary to do so and counsels a discreet silence. It is doubtful whether the Hebrew can bear this interpretation. Ibn Ezra understood the second clause as: 'than a rebuke of love which is administered in secret,' it being less effective because a public reproof will be more deeply felt and have a better chance of producing amendment. A translation which may be suggested as closely fitting the original is: 'Better a rebuke revealed than from love concealed.' It is no mark of true friendship to withhold reproof.

6 Faithful are the wounds of a friend;
But the kisses of an enemy are importunate.

7 The full soul loatheth a honeycomb;
But to the hungry soul every bitter thing is sweet.

8 As a bird that wandereth from her nest,
So is a man that wandereth from his place.

9 Ointment and perfume rejoice the heart;
So doth the sweetness of a man's friend by hearty counsel.

נֶאֱמָנִים פִּצְעֵי אוֹהֵב 6
וְנַעְתָּרוֹת נְשִׁיקוֹת שׂוֹנֵא׃
נֶפֶשׁ שְׂבֵעָה תָּבוּס נֹפֶת 7
וְנֶפֶשׁ רְעֵבָה כָּל־מַר מָתוֹק׃
כְּצִפּוֹר נוֹדֶדֶת מִן־קִנָּהּ 8
כֵּן אִישׁ נוֹדֵד מִמְּקוֹמוֹ׃
שֶׁמֶן וּקְטֹרֶת יְשַׂמַּח־לֵב 9
וּמֶתֶק רֵעֵהוּ מֵעֲצַת־נָפֶשׁ׃

6. *wounds of a friend.* Verbal castigation in correction of faults (Isaiah da Trani).

importunate. A.J.'s intention is probably identical with R.V.'s *profuse,* following Rashi. They seem burdensome to him as though they were many (Isaiah da Trani, Rashi to Gen. xxvi. 21). A.V. has *deceitful,* which appears to be the contrast to *faithful.* Scholars base this on the cognate Arabic root and it resembles Targum (Daath Mikra).

7 HUNGER THE BEST RELISH

the full soul. lit. 'satisfied soul,' sated appetite (see on x. 3).

loatheth. lit. 'trampleth,' rejects with disdain (Targum, Ibn Ezra). More likely, A.J. sees *tabus* as a byform for *tabuz,* 'despiseth,' or 'loatheth' (Ibn Nachmiash).

honeycomb. [Honey would be normally regarded as a welcome and wholesome article of food.]

to the hungry soul. Parallel with the second clause is a Talmudic proverb, 'The dog in his hunger swallows dung.' (Baba Kamma 92b).

8 HARDSHIP OF REMOVAL

from her nest. And has to find a place to build a new nest elsewhere (Isaiah da Trani).

his place. i.e. the place where he is settled. Each removal entailed in ancient times a severe strain, as is expressed in a proverb quoted in the Midrash (Gen. Rabbah 39.15), 'From one house to another a shirt, from one land to another a life.' Removal involves a personal loss proportionate to the distance.

9 VALUE OF SINCERE ADVICE

ointment and perfume. lit. 'oil and incense.' Their sweet odour is diffused and gives pleasure to whoever can smell it (Meiri).

by hearty counsel. lit. 'from advice of the soul,' given with a genuine desire to be helpful (Metsudath David).

10 Thine own friend, and thy father's friend, forsake not;
Neither go into thy brother's house in the day of thy calamity;
Better is a neighbour that is near than a brother far off.

11 My son, be wise, and make my heart glad,
That I may answer him that taunteth me.

12 A prudent man seeth the evil, and hideth himself;
But the thoughtless pass on, and are punished.

13 Take his garment that is surety for a stranger;
And hold him in pledge that is surety for an alien woman.

14 He that blesseth his friend with a loud voice, rising early in the morning,
It shall be counted a curse to him.

10 רֵעֲךָ וְרֵעַ אָבִיךָ אַל־תַּעֲזֹב
וּבֵית אָחִיךָ אַל־תָּבוֹא בְּיוֹם אֵידֶךָ
טוֹב שָׁכֵן קָרוֹב מֵאָח רָחוֹק׃
11 חֲכַם בְּנִי וְשַׂמַּח לִבִּי
וְאָשִׁיבָה חֹרְפִי דָבָר׃
12 עָרוּם ׀ רָאָה רָעָה נִסְתָּר
פְּתָאיִם עָבְרוּ נֶעֱנָשׁוּ׃
13 קַח־בִּגְדוֹ כִּי־עָרַב זָר
וּבְעַד נָכְרִיָּה חַבְלֵהוּ׃
14 מְבָרֵךְ רֵעֵהוּ ׀ בְּקוֹל גָּדוֹל
בַּבֹּקֶר הַשְׁכֵּים
קְלָלָה תֵּחָשֶׁב לוֹ׃

10 HELP FROM FRIENDS

thine . . . father's friend. The text signifies 'thy friend who is thy father's friend,' i.e. an old and tried friend of the family (Metsudath David).

forsake not. And do not rely on appealing to your brother in time of your calamity (Ralbag).

neither go. Better, 'and go not.' The teaching, as in xviii. 24, is that in a grave emergency, look for assistance from a proved friend rather than from a kinsman, even a brother (Metsudath David).

a neighbour that is near. Help may be urgently required, and then the factor of nearness is all-important (Ralbag).

11 EXHORTATION TO A PUPIL

my son. The term in which a teacher addresses his pupil (see on i. 8) (Saadia Gaon, Meiri).

be wise. Act in conformity with the doctrines of wisdom (Malbim).

that I may answer. The worth of a master is estimated from the character of his disciples. If, the speaker urges, I am reproved by a critic, let me be able to point to you as proof of my qualifications (Saadia Gaon).

14 INSINCERE GREETING

with a loud voice. His heartiness conceals feelings of animosity (Ibn Caspi).

rising early in the morning. An idiomatic phrase denoting zeal (cf. Jer. vii. 13), but in this instance it is only feigned (cf. Ibn Caspi, Daath Mikra).

counted a curse to him. The clause is ambiguous and can mean that God will punish the insincere man for his greeting as though it had been a curse; or the translation may be, 'let it be considered

15 A continual dropping in a very rainy day
And a contentious woman are alike;

16 He that would hide her hideth the wind,
And the ointment of his right hand betrayeth itself.

17 Iron sharpeneth iron;
So a man sharpeneth the countenance of his friend.

1 דֶּלֶף טוֹרֵד בְּיוֹם סַגְרִיר
וְאֵשֶׁת מִדְוֹנִים נִשְׁתָּוָה׃
1 צֹפְנֶיהָ צָפַן־רוּחַ
וְשֶׁמֶן יְמִינוֹ יִקְרָא׃
1 בַּרְזֶל בְּבַרְזֶל יָחַד
וְאִישׁ יַחַד פְּנֵי־רֵעֵהוּ׃

v. 15. מדינים ק׳

by him (the man who is greeted) as a curse'—let him not be deceived by the worth. The Rabbis (Arachin 16a) explain this to mean that if one praises his friend in publice for his generosity, his praise will be counted as a curse, for everyone will approach him for handouts and the government will demand much money for taxes. The Midrash (Tanhuma, Balak 15) sees here an allusion to Balaam, who blessed Israel aloud and later sought to bring them into sin (Rashi).

15–16 A QUARRELSOME WIFE

15. *a continual dropping.* The same phrase as in xix. 13 to be rendered, 'a downpour which drives out' the dwellers from a house (see Ibn Ezra).

woman. [The mistress of the house.]

alike. She also, by her nagging, drives the family away (Rashi).

16. *hide her.* This is a more accurate translation than the R.V. *restrain her.* Modern exegetes assert that the text is unintelligible, but the explanation of Metsudath David is simple: Whoever thinks to conceal her character from neighbours is like one attempting to enclose the wind. The effect is only to increase the sound of its howling; similarly this type of woman would raise her voice still louder if she knew that her husband was anxious for others not to hear her.

betrayeth itself. lit. 'calleth.' Metsudath David comments: A person who anointed himself with perfumed oil cannot hide the fact. The right hand, which was used for this purpose, retaining the scent of the oil poured into it, will at once disclose what had been done. So the nature of a quarrelsome woman cannot be kept a secret.

17 EFFECT OF SOCIAL INTERCOURSE

'Just as one piece of iron sharpens the other, so do scholars sharpen one another's mind in the study of the Torah' (Talmud Ta'anith 7a). The Rabbis held that knowledge is more fully and accurately acquired by studying with others.

18 Whoso keepeth the fig-tree shall eat the fruit thereof;
And he that waiteth on his master shall be honoured.

18 נֹצֵר תְּאֵנָה יֹאכַל פִּרְיָהּ
וְשֹׁמֵר אֲדֹנָיו יְכֻבָּד׃

19 As in water face answereth to face,
So the heart of man to man.

19 כַּמַּיִם הַפָּנִים לַפָּנִים
כֵּן לֵב הָאָדָם לָאָדָם׃

20 The nether-world and Destruction are never satiated;
So the eyes of man are never satiated.

20 שְׁאוֹל ואבדה לֹא תִשְׂבַּעְנָה
וְעֵינֵי הָאָדָם לֹא תִשְׂבַּעְנָה׃

21 The refining pot is for silver, and the furnace for gold,
And a man is tried by his praise.

21 מַצְרֵף לַכֶּסֶף וְכוּר לַזָּהָב
וְאִישׁ לְפִי מַהֲלָלוֹ׃

18 REWARD OF INDUSTRY

waiteth on. lit. 'keepeth, observeth,' works conscientiously for his master (Ibn Nachmiash).

honoured. [Or, 'enriched'; he will profit from his fidelity.]

19 THE REFLECTION OF SELF

The Hebrew is literally 'as water the face to the face, so the heart of man to man,' and the translation of A.J. follows A.V. and R.V. Accordingly the sense is: 'As water — the face that you show it, it shows you, so is the heart of man to man,' his friend; according to what man knows that his friend loves him, he shows him a smiling countenance (Rashi). Meiri elaborates on this matter, as follows: Just as the water reflects the exact features of a man's face, and when one looks at the water, he is sure to see an exact replica of his face, so, by looking at his heart, can he tell his friend's attitude to him. If he loves his friend sincerely, he may be sure that his friend loves him just as sincerely.

20 MAN'S INSATIABILITY

the nether-world and Destruction. See on XV. 11.

are never satiated. Cf. XXX. 16. Despite the multitudes that descend to their depths, they clamour for still more (Ibn Nachmiash).

eyes. The organ which arouses desire. The Talmud (Tamid 32b) has a legend about Alexander the Great that, in his travels, he arrived at the gates of heaven. When his demand for admission was reused, he requested a gift to serve as a memento. It took the form of a bone which had the remarkable property of outweighing all the gold heaped upon the other scale of the balance. When, however, the bone was covered with earth, it no longer outweighed the gold. He was told that the bone was that which enclosed the human eye. Only in the grave it ceased to crave for riches.

21 TEST OF CHARACTER

a man is tried by his praise. lit. 'a man is according to his praise.' The meaning given to the pronoun *his,* which can have an objective or subjective force, decides the interpretation. If the former, it signifies 'the praise of him,' the reputation he has among his fellows (Rashi, Metsudath David). According to R.V. margin, 'that which he praiseth' i.e. a test of a man is the kind of person or deed which he commends (Ibn Nachmiash).

22 Though thou shouldest bray a fool in a mortar with a pestle among groats,
Yet will not his foolishness depart from him.

23 Be thou diligent to know the state of thy flocks,
And look well to thy herds;

24 For riches are not for ever;
And doth the crown endure unto all generations?

25 When the hay is mown, and the tender grass showeth itself,
And the herbs of the mountains are gathered in;

22 אִם־תִּכְתּֽוֹשׁ אֶת־הָאֱוִיל ׀ בַּמַּכְתֵּשׁ
בְּתוֹךְ הָרִיפוֹת בַּעֱלִי
לֹא־תָסוּר מֵעָלָיו אִוַּלְתּֽוֹ׃
23 יָדֹעַ תֵּדַע פְּנֵי צֹאנֶךָ
שִׁית לִבְּךָ לַעֲדָרִֽים׃
24 כִּי לֹא לְעוֹלָם חֹסֶן
וְאִם־נֵזֶר לְדוֹר דּֽוֹר׃
25 גָּלָה חָצִיר וְנִרְאָה־דֶשֶׁא
וְנֶאֶסְפוּ עִשְּׂבוֹת הָרִֽים׃

v. 24. ודור ק'

22 FOLLY INERADICABLE

The point of the proverb is clear, viz. the most drastic measures will not remove stupidity from a fool, but the imagery is not so certain. Ibn Nachmiash identifies 'groats' with 'daissa' mentioned in the Talmud. When the groats are beaten with the pestle, their shells fall off. When the fool is beaten, however, his stupidity does not come off. This idea has been expressed above, ix. 8. The only reason for chastising fools is to punish them and to make an example of them so that others learn their lesson, as above, xix. 25. The Midrash renders: 'with raising among groats.' If one chastises a fool, when he raises the rod after striking him the first time, he forgets the first blow, and when he raises the rod after striking him the second time, he forgets the second blow.

23–27 SUPERIORITY OF RURAL LIFE

The purpose of this self-contained section is to advise a young man on the choice of his career. International trading which offered the prospect of large profits was tempting many to abandon the agricultural pursuits of their forefathers. The sage pictures the contentment of the simple life on the land and gives it preference over the luxuries of the city.

23. *state.* lit. 'face,' i.e. appearance, condition. Tend them well (Rashi).

flocks. Of sheep and goats (Daath Mikra).

24. *riches.* Wealth in the form of money derived from profitable business transactions; this is unstable and may be more than counterbalanced by losses (see Metsudath David).

the crown. The honours conferred upon the rich who reside in cities. These are not an enduring heritage, like land, to be bequeathed to descendants (Malbim).

25. *mown.* [Better, 'carried away' to the barn.]

tender grass. [Which grows after the crop of hay has been cut.]

herbs of the mountains. [Cf. Ps. cxlvii. 8. The pasturage of the hill-slopes is intended which is harvested at a later stage.]

The lambs will be for thy clothing,
And the goats the price for a field;

26 כְּבָשִׂים לִלְבוּשֶׁךָ
וּמְחִיר שָׂדֶה עַתּוּדִים׃

And there will be goats' milk enough for thy food, for the food of thy household;
And maintenance for thy maidens.

27 וְדֵי ׀ חֲלֵב עִזִּים לְלַחְמְךָ
לְלֶחֶם בֵּיתֶךָ
וְחַיִּים לְנַעֲרוֹתֶיךָ׃

28 CHAPTER XXVIII כח

'he wicked flee when no man pursueth;
ut the righteous are secure as a young lion.

1 נָסוּ וְאֵין־רֹדֵף רָשָׁע
וְצַדִּיקִים כִּכְפִיר יִבְטָח׃

or the transgression of a land many are the princes thereof;
ut by a man of understanding and knowledge established order shall long continue.

2 בְּפֶשַׁע אֶרֶץ רַבִּים שָׂרֶיהָ
וּבְאָדָם מֵבִין יֹדֵעַ כֵּן יַאֲרִיךְ׃

26. *for thy clothing.* Its wool will provide material for clothes worked by the women of the household (xxxi. 13, 19).

for a field. Additional land (cf. xxxi. 16).

27. *goats' milk.* Mentioned as an article of diet in Deut. xxxii. 14.

for thy maidens. [They will be supported by the produce and have no need to become handmaids to others.]

CHAPTER XXVIII

1 THE WORKING OF CONSCIENCE

the wicked flee. The moral of the verse is that their conscience plagues them, and they flee at the sound of a crackling leaf, imagining that they are being pursued (Ibn Ezra).

2–3 CORRUPT JUDGES

2. *many are the princes.* The modern interpretation is that the verse teaches that a frequent change in the person of the ruler, creating instability in the land, is a punishment for national sin. Rashi explains that the penalty is multiplication of governors who batten on the people, and this is supported by the statement: 'The Arabs have a current anecdote of a wise man who used this imprecation upon his enemies, "May God multiply your sheikhs"—a fearful malediction! No more certain or expeditious plan to ruin one's enemies could be devised. The people familiarly ascribe such a calamity to the greatness of their sins' (Thomson).

established order. This follows Metsudath David. Or, 'right,' justice and equity. In that case, we render: 'a man of understanding, knowing right, will prolong (his days) (Ibn Nachmiash, Isaiah da Trani, J. Kimchi). For the Hebrew word *ken,* see on xi. 19.

3 גבר רש ועשק דלים
מטר סחף ואין לחם׃
4 עזבי תורה יהללו רשע
ושמרי תורה יתגרו בם׃
5 אנשי־רע לא־יבינו משפט
ומבקשי יהוה יבינו כל׃
6 טוב רש הולך בתמו
מעקש דרכים והוא עשיר׃

3 A poor man that oppresseth the weak
Is like a sweeping rain which leaveth no food.

4 They that forsake the law praise the wicked;
But such as keep the law contend with them.

5 Evil men understand not justice;
But they that seek the LORD understand all things.

6 Better is the poor that walketh in his integrity,
Than he that is perverse in his ways, though he be rich.

3. *a poor man.* The exactions of a wealthy ruler are bad enough, but they become much more severe when a poor man grasps power which he uses for self-enrichment (J. Kimchi).

a sweeping rain. 'The illustrative comparison here is most impressive. It is founded upon a phenomenon which I have frequently seen, and sometimes felt. A small black cloud traverses the sky in the latter part of the summer of the beginning of autumn, and pours down a flood of rain that sweeps all before it. The Arabs call it *sale*; we, a waterspout, or the bursting of a cloud. In the neighbourhood of Hermon I have witnessed it repeatedly. . . . Every summer threshing-floor along the line of its march was swept bare of all precious food, cattle were drowned, flocks disappeared. Wherever it came it left no food behind it, and such is the oppression of a poor man that oppresseth the poor. These landlords and sheikhs are generally poor, hungry, greedy, remorseless, and they come in successive swarms, each more ravenous than his predecessor' (Thomson).

4 ATTITUDE TOWARDS THE WICKED

the law. Hebrew *Torah,* again in verses 7 and 9. In these passages the term signifies the 'direction' of the revealed 'law' of God. They who abandon this teaching may be Torah scholars who are not perfectly righteous. They, therefore, fear the prosperous wicked and flatter them (Ibn Nachmiash).

as keep the law. i.e. the perfectly righteous, do not fear the wicked, but con appreciation in its price (Baba Metsia 60b).

5 COMPREHENSION OF JUSTICE

understand not. For the sense of *understand,* see on i. 2. Men who follow evil do not 'distinguish' between justice and its opposite (Ibn Ezra, Ibn Nachmiash).

seek the LORD. To know and obey His will (Ibn Nachmiash).

understand all things. Better, 'understand (it) completely,' because they are sensitive of the distinction between right and wrong (Ibn Nachmiash).

6 HONEST POVERTY PREFERABLE TO DISHONEST WEALTH

better . . . integrity. Identical with the first clause of xix. 1.

his ways. The Hebrew is dual, not plural: 'his two ways,' double-dealing (Daath Mikra).

7 A wise son observeth the teaching;
But he that is a companion of gluttonous men shameth his father.

8 He that augmenteth his substance by interest and increase,
Gathereth it for him that is gracious to the poor.

9 He that turneth away his ear from hearing the law,
Even his prayer is an abomination.

10 Whoso causeth the upright to go astray in an evil way,
He shall fall himself into his own pit;
But the whole-hearted shall inherit good.

7 נוֹצֵר תּוֹרָה בֵּן מֵבִין
וְרֹעֶה זוֹלְלִים יַכְלִים אָבִיו׃
8 מַרְבֶּה הוֹנוֹ בְּנֶשֶׁךְ וּבְתַרְבִּית
לְחוֹנֵן דַּלִּים יִקְבְּצֶנּוּ׃
9 מֵסִיר אָזְנוֹ מִשְּׁמֹעַ תּוֹרָה
גַּם־תְּפִלָּתוֹ תּוֹעֵבָה׃
10 מַשְׁגֶּה יְשָׁרִים ׀ בְּדֶרֶךְ רָע
בִּשְׁחוּתוֹ הוּא־יִפּוֹל
וּתְמִימִים יִנְחֲלוּ־טוֹב׃

v. 8. יתיר ב׳ (וְתַרְבִּית)

7 INSTRUCTION A GUIDE TO THE YOUNG

a wise man . . . teaching. Better, 'He who observeth instruction *(Torah)* is an understanding son'; he discerns his obligation, to gladden his parents' heart by good conduct (see Ralbag).

gluttonous men. See on xxiii. 20. Such men were bad companions and association with them had a demoralizing effect (Ralbag).

8 NO PROSPERITY FROM USURY

interest and increase. Both terms occur in Lev. xxv. 36. The Rabbis drew no distinction between them except in the case of Rabbinical prohibitions. Then, *interest* is the repayment of a larger sum than that loaned. *Increase* is the benefit a purchaser of produce derives from an appreciation in its price (Baba Metsia 60b).

gathereth. God will not allow him to retain the profit, diverting it into the possession of one more worthy to have it (Metsudath David).

gracious to the poor. [Eventually, therefore, the money helps the needy.]

9 PRAYER OF THE WICKED UNACCEPTABLE

turneth away his ear. The action implies a wilful disinclination to heed the teachings of the Torah (Meiri).

his prayer is an abomination. Cf. xv. 8. Since he refuses to hearken to God's instruction, God refuses to hearken to his prayer (Metsudath David).

10 CORRUPTION OF THE GOOD IS PUNISHED

in an evil way. The path of wickedness (as in viii. 13), not harm and misfortune (Saadia Gaon).

fall . . . pit. Cf. xxvi. 27.

whole-hearted . . . good. Cf. ii. 21.

11 The rich man is wise in his own eyes;
But the poor that hath understanding searcheth him through.

12 When the righteous exult, there is great glory;
But when the wicked rise, men must be sought for.

13 He that covereth his transgressions shall not prosper;
But whoso confesseth and forsaketh them shall obtain mercy.

14 Happy is the man that feareth alway;
But he that hardeneth his heart shall fall into evil.

11 חָכָם בְּעֵינָיו אִישׁ עָשִׁיר
וְדַל מֵבִין יַחְקְרֶנּוּ׃
12 בַּעֲלֹץ צַדִּיקִים רַבָּה תִפְאָרֶת
וּבְקוּם רְשָׁעִים יְחֻפַּשׂ אָדָם׃
13 מְכַסֶּה פְשָׁעָיו לֹא יַצְלִיחַ
וּמוֹדֶה וְעֹזֵב יְרֻחָם׃
14 אַשְׁרֵי אָדָם מְפַחֵד תָּמִיד
וּמַקְשֶׁה לִבּוֹ יִפּוֹל בְּרָעָה׃

11 CONCEIT OF THE RICH

wise in his own eyes. Having been successful in business, he forms the opinion that he is clever in all matters and deference must be paid to his views (Ralbag).

searcheth him through. Weighs him up accurately and makes a true estimate of his mental capacity (Ibn Ezra).

12 EFFECT OF GOOD AND BAD GOVERNMENT

when the righteous exult. Because the land is administered justly and they have nothing to fear (Metsudath David).

glory. Better, 'splendour,' referring to the conditions of living. Under just rule taxation is not oppressive and the citizens have money to spend on personal adornment and a comfortable home (Ibn Nachmiash).

the wicked rise. To power; they see in their office an opportunity to grow rich (Metsudath David).

men must be sought for. Render, 'men are searched' for their possessions and plundered (so Ibn Ezra). For this meaning of the verb, cf. Obadiah 6.

13 CONFESSION OF SIN

covereth. He refuses to admit his guilt (see the language of Ps. xxxii. 5).

shall not prosper. Better, 'shall not succeed,' viz. in his repentance (Ibn Nachmiash).

forsaketh. Confession by itself has no efficacy; it must be accompanied by a determination not to repeat the offence. The Rabbis (Yoma 85b) taught the futility of a man saying. 'I will repent, and again sin, and again repent.'

obtain mercy. God will pardon him (Metsudath David).

14 DREAD OF SINNING

feareth. This is not the verb used for 'reverencing' God; it here signifies apprehension of sin and its consequences (Rashi).

hardeneth his heart. He scorns such fear, consciously disregards the thought of God's punishment, and wilfully commits a wrong (Ibn Ezra).

evil. Calamity which is the manifestation of the Divine judgment (Daath Mikra).

As a roaring lion, and a ravenous bear;
So is a wicked ruler over a poor people.

15 אֲרִי־נֹהֵם וְדֹב שׁוֹקֵק
מוֹשֵׁל רָשָׁע עַל עַם־דָּל׃

The prince that lacketh understanding is also a great oppressor;
But he that hateth covetousness shall prolong his days.

16 נָגִיד חֲסַר תְּבוּנוֹת וְרַב מַעֲשַׁקּוֹת
שֹׂנְאֵי בֶצַע יַאֲרִיךְ יָמִים׃

A man that is laden with the blood of any person
Shall hasten his steps unto the pit; none will support him.

17 אָדָם עָשֻׁק בְּדַם־נָפֶשׁ
עַד־בּוֹר יָנוּס אַל־יִתְמְכוּ־בוֹ׃

v. 16. יתיר י׳ (שֹׂנֵא)

15–16 A GRASPING RULER

15. *a roaring lion.* With a victim in its grasp (cf. *Will a lion roar in the forest, when he hath no prey?* Amos iii. 4) (Isaiah da Trani).

a ravenous bear. Or 'a bear roaming' in search of food. The verb is used of swarming locusts (Joel ii. 9) (Ibn Nachmiash).

over a poor people. Weak and helpless (Metsudath David).

16. The translation of A.J. agrees with A.V. which is altered by R.V. margin into, 'O prince that lackest understanding and art a great oppressor, he,' etc. The text best accords with the comment of Ibn Ezra which takes the sentence to be a continuation of the preceding verse: '(He is) a governor lacking understanding and abounding in oppressions; (but) he that hateth,' etc.

that lacketh understanding. Unlike king Solomon (1 Kings iii. 9). The ruler who lacks *understanding* fails to appreciate that only by benign government can he have a happy reign and a secure throne (Rashi).

he that hateth. The *kethib* is plural, alluding to the ruler and the prince (Ibn Ezra).

covetousness. It is greed that often leads to a ruler's tyranny in the form of heavy exactions from the people. When this vice is absent, happy are both ruler and ruled (Meiri).

17 FATE OF A MURDERER

The verse is obscure and most probably deals with the case of a man who, guilty of homicide, is being pursued by the *avenger of blood* (Num. xxxv. 19ff.).

laden with the blood. Rather, 'oppressed because of the blood'; as the consequence of his act, he is being hunted from place to place (Daath Mikra).

shall hasten his steps into the pit. lit. 'unto a pit he shall (or, let him) flee,' *pit* being understood as 'the grave'; i.e. he must remain a fugitive until he dies (Rashi). [But it is doubtful whether *pit* can have this meaning here. Possibly the word *bor* is to be given the sense which it has in Rabbinic Hebrew, 'uncultivated land': let him flee away from the towns to an uninhabited spot. The verse was apparently written when the institution of *cities of refuge* (Num. xxxv) ceased to function.] Daath Mikra, however, renders *bor* as 'dungeon,' referring to the refuge cities, which were like prisons for the murderers.

18 Whoso walketh uprightly shall be saved;
But he that is perverse in his ways shall fall at once.

19 He that tilleth his ground shall have plenty of bread;
But he that followeth after vain things shall have poverty enough.

20 A faithful man shall abound with blessings;
But he that maketh haste to be rich shall not be unpunished.

21 To have respect of persons is not good;
For a man will transgress for a piece of bread.

18 הוֹלֵךְ תָּמִים יִוָּשֵׁעַ
וְנֶעְקַשׁ דְּרָכַיִם יִפּוֹל בְּאֶחָת׃
19 עֹבֵד אַדְמָתוֹ יִשְׂבַּע־לָחֶם
וּמְרַדֵּף רֵיקִים יִשְׂבַּע־רִישׁ׃
20 אִישׁ אֱמוּנוֹת רַב־בְּרָכוֹת
וְאָץ לְהַעֲשִׁיר לֹא יִנָּקֶה׃
21 הַכֵּר־פָּנִים לֹא־טוֹב
וְעַל־פַּת־לֶחֶם יִפְשַׁע־גָּבֶר׃

18 PERVERSITY PUNISHED

walketh uprightly. As in Ps. xv. 2.

saved. From the calamities which surround him (Metsudath David).

perverse in his ways. Cf. verse 6, *ways* being here also in the dual number; a double-dealer (Daath Mikra).

at once. lit. 'in one,' which is most naturally to be connected with *ways.* If he proceeds along the one straight path, he makes progress; should he keep diverging from one path to another, he will stumble in one of them. Classical commentators explain: 'with one misfortune' which will crush him so completely that he cannot recover.

19 ADVANTAGE OF AGRICULTURE

A variant of xii. 11.

shall have poverty enough. A different ending to the verse as compared with xii. 11, but giving a more forceful contrast to *shall have plenty of bread.*

20 HASTE TO GET RICH

a faithful man. Commonly explained as a person who shows fidelity in his transactions; the verse then teaches that 'honesty is the best policy' (see Ibn Ezra).

shall abound with blessings. From others and from God (Ibn Ezra).

shall not be unpunished. For the dishonest acts he committed in his haste. A better rendering is 'shall not be free of guilt'; his eagerness to accumulate wealth quickly will tempt him to commit fraud or theft (Metsudath David).

21 IMPARTIALITY IN JUSTICE

transgress for a piece of bread. The usual explanation is that even a trivial bribe will induce a venal judge to give a false verdict (Meiri). It is better to understand the clause as citing an instance in which a judge might think himself justified in departing from strict justice, viz. a man is driven by hunger to steal a piece of bread. Even in this circumstance, urges the sage, there should be no 'respecting of persons' and the law must be upheld, and his teaching agrees with Exod. xxiii. 3; Lev. xix. 15 (Daath Mikra).

2 He that hath an evil eye hasteneth after riches,
And knoweth not that want shall come upon him.

3 He that rebuketh a man shall in the end find more favour
Than he that flattereth with the tongue.

4 Whoso robbeth his father or his mother, and saith: 'It is no transgression,'
The same is the companion of a destroyer.

He that is of a greedy spirit stirreth up strife;
But he that putteth his trust in the LORD shall be abundantly gratified.

22 נִבֳהָל לַהוֹן אִישׁ רַע עָיִן
וְלֹא־יֵדַע כִּי־חֶסֶר יְבֹאֶנּוּ׃
23 מוֹכִיחַ אָדָם אַחֲרַי חֵן יִמְצָא
מִמַּחֲלִיק לָשׁוֹן׃
24 גּוֹזֵל ׀ אָבִיו וְאִמּוֹ וְאֹמֵר אֵין־פָּשַׁע
חָבֵר הוּא לְאִישׁ מַשְׁחִית׃
25 רְחַב־נֶפֶשׁ יְגָרֶה מָדוֹן
וּבֹטֵחַ עַל־יְהוָה יְדֻשָּׁן׃

22 THE ENVIOUS COME TO WANT

evil eye. One who envies the possessions of others (see on xxiii. 6) (Meiri).

knoweth not. He is unaware that God will punish him by bringing him to a state of destitution (Isaiah da Trani).

23 REPROOF PREFERRED TO FLATTERY

in the end. The Hebrew word is an unusual form of the adverb and means 'afterwards.' The verse teaches that a person may at first be taken in by flattery, but eventually comes to see that he who corrects his faults is his real friend (Rashi). Ibn Ezra renders: 'after me,' meaning 'after Solomon's precepts.' Isaiah da Trani renders: 'behind my back.' Although he should have reproved me to my face rather than behind my back, he is still better than 'he that flattereth with the tongue.'

24 ROBBING PARENTS

it is no transgression. The son acts on the plea that he is entitled to his parents possessions since he will eventually inherit them (Ralbag, Metsudath David). Saadia Gaon explains that one may believe that parents or relatives will overlook the sins of their children and relatives.

companion of a destroyer. Cf. the phrase in xviii. 9. He allies himself with those who destroy other people and rob their property (Metsudath David).

25 HARM CAUSED BY GREED

greedy spirit. lit. 'wide of soul (desire)' (see on x. 3), a person of grasping disposition (Rashi).

stirreth up strife. He is liable to encroach upon his neighbour's rites and so become a cause of contention (Ibn Nachmiash).

trust in the LORD. To provide his needs (Metsudath David).

shall be abundantly gratified. See on xi. 25.

26 **He that trusteth in his own heart is a fool;**
But whoso walketh wisely, he shall escape.

27 **He that giveth unto the poor shall not lack;**
But he that hideth his eyes shall have many a curse.

28 **When the wicked rise, men hide themselves;**
But when they perish, the righteous increase.

26 בּוֹטֵחַ בְּלִבּוֹ הוּא כְסִיל
וְהוֹלֵךְ בְּחָכְמָה הוּא יִמָּלֵט׃
27 נוֹתֵן לָרָשׁ אֵין מַחְסוֹר
וּמַעְלִים עֵינָיו רַב־מְאֵרוֹת׃
28 בְּקוּם רְשָׁעִים יִסָּתֵר אָדָם
וּבְאָבְדָם יִרְבּוּ צַדִּיקִים׃

26 OVERCONFIDENCE

trusteth in his own heart. Relies on his own understanding and is not guided by competent teachers and advisers. He also neglects the principles of wisdom and follows his own judgment (Ralbag, Metsudath David).

walketh wisely. lit. 'walketh in wisdom,' along the path directed by wisdom (Meiri).

shall escape. The harm which comes from too much confidence in self (Meiri).

27 ON CHARITY

shall not lack. On the principle taught in xix. 17.

hideth his eyes. From the distress of the needy (Ibn Ezra).

many a curse. Will befall him. This is the antithesis of *shall not lack.* Instead of saving his money by refraining from giving charity, he will lose it (Metsudath David). cf. 'Reject not a suppliant in his affliction; and turn not away thy face from a poor man. Turn not away thine eye from one that asketh of thee, and give none occasion to a man to curse thee. For if he curse thee in the bitterness of his soul, He that made him will hear his supplication' (Ecclus. iv. 4ff.). A similar thought occurs in Deut. xv. 9.

28 EFFECT OF GOOD AND BAD GOVERNMENT

A variant of verse 12 and cf. xxix. 2.

rise. To power and exercise control over the community (Metsudath David).

men hide themselves. Those not of their group hide themselves from fear of oppression (Metsudath David). Ibn Ezra explains that those who execute justice hide from them. Saadia Gaon sees here an admonition to a king always to appoint righteous judges and aids.

increase. Some understand this to signify increase in power and influence (Ibn Nachmiash). More probably it means increase in numbers; they come into the open and their presence is more noticeable (Metsudath David).

29 CHAPTER XXIX כט

1 He that being often reproved hardeneth his neck
Shall suddenly be broken, and that without remedy.

2 When the righteous are increased, the people rejoice;
But when the wicked beareth rule, the people sigh.

3 Whoso loveth wisdom rejoiceth his father;
But he that keepeth company with harlots wasteth his substance.

4 The king by justice establisheth the land;
But he that exacteth gifts overthroweth it.

אִישׁ תּוֹכָחוֹת מַקְשֶׁה־עֹרֶף 1
פֶּתַע יִשָּׁבֵר וְאֵין מַרְפֵּא׃
בִּרְבוֹת צַדִּיקִים יִשְׂמַח הָעָם 2
וּבִמְשֹׁל רָשָׁע יֵאָנַח עָם׃
אִישׁ־אֹהֵב חָכְמָה יְשַׂמַּח אָבִיו 3
וְרֹעֶה זוֹנוֹת יְאַבֶּד־הוֹן׃
מֶלֶךְ בְּמִשְׁפָּט יַעֲמִיד אָרֶץ 4
וְאִישׁ תְּרוּמוֹת יֶהֶרְסֶנָּה׃

CHAPTER XXIX

1 FATE OF THE STIFFNECKED

he that being often reproved. lit. 'a man of reproofs,' a person who has been frequently cautioned (Ibn Ezra).

hardeneth his neck. The same idiom as in the phrase *a stiffnecked people* (Exod. xxxii. 9); stubborn and unwilling to bend the neck in submission (Metsudath David).

2 GOOD AND BAD GOVERNMENT

when the righteous are increased. The verb has the same force as in xxviii. 28; the righteous are able to assert themselves and take charge of affairs (Ralbag).

the wicked. [lit. 'a wicked man,' referring to an unjust ruler; but the word may be construed collectively. Some Hebrew MSS. read the plural.]

3 EFFECT OF LICENTIOUSNESS

whoso. lit. 'a man.' [Ordinarily the word 'son' occurs in such a connection, e.g. x. 1. The substitution of 'man' in this verse may signify an adult, whose father is advanced in years and dependent upon him.]

loveth wisdom. His life is disciplined by moral principles, and he avoids association with harlots (cf. ii. 1ff., v. 1ff., vi. 24) (Ralbag).

rejoiceth his father. The context suggests that, not having dissipated his money in riotous living, he gladdens his father's old age by maintaining him in comfort (see below).

wasteth his substance. Consequently both he and his father are reduced to penury (Metsudath David).

4 JUST AND OPPRESSIVE RULE

establisheth. lit. 'causeth to stand,' stabilizes and brings prosperity to the country (Ralbag).

he that exacteth gifts. lit. 'a man of exactions.' The Hebrew noun normally denotes parts of the sacrifices assigned to the priests; but in Ezek. xlv. 13, 16, it is employed for the gifts presented to *the prince in Israel* (see Ibn Ezra).

5 A man that flattereth his neighbour
Spreadeth a net for his steps.

6 In the transgression of an evil man there is a snare;
But the righteous doth sing and rejoice.

7 The righteous taketh knowledge of the cause of the poor;
The wicked understandeth not knowledge.

8 Scornful men set a city in a blaze;
But wise men turn away wrath.

9 If a wise man contendeth with a foolish man,
Whether he be angry or laugh, there will be no rest.

5 גֶּבֶר מַחֲלִיק עַל־רֵעֵהוּ
רֶשֶׁת פּוֹרֵשׂ עַל־פְּעָמָיו׃
6 בְּפֶשַׁע אִישׁ רָע מוֹקֵשׁ
וְצַדִּיק יָרוּן וְשָׂמֵחַ׃
7 יֹדֵעַ צַדִּיק דִּין דַּלִּים
רָשָׁע לֹא־יָבִין דָּעַת׃
8 אַנְשֵׁי לָצוֹן יָפִיחוּ קִרְיָה
וַחֲכָמִים יָשִׁיבוּ אָף׃
9 אִישׁ־חָכָם נִשְׁפָּט אֶת־אִישׁ אֱוִיל
וְרָגַז וְשָׂחַק וְאֵין נָחַת׃

5 THE DECEIVER IS PUNISHED

flattereth. lit. 'maketh smooth,' either his words with the aim of misleading (Ibn Ezra), or 'maketh (the path) slippery' for his neighbour to fall (Metsudath David). The latter is preferable.

for his steps. Classical commentators rightly understand this as 'his own steps.' The moral is that of xxvi. 27, xxviii. 10.

6 THE SNARE OF THE WICKED

a snare. Intended for the ruin of another, but the schemer is himself caught in it (Metsudath David).

the righteous. He does not plot against his fellows and is not 'hoist with his own petard'; therefore he can go on his way happy (Metsudath David).

7 THE RIGHTS OF THE POOR

cause. lit. 'judgment,' the just rights (Ralbag).

understandeth not knowledge. As defined in the first clause; pays no attention to the rights of the weak (Ralbag).

8 SCORNERS STIR UP STRIFE

set a city in a blaze. lit. 'blow (fan the flame on) a city'; they take pleasure in accentuating differences among the population to arouse disorder (cf. xxii. 10) (Metsudath David).

turn away wrath. The wise endeavour to smooth out these differences so that a peaceful atmosphere is created (Metsudath David).

9 ARGUING WITH A FOOL IS FUTILE

whether he be angry or laugh. The subject of the verbs is ambiguous. The LXX applies the words to the fool, the Vulgate to the wise man. Ibn Ezra's view accords with the former, explaining that whatever the fool does, whether he be angry or laugh the wise man has no rest from him. Rashi adopts the latter, whether the wise man shows anger to the fool or shows him a friendly countenance, there is no rest from him.

there will be no rest. Better, 'there is no satisfaction,' lit. 'quietness' of spirit. The discussion leads nowhere and is a waste of words (Meiri).

10 The men of blood hate him that is sincere;
And as for the upright, they seek his life.

11 A fool spendeth all his spirit;
But a wise man stilleth it within him.

12 If a ruler hearkeneth to falsehood,
All his servants are wicked.

10 אַנְשֵׁי דָמִים יִשְׂנְאוּ־תָם
וִישָׁרִים יְבַקְשׁוּ נַפְשׁוֹ׃
11 כָּל־רוּחוֹ יוֹצִיא כְסִיל
וְחָכָם בְּאָחוֹר יְשַׁבְּחֶנָּה׃
12 מֹשֵׁל מַקְשִׁיב עַל־דְּבַר־שָׁקֶר
כָּל־מְשָׁרְתָיו רְשָׁעִים׃

10 TREATMENT OF A GOOD MAN

men of blood. Persons who resort to murder to gain their end (Ibn Ezra).

sincere. i.e. a man who recoils from a wrong act when it is to his advantage to do wrong. His strict principles earn him the hatred of the unscrupulous (Ibn Nachmiash).

and as for . . . life. A difficult clause, since the phrase *seek his life* elsewhere means to plot one's death, an act which can hardly be ascribed to *the upright*. Malbim tries to overcome the difficulty not very successfully, by interpreting: 'and as for the upright (they hate them) that seek his life.' Ibn Ezra explains *seek* in the sense of 'demand retribution for,' a signification possessed by the synonymous verb *darash,* which is found in *no man careth for my soul* (Ps. cxlii. 5). Rashi and other commentators assign that meaning to the verb *bikkesh* in this verse, hence R.V. margin, 'but the upright care for his soul.' Whereas evil persons hate a sincere man and desire to harm him, the upright appreciate his qualities and wish to do him good. This is the only satisfactory way to explain the text, and the argument that the phrase has usually the opposite force is not decisive against it.

11 CONTROL OF ANGER

spirit. A synonym for 'anger' as in xvi. 32, xxv. 28. A fool, when roused, gives full vent to his temper and fails to exercise restraint (Metsudath David).

a wise . . . him. A.J. gives a paraphrase rather than a translation. The crucial word is *achor* which commonly means 'backward'; therefore R.V. *a wise man keepeth it back and stilleth it.* It also signifies 'hereafter,' and this suggested A.V. *a wise man keepeth it till afterwards.* Rashi explains: 'But a wise man stilleth it afterwards.' After the fool has let out all his anger, the wise man stills it with his speech. Ibn Nachmiash suggests: 'the wise man stills it by keeping it back.' He stills his own anger by keeping it back instead of venting it.

12 A BAD RULER CORRUPTS

hearkeneth. Pays attention to and acts upon (Metsudath David).

falsehood. [False accusations.]

all his servants are wicked. Because they are liable to take advantage of the ruler's weakness and bring lying charges. Similar is the statement of Ecclus. x. 2, 'As is the ruler of his people, so are his ministers.'

13 The poor man and the oppressor meet together;
The LORD giveth light to the eyes of them both.

13 רָשׁ וְאִישׁ תְּכָכִים נִפְגָּשׁוּ
מֵאִיר עֵינֵי שְׁנֵיהֶם יְהוָה׃

14 The king that faithfully judgeth the poor,
His throne shall be established for ever.

14 מֶלֶךְ שׁוֹפֵט בֶּאֱמֶת דַּלִּים
כִּסְאוֹ לָעַד יִכּוֹן׃

15 The rod and reproof give wisdom;
But a child left to himself causeth shame to his mother.

15 שֵׁבֶט וְתוֹכַחַת יִתֵּן חָכְמָה
וְנַעַר מְשֻׁלָּח מֵבִישׁ אִמּוֹ׃

16 When the wicked are increased, transgression increaseth;
But the righteous shall gaze upon their fall.

16 בִּרְבוֹת רְשָׁעִים יִרְבֶּה־פָּשַׁע
וְצַדִּיקִים בְּמַפַּלְתָּם יִרְאוּ׃

13 EQUALITY BEFORE GOD

The verse is a variant of xxii. 2.

oppressor. lit. 'man of oppressions,' an epithet of the rich who, in Proverbs, are characterized as a class which oppresses the poor (Ibn Nachmiash). Ibn Ezra renders: 'a man broken by poverty.' He suggests: 'a man whose wealth was stolen through oppression and guile.'

meet together. In the streets of the city. The oppressor says, 'The poor man lives frugally, yet he is satisfied with his lot in order to avoid stealing and cheating. Why should I not do the same?' Consequently, he repents of his dishonest ways. The poor man says, 'Look at that thief. He lives only by dishonest means and does not prepare anything for the hereafter. Is not my poverty better than his riches?' Hence, the oppressor repents and the poor man makes peace with his lot (Ibn Nachmiash). Ibn Ezra renders: 'were punished.' They were both punished by God's decree.

giveth light to the eyes. According to Ibn Ezra. 'the LORD giveth light to the eyes of both of them,' by giving them their want. According to Ibn Nachmiash, He *giveth light* to the oppressor by showing him the way of repentance, and to the poor man by giving him courage to endure his poverty.

14 JUST RULE IS STABLE

the king. Hebrew 'a king.' [The monarch was the first judge in the land.]

the poor. The same word as in verse 7. [To secure their rights was the highest test of a just government.]

15 TRAINING A CHILD

the rod and reproof. Daath Mikra construes 'the rod of correction.' It may, however, indicate two different methods of exercising discipline: corporal punishment (xiii. 24) and verbal admonition (Meiri, Ibn Nachmiash).

a child left to himself. lit. 'a lad let go,' to run wild and unchecked (Rashi).

16 THE WICKED OVERTHROWN

are increased. See on verse 2.

shall gaze upon. i.e. shall have the satisfaction of seeing (Ibn Ezra).

17 Correct thy son, and he will give thee rest;
Yea, he will give delight unto thy soul.

18 Where there is no vision, the people cast off restraint;
But he that keepeth the law, happy is he.

19 A servant will not be corrected by words;
For though he understand, there will be no response.

20 Seest thou a man that is hasty in his words?
There is more hope for a fool than for him.

17 יַסֵּר בִּנְךָ וִינִיחֶךָ
וְיִתֵּן מַעֲדַנִּים לְנַפְשֶׁךָ׃
18 בְּאֵין חָזוֹן יִפָּרַע עָם
וְשֹׁמֵר תּוֹרָה אַשְׁרֵהוּ׃
19 בִּדְבָרִים לֹא־יִוָּסֶר עָבֶד
כִּי־יָבִין וְאֵין מַעֲנֶה׃
20 חָזִיתָ אִישׁ אָץ בִּדְבָרָיו
תִּקְוָה לִכְסִיל מִמֶּנּוּ׃

17 REWARD OF TRAINING A CHILD

will give thee rest. The accepted explanation is, will relieve you of anxiety about conduct, and *delight* (lit. 'dainties') is taken in a figurative sense. As Daath Mikra asserts, the verse may deal with the physical comforts which parents enjoy when their son leads a steady life: he gives them rest in their old age by caring for them and providing them with what they need.

18 ATTITUDE TO DIVINE GUIDANCE

vision. The Hebrew word is used specifically of God's medium for the communication of His will through a prophet, and the intention here is that when the Jews are responsible for the cessation of prophecy, they will cast off restraint and adopt evil ways. Accordingly, this refers to the period of the Second Temple, when there were no longer any prophets (Rashi). Ibn Ezra sees *vision* as 'a man of vision.' When there is no man of vision to reprove them, the people cast off restraint. Ibn Nachmiash takes this as an allusion to the episode of the golden calf, when Moses' absence in the camp brought about the making and worshipping of the calf. Interestingly, the word *pera'oh,* 'had let them loose,' (Ex. xxxii. 25) is used in that context (Ibn Nachmiash).

21 He that delicately bringeth up his servant from a child
Shall have him become a master at the last.

22 An angry man stirreth up strife,
And a wrathful man aboundeth in transgression.

23 A man's pride shall bring him low;
But he that is of a lowly spirit shall attain to honour.

24 Whoso is partner with a thief hateth his own soul:
He heareth the adjuration and uttereth nothing.

21 מְפַנֵּק מִנֹּעַר עַבְדּוֹ
וְאַחֲרִיתוֹ יִהְיֶה מָנוֹן׃
22 אִישׁ־אַף יְגָרֶה מָדוֹן
וּבַעַל חֵמָה רַב־פָּשַׁע׃
23 גַּאֲוַת אָדָם תַּשְׁפִּילֶנּוּ
וּשְׁפַל־רוּחַ יִתְמֹךְ כָּבוֹד׃
24 חוֹלֵק עִם־גַּנָּב שׂוֹנֵא נַפְשׁוֹ
אָלָה יִשְׁמַע וְלֹא יַגִּיד׃

21 PAMPERING A SLAVE

delicately bringeth up. [i.e. pampers, rears him in a manner which makes him unfit for the work he will be required to do when grown up.]

a master. The Hebrew word occurs nowhere else and its translation is doubtful. A.J. agrees with Rashi; R.V. *shall have him become a son at last* follows Ibn Ezra, i.e. the slave will conduct himself as though he was a freeborn son of the house.

22 A HASTY TEMPER

an angry man . . . strife. Almost identical with xv. 18.

wrathful man. [One who has a hot temper which he cannot control.]

aboundeth in transgression. In his rage he commits wrongs because his moral sense becomes clouded by the fumes of anger (Metsudath David).

23 PRIDE AND HUMILITY

shall bring him low. Cf. xi. 2, xvi. 18.

shall attain to honour. Cf. xv. 33, xviii. 12. There is a Rabbinic aphorism, 'He who runs after honour, honour flees from him; he who shuns honour, honour pursues him' (source unknown).

24 PARTNERSHIP IN THEFT

hateth his own soul. Is an enemy to himself since he contributes to his own undoing, as below.

the adjuration. The writer has Lev. v. 1 in mind. Although the accessory may not have committed the theft, he has knowledge of it and is in a position to give evidence. When a proclamation is issued calling for witnesses and he fails to respond because he is implicated, he becomes liable to the curse which was pronounced upon those who withhold evidence (Ibn Ezra), or upon those who swear that they have no knowldege of the incident (Metsudath David).

25 The fear of man bringeth a snare;
But whoso putteth his trust in the LORD shall be set up on high.

26 Many seek the ruler's favour;
But a man's judgment cometh from the LORD.

27 An unjust man is an abomination to the righteous;
And he that is upright in the way is an abomination to the wicked.

25 חֶרְדַּת אָדָם יִתֵּן מוֹקֵשׁ
וּבוֹטֵחַ בַּיהוָה יְשֻׂגָּב׃
26 רַבִּים מְבַקְשִׁים פְּנֵי־מוֹשֵׁל
וּמֵיְהוָה מִשְׁפַּט־אִישׁ׃
27 תּוֹעֲבַת צַדִּיקִים אִישׁ עָוֶל
וְתוֹעֲבַת רָשָׁע יְשַׁר־דָּרֶךְ׃

25 EFFECT OF FEAR

the fear of man. An ambiguous translation which can signify the fear a person has of his fellows, or, the fear which paralyses a man's efforts when confronted by an emergency. The latter interpretation is adopted by Ibn Ezra and Metsudath David and is to be preferred.

a snare. On the former interpretation this means that he will be led into wrongdoing; alternatively it indicates that fear hampers his action and prevents him from putting forth his maximum effort.

set up on high. Above the dangers that threaten him (Metsudath David).

26 GOD DECIDES THE ISSUE

the ruler's favour. When they are involved in a suit, to secure a favourable verdict. *Favour* is literally 'face,' and its use in the sense of this phrase is derived from the fact that a man's thoughts and feelings can be read in the expression on his face. By bribery, flattery or self-humiliation many endeavour to make the face of the man who decides their fate well-disposed towards them (see Rashi, Metsudath David).

a man's judgment. The ultimate issue of the case. A corrupt or unjust ruler may condemn an innocent man, but finally God determines his fate (Rashi).

27 THE GOOD AND BAD ARE ANTIPATHETIC

unjust man. lit. 'man of iniquity.'

an abomination. An object of loathing. We may read into the statement the conflict of right and wrong which, throughout history, has been conspicuous in human experience. The virtuous refuse to compromise with the wicked and look upon evil with detestation. Wrong-doers regard the upright as their natural enemies because they condemn their practices (Ibn Nachmiash). [This mutual hostility is the central theme of the Book, and the moral that runs through it is that the fight must continue to a finish, with victory for the righteous in the end.]

With this verse, proclaiming the antagonism of vicious men towards the virtuous and the abhorrence of the evil-doer by the righteous, the Book of Proverbs closes. But three addenda are appended: chapter xxx, *The words of Agur*; xxxi. 1–9, *The words of king Lemuel*; and xxxi. 10–31 Praise of *a woman of valour* (Meiri, Daath Mikra).

1 The words of Agur the son of Jakeh; the burden.
The man saith unto Ithiel, unto Ithiel and Ucal:
2 Surely I am brutish, unlike a man,
And have not the understanding of a man;

1 דִּבְרֵי ׀ אָגוּר בִּן־יָקֶה הַמַּשָּׂא
נְאֻם הַגֶּבֶר לְאִיתִיאֵל
לְאִיתִיאֵל וְאֻכָל׃
2 כִּי בַעַר אָנֹכִי מֵאִישׁ
וְלֹא־בִינַת אָדָם לִי׃

CHAPTER XXX

THE SAYINGS OF AGUR

THE difference of style, language and content in this chapter, as compared with the rest of the Book, is too striking to escape notice. That it is an addition is evident from the heading, but equally so from the author's mode of thought and expression. The feeling created is that the reader is transported to a later age than Solomon's, when the life of the nation had matured and inquiring minds were exercised with the mysteries and problems of human existence. The questions of the prologue are reminiscent of passages in the Book of Job.

1 SUPERSCRIPTION

Agur the son of Jakeh. On the hypothesis that the whole of Proverbs is the work of Solomon, the Midrash discovers an allusion to him in this name: 'He was called *Agur* because he stored up *(agar)* knowledge of Torah, and *the son of Jakeh* because he spewed it out *(hikki)* in that he ignored the warning against multiplying wives.' Some of the later Jewish commentators rejected the identification of Agur with Solomon. Ibn Ezra held that he was a sage, renowned for his piety, who lived during Solomon's reign, and the king incorporated his sayings in Proverbs. Elijah of Wilna asserts that the Men of the Great Assembly incorporated into each Book what was written through Divine inspiration on topics similar to those in the Book, e.g. the Book of Psalms, to which many matters were joined, some of which concerning instruction and admonition, and some of which are songs of praise and thanksgiving to God. Prior to each section, they recorded the name of its author, e.g. Heman, Asaph, and Jeduthun in the Book of Psalms. Similarly, in the Book of Proverbs, they arranged all that was said allegorically in matters of instruction. This section was authored by Agur son of Jakeh, and these are his words.

the burden. Hebrew *ha-massa,* a term for a Divine utterance (Jer. xxiii. 33ff.) or a prophetical declaration (e.g. Isa. xiii. 1, xv. 1). As a noun it is derived from the idiom 'lift up the voice' (cf. Isa. lii. 8; Ps. xciii. 3) and may be used of speech in general. The word occurs again in the superscription of xxxi. Since a descendant of Ishmael was named Massa (Gen. xxv. 14; 1 Chron. i. 30), it has been suggested that Agur and Lemuel belonged to an Arabian tribe and the word is to be translated 'Massaite'; but this is highly conjectural (see Daath Mikra).

unto Ithiel . . . Ucal. The name Ithiel is found in Nehem. xi. 7, but Ucal nowhere else. Agur addressed himself to these two men who were his friends or disciples (Ibn Ezra), and the sayings were deemed worthy of wider publication by the compiler of Proverbs. The name Ithiel is doubled to show his esteem over that of Ucal (Elijah of Wilna).

2–4 THE PROLOGUE

2. *surely.* [Hebrew, 'for, because,' which suggests that something preceded

3 And I have not learned wisdom,
That I should have the knowledge of the Holy One.

4 Who hath ascended up into heaven, and descended?
Who hath gathered the wind in his fists?
Who hath bound the waters in his garment?
Who hath established all the ends of the earth?
What is his name, and what is his son's name, if thou knowest?

3 וְלֹא־לָמַדְתִּי חָכְמָה
וְדַעַת קְדֹשִׁים אֵדָע׃
4 מִי עָלָה־שָׁמַיִם ׀ וַיֵּרַד
מִי אָסַף־רוּחַ ׀ בְּחָפְנָיו
מִי צָרַר־מַיִם ׀ בַּשִּׂמְלָה
מִי הֵקִים כָּל־אַפְסֵי־אָרֶץ
מַה־שְּׁמוֹ וּמַה־שֶּׁם־בְּנוֹ כִּי תֵדָע׃

the verse. Probably only a fragment of Agur's sayings is preserved, and the chapter is a reply to some questions put forward by Ithiel and Ucal about Divine Providence. He answers that he is incapable of understanding the mind of the human being, so how much less dare he presume to try to comprehend the working of the Infinite Mind! Cf. the trend of Job xxxviii-xli.]

I am brutish, unlike a man. For *brutish,* see on xii. 1. *Unlike a man* is lit. 'from (or, than) a man'; A.V. and R.V. *more brutish than any man* (Bechaye). Others render: 'I am too brutish to be a man,' i.e. to reach the status of deserving to be called a man, 'neither have I the understanding of an esteemed man' (Meiri).

3. *I have not learned wisdom.* He does not wish to imply that he has failed to devote himself to the study of wisdom, because what follows plainly contradicts it. Rather he claims that, despite all his efforts to do so, he has not succeeded in mastering the subject (after Metsudath David).

that I should . . . Holy One. Better, 'so should I know the knowledge of the Holy One!' Since he cannot profess to be an expert on *wisdom* (religious ethics), it would be absurd for him to pretend that he is an expert on the *knowledge* of God (the philosophy of religion). For the term *Holy One,* see on ix. 10 (Malbim).

4. The purpose of the series of questions is to point out the impossibility of any man having this *knowledge,* because to do so, he must be able to ascend to heaven, etc. With the verse, cf. Job xxxviii. 4ff. (see Isaiah da Trani).

and descended. Only God has done that (e.g. Gen. xi. 7; Exod. xix. 18), although it is related that Elijah had ascended (Daath Mikra).

gathered the wind. An act of God (Amos iv. 13; Ps. cxxxv. 7) (Daath Mikra).

bound . . . garment. Defined in Job xxvi. 8, *He bindeth up the waters in His thick clouds.* It is God Who arranges for the store of waters to provide the rain without which existence is impossible (Daath Mikra).

established . . . earth. That it rotate on its axis, suspended in space (Malbim).

what is his name? A sarcastic question: if you assert that any man possessed these qualifications, who is he? (Rashi).

what is his son's name? More sarcasm: should you claim that such a person has existed, let me test your knowledge of him; if you give me his name, what more do you know of him? What was his son called? (Rashi).

5 Every word of God is tried;
He is a shield unto them that take refuge in Him.

6 Add thou not unto His words,
Lest He reprove thee, and thou be found a liar.

7 Two things have I asked of Thee;
Deny me them not before I die:

8 Remove far from me falsehood and lies;
Give me neither poverty nor riches;
Feed me with mine allotted bread;

5 כָּל־אִמְרַת אֱלוֹהַּ צְרוּפָה
מָגֵן הוּא לַחוֹסִים בּוֹ׃
אַל־תּוֹסְףְּ עַל־דְּבָרָיו
פֶּן־יוֹכִיחַ בְּךָ וְנִכְזָבְתָּ׃
שְׁתַּיִם שָׁאַלְתִּי מֵאִתָּךְ
אַל־תִּמְנַע מִמֶּנִּי בְּטֶרֶם אָמוּת׃
שָׁוְא ׀ וּדְבַר־כָּזָב הַרְחֵק מִמֶּנִּי
רֵאשׁ וָעֹשֶׁר אַל־תִּתֶּן־לִי
הַטְרִיפֵנִי לֶחֶם חֻקִּי׃

5–6 EXHORTATION TO RELY ON REVELATION

In these verses we have the conclusion which Agur drew from his argument. He advises Ithiel (and Ucal) to be content with what God had revealed to man in the Torah, and not go beyond that with dangerous speculation about the mysteries which baffle comprehension (Malbim, Ibn Ezra).

5. Quoted with a few variations from Ps. xviii. 31, but adapted by Agur to fit his argument.

every word of God. All that He has communicated through Moses and the prophets as teachings for man's intellectual and moral guidance (Ibn Nachmiash).

tried. lit. 'refined' metal, without any alloy (cf. Ps. xii. 7); this should be relied upon (Ibn Ezra).

He is a shield. In all the perplexities which trouble you, turn to Him for direction and He will help you to regain tranquility of mind (Meiri).

6. *add thou not unto His words.* A reminiscence of Deut. iv. 2 where *word* means 'commandment.' Here he urges that no attempt should be made to supplement the Divine doctrines with one's own ideas in that field of thought (Daath Mikra).

He reprove thee. By some misfortune which will manifest His displeasure (Daath Mikra).

thou be found a liar. i.e. He will demonstrate the falsity of your opinions (Metsudath David).

7–9 AGUR'S PRAYER

His advice to rely upon God he enforces by his own example in a touching prayer which expresses his humble aspirations.

7. *before I die.* In Ps. xxxix. 14 the phrase signifies 'I am soon to die,' here 'for the rest of my life' (Metsudath David).

8. *falsehood.* lit. 'vanity,' but as in Ps. xii. 3, xli. 7 it means 'deceit.' To live right he must be a lover of truth and integrity, and not be contaminated by what is false (see Ibn Nachmiash).

mine allotted bread. lit. 'bread of my portion'; the latter noun occurs in xxxi. 15. His needs are small and he begs to be granted a sufficiency to avoid being lured into sin (see Ibn Ezra, Isaiah da Trani).

9 פֶּן־אֶשְׂבַּע ׀ וְכִחַשְׁתִּי
וְאָמַרְתִּי מִי יְהוָה
וּפֶן־אִוָּרֵשׁ וְגָנַבְתִּי
וְתָפַשְׂתִּי שֵׁם אֱלֹהָי׃

Lest I be full, and deny, and say:
'Who is the LORD?'
Or lest I be poor, and steal,
And profane the name of my God.

10 אַל־תַּלְשֵׁן עֶבֶד אֶל־אדנו
פֶּן־יְקַלֶּלְךָ וְאָשָׁמְתָּ׃

10 Slander not a servant unto his master,
Lest he curse thee, and thou be found guilty.

11 דּוֹר אָבִיו יְקַלֵּל
וְאֶת־אִמּוֹ לֹא יְבָרֵךְ׃

11 There is a generation that curse their father,
And do not bless their mother.

12 דּוֹר טָהוֹר בְּעֵינָיו
וּמִצֹּאָתוֹ לֹא רֻחָץ׃

12 There is a generation that are pure in their own eyes,
And yet are not washed from their filthiness.

13 דּוֹר מָה־רָמוּ עֵינָיו
וְעַפְעַפָּיו יִנָּשֵׂאוּ׃

13 There is a generation, Oh how lofty are their eyes!
And their eyelids are lifted up.

v. 10. אדניו ק׳

9. *deny.* My dependency upon God for the satisfaction of my wants (Ibn Nachmiash).

who is the LORD? A less profane way of saying 'there is no God' (Meiri, Metsudath David). cf. the warning addressed to Israel in Deut. viii. 11ff. and the denunciation in Deut. xxxii. 15.

be poor. [Better, 'come to poverty,' as in xx. 13; be reduced to dire straits.]

profane. lit. 'lay hold of.' If *profane* were intended, the usual verb *chillel* would have been expected. However, this verb is found in Targum. In Isaiah liii. 28, for the Hebrew *va'achalel,* we find the Aramaic *we'ethpos,* indicating that these two verbs are interchangeable (Ibn Nachmiash). Ibn Ezra renders: 'I will make mention of God,' if I am accused of stealing and am obliged to swear. Ibn Nachmiash suggests that Agur alludes to the practice of grasping a *Sepher Torah* upon pronouncing an oath required by Biblical law. Agur states, 'I will take hold of (a *Sepher Torah* and swear in) the name of my God.'

slander not a servant. Whereas slandering any person is a reprehensible act, it is especially vile when the victim is a slave, who is helpless and will not be believed when he denies the accusation (Metsudath David, Ibn Nachmish).

and thou be found guilty. Better, 'and thou art guilty,' viz. of the slander and so deserve the curse (Metsudath David).

11–14 FOUR WICKED TYPES

11. *generation.* Hebrew *dor* also signifies 'a class'; cf. Ps. xii. 8, xiv. 5, xxiv. 6 and that is its signification in this passage (Daath Mikra).

13. *how lofty are their eyes.* Cf. vi. 17, xxi. 4.

eyelids are lifted up. They look with contempt upon their fellows (Rashi).

14 There is a generation whose teeth are as swords, and their great teeth as knives,
To devour the poor from off the earth, and the needy from among men.

15 The horseleech hath two daughters: 'Give, give.'
There are three things that are never satisfied,
Yea, four that say not: 'Enough':

16 The grave; and the barren womb;
The earth that is not satisfied with water;
And the fire that saith not: 'Enough.'

דּוֹר ׀ חֲרָבוֹת שִׁנָּיו 14
וּמַאֲכָלוֹת מְתַלְּעֹתָיו
לֶאֱכֹל עֲנִיִּים מֵאֶרֶץ
וְאֶבְיוֹנִים מֵאָדָם׃
לַעֲלוּקָה ׀ שְׁתֵּי בָנוֹת הַב ׀ הַב 15
שָׁלוֹשׁ הֵנָּה לֹא תִשְׂבַּעְנָה
אַרְבַּע לֹא־אָמְרוּ הוֹן׃
שְׁאוֹל וְעֹצֶר רָחַם 16
אֶרֶץ לֹא־שָׂבְעָה מַּיִם
וְאֵשׁ לֹא־אָמְרָה הוֹן׃

14. *great teeth.* The Hebrew appears also in Joel i. 6, where it is translated 'jaw teeth.' The figure is of wild beasts tearing their prey; there are human beings who likewise use their power mercilessly to destroy the helpless (Daath Mikra).

15–16 THE INSATIABLE

A distinctive feature of Agur's teaching is his employment of the quatrain, i.e. the citation of four examples to illustrate an idea. Five instances are included in the chapter, the first relating to insatiable greed.

15. *the horseleech.* This translation of *alukah* is well attested by the ancient Versions, its use in Rabbinic Hebrew and the analogous word in Arabic. Accordingly there is no need to substitute a bloodsucking ghoul as some modern scholars propose. The Midrash explains it allegorically of the netherworld, the *two daughters* being Paradise and Gehinnom (Rashi quoting Midrash Psalms).

hath two daughters. The two daughters of the leech are its two apertures by which it sucks blood. It continues to suck until it is gorged with blood, at which time it falls off. This world is likened to the leech. It has two daughters, as in the following verse. What one gives, the other takes (Meiri).

give, give. A.V. and R.V. insert the word *crying,* and interpret *give, give* as their clamorous demand (so all commentaries). [It is also possible to construe the words as the names of the *daughters,* and the identity of the names indicates the identity of their disposition. The clause therefore points the moral that greed breeds greed.]

16. *the grave.* Hebrew *Sheol.*

the barren womb. lit. 'closing of the womb,' the yearning for children (Metsudath David).

the earth. i.e. the soil dependent upon water for its fertility (Metsudath David).

fire. Which greedily seizes upon any fuel available to keep burning (Ralbag).

17 עין | תלעג לאב
ותבז ליקהת־אם
יקרוה ערבי־נחל
ויאכלוה בני־נשר׃
18 שלשה המה נפלאו ממני
וארבע לא ידעתים׃
19 דרך הנשר | בשמים
דרך נחש עלי צור
דרך־אניה בלב־ים
ודרך גבר בעלמה׃
20 כן | דרך אשה מנאפת
אכלה ומחתה פיה
ואמרה לא־פעלתי און׃

The eye that mocketh at his father,
And despiseth to obey his mother,
The ravens of the valley shall pick it out,
And the young vultures shall eat it.

There are three things which are too wonderful for me,
Yea, four which I know not:

The way of an eagle in the air;
The way of a serpent upon a rock;
The way of a ship in the midst of the sea;
And the way of a man with a young woman.

So is the way of an adulterous woman;
She eateth, and wipeth her mouth,
And saith: 'I have done no wickedness.'

v. 18. וארבעה ק׳

17 FILIAL IMPIETY PUNISHED

the eye. The window to a person's innermost feelings.

mocketh. When the father gives the son advice or reproof (Metsudath David).

young vultures. lit. 'sons of a vulture.' They feed on carcasses, so the punishment implies that the son will meet with a violent end and his body lie unburied to be devoured by birds of prey (see Daath Mikra).

18–20 THE INCOMPREHENSIBLE

18. *too wonderful for me.* To understand how the effect is produced; so Ibn Ezra who also cites an alternative explanation given by Rashi, viz. how no trace is left.

19. *eagle.* Better, 'vulture,' the same word as in verse 17. How can so heavy a bird keep flying without falling to the ground? (Daath Mikra).

serpent. How can it move along without feet? (Ibn Ezra).

way of a man. What a mystery is procreation! (Daath Mikra).

20. This verse is added to point a practical moral. Equally incomprehensible is the lack of sensibility in an adultress who is so degraded as not to feel anything sinful in her act of infidelity (Ibn Ezra). To her, apparently, adultery is nothing more than a physical satisfaction, like eating food. Rashi, based on Talmud (Kethuboth 13a), takes the phrase *she eateth . . . mouth* as a euphemism for intercourse.

21 For three things the earth doth quake,
And for four it cannot endure:

22 For a servant when he reigneth;
And a churl when he is filled with food;

23 For an odious woman when she is married;
And a handmaid that is heir to her mistress.

24 There are four things which are little upon the earth,
But they are exceeding wise:

25 The ants are a people not strong,
Yet they provide their food in the summer;

תַּחַת שָׁלוֹשׁ רָגְזָה אֶרֶץ 21
וְתַחַת אַרְבַּע לֹא־תוּכַל שְׂאֵת׃
תַּחַת עֶבֶד כִּי יִמְלוֹךְ 22
וְנָבָל כִּי יִשְׂבַּע־לָחֶם׃
תַּחַת שְׂנוּאָה כִּי תִבָּעֵל 23
וְשִׁפְחָה כִּי־תִירַשׁ גְּבִרְתָּהּ׃
אַרְבָּעָה הֵם קְטַנֵּי־אָרֶץ 24
וְהֵמָּה חֲכָמִים מְחֻכָּמִים׃
הַנְּמָלִים עַם לֹא־עָז 25
וַיָּכִינוּ בַקַּיִץ לַחְמָם׃

21–23 THE INTOLERABLE

21. *for.* Throughout this quatrain substitute 'under.' i.e. under the rule of the following (Daath Mikra). Metsudath David renders: 'because of,' Isaiah da Trani, 'in the place of.'

the earth. The inhabitants of the earth (Ibn Ezra, Metsudath David).

22. *for . . . reigneth.* Better, 'under a slave when he becomes a king' (see on xix. 10). Such a change of status happened not infrequently in the ancient world; for an example in Israelite history, cf. 1 Kings xvi. 9f. Saadia Gaon mentions the turbulent reign of Herod, who was an Idumean slave.

filled with food. Cf. verses 8f. above for the possible consequences of being well off.

23. *an odious . . . married.* A.J. has followed A.V. and R.V., but the translation is incorrect. The allusion is not to a woman who has had long to wait to secure a husband, but to the kind of circumstance described in connection with Jacob's household. *Odious,* lit. 'hated,' signifies a wife in a polygamous family who is less favoured by the husband (see on xiii. 24). When a wife, who had been neglected by her husband for a favourite rival, is re-established in his affections, she gives herself insufferable airs (Isaiah da Trani).

handmaid . . . mistress. And so becomes a mistress, acting in the same manner as a slave who becomes a king (Isaiah da Trani). Another interpretation is that she displaces her mistress in the husband's favour and takes her place as his wife (Daath Mikra).

24–28 FOUR CREATURES SMALL BUT WISE

Attention is drawn to the animal kingdom for men to learn useful lessons from the habits that can be witnessed there.

24. The thought to be derived is that bigness is not the same as greatness, and there is much good in what is usually despised on account of its smallness.

25. See on vi. 8.

a people. [i.e. a species.]

26 The rock-badgers are but a feeble folk,
Yet make they their houses in the crags;

26 שְׁפַנִּים עַם לֹא־עָצוּם
וַיָּשִׂימוּ בַסֶּלַע בֵּיתָם׃

27 The locusts have no king,
Yet go they forth all of them by bands;

27 מֶלֶךְ אֵין לָאַרְבֶּה
וַיֵּצֵא חֹצֵץ כֻּלּוֹ׃

28 The spider thou canst take with the hands,
Yet is she in kings' palaces.

28 שְׂמָמִית בְּיָדַיִם תְּתַפֵּשׂ
וְהִיא בְּהֵיכְלֵי מֶלֶךְ׃

29 There are three things which are stately in their march,
Yea, four which are stately in going:

29 שְׁלֹשָׁה הֵמָּה מֵיטִיבֵי צָעַד
וְאַרְבָּעָה מֵיטִבֵי לָכֶת׃

30 The lion, which is mightiest among beasts,
And turneth not away for any;

30 לַיִשׁ גִּבּוֹר בַּבְּהֵמָה
וְלֹא־יָשׁוּב מִפְּנֵי־כֹל׃

26. *rock-badgers.* lit. 'hiders,' an animal prohibited for consumption (Lev. xi. 5) which makes its home in the rocks (Ps. civ. 18, translated *conies*). Being weak and without means of defence against stronger animals, it wisely dwells in inaccessible places (Metsudath David).

27. *by bands.* lit. 'dividing' themselves into companies (cf. the graphic description in Joel ii. 2ff., especially verse 7 where they are likened to a trained army). These insignificant creatures have an instinct which teaches them that unity and discipline in their ranks make them formidable (Daath Mikra).

28. *spider.* So Rashi. Modern scholars prefer to translate 'lizard.' So Targum Jonathan to Lev. xi. 30. The word has both meanings in Rabbinic Hebrew and either would suit the context.

thou canst take with the hands. It is so small that one can take hold of it and crush it in his hand (Gerondi, quoted by Ibn Nachmiash). This is better than A.V. *taketh hold with her hands,* which follows Rashi. On this interpretation the feet are called *hands* because they are so employed, and by their means the insect has the power to climb walls and gain entry into a palace.

palaces. The grandest type of building is mentioned to present the fullest contrast with the tiny insect, which is yet able to secure admission (Ibn Nachmiash).

29–31 FOUR STATELY BEINGS

29. *stately in their march . . . going.* lit. 'makers good of step . . . makers good of going.'

30. *turneth not away.* In fear of any other animal as it goes its way (Ibn Nachmiash).

31 The greyhound; the he-goat also;
And the king, against whom there is no rising up.

32 If thou hast done foolishly in lifting up thyself,
Or if thou hast planned devices, lay thy hand upon thy mouth.

33 For the churning of milk bringeth forth curd,
And the wringing of the nose bringeth forth blood;
So the forcing of wrath bringeth forth strife.

זַרְזִיר מָתְנַיִם אוֹ־תָיִשׁ 31
וּמֶלֶךְ אַלְקוּם עִמּוֹ׃
אִם־נָבַלְתָּ בְהִתְנַשֵּׂא 32
וְאִם־זַמּוֹתָ יָד לְפֶה׃
כִּי מִיץ חָלָב יוֹצִיא חֶמְאָה 33
וּמִיץ־אַף יוֹצִיא דָם
וּמִיץ אַפַּיִם יוֹצִיא רִיב׃

31. *greyhound.* So Ralbag. The Hebrew appears to mean 'girt of loins.' Other proposed translations are 'warhorse,' 'cock' (LXX, Targum), 'starling' and 'zebra.' It is impossible to decide with certainty.

he-goat. 'The stately march of the he-goat before the herd, and his haughty bearing, as well as the dauntless stare with which he scrutinizes a stranger, are well known to all familiar with the East; and the he-goat is still commonly applied by Arabs as a simile for dignity and bearing' (Tristram).

and the king . . . rising up. For this translation the Hebrew word *alkum* is construed as two words, *al* 'not' and *kum* 'rising' (Ibn Ezra, Metsudath David). More acceptable is R.V. margin, when his army is with him,' *alkaum* being Arabic for 'a people, body of men.' The king at the head of his troops may well be an illustration of stateliness (Daath Mikra).

32–33 EXERCISE RESTRAINT

32. *hast done foolishly.* Behaved like a *nobal* (see on xvii. 7), acted basely (Ibn Ezra).

in lifting up thyself. In asserting thyself against an opponent (Ibn Ezra).

or if thou hast. Better, 'and if thou hast,' i.e. thou intendest to act in this knavish manner (Ibn Ezra).

lay thy hand upon thy mouth. lit. 'hand to mouth,' check thyself and desist (Ibn Ezra).

33. *for the churning.* As churning milk produces curd and nose-wringing causes a flow of bood, so 'squeezing anger (so lit.) starts a quarrel.' Avoid this by putting thy hand to thy mouth to suppress angry words (Rashi, Metsudath David).

wringing . . . forth. [In the Hebrew the verbs are the same and identical with *churning.* An important point is made here, viz. strife is not a natural tendency in man but is often deliberately created by him. As curd is manufactured from milk and as blood is forced from the nose, so is a quarrel wilfully brought into being. It need not happen and can be averted. This being true of the individual, is it not true also of international conflict?]

nose . . . wrath. A play on words is intended, because the Hebrew of the latter is the dual of the former (Daath Mikra).

1 The words of king Lemuel; the burden wherewith his mother corrected him.

2 What, my son? and what, O son of my womb?
And what, O son of my vows?

3 Give not thy strength unto women,
Nor thy ways to that which destroyeth kings.

4 It is not for kings, O Lemuel, it is not for kings to drink wine;
Nor for princes to say: 'Where is strong drink?'

1 דִּבְרֵי לְמוּאֵל מֶלֶךְ
מַשָּׂא אֲשֶׁר־יִסְּרַתּוּ אִמּוֹ׃
2 מַה־בְּרִי וּמַה־בַּר־בִּטְנִי
וּמֶה בַּר־נְדָרָי׃
3 אַל־תִּתֵּן לַנָּשִׁים חֵילֶךָ
וּדְרָכֶיךָ לַמְחוֹת מְלָכִין׃
4 אַל לַמְלָכִים ׀ לְמוֹאֵל
אַל לַמְלָכִים שְׁתוֹ־יָיִן
וּלְרוֹזְנִים או שֵׁכָר׃

v. 4. אי ק׳

CHAPTER XXXI

1–9 THE SAYINGS OF LEMUEL

1 SUPERSCRIPTION

Lemuel. As with Agur, the traditional opinion is that Lemuel is a name of Solomon, meaning 'towards *(lemo)* God *(el),*' one who is dedicated to Him (Isaiah da Trani, Metsudath David). Nothing is known of a king of this name.

his mother. A story in the Midrash relates that Solomon married Pharaoh's daughter on the day of the Temple's dedication. She kept him awake the whole night with music so that he slept late into the morning; and since he kept the keys of the Temple gates under his pillow, the morning sacrifice was delayed. Whereupon his mother came and gave him the exhortation that follows.

2 INTRODUCTORY REMARK

what. Perhaps abbreviated for 'what am I to say unto thee?' (Isaiah da Trani).

3–7 AVOID DEBAUCHERY

3. *thy strength.* Do not exhaust thy physical powers in the harem and so become unfitted for the duties which a king has to discharge (Isaiah da Trani).

to that which destroyeth kings. lit. 'to the causing of kings to be blotted out' (Yalkut Machiri) i.e. to behaviour which leads to the revolt of the population and the destruction of a dynasty. The plural termination of *kings* has the Aramaic form (Ibn Ezra).

4. *it is not for kings.* It is not seemly for kings to be intoxicated; it makes them undignified and loses for them the respect of their subjects, as well as dulls their judgment in the exercise of their royal functions, as below.

Lemuel. The Hebrew form of the name here is *Lemoel,* perhaps with an allusion to its derivation; as though to say, 'This is particularly unbecoming in one who bears a name with the signification "(dedicated) to God"' (see Rashi).

to say. Lacking in the text but required by the *kerë, where is?* (Ralbag, Isaiah da Trani).

5 Lest they drink, and forget that which is decreed,
And pervert the justice due to any that is afflicted.

6 Give strong drink unto him that is ready to perish,
And wine unto the bitter in soul;

7 Let him drink, and forget his poverty,
And remember his misery no more.

8 Open thy mouth for the dumb,
In the cause of all such as are appointed to destruction.

9 Open thy mouth, judge righteously,
And plead the cause of the poor and needy.

פֶּן־יִשְׁתֶּה וְיִשְׁכַּח מְחֻקָּק
וִישַׁנֶּה דִּין כָּל־בְּנֵי־עֹנִי׃
תְּנוּ־שֵׁכָר לְאוֹבֵד
וְיַיִן לְמָרֵי נָפֶשׁ׃
יִשְׁתֶּה וְיִשְׁכַּח רִישׁוֹ
וַעֲמָלוֹ לֹא יִזְכָּר־עוֹד׃
פְּתַח־פִּיךָ לְאִלֵּם
אֶל־דִּין כָּל־בְּנֵי חֲלוֹף׃
פְּתַח־פִּיךָ שְׁפָט־צֶדֶק
וְדִין עָנִי וְאֶבְיוֹן׃

strong drink. See on xx. 1.

5. *they drink, and forget.* The Hebrew is singular, 'each of them drinks and forgets' (Daath Mikra).

that which is decreed. The national laws and act unconstitutionally (Meiri).

any that is afflicted. lit. 'all the sons of affliction'; they look to the king to uphold their rights (Malbim).

6. *give strong drink.* Although overindulgence has been deprecated and drunkenness severely denounced (xxiii. 29ff.), it was appreciated that intoxicants had their proper use. Wine *maketh glad the heart of man* (Ps. civ. 15) and was created by God for that purpose. If the king had to practise abstinence, he also had the duty of supplying wine to those who needed to benefit from it (Saadia Gaon).

unto him that is ready to perish. [From want; to him strong drink would be a restorative.]

bitter in soul. Suffering mental anguish; upon him wine would act as a stimulant (Rashi).

7. *his misery.* Rather, 'his trouble, suffering,' with particular reference to *the bitter in soul* (Metsudath David).

8–9 RULE JUSTLY

8. *the dumb.* Employed figuratively of the person who for any reason is unable to plead his own cause (Metsudath David).

all such . . . destruction. lit. 'all sons of passing,' which Rashi explains as orphans who have lost their defenders, and Ibn Ezra as men liable to the death penalty. Meiri and Isaiah da Trani explain as 'all mortals,' who will eventually pass from the world.

9. *plead the cause of.* Better, *minister judgment to* (R.V.).

A woman of valour who can find?
For her price is far above rubies.

The heart of her husband doth safely trust in her,
And he hath no lack of gain.

She doeth him good and not evil
All the days of her life.

She seeketh wool and flax,
And worketh willingly with her hands.

10 אֵשֶׁת חַיִל מִי יִמְצָא
וְרָחֹק מִפְּנִינִים מִכְרָהּ׃
11 בָּטַח בָּהּ לֵב בַּעְלָהּ
וְשָׁלָל לֹא יֶחְסָר׃
12 גְּמָלַתְהוּ טוֹב וְלֹא־רָע
כֹּל יְמֵי חַיֶּיהָ׃
13 דָּרְשָׁה צֶמֶר וּפִשְׁתִּים
וַתַּעַשׂ בְּחֵפֶץ כַּפֶּיהָ׃

10–31 THE IDEAL WIFE

Mention has been so often made of the unfaithful wife in Proverbs, that the compiler may have thought it advisable to end the Book with a glowing tribute to the good wife. That it is a separate and self-contained composition is evident from the fact that it is constructed within the framework of an alphabetical acrostic. The ideal wife is described as the skilful manager of the home and a blessing to her family. Her husband is enabled to devote himself to public affairs and is a respected member of the community. Her life is not self-centred; she is charitable to the poor and kindly to all. It has been truly said, 'Nothing in ancient literature equals this remarkable attestation to the dignity and individuality of woman' (Abrahams). Quite possibly the poem was the work of a teacher who advocated a monogamous home; at any rate, consonant with the view held throughout Proverbs, the household is ruled over by one wife. According to traditional usage, this poem is recited in the Jewish home on the Sabbath eve *(P.B.,* p. 123). It set a high standard of wifehood which was widely adopted and was a reality in many Jewish homes.

who can find? the Hebrew is construed as a question, as though the writer's intention was 'a good wife is not easily found, but when she is found, she is of inestimable value.' The sense may also be: whoever has married such a woman knows from his experience how priceless is her worth (Meiri).

11. *doth safely trust in her.* The husband has full confidence in her management of the domestic economy (Metsudath David).

he hath no lack of gain. Better, 'gain shall not be lacking to him.' The word for *gain* is the ordinary term for 'spoils' of war. Daath Mikra suggests that it connotes an increase of wealth which does not result from one's personal labours, and is therefore selected here because it is wealth which accrues to the man from his wife's enterprise.

12. *she doeth him good.* [She fully justifies the confidence he places in her.]

13. *seeketh.* The meaning is: she concerns herself to see that there is an ample supply of material from which to make the necessary clothing (Rashi, Metsudath David).

worketh willingly with her hands. lit. 'she makes according to the pleasure of her hands'; she works the material into the best garments, her labour being one of 'pleasure.' It is as though the hands themselves have pleasure from the work (Rashi).

14 She is like the merchant-ships;
She bringeth her food from afar.

15 She riseth also while it is yet night,
And giveth food to her household,
And a portion to her maidens.

16 She considereth a field, and buyeth it;
With the fruit of her hands she planteth a vineyard.

17 She girdeth her loins with strength,
And maketh strong her arms.

18 She perceiveth that her merchandise is good;
Her lamp goeth not out by night.

הָיְתָה כָּאֳנִיּוֹת סוֹחֵר
מִמֶּרְחָק תָּבִיא לַחְמָהּ׃
וַתָּקָם ׀ בְּעוֹד לַיְלָה
וַתִּתֵּן טֶרֶף לְבֵיתָהּ
וְחֹק לְנַעֲרֹתֶיהָ׃
זָמְמָה שָׂדֶה וַתִּקָּחֵהוּ
מִפְּרִי כַפֶּיהָ נָטַע כָּרֶם׃
חָגְרָה בְעוֹז מָתְנֶיהָ
וַתְּאַמֵּץ זְרוֹעֹתֶיהָ׃
טָעֲמָה כִּי־טוֹב סַחְרָהּ
לֹא־יִכְבֶּה בַלַּיְל נֵרָהּ׃

v. 16. נטעה ק׳ v. 18. בלילה ק׳

14. *like the merchant-ships.* Which import goods from distant lands; similarly she does not depend for her supplies upon sources near at hand, but seeks them from afar to obtain the choicest obtainable (Daath Mikra).

15. *while it is yet night.* Before daybreak to bake the bread and prepare the food required during the day (Malbim).

her maidens. The maidservants of the household; they, too, are the objects of her industrious care (Malbim).

16. *considereth.* She examines the value of a piece of land which is for sale and, being satisfied with it, adds it to the family estate (see Metsudath David).

the fruit of her hands. The money accumulated from her skilful management (Metsudath David).

she planteth. Like the statement, *the house which I* (Solomon) *have built* (1 Kings viii. 44), this does not imply that the work of planting was done with her own hands (so Ibn Ezra).

vineyard. Part of a properly equipped homestead (cf. the ideal scene of 1 Kings v. 5, *every man under his vine).*

17. The verse draws a picture of her setting about her tasks with vigour.

girdeth . . . strength. Ibn Ezra and Metsudath David understand this as a figure of speech, 'with strength as a girdle.' It is so used of God in Ps. xciii. 1: *He hath girded Himself with strength.*

18. *perceiveth.* lit. 'tasteth,' finds from experience (cf. Ps. xxxiv. 9, where the verb is translated *consider).*

her lamp . . . night. Metsudath David interprets the words as: she works during the earlier part of the night, and rises early (verse 15) to increase her earnings with which to do business. [Possibly the reference is to do the practice in the East to keep a light constantly burning in the house (cf. Jer. xxv. 10; Job xviii. 6), its going out being considered an omen of misfortune. A modern Bedouin saying is 'He sleeps in darkness,' to indicate a condition of abject poverty.]

She layeth her hands to the distaff,
And her hands hold the spindle.

She stretcheth out her hand to the poor;
Yea, she reacheth forth her hands to the needy.

She is not afraid of the snow for her household;
For all her household are clothed with scarlet.

She maketh for herself coverlets;
Her clothing is fine linen and purple.

Her husband is known in the gates,
When he sitteth among the elders of the land.

She maketh linen garments and selleth them;
And delivereth girdles unto the merchant.

19 יָדֶיהָ שִׁלְּחָה בַכִּישׁוֹר
וְכַפֶּיהָ תָּמְכוּ פָלֶךְ׃
20 כַּפָּהּ פָּרְשָׂה לֶעָנִי
וְיָדֶיהָ שִׁלְּחָה לָאֶבְיוֹן׃
21 לֹא־תִירָא לְבֵיתָהּ מִשָּׁלֶג
כִּי כָל־בֵּיתָהּ לָבֻשׁ שָׁנִים׃
22 מַרְבַדִּים עָשְׂתָה־לָּהּ
שֵׁשׁ וְאַרְגָּמָן לְבוּשָׁהּ׃
23 נוֹדָע בַּשְּׁעָרִים בַּעְלָהּ
בְּשִׁבְתּוֹ עִם־זִקְנֵי־אָרֶץ׃
24 סָדִין עָשְׂתָה וַתִּמְכֹּר
וַחֲגוֹר נָתְנָה לַכְּנַעֲנִי׃

19. This verse is to be connected with what follows. No time is wasted in idleness. Her other work being finished, she spends her leisure in spinning and making garments for the poor and the members of her household (Malbim).

20. *her hand.* Although she is occupied with her work, she does not disregard the poor and needy who approach her, but she stretches out her hand to give them alms. Alternatively, the profit she has gained from her work, she does not hesitate to give to the poor (Meiri).

21. *snow.* Cold weather (Metsudath David, Rashi).

scarlet. Luxurious clothing (cf. 2 Sam. i. 24; Jer. iv. 30). Since the family ordinarily wore these expensive garments they were obviously provided with warm clothing for the winter (see Isaiah da Trani).

22. *coverlets.* Cf. vii. 16.

fine linen and purple. She was herself attired in the costliest garments (Metsudath David).

23. *is known.* For the excellence of his clothes (Rashi) which raises him in the estimation of his townsmen.

elders of the land. The sages of the land (Ralbag).

24. *linen garments.* The word occurs again in Judges xiv. 12f.; Isa. iii. 23. In the latter passage it is included in a list of women's apparel. It was a square or rectangular piece of fine linen worn as an outer garment or as a wrapper around the body when in bed (see Daath Mikra).

delivereth. lit. 'gave.' The verb is translated *tradeth* in Ezek. xxvii. 12 and that is its force here (see Daath Mikra).

25 Strength and dignity are her clothing;
And she laugheth at the time to come.

26 She openeth her mouth with wisdom;
And the law of kindness is on her tongue.

27 She looketh well to the ways of her household,
And eateth not the bread of idleness.

28 Her children rise up, and call her blessed;
Her husband also, and he praiseth her:

25 עֹז־וְהָדָר לְבוּשָׁהּ
וַתִּשְׂחַק לְיוֹם אַחֲרוֹן׃
26 פִּיהָ פָּתְחָה בְחָכְמָה
וְתוֹרַת־חֶסֶד עַל־לְשׁוֹנָהּ׃
27 צוֹפִיָּה הֲילכוֹת בֵּיתָהּ
וְלֶחֶם עַצְלוּת לֹא תֹאכֵל׃
28 קָמוּ בָנֶיהָ וַיְאַשְּׁרוּהָ
בַּעְלָהּ וַיְהַלְלָהּ׃

v. 27. הליכות ק'

girdles. [Like *linen garments* the noun is the collective singular. Sashes or belts were commonly worn around the waist, and for the wealthy were elaborately embroidered.]

the merchant. [Hebrew, 'the Canaanite,' a Phoenician trader.]

25. *strength and dignity.* [A strong financial position and the esteem which comes from it.]

are her clothing. These characteristics are borne by her as one wears clothes (Ibn Ezra). cf. *Thou art clothed with glory and majesty* (Ps. civ. 1); *Let Thy priests be clothed with righteousness* (Ps. cxxxii. 9).

laugheth at the time to come. lit. 'at a latter day.' The future causes her no anxiety because of her secure financial position (Ibn Ezra, Meiri).

26. *openeth her mouth with wisdom.* When she speaks, her words are distinguished by good sense and discretion (Meiri).

the law of kindness. i.e. instruction of kindness; she gives her directions to children and servants to practice acts of kindness (Metsudath David).

27. *looketh well to the ways.* In addition to giving orders, she sees that they are duly carried out and supervises every detail of the home that it be with modesty and fear of God (Metsudath David).

eateth not the bread of idleness. She is full of energy and always well occupied (Metsudath David).

28. *rise up.* Ibn Ezra understands the verb as 'rise up in the morning,' and finding everything well prepared, the children express their thankfulness to her. It might signify 'stand up' in her presence as a mark of respect (cf. Lev. xix. 32). the Talmud (Kiddushin 31b) relates of a Rabbi that, whenever he heard his mother's footsteps, he used to exclaim, 'I stand up before the Shechinah (the Divine Presence).'

call her blessed. More lit. 'and praise her.' Cf. Ps. lxxii. 17, Cant. vi. 9.

her husband also. Supply the verb 'riseth up' (Metsudath David).

'Many daughters have done valiantly,
But thou excellest them all.'

Grace is deceitful, and beauty is vain;
But a woman that feareth the LORD, she shall be praised.

Give her of the fruit of her hands;
And let her works praise her in the gates.

29 רַבּוֹת בָּנוֹת עָשׂוּ חָיִל
וְאַתְּ עָלִית עַל־כֻּלָּנָה׃
30 שֶׁקֶר הַחֵן וְהֶבֶל הַיֹּפִי
אִשָּׁה יִרְאַת־יְהוָה הִיא תִתְהַלָּל׃
31 תְּנוּ־לָהּ מִפְּרִי יָדֶיהָ
וִיהַלְלוּהָ בַשְּׁעָרִים מַעֲשֶׂיהָ׃

29. The verse gives the wording of the husband's praise (Daath Mikra).

daughters. Poetical synonym for *women* (Gen. xxx. 13, xxxiv. 1, Cant. ii. 2, vi. 9). As is apparent from our verse, this does not refer only to unmarried women, who are still members of their fathers' household, but also to married women, the peers of our 'woman of valour.' Neither is it to be conjectured that even after marriage the woman remained always a member of her father's family, and was therefore called his daughter, since it is evident from Num. xxxvi. that among the Hebrews the daughter, on marriage, not only passed from her father's house, but also from his tribe.

30. The concluding verses are the poet's reflection upon the picture he has drawn and the lesson he wishes to impress upon the reader. He does not decry feminine beauty, but it is not the essential or most important qualification in a wife; character is the true criterion (Isaiah da Trani).

grace is deceitful. A graceful exterior is no index of a woman's nature. Beauty is skin deep. Rabbinic literature preserves a report that on two occasions in the year, 'the daughters of Jerusalem used to go out dressed in white garments which were borrowed, so as not to put to shame anybody who did not possess her own. The daughters of Jerusalem would go out and dance in the vineyards. (The beautiful women would cry), 'Young man, raise thine eyes and see whom thou wilt choose as thy wife.' (The women of distinguished families would cry,), 'Pay not attention to beauty, but rather to family,' and (the homely ones, possessing neither beauty nor nobility) quoted this verse. The criterion of 'family' indicated that the girl had a good heredity and upbringing and was therefore likely to be of good character.

vain. lit. 'a breath'; it does not endure and soon passes (Ramban, Eccles.).

that feareth the LORD. This is the indispensable characteristic to be possessed by a wife who is to deserve the above praise (Isaiah da Trani).

31. *give her.* Let her have full credit for all she does (Metsudath David).

and let . . . gates. Although her activities are confined to the home, due recognition should be paid publicly *(in the gates)* to the vital contribution she makes to the welfare of the community (after Rashi).

AUTHORITIES QUOTED

Abrahams, I. (Anglo-Jewish Scholar), *A Companion to the Authorized Daily Prayer Book.*
Aboth—*Pirke Aboth, Sayings of the Fathers*: Mishnaic tractate.
Alschich, Moshe (sixteenth century Bible commentator) *Rab Peninim.*
Amos—One of the Minor Prophets.
Anaf Yosef—Anthology on Tractate Aboth, by Enoch Zundel, noted anthologist.
Arachin—Talmudic tractate.
Baba Bathra—Talmudic tractate.
Baba Metsia—Talmudic tractate.
Baba Kamma—Talmudic tractate.
Bechaya, ben Asher (fourteenth century Bible exegete) Commentary on Proverbs compiled by Judah Aryeh Leib Heine from Bechaya's various works.
Berachot—Talmudic tractate.
Chotam Tochnit—Hebrew Synonyms, by Abraham Bedarschi (13th century).
Daath Mikra, (contemporary Jewish commentary) Mosad HaRav Kook, 1983.
Eitan, I. (Jewish Orientalist) *A Contribution to Biblical Lexicography.*
Elijah of Wilna (1720–1797), Annotator of the Bible and Talmud, Commentary on Proverbs.
Gerondi, Jonah (thirteenth century Talmudist, ethicist and Biblical exegete) Commentary on Proverbs.
Esther—Book of the Bible, one of the Five Scrolls.
Gittin—Talmudic tractate.
Hagigah—Talmudic tractate.
Hirsch, Samson Raphael (nineteenth century leader of German Orthodoxy).
Hullin—Talmudic tractate.
Ibn Caspi, Joseph (1279–1340, Bible commentator) *Chatzotzeroth Keseph.*
Ibn Ezra, Abraham (1092–1167, Bible commetator), Commentary on Proverbs. Commentary usually attributed to him is believed to have been authored by Moses Kimchi, a twelfth century grammarian and Bible commentator and brother of David Kimchi.
Ibn Ganah, Jonah (11th century grammarian and lexicographer) *Shorashim.*
Ibn Nachmiash (fourteenth century exegete) commentary on Proverbs.
Isaiah of Trani (thirteenth century Bible commentator) commentary on Prophets and Hagiographa.
Job—Book of the Bible.
Joel—One of the Minor Prophets.
Jonah—One of the Minor Prophets.
Judges—Book of the Bible.
Josephus, Flavius (Jewish historian, 1st century C.E.) *Antiquities.*
Kimchi, David (1160–1235, Bible commentator, grammarian, and lexicographer) *Shorashim.*
Kimchi, Joseph (12th century Bible commentator and grammarian) *Sefer Chukah.*
Kethuboth—Talmudic tractate.
Kiddushin—Talmudic tractate.
Kings—Book of the Bible, divided into 1 Kings and 2 Kings.
Likutei Yehudah (Recent anthologized Chasidic commentary on Proverbs from Rabbis of Ger) by Judah Aryeh Leib Heine.
Maimonides, Moses (1135–1204, Jewish philosopher) *Guide to the Perplexed.*
Makkoth—Talmudic tractate.
Malbim, Meyer Leibush (1809–1879) famed Bible commentator.
Mechilta—Rabbinical commentary on Exodus.
Megillah—Talmudic tractate.

Meiri, Menachem (13th century Talmudist and Bible commentator) commentary on Proverbs.
Metsudath David ('Tower of David'), Hebrew commentary on Books of the Bible by David Altschul (17th century).
Metsudath Zion ('Tower of Zion'), Hebrew definition of words of the Bible by David Altschul.
Micah—One of the Minor Prophets.
Michlol Yofi (commentary on the Bible, anthologized from earlier grammarians and lexicographers) by Shlomo ben Melech.
Midrash—Rabbinic Homilies on Proverbs, the Pentateuch, etc.
Mishnah—Codification on Jewish law (c. 200 C.E.).
Nedarim—Talmudic tractate.
Obadiah—One of the Minor Prophets.
Pesahim—Talmudic tractate.
Ralbag (Rabbi Levi ben Gershon, 1288–1344, commentator and philosopher).
Ramban (Rabbi Moshe ben Nachman, thirteenth century Talmudist, Kabbalist, and Biblical exegete) Discourse on Eccles.
Rashi (Rabbi Solomon ben Isaac, 1040–1105, French Bible commentator), *Commentary on Proverbs.*
Ruth—Book of the Bible, one of the Five Scrolls.
Saadia Gaon (882–942, Bible exegete and philosopher), *Commentary on Proverbs.*
Sanhedrin—Talmudic tractate.
Septuagint, the Greek translation of the Bible, made by the Jews in Egypt in the third century B.C.E.
Siphre—Ancient Rabbinical commentary on Numbers and Deuteronomy.
Shabbath—Talmudic tractate.
Sotah—Talmudic tractate.
Sukkah—Talmudic tractate.
Taanith—Talmudic tractate.
Talmud—Corpus of Jewish law and thought (compiled at the end of the 5th century C.E.)
Tamid—Talmudic tractate.
Tanna de be Eliyahu—Midrash attributed to Elijah the prophet, as revealed to Rav Anan, early Amora.
Tosefta—Tannaitic compilation, elaborating on the Mishnah.
Targum, Aramaic translation of the Bible (1st and 2nd centuries C.E.)
Thomson, W.M., (Traveller), *The Land and the Book.*
Tristram, H.B. (Natural Scientist), *The Natural History of the Bible,* 1873.
Uktsin—Mishnaic tractate.
Vulgate—Latin translation of the Bible by Jerome (4th century C.E.).
Wertheimer—Solomon Aaron—scholar and lexicographer (1862–1935). *Synonyms in the Bible.*
Yalkut Machiri—Midrashic Compilation (Late 13th–early 14th century) by Machir ben Abba Mari.
Yerushalmi—Jerusalem Talmud, compiled in the Holy Land before the Babylonian Talmud, attributed to Rabbi Johanan, early Amora.
Yebamoth—Talmudic tractate.
Yoma—Talmudic tractate.